BACKROADS & BYWAYS
OF
HAWAII

Oct 2013

BACKROADS & BYWAYS OF HAWAII

Drives, Daytrips & Weekend Excursions

Michele Bigley

FIRST EDITION

THE COUNTRYMAN PRESS
WOODSTOCK, VERMONT

Interior photographs by the author unless otherwise specified
Frontispiece photo: Kaua'i's North Shore
Maps by Erin Greb Cartography, © The Countryman Press
Book design by Susan Livingston
Composition by Chelsea Cloeter

Published by The Countryman Press,
P.O. Box 748, Woodstock, VT 05091

Distributed by W. W. Norton & Company, Inc.,
500 Fifth Avenue, New York, NY 10110

Printed in the United States of America

10 9 8 7 6 5 4 3 2 1

Backroads & Byways of Hawaii
ISBN 978-1-58157-184-4

FOR EDDIE, KAI, AND NIKKO, MY *OHANA*. YOU ARE LOVED.

The Na Pali Coast

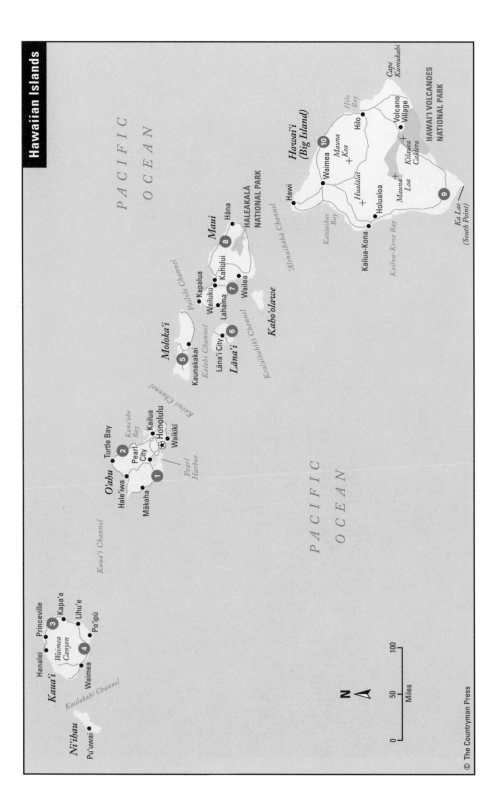

Hawaiian Islands

Ni'ihau

Pu'uwai

Kaua'i

Hanalei
Princeville
Kapa'a
Līhu'e
③
Waimea Canyon
④
Po'ipū
Waimea

Kaulakahi Channel

Kaua'i Channel

PACIFIC OCEAN

PACIFIC OCEAN

O'ahu
Turtle Bay
Hale'iwa
②
Pearl City
Kailua
Kāne'ohe Bay
★ Honolulu
Waikīkī
Mākaha
①
Pearl Harbor

Kaiwi Channel

Moloka'i
Kaunakakai
⑤

Kalohi Channel

Lāna'i
Lāna'i City
⑥

Kaululakahiki Channel

Maui
Kapalua
Wailuku
Kahului
⑦ Wailea
Lahaina
⑧
Hāna
Pailolo Channel

Kaho'olawe

HALEAKALĀ NATIONAL PARK

'Alenuihāhā Channel

Hawai'i (Big Island)
Hawi
Waimea
⑩
Mauna Kea ✛
Hualālai ✛
Holualoa
Kailua-Kona
Mauna Loa ✛
Kīlauea Caldera ✛
⑨
Ka Lae (South Point)

Hilo Bay
Hilo
Volcano Village
Volcano
Cape Kumukahi

HAWAI'I VOLCANOES NATIONAL PARK

Kawaihae Bay
Kailua-Kona Bay

N

0   50   100
Miles

© The Countryman Press

CONTENTS

On Maui's road to Hana

ACKNOWLEDGMENTS

Many *mahalos* are necessary for the wealth of generous people who helped birth this gigantic project. First and foremost, a big dollop of appreciation goes out to Kermit Hummell, Lisa Sacks, Doug Yeager, Laura Jorstad, and the entire Countryman Press crew for believing in the need for a responsible travel guide to the state of Hawai'i. Humble thanks to Kim Grant for being a mentor since day one.

This book could not have been possible without the wisdom and guidance of those who offered insight throughout the research and writing. The following people deserve many *mahalos*: Nathan Kam, Emele Freiberg, Keli'i Brown, Alicia Yoshikami, Lindsay Chambers, Joanna Blume, Dania Katz, the guys behind Beat of Hawaii, Kelley Cho, Noreen Kam, Daniela Powers, Rosemary and Norbert Smith, Carol Fowler, Don Hill, Beverly Clemente, Elizabeth Ferrer, Tom Corson-Knowles, Bonnie Friedman, Yvonne Biegel, Joelle Keller, Marilyn Jansen Lopes, James McDonald, Charity Texeira, Roxanne Darling, Bob Bone, Roxanne Murayama, Julie Bicoy, Bree Dallwitz, Paul Garcia, Calee Brean, Andrea Oka, Michelle Edwards, Carlton Kramer, Kim Markham, Jane Flandez, Lono, Dusty Grable, Candy Aluli, Lisa Reasoner, Lori Michimoto, and the hundreds of other people whom I may not have listed, but whose aloha helped create these pages.

Deep appreciation goes out to Carrie Kellerby, Lindsay Barels, and the amazing Rachel Edgar for pulling through at the last minute with those tedious details. Coralissa and Ivan Delaforce, you always inspire me; much aloha is coming at you! Mom, Dad, Baba, Ali, Andrea, and my amazing cadre of friends and family have helped in myriad ways, and for this I thank you with all my heart.

Kai and Nikko, I am so proud of my little world travelers for visiting all the Hawaiian Islands with me and placing your stamp of approval on almost every destination, even the spooky ones. You help me view my favorite state with new eyes, laughing through challenging travel days. I appreciate every moment I get to experience the world with you.

And to Eddie, my love, thank you for embarking with me on yet another wild journey. Once again you helped me pull it off—without you, nothing would be possible.

Canoe plants like these taro thrive in Hawai'i.

INTRODUCTION

Nowhere else on the planet evokes as many visions of grandeur as the Hawaiian Islands. Charmed with so many of the planet's bests—from beaches to waterfalls, hiking trails to campsites, lava flows to restaurants, luxury resorts to hidden hideaways—Hawai'i attracts not only those on the prowl for a tropical vacation, but also the intrepid travelers on the prowl for adventure.

Historically, Hawai'i has been luring visitors since its creation. Polynesians arrived somewhere between a.d. 500 and 800, bringing along in double-hulled canoes a battery of breadfruit (to make surfboards, sandpaper, and instruments), coconut, bananas, taro, *ti*, sweet potatoes, sugarcane, plus chickens, pigs, and rats. These plants and animals thrived on the islands and quickly became synonymous with the environment. For the next thousand years, the Polynesians lived off the islands' resources, believing that the land was chief and the humans were the servants. They saw themselves as part of, not separate from, nature. And though they used trees to make everything from canoes to spoons, weapons to sandpaper, houses to clothing, they would only use one tree at a time for fear of angering the spirit god that resided in the forest. In fact, every time they cut down a tree from the upland sacred forest, they made a human sacrifice.

The Polynesians also implemented a new belief system to worship four major gods: Ku (the god of war, ancestors, sunrise, and fishing), Lono (god of rain, harvest, fertility, and peace), Kane (who created the first man), and Kanaloa (ruler of the underworld). The

---

THE *'AUMAKUA* By Lilly Barels

Long before missionaries introduced their concept of God to Hawai'i, Polynesians believed in a nature-based spiritual system. A family of deities called *'aumakua* were prayed to and summoned for protection and comfort. These deities were the spirits of ancestors manifesting as sacred earth dwellers like the shark, sea turtle, octopus, eel, caterpillar, and owl. It's common to hear modern stories like one of a local canoe paddler who evaded danger because of guidance from his shark *'aumakua*. When visiting the islands, it is important to understand where the deep respect comes from for these seemingly ordinary creatures of land and sea.

chief ruler also started the *kapu* system, which set up a unified set of laws (most of which applied to commoners and were punishable by death). They also created *heiaus* (sacred houses of worship) and the caste system, where people were divided into four categories: *Ali'i* (royalty), *Kapuna* (high priests), *Maka'ainana* (commoners), and *Kauwa* (outcasts). People were born into a caste and could not move freely between these categories.

In the late 1700s, in sailed Captain Cook. Believing he was the god Lono returning on a floating island, the Hawaiians canoed out to the ships with an abundance of offerings. This proved a fateful turning point in Hawaiian history. Not only did Cook and his crew trade iron, weaponry, and nails for sweet potatoes and fish, but they also left a scar on the pure Hawaiian population: a nasty bout of syphilis.

Leaving weapons and sickly people behind, Cook and his crew took off for the Arctic, dubbing the friendly islands to the south the Sandwich Islands, to honor his patron the Earl of Sandwich. However, the weather forced Cook to turn back, and he returned to the Big Island. Once again the sailors received a warm welcome, filled with the finest foods and women. But soon the people suspected this farm boy wasn't a god (since the

ANCIENT *KAPU*

Ancient Hawaiian people had many *kapu* (taboos) that commoners could be killed or punished for breaking. They might seem ridiculous to our modern society, but the system provided a unified way to rule the tribes. This belief system lasted until 1819, when King Kamehameha II ended the *kapu* system of law by eating with women. Afterward, the Kaua'i people, left with a spiritual void, turned to Christianity.

Some examples of *kapu* actions:

❖ It was forbidden for men and women to eat together.

❖ A commoner could not touch the food of a chief, or enter his house.

❖ If the shadow of a commoner fell across the chief (or chief's shadow), it meant death for the commoner.

❖ If people were in a house when someone died, they had to leave immediately; they became contaminated and could not enter another house, eat another's food, work, or touch anyone.

❖ During ceremonies, if people interrupted or created even a small disturbance, they were sent to die.

❖ During hula training, it was *kapu* to eat sugarcane, taro tops, some types of seaweed, and squid. Also, sex was prohibited. Fingernails could not be cut, hair couldn't be trimmed, and men could not shave.

❖ Women could not prepare any food but sweet potatoes.

pious didn't actually *need* women, and the crew members broke an infinite number of *kapu*); finally, after Cook had set sail for the north once more then was forced to return due to rough seas, the locals grew angry and started stealing iron from the ships. Cook then made a series of unfortunate decisions, which ultimately led to a battle with the Hawaiians that killed him. Cook's crew went ballistic, burning a village and beheading natives. Ultimately, realizing the explorer was a highly respected man, King Kalaniopu'u returned Cook's bones so he could be buried at sea.

Besides a legacy of venereal disease, Cook and his crew left Hawaiians with a taste for violence, with weapons to boot. From 1786 to 1795, war and chaos ravaged the islands. Mostly this was because of young warrior King Kamehameha I, who ruled the Windward Islands and desired the Leeward Islands of Kaua'i and Ni'ihau for his empire. Prophets and high priests warned him to be content with what he al-

An ancient *heiau* on the Big Island

ready had, but the greed got the best of him and he set out to conquer the leeward duo. As Kamehameha was failing at "uniting" the islands, the *kapu* system was going kaput, chiefs lost power, and the local people needed spiritual guidance. The Reverend William Ellis, who knew how to speak and write Tahitian, quickly picked up the Hawaiian language and started preaching to natives in their own tongue. The amazed Hawaiians then attended missionary schools, while Ellis established a written Hawaiian language. By 1831, two-fifths of the population was students. Because of a shortage of teachers and supplies, once a Hawaiian could read, he became a teacher. And rumor has it that at least one school used surfboards as desks.

The local people, needing this spiritual structure, opened their world to the missionaries, who quickly became powerful in the construction of industry. Builders with ties to the church created the first sugar plantations. Missionaries encouraged (read: forced) sugar barons to hire local Hawaiians. This type of work was a new thing for the islanders, who looked at company leaders as chiefs.

O'ahu's Hanuama Bay Nature Preserve gets you up close with tropical fish.

In 1819, the combination of missionaries sailing in and the death of Kamehameha led to a new era of schooling, religion, and sugar. In the mid-1800s, the Royal Hawaiian Agricultural Society, looking for staff, brought Chinese, Japanese, Portuguese, Filipino, German, and Gilbert Islander workers. But with this new influx of workers came opium, smallpox, leprosy, a rise in crime and rebellion, and of course resentment.

Though the plantation owners essentially acted as the leaders of the small societies, Hawai'i was still a monarchy—albeit a dying one. In 1887, Queen Lili'uokalani (the last monarch of the islands), believing that the United States had too much control over the islands, created a constitutional monarchy. Unfortunately for her, a coup, inspired by US planters, overtook her. US soldiers then arrived for "peacekeeping" measures, and made Sanford Dole the provisional president of the Hawaiian Republic.

The provisional government set up voting rights, but only for people who had a certain amount of income and property value. Most commoners still wanted Hawai'i to stay a monarchy. But they were not permitted to vote. So the islanders had to abide by US laws, whether they liked it or not. One wealthy native, Prince Kuhio, the Kaua'i-born great-grandson of the former king of the island Kaumuali'i, tried to restore the monarchy, but was imprisoned (later he was elected to Congress; his birthday is still celebrated today). Other than that little wave, it was smooth sailing in 1898, when President McKinley was able to secure the annexation of Hawai'i for the United States.

Strangely, it was the Pearl Harbor attack that led Hawaiians into a movement to become more than a territory. They had suddenly become American, wanting the voting power and rights that came with being a state. Thus a movement was born, one that would take 18 years to accomplish its goal: statehood. The common people, the elites, and the American Japanese studying on the GI Bill all agreed, voting by an overwhelming majority to become a state. On August 21, 1959, President Eisenhower granted the small but desired chain of islands entrance into the club, as the 50th state.

If you listen closely to the voice of the native Hawaiian people, you might hear the phrase *Pae'aina o Hawai'i Loa*. This indicates the growing (and persistent) movement toward a sovereign nation of Hawai'i. Where once countless people voted to become a part of the United States, now indigenous people want their own nation, free from the control of the red, white, and blue.

There have been a number of official government gestures in response to the movement, but who in the United States really wants to part with this tropical paradise? Just in time for the 100th anniversary of the monarchy's overthrow, the US Congress offered the "Apology Bill" to Hawaiians, comprising little more than its name. Though the debate rages on, this doesn't stop the Hawaiian people from recognizing their place in American culture. They vote, celebrate national holidays, and generally offer their aloha spirit freely. Rocky times may be ahead, however. With the boom in mainlanders moving to the islands and buying up precious property, indigenous people cannot afford ascending costs of modern life. Many are forced to move to the Big Island, Las Vegas, and Oregon, where property is affordable. This cultural earthquake, plus the shrinking of the native forest, is leading Hawai'i to a new stage in its dramatic history.

HOW THIS BOOK WORKS

By some measure, this book's title is misleading. Hawai'i has no byways to speak of, and the majority of "backroads" are privately owned. And while much like you explorers I typically spend my holidays hunting for the hidden waterfalls or uncharted territory, in Hawai'i I stick to destinations that are tried and true. There are a few reasons for this. First and foremost, there is not much that has not been "found" on Hawai'i. Explorers have been plunging inland, trekking to secret beaches and waterfalls, and venturing off roads since ancient times—there is only so much land to explore. All beaches are public, even those that require you to cross private land to access them. So in essence there is not much left to find.

To be frank, Hawaiians have a love–hate relationship with tourism. Locals need our dollars, but they also see on a daily basis the impact of our footprints on the landscape: from our disrespect of sacred destinations to our need to hike down unsafe trails to waterfalls, or swim in rough current–filled seas. As someone who loves and respects this archipelago, I cannot lead you on this type of adventure. Instead, with this book I offer ways to experience Hawai'i both safely and respectfully: You will spend the majority of your time driving the islands' roads to an array of quiet beaches or less-visited hiking

HOW TO BE A GRACIOUS GUEST ON THE ISLANDS

I am sure you are a wise ambassador for wherever you come from, but it's important to do your part to understand the impact, both positive and negative, of your footprint on the most fragile and beautiful environment in the U.S.

As a surfboard stuck up on the trees on the way to Kaua'i's 'Anini Beach reads: SLOW DOWN. Take off your watch. Turn off your cell phone and just be okay with Hawai'i Time. Things move slower here. Meals take time. Grocery store clerks want to talk story. People (except for some locals, but don't take their lead) drive slower. There is nothing to hurry for. Really.

Hemo da slippahs. Whenever you are invited into a home (or enter your lodging), take off your shoes.

Even though it feels like you have exited the United States, be aware that Hawai'i is a valuable part of the USA. So when talking about home, try not to say, "In America...." Instead try, "On the Mainland...."

Respect nature. Okay, I mean that in the hippie way of being green and not picking all the flowers or taking home shells, but I also mean this for your safety. Pay attention to the weather report. If it says rain, you probably should not go hiking. If the waves or currents are too strong, even if you are an experienced swimmer, don't swim. There is a catchphrase in Hawai'i: *When in doubt, don't go out.* Follow this phrase like your life depends on it. Locals do.

I am a traveler who wants to find every unexplored spot. Except here. Lately, there has been a lot of controversy about guidebooks telling people how to get to "secret" spots. Unfortunately tourists visiting these places have caused some trouble. First off, many people have died or been seriously injured by visiting some of these "secret" adventure spots. This happens in a variety of ways. Visitors unused to the moods of a particular waterfall will rope-swing into the water, not knowing that the water level is unusually low; or they will take a wrong turn on an unkempt trail. If you talk to locals, chances are they will tell you about (and sometimes even take you to) their favorite spot. But when you just arrive, locals feel territorial—this is their backyard. Those of us who live in big cities may not understand this type of mentality. But in Hawai'i people see land as sacred, something to respect, and something that belongs to them. If you can respect that you are visiting another culture, your visit will be as rich as the soil.

Wear sunscreen and mosquito repellent. We can always spot the tourists. Aside from being armed with a map and a camera, they always have this lobster hue to their shoulders. The Hawai'i sun is dangerous, even when it is cloudy. Always wear sunscreen of more than SPF15. And as you might guess, with rain comes mosquitoes, a lot of the nasty buggers. Wear repellent, especially in gardens.

Leave the pidgin dialect to the locals. It is okay to practice pronouncing Hawaiian words (and even appreciated), but when *haoles* start chatting away in pidgin, it is like traveling to Britain and taking on a cockney accent.

Kaua'i's Na Pali Coast *Oliver Reyes*

trails, but you will also be primarily supporting locally owned businesses along the way and getting to know the real Hawai'i.

Set up in 10 chapters, each a themed itinerary, this book encourages you to unearth Moloka'i's charms, unravel Lana'i's spooky side, or traipse into Maui's Upcountry to learn about the rich foodie scene on this beach lover's isle. And of course, this would not be an honest portrayal of Hawai'i without accurate information on how to enjoy the state's most alluring sites, including how to best explore the Big Island's Hawai'i Volcanoes National Park, Kaua'i's Na Pali Coast, Waikiki's beaches, and Maui's Hana Highway.

Each chapter is an itinerary for a road trip designed to last a weekend or a week. With this book you'll be armed with tailored itineraries to suit varied needs. You can play on Maui's strands and hike along the lip of Haleakala crater; party all night in O'ahu's Chinatown or stroll the Windward Coast beaches without running into another soul; listen to Moloka'i elders serenade you and hike to Kalaupapa; get a massage treatment on Lana'i and go four-wheel-driving to a ghost town; listen to a slack key guitar concert in Kaua'i's funky Hanalei or take a helicopter ride over Waimea Canyon. These itineraries take you off the beaten track and into parts of Hawai'i that locals don't even know exist, and hopefully, by getting on some of the United States' most beautiful roads, you too will find excuses to return and craft your own itineraries.

THE HAWAIIAN LANGUAGE

With only 12 letters and two punctuation marks, the Hawaiian language is relatively simple to speak and understand. Though English is the primary language spoken, Hawaiian is experiencing a renaissance, in order to save it from obscurity. To immerse yourself in the culture, you might consider adding a few useful Hawaiian words to your vocabulary.

Local Hawaiians, however, speak a combination of English, Hawaiian, and slang. Pidgin, as it is called, is difficult to understand. You won't hear it at resorts or even when being served at local restaurants. But hang on the beach next to some surfers, or pay attention to locals talking story, and you'll soon be scratching your head, trying to make sense of the one rapid thing on the island—this language.

Here are a few basic pronunciation rules to make your travels easier.

CONSONANTS

h, l, n, m	pronounced the same as English
k, p	pronounced with less breath
w	usually pronounced like a soft *v*, though at the beginning of the word or after an *a* can be pronounced like a *v* or *w*

VOWELS (UNSTRESSED)

a	*a* as in *above*
e	*e* as in *bet*
i	*y* as in *pity*
o	*o* as in *hole*
u	*u* as in *full*

VOWELS (STRESSED)

When two vowels appear next to each other, stress the first vowel a little less than you would in English.

a	*a* as in *bar*
e	*ay* as in *play*
i	*ee* as in *see*
o	*o* as in *mole* (but slightly longer)
u	*oo* as in *soon*

THE USE OF THE *OKINA*, OR GLOTTAL STOP

Though I don't speak fluent Hawaiian, I promised a friend I would attempt to honor the written language as much as possible. In this book, you will notice the use of the *okina* or glottal stop ('). This punctuation mark indicates a pause in the pronunciation of a word. For example, *haoles* pronounce Hawai'i as *Ha-why*, when locals say *Ha-wai-ee*. I have tried to stay true to this mark even when street signs and company names don't include it. The other Hawaiian punctuation mark is the *kahako*, which looks like a straight line over a vowel. When the *kahako* is used, hold the vowel sound slightly longer than other vowels.

COMMON WORDS

The best Hawaiian electronic dictionary can be found at http://wehewehe.org. The *New Pocket Hawaiian Dictionary*, by Mary Kawena Pukui and Samuel Elbert, published by the University of Hawai'i Press, is a wonderful resource as well.

Below is a list of commonly used Hawaiian and pidgin words.

'ae	to say yes or offer consent
ahupua'a	a triangular division of land reaching from the mountains to the ocean—with the largest piece being oceanfront
'aina	land or earth
akua	god, goddess, or spirit
ali'i	Hawaiian chief, royal, or person of high rank
aloha	welcome, hello, good-bye, love, or friendship
a'ole	no, never, not
brah	pidgin for friend
da kine	pidgin for thingamajig, whatchamacallit
e komo mai	welcome
halau	a hula group or school
hale	house or building
haole	Caucasian, mainlander, or foreigner
hapu'u	tree fern
heiau	ancient temple or place of worship
hemo da slippahs	take off your shoes
ho'ike	information
holoholo	cruising
hui	group or club
hula	a form of dance and music
kahuna	priest or priestess; a person well versed in any field
kai	sea
kama'aina	resident of Hawai'i
kane	man
kapa	cloth made from bark
kapu	sacred or forbidden
kapuna	older person
keiki	young child
kiawe	mesquite

koa	rare hardwood tree
kona	leeward
kuapapa	ancient
kukui	candlenut tree
lanai	balcony or patio
lau	leaf
lei	wreath of flowers or shells worn around the neck
mahalo	thank you
makai	toward the sea (used as a directional signifier)
makana	gift
malihini	stranger or newcomer
mana	a kind of spiritual power
mauka	toward the mountain (used as a directional signifier)
mea ho'onanea	relax
mele	ancient chant
Menehune	legendary, dwarf-like ancient Hawaiian people
mu'umu'u	loose-fitting gown or dress
Na pana kaulana	the famous places
nui	significant or important
'ohana	family
pali	cliff-like mountain
paniolo	cowboy
pau	finished or done
pili	a kind of grass
puka	hole or door
tutu	grandparent
wahine	woman
wai	water
wikiwiki	fast

FOOD TERMS

ahi	yellowfin tuna
aku	bonito (tuna)
'awapuhi	ginger
azuki beans	Japanese sweet red beans used in desserts like *mochi* and shave ice
bento	a Japanese-style box lunch with meat or fish, rice, and vegetables
crack seed	Chinese sweet-and-sour preserved fruit snack
haupia	sweet coconut pudding

Hawaii's state bird, the *nene*

imu	pit-style oven
kalua pork	preparation for pork cooked in *imu* pit for an extended period of time
kapahaki	cooked Hawaiian food
kaukau	Hawaiian food
ko'ala	broiled food
laulau	pork, chicken, or fish wrapped in *taro* or *ti* leaves then steamed
liliko'i	passion fruit
limu	seaweed
loco moco	two scoops of white rice, a hamburger patty with a fried egg, topped with sausage gravy
lomilomi	raw salmon salted and minced, then mixed with green onions and tomatoes
lu'au	traditional Hawaiian meal
mahi mahi	the white fish called dolphin, though it really isn't one
mai tai	an alcoholic beverage made with rum, grenadine, lemon (or orange), and pineapple juice
malasadas	Portuguese doughnuts
mochi	Japanese sticky rice dumpling, often served sweet or filled with ice cream
nori	dried seaweed
ono	wahoo fish

'ono	delicious
'opae	shrimp
'opakapaka	blue snapper
pao dolce	Portuguese sweet bread
plate lunch	two scoops of rice, meat or fish, and macaroni salad
poi	a basic Hawaiian food made from pounded taro root
poke	raw fish (usually *ahi*) with *shoyu*, sesame oil, salt, onions, and "special" ingredients
pua'a	pig
pupu	snack or appetizer
saimin	the Hawaiian version of noodle soup with pork, scallions, and *nori*
shave ice	a traditional Hawaiian dessert consisting of finely shaved ice smothered in sweet sugary syrup on top of either ice cream or sweet *azuki* beans
shoyu	soy sauce
star fruit	a yellowish green fruit shaped like a star (with five points)
taro (or *kalo*)	hearty starchy vegetable similar to potatoes or corn
'uala	sweet potato
'ulu	breadfruit

WEATHER, PACKING, AND ROAD CONDITIONS

Most of Hawai'i is a tropical paradise with temperatures averaging in the 70s (Fahrenheit) in winter and in the 80s in summer. That being said, winter evenings can get chilly, especially in the upcountry of any island, so bring a sweater. You can expect rain year-round, especially on the north shores of the islands, and so you'll want a raincoat, closed-toe shoes, and at least one pair of pants to go along with those sandals and shorts. The

CAMPING DETAILS

Local Hawaiians have a long tradition of sleeping outdoors. Campsites are open year-round, though those on the north shores of the islands get a ton of wind and rain in winter. For all campsites, you need a permit. The good news, though, is that camping is cheap. At county beach parks, permits are good for up to seven days per campground. Contact the Division of Parks and Recreation (www.hawaiicounty.gov) for each island in advance. For state parks, contact the Department of Land and Natural Resources Division of State Parks (www.hawaii.gov/dlnr). Here, camping is limited to five consecutive nights per site.

Hawai'i Volcanoes National Park

main exception is if you are traveling to the Big Island or Maui. In Upcountry and in and around the volcanoes, you can expect startlingly cold weather—it snows on the Big Island's Mauna Kea in winter!—so bring a very warm jacket if you want to hike Maui's Haleakala, or summit Mauna Kea.

As for driving, one of the biggest surprises on the islands is traffic. O'ahu, Kaua'i, Maui, and the Big Island are plagued with bumper-to-bumper conditions throughout the day. Be sure to remember that you are on vacation, give yourself plenty of time to get between destinations, always follow the road rules, and let locals pass—they are more familiar with the twists and turns of the roads and thus drive way faster than we should. For more on driving one-lane highways, see chapter 3. Throughout this book, I have used the Hawaiian terms *mauka* (mountain side) and *makai* (ocean side) as directional signifiers.

ONE LAST NOTE

While this book is my love note to Hawai'i, it is also a work in progress. Hotels close, restaurants open, and outfitters change hands. If you notice a mistake, a glaring omission, or a bit of incorrect information, please send me your thoughts and I'll remedy that for the next edition. I also love feedback about itinerary ideas, great new finds, and places that have let service slide dramatically, so feel free to drop me a line. Happy travels!

Michele Bigley
michele@michelebigley.com
www.michelebigley.com
Twitter: @michelebigley

A *keiki* at Kailua Beach

1 O'ahu's Town and Country
EXPLORING WAIKIKI, HONOLULU, AND THE WAI'ANAE COAST

Estimated length: 46 miles

Estimated time: 5–7 days

Getting there: Honolulu International Airport receives flights from almost 30 different national and international airlines. The lines are epic, and staff recommend getting to the airport at least two hours before your mainland flight departs. If you have a long layover at the airport, there's a lovely grassy area in the center of the departure area, ideal for picnicking and soaking up those last Hawaiian rays of sun.

Avis (www.avis.com), Budget (www.budget.com), Dollar (www.dollar.com), Enterprise (www.enterprise.com), Hertz (www.hertz.com), and National (www.nationalcar.com) all have car rental desks at the airport. Reserve in advance, and check in at the baggage claim desks before hopping on the bus to the car rental office.

As for driving, Honolulu's main highways include H1, H2, and H3, which can be severely congested throughout the day. If you need to get somewhere on these highways, plan extra travel time.

Highlights: O'ahu's foodie scene; honoring US soldiers at Pearl Harbor; viewing the largest collection of Hawaiian artifacts at the Bishop Museum; Waikiki's stellar beaches; a funky art community of Chinatown; the rugged Wai'anae Coast.

Arriving on O'ahu is a jolt to the senses. Home to the bustling metropolis of Honolulu and the tourist hub of Waikiki, there is no other American city that so defies expectation. Here you'll find some of the best Asian fusion food on the planet, impossibly beautiful beaches, hiking trails through the city's mountains to access gushing waterfalls, and so much art—street art, ancient crafts, a fashion scene to take note of, and music that lingers in your heart. Yet the allure of O'ahu doesn't end with its urban vibe. Like the other Hawaiian Islands, O'ahu houses a bounty of nature; but unlike the other isles, O'ahu

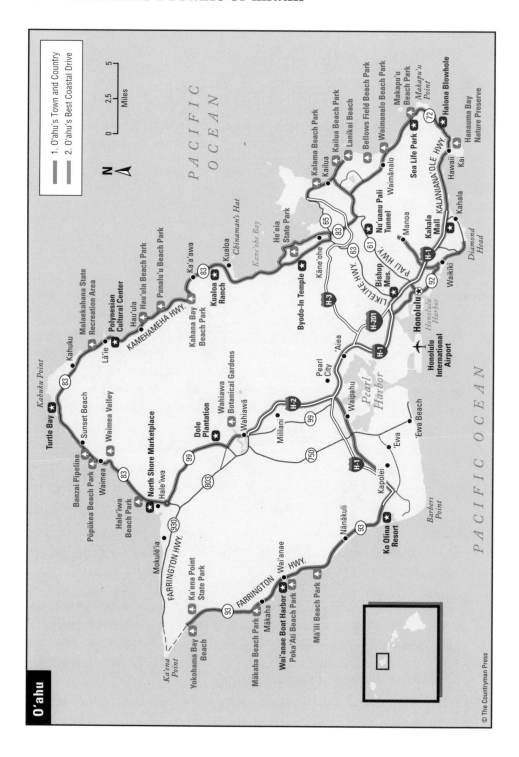

© The Countryman Press

doesn't feel so remote that you struggle find a good latte or a performance by a major recording star.

In its beginnings, O'ahu was a quiet place presided over by farmers and fishermen. When King Kamehameha I took over O'ahu, he moved his royal court from Lahaina to Honolulu, and seven Hawaiian monarchs later Honolulu still held favor with ancients as the royal stomping grounds. However, in the 1800s, missionaries and opportunists brought crops, disease, religion, and weaponry to the islands. Once the sugar industry got wind of the fertile landscape on O'ahu, the big names of the industry whooshed in and built empires. Workers from around the Pacific sailed in to earn their keep. In the early 1900s, innovative entrepreneurs started building hotels. Hoping to cash in on tourism, Waikiki boomed. Unfortunately, hopes for development were shattered when Japanese bombers destroyed Pearl Harbor. Martial law was placed on the locals, civil rights were thrown into the palm trees, and Japanese people were put in internment camps, not to be given equality for decades. Fortunately, O'ahu didn't bury its face; instead, banking on the sunny shores and idyllic island vibe, O'ahu found its place in the sun as the favored destination of Americans and Japanese travelers.

Getting your bearings on the island, especially in a jet-lagged state, can be challenging. My first stop is always Nico's at Pier 38. Hop on H 92 east for just under 4 miles to find the harbor and this thriving fish market and restaurant. Order *furikake-*

Waikiki from above

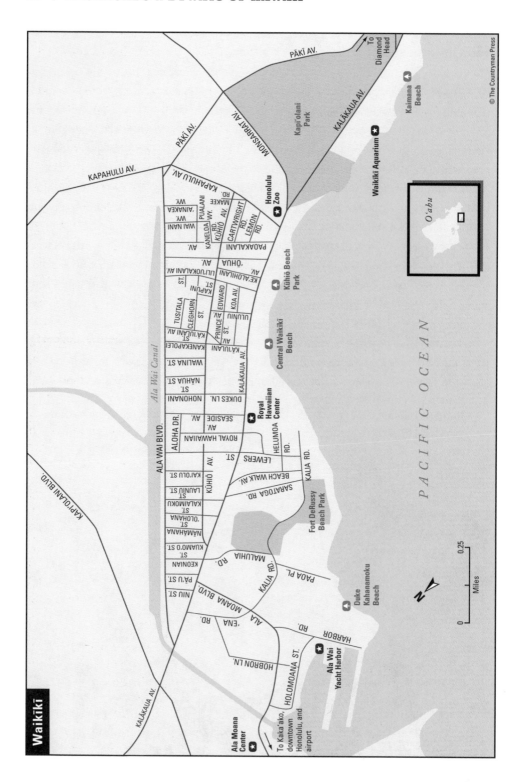

Waikīkī

© The Countryman Press

crusted *ahi* at the counter and ignore the Styrofoam containers as you sip small-batch brews, listen to live slack key guitar, watch basketball on TV, and begin to adjust to Hawai'i Time.

With your belly full, take H 92 southeast for 4 miles, bypassing downtown Honolulu (you'll be back). Turn onto Kalakaua Avenue to arrive in Waikiki. Of course there is nothing off-the-beaten-path about Waikiki: High-end shops line the well-lit malls backing the intoxicating Waikiki Beach; scores of hotels and condos populate the area. Chain restaurants rub elbows with hole-in-the-wall Japanese eateries on par with those you'll happen upon in Osaka. Yet this is where the majority of O'ahu visitors come to sleep, and this well-worn path offers a number of hidden gems alongside those tried-and-true brand hotels. It is wise to know that parking in Waikiki is obscenely expensive. Most hotels will park your car for you for a ridiculous fee. You can occasionally find free parking around Honolulu Zoo, along Ala Wai Canal, and near Hilton Hawaiian Village's lagoon. Otherwise, park at Aston Waikiki Banyan's lot on Ohua Street, which is considerably less than other lots.

BRAND HOTELS IN WAIKIKI

It's my experience that those buying a *Backroads and Byways* guidebook aren't too interested in staying at the lovely Waikiki Sheraton; you crave that uniquely Hawaiian experience. However, there are a few notable exceptions worth mentioning. The city-sized Hilton Hawaiian Village is so big it can afford to ignite fireworks on weekends; it also has its own lu'au, a battery of restaurants, a spa, and a lagoon. The Hawai'i brand Outrigger manages 10 Waikiki properties, of which my favorites are Outrigger Waikiki on the Beach for its oceanfront address, and Outrigger Regency on Beachwalk for well-kept condos with resort amenities along the shore.

Despite the brand name tacked on the front of the historic Westin Moana Surfrider, Waikiki's first hotel struts her stuff at every turn. From the white-columned lobby framing the impressive banyan-covered courtyard, restaurant, and pool, to the spacious porches dotted with laptop-toting travelers and kids playing on rocking chairs, this property slows you down. A central address on Waikiki Beach, the best coffee shop in Waikiki (Honolulu Coffee Company), and a world-class spa are some of the perks.

Lastly, the humongous Hyatt Regency Waikiki sits across from Waikiki Beach, with many of the rooms in the 40-story towers offering at least a peek at the sea or Diamond Head. This sprawling mega-resort houses the yummy Japengo and the locally sourced Shor restaurants, a small pool, cultural programs and hula shows, a ground-floor mall that features the only UGG store in Hawai'i, and the fantastic Na Ho'ola Spa, staffed by masters of massage.

The iconic Duke statue in the heart of Waikiki

For those with cash to burn, the beachfront Halekulani is the epitome of luxury. The 453 rooms were renovated in 2012 in seven shades of white, with elegant furnishings, divine bedding, and wide windows framing the robin's-egg-blue sea. The three restaurants (more on these farther along) cater to romance seekers with long lines of credit. Even if you are not splurging on a room, grab a cocktail at House Without a Key, or arrange a decadent spa treatment at Spa Halekulani (the rooftop terrace's views are second only to Diamond Head's).

Overlooking the outrigger canoe clubs traveling down the canal, Coconut Waikiki Hotel offers spacious rooms with kitchenettes, lanais, free Wi-Fi, flat-screen TVs, and retro-themed interiors sure to blast you back to the 1950s. A small pool and a reasonable price tag make this a favorite with young couples.

Occupying a premier address on Sans Souci Beach, New Otani Kaimana Beach Hotel's rooms are compact with an extra-large balcony overlooking Waikiki. Basic amenities like free Wi-Fi, refrigerators, and complimentary beach gear please travelers. The on-site Hau Tree Lanai is a historic eatery under a leafy tree on the sands of the beach with an adjacent bar for simple bar food and a strong *mai tai*. Their Miyako Restaurant serves pricey Japanese favorites. It is wise to have a car if you are staying here, as it's a bit of a walk to Waikiki's main drag.

Urbanites flock to Modern Honolulu. The sleek lobby boasts reclaimed wood walls, broken surfboards morphed into art, and "Study" for cocktails and morning coffee, iPad surfing, and concierge consulting. There are two pools: One is geared toward hipsters who crowd the lounge chairs hovering over the pool during the day and populate Addiction Nightclub after dark. On the ground-floor level, the saltwater family pool has an outdoor café and bar for impeccable drinks like the deconstructed *mai tai*. Rooms are done up in white, with 48-inch flat-panel TVs and a splash of whimsy in the colorful ukuleles and sarongs along the walls. While the hotel is not in the heart of Waikiki, the lively atmosphere won't leave you wanting.

Afternoons in Waikiki mean one thing: the beach. Waikiki's beaches are an unbelievably lovely 2 miles of white sand, with plentiful surfing, bodyboarding, swimming, and even enclosed areas for *keikis*—however, if you're imagining a quiet slice of peace to sun yourself, you'll want to excuse yourself from Waikiki's lively strands. The charm of this string of beaches is the anything-goes vibe, complete with vacationers attempting darn near any feat that can be achieved on or under water, and locals soaking up the energy of one of Hawai'i's most exciting outdoor spaces.

A typical afternoon at the office

The superstar attraction of Central Waikiki Beach doesn't need any introduction: You'll notice the massive statue of Duke Kahanamoku, Hawai'i's most legendary surfer and Olympian who put the state's surf scene on the map, his arms draped with leis; plus there's a staggering collection of outfitters hawking catamaran trips, surf lessons, your name stitched out of palm leaves…you get the picture. Families love the enclosed lava rock walls; sunbathers appreciate the lounge chairs for hire; swimmers favor the calm waters; and surfers delight in the breaks along the offshore reef.

The area west of the statue is a bit less crowded and is known as Kuhio Beach Park. Musicians set up on the large stage area on Sunday afternoons. The beachfront walk picks up here, running along the sea and connecting to the east with Kapiolani Beach Park, which offers access to sand, grassy areas ripe with yogis and dog walkers, and so many tropical fish fluttering in the sea. Last time I was walking here, I saw three *humuhumunukunukuapuaas* (Hawai'i's state fish) swimming in the ocean just offshore. Locals paddle out to catch waves at Queen's Surf Beach and Publics.

This large saltwater pool was once a lively lap-swimming area fed by tides. Today is it off limits and in dire need of some TLC. Finally, the favorite of locals for ample free parking and mellow swimming is Sans Souci Beach.

If Waikiki makes you want to ride a wave, Hans Hedemann Surf School, Hawaiian Fire Surf School, Girls Who Surf, and Big Wave Dave offer surfing lessons and board rentals (many of these outfitters are included in the Go O'ahu card deals—see the chapter 2 sidebar). Na Hoku II docks its catamarans on the western edge of Waikiki Beach, and provides boozy cruises throughout the day and evening; most of the time, you can walk up and hop on a boat.

As the sun sets, the *tiki* torches blaze up along the sea. Scrubbed people dressed in their best linen and summer dresses descend upon Waikiki's eateries, which offer something to please every palate. Budget seekers and those with an affinity for Asian food are in luck. Waikiki caters to their biggest tourist market with style. Marukame Udon is *the* spot for savory bowls of soup. Don't let the line scare you away; it moves surprisingly quickly past the chefs making the noodles, then throwing them in a bowl, adding *musubi* and tempura, squirting on broth and sauce, and sending you along to slurp up the goodness. A bit more upscale, Matsugen is an expensive but delicious choice for handmade soba. Go early, or you'll be waiting for ages. In Aston Waikiki Joy Hotel, in-the-know Japanophiles can't get enough of the deliciously hip Tokyo favorite Kimukatsu. Order up the 25-layer pork cutlet *okonomiyaki*-style, taro tempura, and Japanese *panna cotta*.

Over in the Kapahulu Avenue area, Uncle Bo's is Waikiki's hippest eatery. Grind on farm-to-table Hawaiian fusion cuisine in the shadows of a pink backlit bar, or order up a fancy cocktail and gaze at O'ahu's beautiful hipsters. Directly next door is Irifune, a local spot for reasonably priced fusion meals. Don't miss "the number three" plate with seared garlic *ahi* sitting on a bed of fresh spinach. If you go to celebrate a birthday, get ready for oohs and aahs as the lights are turned off and the glow-in-the-dark stars shine

San Souci Beach and the Natatorium

on the ceiling while the staff sings. Up the street, the casual Rainbow Drive-In is Waikiki's favored eatery for *loco moco*, burgers, and teriyaki. I've yet to find a better macaroni salad.

For an upscale dinner, in Modern Honolulu, Morimoto Waikiki assumes a flashy demeanor with hovering coral fossils hanging from the ceiling and massive windows gazing upon the harbor. Chef Masaharu Morimoto didn't become a celebrity chef for nothing. Splurge on the

Public art on the Waikiki sidewalk

yellowtail bim bim bop, cooked at your table, or the tuna pizza. Cocktails are strong and as pricey as the food. Alternatively, Nobu Waikiki might be a part of the Iron Chef's dynasty, but there is nothing cookie-cutter about this slick eatery in Waikiki Parc Hotel. Expect to be wowed by his signature black cod with *miso*. Another outpost of a superstar chef is the venerable Roy's Waikiki. Sure, local icon Roy Yamaguchi has brought his house of Hawaiian regional cuisine to an urban center near you, but there is something charming about enjoying his pineapple martini, his signature *miso* butterfish, and topping it all off with chocolate soufflé in Hawai'i.

Rumor has it that unless you take your own fishing boat out into the sea, catch, gut, and eat your *opah* right there and then, you might not find a fresher seafood dinner on O'ahu than at the gorgeous Azure restaurant. Chef Matsubara is up at 5:30 a.m. selecting the best fish to serve that night from the Honolulu Fish Market. Tropical flavors dominate the menu, but don't be ashamed to sample the more traditional preparations, especially when the waiters recommend a particular cut of fish. Reservations required.

Spending years at the top of Hawai'i's *Best Of* lists as one of the most romantic dining destinations…ever, Halekulani's La Mer is a wise choice for celebratory dinners. Most mere mortals will not fancy shelling out a hunk of change for the exquisite tasting menu served in a plush dining room with million-dollar views. But if you want to pop the question, look no farther. Book well in advance, dress to the nines, bring your credit card, and expect to be enchanted by the French magnificence at one of O'ahu's best restaurants.

On Tuesday, Thursday, Saturday, and Sunday nights, there's a free beachfront Kuhio Beach Hula Show at 6:30, complete with live musicians, a serenade by local birds fluttering around the banyan tree, and plenty of bootie shaking. Another free evening hula show can be found at Royal Hawaiian Center and features venerable local musicians giving an informative (and entertaining) lesson on the history of music and hula in the state. Most major hotels offer live music in the evenings, so check *Honolulu Weekly* for specifics. Often you'll find famed crooners Jake Shimabukuro, Vergel Jepas, or Tahiti Rey populating the lounges of large hotels. Favorite venues to catch a live show in Waikiki include the poolside lounge at Modern Honolulu, the Banyan Tree Bar at Westin Moana Surfrider, Lulu's Surf Club, and Hilton Hawaiian Village's Tapa Bar. For those who want to dance under the stars, head over to the gay-friendly Hula's Bar and Lei Stand. There are a couple of dinner shows in Waikiki, which frankly are all too pricey for me to enthusiastically give a nod to, but if you *must*, head over the Waikiki Starlight Lu'au at Hilton Hawaiian Village for an energetic show of fire dancing and hula.

In general, breakfast in Waikiki is overpriced, with excruciatingly long waits for mediocre food. A fantastic, albeit pricey, option along the Ala Wai Canal is Cream Pot, a precious eatery that manages to feel like you entered a Hobbit's country abode. Order the overly sweet soufflé pancakes or the burgundy beef omelet. On the more casual side, locals swear by the greasy breakfast fare at Wailana Coffee House where you can carboload for that morning surf or hike. Portions are lumberjack sized and you probably won't tweet about the meal, but the guava-stuffed French toast is better than pretty much anything you find at one of those gigantic resort buffets. Your best bet is to travel away from the beach, up Kapahulu Avenue, to enjoy house-made specialties at the homey Sweet E's Café, hidden in the back of a strip mall with pictures of the owner's family lining the

WHAT THE HECK IS THE GREEN FLASH?

You'll hear sunset-watchers murmur about the phenomenon of the green flash. Often enough, applause will follow a sunset, making you wonder if you are crazy for not having seen something besides a beautiful ball of gas dissolving into the sea. The green flash is a mirage, an optical illusion of sorts, but that does not mean it isn't real. I've seen it. Twice. And both times I was completely sober. Here's how it happens: Usually as the sun sets over the horizon (it's best over the ocean), just a second or two after the sun is gone from sight, a ray of green seems to bloom over the spot where the sun just was. It requires careful attention and literally thousands of sunsets before you glimpse this unusual occurrence. Keep your eyes peeled and soon you too will join the "green flash club."

Sunsets like this might offer a glimpse of the green flash.

Diamond Head crater

walls. Be prepared to wait on weekends for the freshly crafted corned beef hash and banana pancakes.

From Kalakaua Avenue, travel south; the road turns into Monsarrat Avenue and then
Diamond Head Road; continue until it ends. Park in the lot (go early, as the parking lot
fills up by late morning) and get ready to ascend O'ahu's most vivid landmark: Diamond
Head State Monument. Created by a fierce lava flow, the crater has held sacred significance for locals since ancient times. Today thousands climb up the steep 0.8-mile trail
to reach the crowded peak, which offers stellar views of Kahala, Koko Head, Waikiki, and
Honolulu. Bring lots of water and sunscreen and reschedule if rain is in the forecast.
While the century-old trail is paved, it can get slippery, especially in the dark tunnel
about three-quarters of the way up the hill. The entire hike should take between an hour
and two hours depending on your fitness ability.

If you cannot tell already, O'ahu is all about food. So on the way back to Waikiki, going
over Diamond Head Road you'll spot crowds lingering outside Diamond Head Market
and Grill, a gourmet market with a decent hot food selection and a glorious selection of

OCEANARIUM RESTAURANT'S BRUNCH

Birthday celebrations are de rigueur at Pacific Beach Hotel's Oceanarium Restaurant. The under-the-sea-themed brunch spread sits in the shadows of a massive floor-to-ceiling aquarium, packed with tropical fish and coral. Just when you thought the experience could not get any wackier, the "mermaids" appear in the tank, holding up signs to wish people happy birthday and swimming around while you eat crab legs. *Only in Waikiki....*

snacks. In the Kapahulu Avenue area, Ono Seafood is known for outstanding fresh *poke* that often sells out after the lunch rush (I like to grab a container to take away for afternoon beach *pupus*).

Back in Waikiki, Iyasume Musubi-Ya is lodged behind Hyatt Regency on the bottom floor of an apartment complex. This hole-in-the-wall is *the* place for cheap and delicious Japanese favorites like *musubi*, curry, and rice bowls. For those prowling Waikiki's streets for organic grub, look no farther than Ruffage Natural Foods. Sure the prices are outrageous, but the *ahi* bowls, heaping turkey sandwiches stuffed with locally grown avocados, and the banana and peanut butter smoothies will please those who consider their body a temple of health. For decent Thai food, Siam Square delivers salty noodle dishes, fiery curries, and hearty meat and veggie plates.

Besides restaurants, Kapahulu Road shelters some of Waikiki's most interesting shops. For the largest selection of vintage and new aloha shirts maybe on the planet, stop

Just one angle of the 360-degree view from atop Diamond Head

FARM-FRESH EVERYTHING

Get up early on Saturday morning and motor up to KCC Saturday Farmers' Market, at the community college next to the entrance of Diamond Head. Keep an eye out for Pig & the Lady's *poke* with fried kale chips, pineapple sausage at the sausage company, and Grandma G's *char sui* fried rice. It is super crowded and parking is *cra*-zy! But what other farmers' market offers complimentary straw mats to picnic on, locally grown and roasted coffees, and starfruit to sample?

---

at Bailey's Antiques and Aloha Shirts. Another favorite is Somace Design, a small home décor shop that never fails at making me want just about everything—it's all beach style here, but *style* is the word of note in that phrase.

Back in downtown Waikiki, expect many of the swanky shops you'd see at any international destination—a Ferrari Store, an Apple Store, Anna Sui, Gucci, alongside a super-cheesy International Market Place, ground zero for *keiki* hula skirts, Hawai'i beach towels, and license plates. Musicians should save some time to admire Bob's Ukulele in the Marriott; the rest of you might want to hold off until you reach Honolulu, where there are more unique boutiques.

Sure, most of you head to Waikiki to laze away on the beach, but what do you do when it rains, or if you are too sunburned to enjoy the beach? While on the small side, Waikiki Aquarium features a collection of tropical fish that will make the child in you gleefully scream, "There's Nemo!" There are monk seals and sharks on hand as well. Across the street, at Kapi'olani Park, laze under a banyan and spot the resident parrots, listen to live music at the bandstand, and then take a tour of Honolulu Zoo. Though most the of zoo is outside and I have been caught in many storms here, don't let that sway you; the animals get frisky in the rain and do their part to entertain visitors.

Once you've had your fill of Waikiki—and chances are you will tire of the endless crowds, weak *mai tais*, and time-share salespeople vying for your attention—travel west on Ala Wai Boulevard, right on McCully Street, and then turn left on Kapiolani Street to find Ala Moana Center. The pulse of O'ahu, this three-story outdoor shopping area features live hula

---

THE SWEETEST TREATS IN WAIKIKI

It's impossible to be in O'ahu and not experience the historic Leonard's, O'ahu's legendary home of *malasadas*—a sweet fried ball of dough stuffed with flavored crèmes. Tour buses, locals, families, and fans of all things sweet cram into the retro doughnut shop, and you should too.

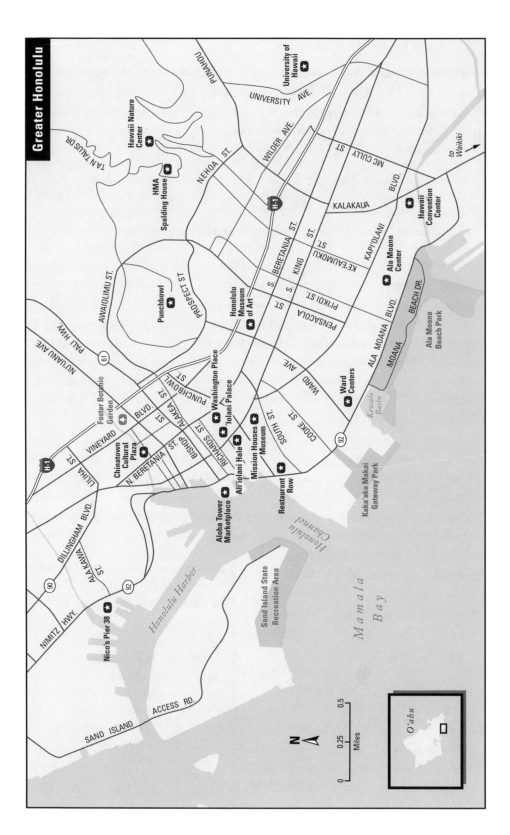

Greater Honolulu

DETOUR: KAIMUKI'S FARM-TO-TABLE RESTAURANTS

The nondescript Waialae Avenue highlights some of O'ahu's best farm-to-table restaurants. At the helm is Ed Kenney's spectacular Town Restaurant. Besides being the choice O'ahu chef for the Obamas, Kenney is a guiding light in serving fresh-off-the-farm breakfast, lunch, and dinner in a spare yet artsy dining room. Breakfasts show off banana pancakes and fried rice with eggs. Lunches and dinners favor risotto cakes topped with *ahi tartare*, or a limited selection of gnocchi with Kulana beef ragout.

Up the road, 12th Ave Grill is at once neighborhoody and sophisticated, sourcing its produce from local farms to craft New American Cuisine with a Hawaiian twist. I often order a bunch of appetizers like baked mac and cheese and beer-battered avocado, and then share an organic Jidori-marinated chicken breast lathered in honey, mustard, and spinach. No one does chocolate like these guys, so save room for dessert.

In 2012, Salt Bar + Kitchen came onto the scene. Like its neighboring restaurants, this venture uses local ingredients, but they take it one step farther, with artisan cocktails like Smoking Goat to pair with *chiccharones* and house-made charcuterie. You can't go wrong with the duck ramen, nor the brick-pressed Jidori chicken with Mexican spices and sweet corn. Open late, this is the kind of place locals like to whisper about for fear that the word will get out and too many people will crowd the slick bar area.

shows and Hawaiian music on select afternoons, as well as a hopping Mai Tai Bar, two food courts, and some haute cuisine (Alan Wong's Pineapple Room is *the* locally favored eatery for the work crowd). The ground floor hawks an array of kitschy tourist-centered shops for that last-minute turtle magnet, while the upper floors feature everything from Balenciaga and a Shirokiya Department Store to local boutiques like Cinnamon Girl and Sand People.

Speaking of the mall's Shirokiya Department Store, a visit to Ala Moana would not be complete without a stop at their Japanese food court. Line up for *takoyaki* (octopus balls) cooked in front of you; when they are ready, the chef hits a drum and announces, "Come and get them"—in Japanese of course. The *gyoza* stand is quite good. There's ramen, bento, *okonomoyaki*, *udon*, sushi, and a host of sweet and savory snacks (I like to grab airplane food here). Plus, the food court occasionally invites guest chefs from Japan to sling favorites.

While you likely won't have time to visit, it is helpful to know that, almost next door to the mall, Ward Centers houses a host of additional shops, a cinema favored by locals on rainy days, and a few eateries. Na Mea Hawai'i sells native Hawaiian books and locally made crafts and clothing. Also in the massive shopping area, you'll find shops like

Rainbowtique for all your U of H gear, Honolulu Chocolate Company for yummy cocoa treats, and Nohea Gallery's inspiring collection of art.

Across the street from Ala Moana Mall is Honolulu's beach, an ideal post-shopping destination, especially as the sun sets and locals come out for picnics, ukulele strumming, and to catch waves. Ala Moana Beach Park is part grassy park, with a pond for remote-control boats, picnic areas, jogging trails, and sporting areas, and part world-class beach with dependable waves for surfers, white sand, and a fun atmosphere. After a bit of shopping, go for a sunset swim or jog.

When you are ready for your evening meal, one of the most famous restaurants in O'ahu, Alan Wong's, is just a short drive away. This world-class eatery serves dependable Hawaiian regional cuisine like twice-cooked *kalbi* short ribs, albeit without those superstar views of some of his peers' restaurants. The cooking speaks louder than any view could, which is a testimony to Wong's talents. If you are in town for Wong's Farmers Series Dinners, which highlight (you guessed it) the wealth of produce found on O'ahu, book a spot at his table well in advance.

Another esteemed dining destination, Chef Mavro presents the local bounty spruced up by George Mavrothalassitis's French upbringing and training. Imagine a caviar menu fit for *ali'i*, abalone *yuzu*, and *lilliko'i malasadas*, all served via a four- or six-course tasting menu. One of O'ahu's most romantic restaurants, this pricey option is a great choice for celebratory dinners, though not fit for families.

Nanzan GiroGiro specializes in *kaiseki*—ceremonial small plates devoted to the art and craft of Japanese cooking. Rumor has it that chef Yoshihiro Matsumoto not only handmakes the plates that food is served on, but also crafts your dinner in an open-air kitchen surrounded by the restaurant's 30 seats. Reservations are required. Dishes like eggplant topped with cured *maguro*, *uni*, tofu skin, and *mizuna* inspire.

For something a bit less extravagant,

While not native, a hibiscus flower is a common sight on the islands.

USEFUL WEBSITES

❖ Beat of Hawaii, www.beatofhawaii.com
❖ Hawai'i Tourism Authority, www.gohawaii.com
❖ *Honolulu Star Advertiser*, www.staradvertiser.com
❖ Na Ala Hele, hawaiitrails.ehawaii.gov

but no less in demand, pop into Side Street Inn (they also have a Kapahulu Avenue location, for those wanting to eat a bit closer to Waikiki's main drag). Late in the evening chefs populate the vinyl booths, watching sports and pigging out on the huge plates of pork chops, *kimchi* fried rice, and fried butter pound cake (sounds like just the ticket for those wanting to squeeze into a bikini, huh?). All plates are large enough to share.

Fans of Japanese cuisine swear by the sashimi, baked king crab, grapefruit soju, and seared salmon at Sushi Izakaya Gaku. You'll have to make a reservation for dinner, unless you don't mind waiting for ages, as this is one of O'ahu's most noteworthy tables. Another local favorite, Sushi Sasabune is more expensive, but is rumored to be the best sushi in the state—one friend calls this "the Holy Grail of raw fish." Though I'm not sure I'd go that far, their squid stuffed with blue crab is phenomenal. Tables are hard to get: Reservations are highly recommended. A bit farther out in the university area, Imanas Tei Restaurant is known for friendly service and delicious *chanko nabe*, a traditional stew that helps sumo wrestlers gain weight. Make a reservation well in advance, as this dinner only favorite fills quickly with students, families, and people snapping photos of their seafood dynamite.

When the sun sets, the area surrounding Ala Moana does not turn its lights out. Sure, you'll find better drinking establishments in Chinatown, but don't tell the party at V Lounge, where head-bobbing hipsters hang until well past bedtime enjoying wood-fired pizzas crafted by a true *pizzaiolo* and late-night grooves.

In the morning, travel up to Punahou Street, weaving uphill through Manoa, one of Honolulu's poshest neighborhoods. Punahou turns into Manoa Road; veer on East Manoa Road to reach O'ahu's best coffee shop, Morning Glass Coffee. The open-air café features local art, groovy tunes, and the best lattes around. They serve pastries made from locally sourced fruits, and on weekends they have a minimal brunch menu. Fill up your belly and then continue on Manoa Road (you'll want to travel back to the fork where it became East Manoa Road). Drive until you reach the parking lot for Manoa Falls. This is easily O'ahu's most rewarding hike, as halfway into the 1.6-mile round-trip experience you are greeted with a gushing waterfall plunging into a crystal pool—though don't swim in it, as leptospirosis has been found in most of the island's freshwater pools. On

Manoa Falls is just a short hike from Honolulu.

the way back to the car, detour up to the Lyon Arboretum. Managed by UH Manoa, this lovely 200-acre green space showcases native plants in a less manicured way than you'll see in most botanical gardens. You could easily turn your visit into a three-hour adventure exploring the grassy hills and hidden waterfalls, though I generally get too hungry to do more than snap a couple of pictures before heading back downhill. Bring mosquito repellent.

As you travel back downhill, Wai'oli Tea Room lounges in a shady nook against a sea of trees. This breakfast and lunch spot has been slinging salads and sandwiches since 1922; the teas, quiet ambience, and bakery goods make for a relaxing post-hike stop, though once the novelty wears off I prefer to eat elsewhere.

If you can hold off your hunger until you descend into the University District along King Street, health food junkies should make their way to Down to Earth Natural and Organic Grocery. This massive market not only features all you'll need for a picnic, but also offers smoothies, fruit and veggie juices, hot vegetarian cuisine, and heaping sandwiches. For some serious Hawaiian fare without any pretense, line up at Da Kitchen for artery-clogging outlandishly big plates of deep-fried Spam *musubi*, chicken long rice, and *shoyu* chicken. After lunch, be sure to pop into Bubbies for traditional Japanese-style *mochi* ice cream and tropical ice creams sure to delight the goofy kid in you.

With your belly full, drive north to Beretania Street and travel west for 2 miles. You need at least half a day to *fully* explore the Honolulu Museum of Art (though without the extra tour of Shangri La, you can do this in about three hours). This 75-year-old-museum pleases families and art lovers with collections from around the globe. View masters like O'Keeffe and Monet as well as some of the world's most interesting ancient and modern works by Pacific Islanders. There's a café for snacks and coffees. It is possible to save your tour of the main museum for the weekend Art After Dark parties (check online for details). The museum hosts the Doris Duke Theatre, which features live music and artsy films on select nights. You'll have to reserve in advance to take a guided tour of the museum's Doris Duke's Shangri La estate near Diamond Head. The 5-acre 1937 estate of tobacco-heiress Doris Duke houses an impressive collection of Islamic art and is considered one of Hawai'i's most architecturally significant homes.

Serious art fans might also budget time to motor up into the hills over Honolulu to view the HMA's Spalding House. The Asian-inspired grounds lead to a collection of modern art by David Hockney, Japanese woodblock prints, and inspiring creations by Hawaiians. There is a small café on site for a coffee and pastry should you want to stay awhile. Your admission fee gets you into both the Honolulu Museum of Art and the Spaulding House on the same day.

By this point, you are probably ready for some sustenance, and while you are near many of the other eateries suggested earlier, I have one more worth consideration. Travel west on South Beretania to Ward Avenue (turn left); turn right on Ala Moana Boulevard, and then right on Keawe. Nestled in an industrial area is Whole Ox Deli and Butcher Shop. Foodies rally around this sleek café, lining up for all parts of the cow served between slices of hearty bread, the 21-day dry-aged burger, or the fried chicken sandwich. If you're uninterested in meat, the last time I was here the "falafel" sandwich blew me away. They have limited hours, so check the website to make sure they are serving dinner. Afterward, head over to Restaurant Row's Hiroshi's Eurasian Tapas for sangria.

Downtown Honolulu might look like it is geared toward the lunch crowd, but don't be fooled: You can score a yummy breakfast as well. Start with a coffee at Honolulu Coffee Company's downtown location, or sample a microbrewed Hawaiian cup of joe at Beach Bum Cafe. Then gear up for belly-filling pancakes packed with fruit at Café Kaila. For a Japanese breakfast and lunch highlighting *musubi*, Manu Bu's is considered addictive in some circles—they close when they run out of those small rice balls filled with salty ingredients like salmon, often before 1 p.m., so go early. Tango Café serves three meals a day, but I fancy their breakfast benedicts and *loco moco* above all else. A bit far out of downtown, though still in Honolulu, Liliha Bakery is famous for

O'AHU'S *TIKI* BAR

It's tough not to immediately fall in love with La Mariana Sailing Club. Located on a private marina along Sand Island, this funky *tiki* bar serves up *mai tais* in hand-carved mugs. The Hawaiiana lining the walls, ocean views, and live music add to the allure. There's food as well, though I usually just opt for a *pupu* during the sunset and then have a bigger meal later in another location.

EAT THE STREET

On the last Friday of the month, from 4 to 9 p.m., don't miss the 250 food trucks that participate in Eat the Street. This food festival features some of O'ahu's most innovative chefs. Favorite edibles include the *kalua* pork from Simply Ono, anything from Girls Who Bake Next Door Dessert Truck, the Malasada Burger truck, Ono To Go, Ono Pops, and Camille's on Wheels fusion tacos.

coco puffs and Chantilly banana bread, long waits, and late-night hours. Go early, as the tour buses bring visitors here throughout the day.

Most bypass Honolulu's historic attractions. Don't make that mistake. Plan a day (or two) to really see Greater Honolulu. It isn't called "the gathering place" for nothing. In the bustling streets you'll find businesspeople in Hawaiian shirts, the USA's last remaining palace, parks, cultural attractions, and some of the state's best restaurants. Because of car break-ins, I recommend paying to park in the Ali'i Place lot on Alakea Street. The compact downtown area allows for you to walk between many destinations.

The centerpiece of Honolulu is 'Iolani Palace—the only royal palace on American soil. Built by King Kalakaua's devotees in 1882, this palace has long been a symbol of Hawai'i's current state. After the sugar barons took over the islands, they imprisoned Queen Lili'uokalani here and then allowed the palace to fall into shambles. Local historians have reinvigorated the place, offering guided tours by reservation (independent-

'Iolani Palace stands guard over downtown Honolulu. *Eddie Broitman*

minded readers can also take self-guided explorations—check the website for times). The palace showcases historical photos and artifacts, plus a refurbished kitchen and office. Children under five are not allowed inside. The 'Iolani Palace grounds beckon, especially at lunchtime on Friday when there is often live Hawaiian music by Royal Hawaiian Band. Take a seat under the banyan tree and view the statues of Moloka'i saint Father Damien and Queen Lili'uokalani (Hawai'i's last ruling queen) guarding the State Capitol Building.

Across the street, Washington Place is a colonial mansion constructed in 1846 for Queen Lili'uokalani and her *haole* husband. Today the governor calls the mansion home. Call for reservations to tour the building.

Just on the edge of the grounds on Richards Street, Hawai'i State Art Museum (HiSAM) is one of the few state-sponsored museums in the country. HiSAM, Hawai'i's newest museum, presents a staggeringly large collection of work by Hawai'i artists. Essentially HiSAM is a "museum without walls," allowing visitors to interact with the art of Pacific Islanders, with a wealth of cultural activities like family art days, First Friday Art Nights, lectures, and live music performances. The museum store, Showcase Hawai'i, showcases innovative crafts. Grab a snack at Grand Café & Bakery, which serves Hawaiian food from the 1920s; or head over to Café Julia located next door at the Julia Morgan–

DETOUR: EXPLORING THE HILLS ABOVE HONOLULU

Hikers can spend days exploring the trails above Honolulu. However, since most of you have limited island time, you can still get the Upper Manoa Valley vistas without taking too much time away from your beach days. An easy scenic drive starts just 2 miles above downtown Honolulu. Take Tantalus Drive uphill to Hawai'i Nature Center, where local families and school groups depart for guided hikes and outdoor adventures. Pop into the center to learn about the flora and fauna of this fertile valley, or to inquire about excursions you can join. If you'd prefer to throw those hiking shoes back on, from here the Makiki Loop Trail explores 2.5 miles of lush forests, connecting you to Nu'uanu Valley Lookout. Grab a map from the Nature Center if adventure inspires you to take the long road. Drivers should continue up the very twisty Tantalus Drive, where (if the tropical forest makes you want to dive in and hike all morning) you can catch any number of trails that circle Mount Tantalus and provide budding photographers with a bird's-eye view of Honolulu. The road continues for 8.5 miles into Pu'u 'Ualaka'a State Wayside, where you can hike the Pu'u 'Ohi'a Trail to Nu'uanu Valley Lookout, which offers glorious views of southern O'ahu. You can still access the lookout and snap those memorable photos as you drive. Just know the road turns into Round Top Drive as it descends back toward Honolulu.

designed YWCA. Sourced with organic and locally grown produce, Café Julia is a favorite with the lunch crowd for their huge burger, *loco moco*, pork chops, and wild-caught salmon.

In front of Ali'iolani Hale (which means "house of heavenly chefs"), notice the massive bronze statue of King Kamehameha. On King Kamehameha Day, June 11, this statue is wreathed in leis, and is the centerpiece of the statewide celebration of the legendary king. Ali'iolani Hale is Hawai'i's oldest government building, built in 1874, and now houses the Hawai'i Supreme Court.

On Wednesday at noon, St. Andrews Cathedral features musicians, who pound out tunes on the massive pipe organ for free. Otherwise, you can make arrangements to tour this 1861 French Gothic church on Sunday. The building was commissioned by King Kamehameha IV and Queen Emma to prove their faith. O'ahu's oldest tribute to Christianity, Kawaiaha'o Church, was constructed over 170 years ago. Made of more than 14,000 coral pieces, this project took divers and builders four painstaking years to complete. Also on the grounds you'll see the resting place for missionaries, King Lunalilo, and Sanford Dole. Donations are accepted.

Next door, take a step back in time to explore the social history of early Hawai'i at Mission Houses Museum. The New England–style saltbox Frame House is the oldest existing house in Hawai'i, built in 1821. You can view a replica of the Ramage hand press used to print the first Hawaiian laws, newspapers, Bibles, and schoolbooks.

Take H1 west to Kalihi Street north; turn right onto Bernice Street to find Hawai'i's tribute to natural history at the Bishop Museum. Explore the world's largest collection of Hawaiian and Pacific artifacts. There's a hall of sea mammals as well. The attractive grounds and historic buildings feature rotating exhibits for kids and grown-ups. Don't miss the lava exhibit, where the staff actually *makes lava* right in front of you. There's a modest store for crafts and books, as well as a planetarium. Check the website for weekly events.

Make your way to South Vineyard Street, in the outskirts of Chinatown, to reach Foster Botanical Gardens. Home to two kapok trees, this is the tree museum of Joni

REAL HAWAIIAN COMFORT FOOD

Lunchtime is serious business at Helena's Hawaiian Food, open since 1946. Winner of the James Beard Award, chef Helen Kwock Chock doesn't mess around. Lip-smacking deliciousness is served here for way less (and it's way better tasting) than you'll find at any lu'au. This is where you should try poi, *kalua* pork, *lomilomi* salad, and *haupia*. They have limited hours, so check the website before trekking out here.

The Bishop Museum

Mitchell's song "Big Yellow Taxi." Thirteen acres of some of the planet's most unusual, most fragrant, and most beautiful plants can be found here. Garden fans can spend hours wandering through the orchid gardens, inhaling the vanilla, and marveling at the array of trees that thrive in the Pacific. At the entrance is the Buddhist Kuan Yin Temple, adorned inside with flowers, fruit, and incense.

When you've exhausted your trip into the past, now is the time to experience O'ahu's haven of hip—Chinatown. What began as the home of Chinese laborers is now a vibrant blend of Southeast Asian immigrants and fashion-forward boutiques, galleries and antiques shops, thriving eateries, homey noodle shops, and the state's best nightclubs. The area in and around North Hotel Street can be somewhat dodgy, especially after dark—the street doubles as skid row.

Park in Chinatown Cultural Plaza, a modern outdoor mall of sorts, with statues of Kuan Yin and Chinese revolutionary Dr. Sun Yat-sen. While you can stroll the interior of the mall hunting for the best acupuncturist or flight deals to Beijing, opt for the River Promenade (which is a somewhat stinky and dirty area with picnic tables dotted with elderly Chinese men playing cards and *mah-jongg*) to grab a few *char-siu* pork or red bean buns at Royal Kitchen's take-out counter.

Wander along Maunakea Street, noticing the ladies stringing flower leis—this is the cheapest place to get these fragrant flower necklaces, used as a symbol of dignity, or to

---

FIRST FRIDAY ART WALK

The monthly First Friday Art Walk put Chinatown on the map for the beautiful people of Honolulu. Today hordes congregate in Chinatown on the first Friday of the month when boutiques and galleries stay open until 9 p.m. Download the map at www.firstfridayhawaii.com. Galleries worth a peek inside include the ARTS at Marks Garage (for funky mixed-media art), Pegge Hopper Gallery (for female-centered paintings), and thirtyninehotel (where local artists reinvent the entire club and bar every three months). Even if you don't make it here on the first Friday, you can always visit the galleries earlier.

---

mark a special day like a birthday, anniversary, or graduation. If you'd like to see what it feels like to be in a Chinese marketplace without traveling to Shanghai, Maunakea Marketplace won't let you down. There's an Asian food court here, but if I were you, I'd hold off—there is better food in your future. At North King and Kekaulike Streets, O'ahu Market is home to the fresh-caught fish reeled in every morning.

Weaving through the streets, travel away from the river to reach Nu'uanu Avenue. If you're the type who can spend eons exploring Hawaiiana and funky clothing, you'll love Chinatown's antiques shops and boutiques. La Muse lures urbanites with creative jewelry and fun bikinis. On Bethel Street, Homecoming hawks funky dresses, T-shirts, and jackets, ideal for the artists who line Chinatown's streets after dark. On the same block, Blank Canvas caters to skaters and surfers, or those interlopers wanting to dress like one.

It's hard not to become smitten with the sheer abundance of good food in this 1-mile stretch of O'ahu. Lucky Belly is the brainchild of Jessie Cruz and Dusty Grabble, both locals with fine-dining experience, who wanted to create a space where you could grab an affordable bowl of ramen alongside Bordeaux or a peaty Scotch from Islay. Throw in an industrial space with thoughtful—almost racy—artwork, a glorious sake menu, and some of O'ahu's best pork buns.

Next door, Little Village Noodle House reels them in with less creative but dependable seafood noodle dishes bathed in garlic, fried rice, and honey walnut shrimp. I order something different every time and have always been impressed. Late-night meal service packs them in. If you prefer dim sum, Legend Seafood

Lucky Belly's spicy ramen satisfies.

Pearl Harbor

Restaurant might be starting to lose its luster, but the sheer array of Chinese favorites like potstickers, bao, garlic noodles, and chicken feet will allow you to experience the essence of Chinatown.

Hang around Chinatown long enough and you hear about Indigo, vital in the emergence of this community as a dining destination. Indigo has a devoted following for its fusion *pupus* like goat cheese wontons, as well as fantastic happy-hour martini specials (the *lychee* is a house favorite). The bar is packed on Friday nights when drinks and live music flow freely.

After dark, check *Honolulu Weekly* for event listings. There's often live music to be found at the historic art deco Hawai'i Theatre and thirtyninehotel (which also boasts one of the islands' most innovative mixologists). Live music and 150 bottles of

THE ISLAND'S BEST SOUVENIRS

To purchase souvenirs on a Wednesday, Saturday, or Sunday before 3 p.m., Aloha Stadium Swap Meet is the one-stop shop for *cheap* Hawaiiana and some serious *ono kine grindz* whipped up in some of the state's best food trucks. The stadium is just off H1, along Highway 99 in 'Aiea.

beer enliven Bar 35. Part art gallery, part coffee shop, and part bar, with live music and an inventive *mai tai* sure to change your perception of the fruity cocktail, Manifest reels in the cool kids.

If you don't have too much of a headache in the morning, take H1 west, bypassing the airport and following the signs to Pearl Harbor's World War II Valor in the Pacific National Monument. Established on O'ahu in 1949, the monument commemorates all World War II military veterans who died in the attack on Pearl Harbor. On December 7, 1941, over 350 Japanese planes flew over O'ahu. They showered bombs on the Pacific fleet, sinking the USS *Arizona* in nine minutes, trapping the crew inside the tomb of a ship. The two-hour attack destroyed 20 other ships and over 300 aircraft.

Today Pearl Harbor's four attractions are Hawai'i's number one tourist destination. To avoid crowds, try to time your visit as early as you can on a weekday, and buy tickets in advance—only a third of tickets are available for walk-ins. You need a few hours to fully tour this massive tribute to the military. The entire experience can be emotional, especially as you walk through the new visitors center and see the faces of the people who perished here. Also intense is the 23-minute movie explaining the Japanese attack, followed by the boat ride to see the sunken USS *Arizona* and the stunning white memorial built atop the ship. You'll see a reef growing on the ship, tropical fish swimming below, plenty of oil that remains in the water to this day, and flowers floating in the sea (though this is harmful to the fish, it is lovely). When you arrive at Pearl Harbor, you must check in with the visitors center to get the time of your boat trip to the memorial—expect to wait a bit before your launch.

Those really in the military spirit can tour USS *Bowfin* Submarine and Museum. Learn about the history of these underwater vessels and actually enter this historic sub. Another stop on the itinerary should be the Battleship *Missouri* Memorial. To get out to this former battleship, just beyond the memorial, purchase tickets at Bowfin Park and board the visitors shuttle. Take a self-guided tour of this giant ship, which was present in both the battles of Iwo Jima and Okinawa. You'll also need to grab tickets at Bowfin Park to tour the Pacific Aviation Museum's collection of Japanese bombers, WWII memo-

---

DETOUR: NATIONAL MEMORIAL CEMETERY OF THE PACIFIC

The Punchbowl crater, just a mile from downtown Honolulu, was one of the ancient locations for human sacrifices. Today it is the final resting place for thousands of US soldiers, many of them casualties from World War II. You may walk around the cemetery, soaking up the quiet, the views, and the chance for a bit of introspection after a wild night in Chinatown.

DETOUR: KEA'IWA HEIAU STATE RECREATION AREA

If you fancy a hike in the hills atop Pearl Harbor, take H1 west from Honolulu and merge onto Highway 78. Get off on Moanalua Road (this is exit 13A) and turn right on 'Aiea Heights Drive. Continue for just over 2 miles until you reach Kea'iwa Heiau State Recreation Area. The ancients used this sacred *heiau* to grow medicinal herbs. The healers then used the herbs to treat everything from fevers to heart disease. While today it's no more than a pile of rocks with medicinal plants rising around them, this is considered a sacred site by Hawaiians, so please respect the area.

Locals use the 4.5-mile 'Aiea Loop Trail to stay in shape, running, hiking, and mountain biking. The views from up here are worth the trek, and history buffs keep an eye out for the wreckage of a military cargo plane that crashed in the 1940s. However, avoid the hike if it has been raining, and bring rain gear year-round.

---

rabilia, and remnants from recent aviation history. For all of these attractions, you are not allowed to bring in any bags or backpacks, so leave them in the car.

When it comes time for lunch, head over to Waipahu, O'ahu's former capital, to find Tanioka's Seafoods and Catering. Known for *poke*, fried chicken, *musubi*, and long lines of hungry eaters waiting for their fix, this choice eatery is a great antidote to a contemplative morning. Another Waipahu favorite is Poke Stop, which boasts over 20 kinds of *poke*, *bentos*, hearty steaks, and *kalbi* short ribs. They have another location in Mililani. While you are in the area, check out Hawai'i Plantation Village in Waipahu Cultural Garden Park. This living museum educates about Hawai'i's sugar history. Explore 30 homes that are authentic replicas of immigrant dwellings and take in the simplicity of the past. Around Halloween this museum has a freaky haunted house.

From Waipahu, take Farrington Highway west toward the Leeward Coast. O'ahu's least-visited region is the industrial center of the island, but this is also where a vast majority of the state's native Hawaiians live. To some, this is the real Hawai'i, devoid of tourists (except in the Ko Olina Resort area), with beach parks packed on weekends with picnickers, kids running around grassy parks, and beach shacks hugging the highway. Many tourists might consider the lack of breezy lanais, adventure outfitters, and *mai tais* dull or, worse, distressing, but the reason people live here is because this is where they can afford to live. Locals are territorial of their last slice of their island.

Off Farrington Highway in Kapolei is Wet 'n' Wild Hawai'i, the state's only water park. Thrill yourselves with exhilarating slides, lazy rivers, and a wealth of ways to cool off in the heat of the day. Pools vary by age, so adults can enjoy quieter soaks while the *keikis* can splash to their hearts' content. This outdoor wonderland is quite expensive, so

Around Ko Olina Resort area, the beaches turn a bit more rugged.

plan to stay long enough to get your money's worth. This is best enjoyed if you are staying at Ko Olina, or want to head here after a trip to Pearl Harbor before trekking back to Waikiki.

Continuing on Farrington Highway, follow the signs to Ko Olina Resort area. Worlds away from the dry, almost desolate Leeward Coast farther north, this manicured resort area is home to a collection of upscale resorts, condos, and a golf course. For those who want luxury, or to escape the crowds of Hawai'i's largest metropolis, Ko Olina makes a great base—it is just 40 minutes from Waikiki and Honolulu's fine restaurants.

Ko Olina houses four man-made lagoons, hugged by that perfect Hawaiian sand. These lagoons are ideal for swimming, snorkeling in the mornings, and learning to stand-up paddle. There's a paved path connecting the lagoons, as well as dirt trails leading to hidden beaches frequented by endangered Hawaiian monk seals. Families and hesitant swimmers can visit these lagoons to enjoy soaking in the sea without fear of waves.

Other than Ko Olina Golf Club, this area is about pure bliss and relaxation. Those hunting for romance or quiet have JW Marriott Ihiani Resort all to themselves now that Disney's Aulani moved in next door and swooped up the family travel business. This upscale resort is bathed in white and occupies a prime perch above the sea. Typical luxuries like tropical room décor, a pool and spa, four restaurants, a couple of posh lounges, and tennis courts add to the allure.

Disney's Aulani Resort seems to have thought of everything: a tropical-fish-and-coral-filled saltwater pool for guests to snorkel with *humuhumunukunukuapuaas*; architecture that focuses on Hawai'i's past with thatched-roof high-rises and petroglyphs on the wallpaper and carpets; and abundant flowers leis left around the property for guests to try on at will. Rooms provide upscale amenities like private lanais and plush bedding, throwing in extra perks like after-sun lotion and foot cream. There's a great kids' club, a fun spa for grown-ups and teens, a scavenger hunt using the hotel's smartphones to make paintings come alive (this is Disney), and the best pool area in the state (with a huge lazy river to inner-tube down, a thrilling waterslide, water play areas, a shave ice stand and snack food, and a lively poolside bar); plus there are four restaurants, including the signature 'Ama 'Ama Restaurant, which serves a pricey oceanfront Japanese breakfast, fruity pancakes and omelets. If you can get over the sticker shock of this resort, you'll be rewarded with a Hawaiian experience like no other.

Across the street, Ko Olina Center offers the only non-resort services in these parts. Stock up with groceries at Island Country Market—a spruced-up ABC Store. The only restaurant I *love* over here is Maui farm-to-table chef Peter Merriman's Monkeypod Kitchen—an open-air, two-story megalith, with live Hawaiian music, *tiki* torches, outstanding wood-fired pizzas, *poke* and seafood entrées. The cocktail menu is as well thought out as the food. Make a reservation.

If you are not staying in one of the Ko Olina resorts, hop back on the highway, passing Kahe Point (notable for its giant power plant). Continue through the community of Nanakuli, passing Nanakuli Beach, where locals handwrite posters selling *shoyu* chicken and BBQ, and families gather on the grass to celebrate just about everything. A bit down the road is Wai'anae, the center of activity for this stretch of coast. The area can appear dreary to some, with no resorts or upscale eateries banking on your cash. For

---

NO PANIC GO ORGANIC AT MA'O FARMS By Lilly Barels

Take a farm tour and relish the full-body stimulation: the grand view of the majestic Wai'anae mountains, the delicious fresh taste of freshly harvested organic fruits and vegetables, the rumbling sound of the waves, and the feel of the red earth under your feet. Ma'O Farms offers opportunities like GIVE days when you can join other volunteers and try your hand at organic farming. Visit http://maoorganicfarms.org for more info.

THE EFFECTS OF SWIMMING WITH DOLPHINS

There isn't much that rates as high on the excitement scale as getting to frolic in waves with a pod of playful dolphins. I get giddy just thinking about it. Many local outfitters promise to motor you out to the secret spots where these mammals congregate and then instruct you how to quietly enter the water and be surrounded by dolphins. Research shows that usually these dolphins are taking a much-needed rest away from predators, and when humans show up to swim with them, it stresses them out.

However, at the end of the day, it's your call. I know it is hard to pass up this once-in-a-lifetime adventure. In my experience, the most reputable of these outfits is Wild Side Specialty Tours. The husband-and-wife crew of the *Island Spirit* catamaran promise to educate and feed you, and then deposit you into the water to swim with free-roaming dolphins. If you opt for this adventure, please be respectful of these animals.

those on the prowl for a place to jump in that gorgeous ocean, the beloved Poka'i Beach Park grants access to the sandy-bottomed sea, without the treacherous waves that characterize this stretch of coastline.

Though you may find the occasional food truck to dull the monotony, fast food dominates the landscape. To access Wai'anae's refreshing alternative, travel 2 miles *mauka* on Ma'ili'ili Road and find Kahumana Café. On an organic farm, this casual and cozy eatery offers healthful salads and pastas, as well as a mean cheesecake—the *lilliko'i* is to die for. They have limited hours, so call ahead.

Makaha Beach Park's wild waves

Power north on the highway to Makaha Beach Park, the Leeward Coast's ferocious surf beach, where big wave surfing on O'ahu earned its chops as the host to the island's first surf competition. In winter, you can peep at the massive waves sans crowds, and the daring can brave the pounding whitewater.

As you continue north on the highway, the area becomes more and more desolate. You'll pass through Makua Valley, popular with hunters and littered with the remains of explosives left over from military training. Makua Beach, while lovely, is not recommended for swimming, nor for hanging out—this is a fiercely local beach. Ahead Ka'ena Point State Park looms, an imposing jut of land with mystical significance to ancients, who say this is where the soul departs for the other land after you die. At the end of the road, Yokohama Bay Beach is a surf beach, though in win-

The rough West Shore waves inspire respect.

ter even O'ahu's kamikazes don't try to surf these waves. Hiking, however, is a worthy venture, especially along O'ahu's northernmost tip, Ka'ena Point. This undeveloped area connects Wai'anae Coast with the North Shore; the only way to see it is by taking the windy 2.5-mile trail to the point and then continuing another couple of miles to the North Shore. Don't leave anything in your car; in fact, leave your car unlocked to minimize the chance of a break-in. If you brave this trail, bring plenty of food and water. As the win-

DETOUR: KANE'AKI HEIAU: A TRIBUTE TO LONO

Bishop Museum staff took the desolate Kane'aki Heiau and lovingly restored this house for those who had committed *kapu* (taboos), the prayer towers, and an altar. The *heiau* was a temple built to honor the god of fertility and agriculture, Lono. As with most sacred sites in Hawai'i, it then became the site of human sacrifices. Travel *mauka* to Makaha Valley Road, which merges onto Huipu Drive. Turn right at Mauna Olu Street. Pass through the estates, and tell the guard you are visiting the *heiau*. If it is raining, don't bother.

ter surf pounds the rocks, native birds fly overhead, and the occasional monk seal lazes away on the sand, you'll likely agree that this is as good as it gets on O'ahu—a spot where you can escape the masses for the day and then motor back to civilization for a four-star dinner under the stars.

IN THE AREA

ACCOMMODATIONS

Coconut Waikiki Hotel, 450 Lewers St., Waikiki. Retro rooms with a dash of whimsy. Expect designer flair, complimentary Wi-Fi and continental breakfast, a pool, and parking (for a fee). Call 866-974-2626. Website www.jdvhotels.com/hotels/hawaii/coconut-waikiki-hotel.

Disney's Aulani Resort, 92-1185 Ali-inui Dr., Kapolei. One of the state's best family hotels is home to a gorgeous beach, a lazy river and waterslide, a slew of restaurants, and surprisingly sophisticated décor. Call 808-674-6200. Website www.resorts.disney.go.com.

Halekulani Hotel, 2199 Kaila Rd., Waikiki. The island's most upscale property offers the Hawaiian royal treatment, with a world-class spa, one of the state's best restaurants and lounges, and rooms that will inspire. Call 808-923-2311. Website www.halekulani.com.

Hilton Hawaiian Village, 2005 Kalia Rd., Waikiki. A megaresort perched on a lovely lagoon on the west edge of Waikiki, with restaurants, shops, and its own lu'au. Call 808-949-4321. Website www.hiltonhawaiianvillage.com.

Hyatt Regency Waikiki, 2424 Kalakaua Ave., Waikiki. One of the state's largest hotels, in the heart of Waikiki, the hotel provides upscale shopping, a small pool, and two great eating options. Call 808-923-1234. Website www.hyattregency waikiki.com.

JW Marriott Ihiani Resort, 92-1001 Olani St., Kapolei. A gorgeous oceanfront property in an isolated beach area, this upscale Marriott features an oceanfront pool, restaurants, a spa, and tech-savvy rooms. Call 808-679-3321. Website www.ihilani.com.

Modern Honolulu, 1775 Ala Moana Blvd., Waikiki. Waikiki's hippest hotel boasts a nightclub, two designer pool areas, a lounge, a restaurant, and smallish rooms fit for magazine spreads. A bit out of the heart of Waikiki, but since the party comes to the Modern on select nights, who cares? Call 808-943-5800. Website www.themodernhonolulu.com.

New Otani Kaimana Beach Hotel, 2863 Kalakaua Ave., Honolulu. A boutique hotel for in-the-know travelers wanting to stay on one of Waikiki's best beaches, with slick rooms with wide lanais and small bathrooms as well as two restaurants and a bar. Call 808-923-1555. Website www.kaimana.com.

Outrigger Regency on Beachwalk, 255 Beach Walk, Honolulu. Chic condos with fully equipped kitchens and private lanais. The only downside is that there are no bathtubs. Call 866-263-4421. Website www.outrigger.com.

Outrigger Waikiki on the Beach, 2335 Kalakaua Ave., Honolulu. Adjacent to Waikiki's convention center, this full-service beachfront resort offers cultural activities, a pool, and stately rooms decked out in autumnal hues. Call 808-923-0711. Website www.outriggerwaikiki hotel.com.

Westin Moana Surfrider, 2365 Kalakaua Ave., Honolulu. Waikiki's most historic hotel set in a stark white plantation-style oceanfront building, with a large porch dotted with rocking chairs, and a huge banyan tree covering the restaurant and bar area. Additional perks include a pool, a spa, and lovely rooms (many with ocean views). Call 808-922-3111. Website www.moana-surf rider.com.

ATTRACTIONS AND RECREATION

Ala Moana Center, 1450 Ala Moana Blvd., Honolulu. The state's biggest mall.

Ali'iolani Hale, 417 S. King St., Honolulu. The former seat of government for the Hawai'i monarch now houses the state Supreme Court. Call 808-539-4999.

Aloha Stadium Swap Meet, 99-500 Salt Lake Blvd., Aiea. Hundreds of merchants sell their vintage, secondhand, and artistic endeavors. Website www .alohastadiumswapmeet.net.

ARTS at Marks Garage, 1159 Nuuanu Ave., Honolulu. A hip art gallery in Chinatown. Call 808-521-2903. Website www.artsatmarks.com.

Bailey's Antiques and Aloha Shirts, 517 Kapahulu Ave., Honolulu. Score vintage Hawaiian shirts. Call 808-734-7628. Website www.alohashirts.com.

Battleship *Missouri* Memorial, 63 Cowpens St., Honolulu. Open 8–4 daily (and until 5 in summer). Take a shuttle from Pearl Harbor Visitors Center to tour the battleship that acted as the site of the Japanese surrender during World War II. Call 808-455-1600. Website www.ussmissouri.com. Buy tickets at www.pearlharborhistoricsites.org.

Big Wave Dave, 2410 Koa Ave., Waikiki. Surf lessons and rentals. Call 808-386-4872. Website www.bigwavedavesurfco .com.

Bishop Museum, 1525 Bernice St., Honolulu. Tour the Romanesque buildings that make up Hawai'i's largest natural history and cultural museum. Check the website for upcoming exhibits and events. Call 808-847-3511. Website www.bishopmuseum.com.

Blank Canvas, 1145 Bethel St., Honolulu. Grab skater or surf gear at this Chinatown boutique. Closed Wednesday. Call 808-780-4720.

Bob's Ukulele, Waikiki Marriott, 2552 Kalakaua Ave., Waikiki. Part gallery, part store, this tribute to Hawai'i's iconic instrument is *the* place to find a professional-level ukulele to bring home. Call 808-372-9623. Website www.bobsukulele .com.

Foster Botanical Gardens, 180 N. Vineyard Blvd., Honolulu. Offering a prehistoric collection, a fantastic orchid garden, and enormous trees. Call 808-522-7065. Website www1.honolulu.gov.

Girls Who Surf, 1020 Auahi St., Honolulu. Surf lessons and rentals from Waikiki's best surfer gals. Call 808-772-4583. Website www.girlswhosurf.com.

Hans Hedemann Surf School, 134 Kapahulu Ave., Waikiki. Arguably O'ahu's most reliable surf school. Call 808-924-7778. Website www.hhsurf.com.

Hawai'i Nature Center, 2131 Makiki Heights Dr., Honolulu. Informative educational and interpretive nature center. Call 808-955-0100. Website www.hawaii naturecenter.org.

Hawai'i State Art Museum (HiSAM), 250 S. Hotel St., Honolulu. One of the state's premier art houses, considered the best place to view Hawaiian art. Call 808-586-0900. Website hawaii.gov.sfca .HiSAM.

Hawai'i Theatre, 1130 Bethel St., Honolulu. Gorgeous old revival theater that's rich with history; this is a great spot to view live music or theater events. Call 808-528-0506. Website www.hawaii theatre.com.

Hawaiian Fire Surf School, 3318 Campbell Ave., Honolulu. Surf lessons and rentals. Call 808-737-3473. Website www.hawaiianfire.com.

Homecoming, 1191 Bethel St., Honolulu. Funky Chinatown boutique. Closed Sunday. Call 808-536-6000.

Honolulu Museum of Art, 900 S. Beretania St., Honolulu. Modern and classic artwork populates the three venues of this major museum. Tours of Doris Duke's Shangri La estate depart daily. Your admission fee also gets you in the Spalding House on the same day. Call 808-532-8734. Website www.honolulu museum.org.

Honolulu Zoo, 151 Kapahulu Ave., Waikiki. Tropical gardens, plenty of animals (including elephants, tigers, and a black rhino), a café, and a playground please families. Call 808-971-7171. Website www.honoluluzoo.org.

'Iolani Palace, 364 S. King St., Honolulu. Tour the 1882 palace, experience live music in the gardens on Friday afternoons, or shop in the Palace Store. Closed Sunday. Call 808-522-0822. Website www.iolanipalace.org.

Kawaiaha'o Church, 957 Punchbowl St., Honolulu. Historic church in downtown Honolulu. Call 808-522-1333. Website www.kawaiahao.org.

Kicks/HI, 1530 Makaloa St., Honolulu. Get new tennis shoes. Call 808-941-9191. Website www.kickshawaii.com.

La Muse, 1156 Nuuanu Ave., Honolulu. A decent selection of women's apparel. Call 808-536-0818. Website www.lamuse hawaii.com.

Lyon Arboretum, 3860 Manoa Rd., Honolulu. Explore the trails at University of Hawai'i's botanical gardens. Closed Sunday. Call 808-988-0456. Website www.hawaii.edu/lyonarboretum.

Mission Houses Museum, 553 S. King St., Honolulu. Explore the former missionary houses of Honolulu. Closed Sunday and Monday. Call 808-447-3910. Website www.missionhouses.org.

Na Hoku II, 2335 Kalakaua Ave., Waikiki. Booze cruises, sunset sails, and catamaran tours of the Waikiki area. Call 808-554-5990. Website www.nahokuii .com.

National Memorial Cemetery of the Pacific, 2177 Puowaina Dr., Honolulu.

Visit this final resting place of soldiers. Call 808- 532-3720.

Pearl Harbor, 1 Arizona Memorial Place, Honolulu. Take an audio tour of the memorial and museums. Visiting the memorial is free. Get here early (they open at 7 a.m.)—tickets often sell out as the day progresses. No bags allowed in the entire area. Buy tickets for all four attractions at www.pearlharborhistoric sites.org.

Pegge Hopper Gallery, 1164 Nuuanu Ave., Honolulu. One of Chinatown's most iconic galleries. Call 808-524-1160. Website www.peggehopper.com.

Royal Hawaiian Center, 2201 Kalakaua Ave., Waikiki. Website www .royalhawaiiancenter.com.

Somace Design, 1016 Kapahulu Ave., Waikiki. A charming collection of beach chic trinkets to decorate the house. Call 808-593-8780. Website www.somace design.com.

Spalding House, 2411 Makiki Heights Dr., Honolulu. A tribute to contemporary art in the Honolulu hills, known for its David Hockney gallery. Call 808-532-8700. Website www.honolulumuseum.org.

St. Andrews Cathedral, 229 Queen Emma Square, Honolulu. Lovely historic church in the heart of downtown. Call 808-524-2822. Website www.saint andrewscathedral.net.

USS Bowfin Submarine and Museum, 11 Arizona Memorial Dr., Honolulu. Explore the historic submarine and the adjacent museum, located in the Pearl Harbor complex. No bags allowed. Call 808-423-1341. Website www.bowfin .org; www.pearlharborhistoricsites.org.

Waikiki Aquarium, 2777 Kalakaua Ave., Waikiki. A small but sweet look at the archipelago's resident mammals and tropical fish. Call 808-923-9741. Website www.waquarium.org.

Ward Centers, 1200 Ala Moana Blvd., Honolulu. Call 808-591-8411. Website www.wardcenters.com.

Wet 'n' Wild Hawai'i, 400 Farrington Hwy., Kapolei. Everything from exciting waterslides to relaxing pools and rivers can be experienced at Hawai'i's only water park. Closed Wednesday. Call 808-674-9283. Website www.hawaii.mywetnwild.com.

Wild Side Specialty Tours, 87-1286 Farrington Hwy., Waianae. The best snorkel cruise on the island offers naturalist-led intimate trips to swim with free-roaming dolphins. Call 808-306-7273. Website www.sailhawaii.com.

DINING AND DRINKING

12th Ave Grill, 1145C 12th Ave., Honolulu. Contemporary American cuisine using locally sourced ingredients; house-cured meats star on the menu. Open for dinner. Closed Sunday. Call 808-732-9469. Website www.12thavegrill.com.

Alan Wong's, 1857 S. King St., #208, Honolulu. Splurge on the five-course tasting menu, or order à la carte items like coconut lamb or the *foie gras* with macadamia nuts. Super expensive and insanely popular; reservations are required. Call 808-949-1939.

Alan Wong's Pineapple Room, 1450 Ala Moana Blvd., Ste. 1300, Honolulu. One of Hawai'i's premier chefs offers a more casual taste of Asian fusion cuisine in the Ala Moana Mall. Reserve a table. Call 808-945-6573. Website www.alanwongs.com.

Azure, 2259 Kalakaua Ave., Waikiki. Dramatic oceanfront fine dining, relying on dishes like Kona lobster tail risotto and Wagyu filet to draw romance seekers. Very expensive and reservations required. Dinner only. Call 808-931-7440. Website www.azurewaikiki.com.

Bar 35, 35 N. Hotel St., Honolulu. Indoor and patio bars, ideal for enjoying live music; over 150 beers in stock, along with some of the best pizza in China-town. Call 808-537-3535. Website www.bar35hawaii.com.

Beach Bum Café, 1088 Bishop St., Ste. 101, Honolulu. Microbrew coffeehouse. Call 808-521-6699. Website www.beachbumcafe.com.

Bubbies, 7192 Kalanianaole Hwy., Ste. D103, Honolulu. Homemade ice cream and desserts. Sample the Kona coffee—yum. Call 808-396-8722. Website www.bubbiesicecream.com.

Café Julia, 1040 Richards St., Honolulu. Organic food served in a historic YMCA draws the lunch crowd yearning for smoked salmon sandwiches or shrimp pasta. Closed Saturday. Check the website for hours, as they are only occasionally open for dinner. Call 808-533-3334. Website www.cafejuliahawaii.com.

Café Kaila, 2919 Kapiolani Blvd., Honolulu. Breakfast and brunch joint serving dishes made with love. Excellent waffles topped with fresh fruit. Call 808-732-3330.

Chef Mavro, 1969 S. King St., Honolulu. One of the state's most romantic restaurants, specializing in Hawaiian seafood cooked with French panache. Children over five years old are welcome. Call 808-944-4714. Website www.chefmavro.com.

Cream Pot, 444 Niu St., #104, Waikiki. This charming breakfast and brunch restaurant along the Ala Wai Canal is known for soufflé pancakes. Closed Tuesday. Call 808-429-0945.

Da Kitchen, 925 Isenberg St., Honolulu. Lunches and dinners pack this casual plate lunch joint that is one of President Obama's favorite Hawaiian eats. Call 808-957-0099. Website www.da-kitchen.com.

Diamond Head Market and Grill, 3575 Campbell Ave., Waikiki. Gourmet market has a nice selection of picnic fixings for a beach outing or a Diamond Head hike. Call 808-732-0077. Website www.diamondheadmarket.com.

Down to Earth Natural and Organic Grocery, 2525 S. King St., Honolulu. Call 808-947-7678. Website www.downto earth.org.

Hau Tree Lanai, 2863 Kalakaua Ave., Waikiki. Sit along Sans Souci Beach under a leafy tree to enjoy three traditional (and very expensive) meals a day. Reservations recommended for dinner. Call 808-921-7066. Website www .kaimana.com/hautreelanai.htm.

Helena's Hawaiian Food, 1240 N. School St., Honolulu. One of the state's best examples of Hawaiian cuisine. Nothing fancy here, just lots of yummy plate lunch fixings and big crowds. Only open Tue.–Fri. 10:30–7:30. Call 808-845-8044. Website www.helenashawaiian food.com.

Hiroshi Eurasian Tapas, Restaurant Row, 500 Ala Moana Blvd., Honolulu. Dinners are popular at this tapas eatery, which serves dishes like foie gras sushi. The bar area is fun for evening cocktails. Call 808-533-4476. Website www.hiroshi hawaii.com.

Honolulu Coffee Company, 1450 Ala Moana Blvd., Honolulu (also in Westin Moana Surfrider Hotel in Waikiki, see above). Call 808-949-1500. Website www.honolulucoffee.com.

House Without a Key, Halekulani, 2199 Kalia Rd., Waikiki. Waikiki's most upscale bar and lounge. Call 808-923-2311. Website www.halekulani.com.

Hula's Bar and Lei Stand, 134 Kapahulu Ave., Waikiki. A gay-friendly beach bar with views of the ocean, fun music, and drinks flowing until late. Call 808-923-0669. Website www.hulas.com.

Imanas Tei Restaurant, 2626 S. King St., Honolulu. This dinner-only hot spot is known for its chanko nabe. Make reservations. Closed Sunday. Call 808-941-2626.

Indigo, 1121 Nuuanu Ave., Honolulu. Chinatown's popular bar and restaurant specializes in Asian fusion cuisine and an urban ambience. Call 808-521-2900. Website www.indigo-hawaii.com.

Irifune, 563 Kapahulu Ave., Honolulu. This Kaimuki restaurant is a local fave for garlic ahi fried rice. Save room for dessert—the ice cream crepe with banana and homemade haupia yogurt rocks. BYOB. Call 808-737-1141.

Island Country Market, 92-1048 Olani St., Kapolei. Stock up your fridge with groceries. Call 808-671-2231.

Iyasume Musubi-Ya, 2410 Koa Ave., Honolulu. A hole-in-the-wall that tops locals' lists of the best musubi, curry, and rice bowls. Open daily 6:30–4. Call 808-921-0168.

Japengo, Hyatt Regency Hotel, 2424 Kalakaua Ave., Waikiki. Slick eatery has recently been spruced up to highlight an ambitious Japanese menu. Open for dinner. Reservations highly recommended. Call 808-923-1234. Website www.waikiki .hyatt.com.

Kahumana Café, 86-660 Lualualei Homestead Rd., Wai'anae. Organic eats on a farm in the hills above Wai'anae, only open Tue.–Sat. 11:30–2 and 6–7:30. It is wise to call ahead to see if the ovens are fired up. Call 808-696-8844. Website www.kahumanafarms.org.

KCC Saturday Farmers' Market, Kapiolani Community College, 4303 Diamond Head Rd., Honolulu. Open 7:30–11 a.m.

Kimukatsu, Aston Waikiki Joy Hotel, 320 Lewers St., Honolulu. This relatively new katsu eatery has been transplanted from Japan. Open for lunch and dinner. Call 808-922-1129. Website www.kimu katsu.com.

La Mariana Sailing Club, 50 Sand Island Access Rd., Honolulu. A historic and fun tiki bar-restaurant laden with kitsch. Call 808-841-2173. Website www.lamarianasailingclub.com.

La Mer, Halekulani Hotel, 2199 Kalia Rd., Waikiki. One of Waikiki's most romantic tables features super-fresh seafood, with sea views. There is a dress code, and no children under eight are allowed. Reservations required. Call 808-923-2311. Website www.halekulani.com.

Legend Seafood Restaurant, 100 N. Beretania St., #108, Honolulu. Dim sum eatery in Chinatown draws families wanting chicken feet, dumplings, and other Chinese celebratory treats. Call 808-532-1868. Website www.legend seafoodhonolulu.com.

Leonard's, 933 Kapahulu Ave., Waikiki. Hawai'i's most famous stop for *malasada* doughnuts. Call 808-737-5591. Website www.leonardshawaii.com.

Liliha Bakery, 515 N. Kuakini St., Honolulu. Pastries like the über-sweet coco puffs are so good, they should be illegal. Closed Monday. Call 808-531-1651. Website www.lilihabakeryHawaii.com.

Little Village Noodle House, 1113 Smith St., Honolulu. O'ahu's best Chinese restaurant does just about every dish right, though the noodles bathed in black bean sauce are my favorite. Call 808-545-3008. Website www.littlevillage hawaii.com.

Lucky Belly, 50 N. Hotel St., Honolulu. Perfectly crafted ramen and pork buns served in an artsy Chinatown location with a great selection of spirits. Open late for hungry night owls. Call 808-531-1888. Website www.luckybelly.com.

Lulu's Surf Club, 2586 Kalakaua Ave., Waikiki. A typical vacation beach bar with a dash of Waikiki spirit to bring authenticity. Food is served 7 a.m.–11 p.m., and drinks continue well past midnight. Call 808-926-5222. Website www.lulus waikiki.com.

Manifest, 32 N. Hotel St., Honolulu. During the day, this funky joint is a coffee shop and art gallery; at night it becomes a thumping club and bar. Call 808-523-7575. Website www.manifest hawaii.com.

Manu Bu's, 1618 S. King St., Honolulu. Get here early (and I mean like 7 a.m.) for *musubi*, as this takeout joint often sells out and they close by 1pm. Call 808-358-0287. Website www.hawaii musubi.com.

Marukame Udon, 2310 Kuhio Ave., Waikiki. Insanely busy throughout the day as hordes line up for cafeteria-style *udon* and tempura. Call 808-931-6000.

Matsugen, 255 Beach Walk, Waikiki. Lunch and dinner relies on authentic handmade soba to make this one of Waikiki's best Japanese eats. Don't miss the traditional *natta* (fermented soy beans). Call 808-926-0255.

Morimoto Waikiki, in Modern Honolulu, 1775 Ala Moana Blvd., Waikiki. Upscale Asian fusion cuisine from celebrity Iron Chef Masaharu Morimoto in a sleek setting. Open for three meals daily. Reservations required for dinner. Call 808-943-5900. Website www.mori motowaikiki.com.

Monkeypod Kitchen, 92-1048 Olani St., Ko Olina. Peter Merriman's fun, casual restaurant serves farm-fresh pizza, pastas, and seafood in a lively atmosphere. Call 808-380-4086. Website www .monkeypodkitchen.com.

Morning Glass Coffee, 2955 E. Manoa Rd., Honolulu. O'ahu's best coffee shop is up in the Manoa hills and serves Portland micro-roaster Stumptown's beans. Call 808-673-0065. Website www.morning glasscoffee.com.

Nanzan GiroGiro, 560 Pensacola St., Honolulu. An upscale *kaisake* coursed dinner house, known for creative Japanese dishes sourced with local ingredients. Reservations required. Dinner only. Call 808-524-0141.

Nico's at Pier 38, 1129 N. Nimitz Hwy., Honolulu. Casual French-inspired dining by Lyon-born chef Nico Chaize. Reasonably priced favorites like *furikake*-crusted *ahi* win hearts. Call 808-540-1377. Website www.nicospier38.com.

Nobu Waikiki, 2233 Helumoa Rd., Waikiki. Chef Nobu Matsuhisa's eatery crafts dishes like sashimi tacos and compressed nashi pear napoleon. Dinner only. Reservations recommended. Call 808-237-6999. Website www.nobu restaurants.com/waikiki.

Oceanarium Restaurant, 2490 Kalakaua Ave., Waikiki. Dine before a massive floor-to-ceiling aquarium as manta rays and mermaids flutter by. Call 808-921-6111. Website www.pacific beachhotel.com.

Ono Seafood, 747 Kapahulu Ave., Waikiki. Grab *poke* and seafood for a picnic. They often sell out, so go early. Closed Tuesday and Sunday. Call 808-732-4806.

Poke Stop, 94-050 Farrington Hwy. E4, Waipahu. Elmer Guzman's take on Hawaiian comfort food, with an array of inventive *pokes*. They also have a Mililani location (95-1840 Meheula Pkwy.). Call 808-676-8100. Website www .poke-stop.com.

Rainbow Drive In, 3308 Kanaina Ave., Waikiki. A local mainstay for plate lunch in a retro outdoor setting. Open for three meals daily. Call 808-737-0177. Website www.rainbowdrivein.com.

Royal Kitchen, 100 N. Beretania St., Honolulu. A take-out joint that has been hawking steamed buns since 1974. Open 5:30 a.m.–4 p.m. Call 808-524-4461. Website www.royalkitchenHawaii.com.

Roy's Waikiki, 226 Lewers St., Honolulu. Iconic Hawaiian regional cuisine at big prices from the Roy's brand—seafood stars on the menu. Reservations highly recommended. Call 808-923-7697. Website www.roysrestaurant.com.

Ruffage Natural Foods, 2443 Kuhio Ave., Waikiki. Healthy eaters love this take-out sandwich shop that also features minimal groceries and healthful rice bowls and smoothies. Call 808-922-2042.

Salt Bar + Kitchen, 3605 Waialae Ave., Honolulu. This fun foodie haven offers fresh-cured meats, sustainable oxtail empanadas, and creative cocktails. The restaurant/lounge is a late-night favorite. Call 808-744-7567. Website www.salthonolulu.com.

Shor, in Hyatt Regency Waikiki (see above). Dine alfresco with views of the sea. The wine list is impressive, and an intelligent kids' menu pleases parents. Reservations recommended. Call 808-237-6145. www.shorgrill.com.

Siam Square, 408 Lewers St., Waikiki. No-frills Thai food in the heart of Waikiki offering favorites like papaya salad and *pad see ew* for reasonable prices. Call 808-923-5320. Website www.siamsquaredining.com.

Side Street Inn (two locations), 614 Kapahulu Ave., Waikiki; 1225 Hopaka St., Honolulu. Gigantic portions of Hawaiian comfort food and great beers. (Waikiki) 808-739-3939; (Honolulu) 808-591-0253. Website www.sidestreetinn.com.

Sushi Izakaya Gaku, 1329 S. King St., Honolulu. Consistently perfect presentations of sushi draw devotees. Call 808-589-1329.

Sushi Sasabune, 1417 S King St., Honolulu. Discerning sushi lovers splurge for the *omakase*-style dinner. Sit at the bar and allow the chefs to do their magic. Reservations required, well in advance. Call 808-947-3800.

Sweet E's Café, 1016 Kapahulu Ave., Waikiki. Hidden in a strip mall, this little café delivers freshly made breakfast and lunch specialties in a homey atmosphere. Call 808-737-7771.

Tanioka's Seafoods and Catering, 94-903 Farrington Hwy., Waipahu. Get here early, as they usually run out of the famed *musubi* and bentos by 1 p.m. Call 808-671-3779. Website www.taniokas .com.

Tango Café, 1288 Ala Moana Blvd., #120, Honolulu. Everything from Swedish pancakes to Hamakua mushroom risotto pleases the fans of this cute café. Call 808-593-7288. Website www.tangocafehawaii.com.

Thirtyninehotel, 39 N. Hotel St., Honolulu. A funky gallery, bar. and restaurant that seems to have its finger on the pulse of what O'ahu young people need for a fun night out. Call 808-599-2552. Website www.thirtyninehotel.com.

Town, 3435 Waialae Ave., #104, Honolulu. Farm-fresh organics served from morning to night. Reservations recommended for dinners. Call 808-735-5900. Website www.townkaimuku.com.

Uncle Bo's, 559 Kapahulu Ave., Waikiki. Ask hipsters where they go after work and Uncle Bo's generally tops the list for *pupus* and amazing cocktails. Call 808-735-8311. Website www.unclebos restaurant.com.

V Lounge, 1344 Kona St., Honolulu. *Kiawe* wood-fired pizzas, a hopping late-night bar, and one of those urban vibes that lures the beautiful people. Call 808-953-0007. Website www.vloungehawaii.com.

Wailana Coffee House, 1860 Ala Moana Blvd., Waikiki. The price is right and the plates are Hawaiian sized at this greasy spoon. Call 808-955-1764.

Wai'oli Tea Room, 2950 Manoa Rd., Honolulu. In the Manoa hills, this historic teahouse and bakery makes a lovely pit stop after a Manoa Falls hike. Call 808-988-5800. Website www.the waiolitearoom.net.

Whole Ox Deli and Butcher Shop, 327 Keawe St., Honolulu. This butcher shop is graced with a bounty of sustainable meats and produce, which they use to churn out heaping sandwiches. Call 808-699-6328. Website www.wholeox .deli.com.

OTHER CONTACT INFORMATION

O'ahu Visitors Bureau. Call 800-GO-HAWAII. Website www.gohawaii.com.

An Oʻahu sunset

2 O'ahu's Best Coastal Drive
THE WINDWARD COAST AND THE NORTH SHORE

Estimated length: 109 miles
Estimated time: 1–4 days

Getting there: From Honolulu or Waikiki, take H1 east to Highway 72 toward Kailua. From Kailua, take Highway 630 west and connect to Highway 83 west into Hale'iwa. Then travel south on Highway 99 to meet up with H2 in Honolulu.

Highlights: O'ahu's most gorgeous coastal drive; exploring Hawai'i's coral reef alongside tropical fish; bodysurfing like President Obama at Kailua Beach; sampling Kailua's up-and-coming eateries; watching big-wave surfers brave the North Shore; and shopping for ridiculously fresh produce at Hale'iwa Farmers' Market.

While it seems everything on O'ahu centers on Honolulu and Waikiki, you can escape the urbanity in an instant. Devoid of the trappings of a bustling metropolis, the leisurely coastline delivers jaw-dropping vistas, posh neighborhoods, and the Hawai'i you may have dreamed about when booking this holiday. Whether you focus the majority of your trip on this itinerary, or make a day trip to loop up from Waikiki through Kailua and the North Shore, you won't regret your efforts.

Just beyond Waikiki, upscale Kahala sits in Diamond Head's shadow, soaking up her proximity to Waikiki's attractions while owning a quiet sophistication coveted by the island's most elite visitors, who have laid their heads at the regal Kahala Hotel and Resort. This isolated property boasts a peaceful swimmer-friendly beach, as well as oceanfront restaurants like Hoku's for east–west fusion cuisine and Plumeria House's buffet. Rooms ooze comfort, with gazillion-thread-count sheets atop beds you could melt into, soaking tubs, electric toilets that clean parts of you you never knew you had, walk-in rain showers, large balconies, and Wi-Fi. Get a room around the dolphin lagoon to marvel at the Dolphin Quest mammals that murmur quietly through the night; through-

Kahala Resort's upscale interiors

out the day visitors delight in the chance to swim with and train these amazing creatures (if you choose to participate, make reservations in advance). There is a spa, two small pools and a hot tub, a lively bar, and access to the golf course, which hosts the annual Sony 500. If you can splurge on a night (or a week here), your body and mind will thank you.

Since in Kahala food choices are limited to Kahala Mall's Whole Foods (you might want to grab a picnic here before continuing on), Olive Tree Café for authentic Greek food, and Lanikai Juice for *acai* breakfast bowls and smoothies, keep going: Nearby Hawai'i Kai houses plenty of restaurants sure to satisfy.

Take Highway 72 east to Hawai'i Kai, one of O'ahu's most posh addresses. Here you'll likely feel like you've arrived in Southern California. Large mini malls dominate the landscape; canals lead to houses and private boat launches. In essence, Hawai'i Kai feels like a playground for the 1 percent.

For now, bypass the turnoffs to Hawai'i Kai, and as long as it is not Tuesday, head over to Hanauma Bay Nature Preserve. Spend hours snorkeling in this mellow coral-infused bay as yellow tangs, sea turtles, parrotfish, and wrasses flutter past your mask. This is O'ahu at its finest, complete with an educational film detailing the environmental concerns of your visit (a must for first-time visitors), a bus to cart less-able-bodied vis-

THE INDIGENOUS SOAP COMPANY AT WHOLE FOODS
By Lilly Barels

While stocking up on earth-conscious, low-carbon-footprint groceries, be sure to buy a few bars of Indigenous Soap. Created on the island of O'ahu, these organic, synthetic-free soaps are made with native medicinal oils and herbs to create a healing product sure to soothe your sun-kissed skin. Read more at www.indigenoussoap.com.

itors down the hill before diving in the sea, and a shady sand-and-grass area popular with families. However, as is the case at most popular Hawai'i destinations, visitors are affecting the land and sea. Thousands of people visit the bay each day, and while it's achingly beautiful, few consider the impact of their footprint. Those who crave privacy should either arrive early in the morning (like 6 a.m.) on a Thursday or Friday, or bypass the bay entirely to snorkel elsewhere.

If you didn't grab a picnic to enjoy at the beach, take a quick detour back to Hawai'i Kai's Kona Brewing Company. If you followed my advice and snorkeled early, Moena Café serves a good breakfast with favorites like short rib *loco moco* and banana Chantilly pancakes. If you spent the entire day at the beach and want a gorgeous dinner, there's an outpost of the venerable Roy's chain here that inspires the fancy Hawai'i Kai people to sport their finest resort wear and gussy up for Roy's signature *miso* butterfish; unfortunately, the restaurant is only open for dinner.

> ### DETOUR: A QUICK AND QUIET HIKE
>
> There's hiking up in the hills west of Hawai'i Kai, which you can access by traveling *mauka* on Kuli'ou'ou Road for a mile to the trailhead. Views are well worth the schlep; however, those undertaking this whole itinerary in a day or two should skip the 5-mile round-trip Kuli'ou'ou Ridge Trail and forge ahead.

Hanauma Bay Nature Preserve

The views along the coastal road

Back on Highway 72, the highway teams up with the coast and sinews along the emerald mountains. It's impossible to decide which direction to look. Use the turnoffs liberally, as you'll likely recall this drive long after your plane heads back to the mainland. Half a mile past Hanauma Bay is Lana'i Lookout, where you can spot Lana'i, Maui, and Moloka'i. On the left side for the highway, Koko Crater arcs 645 feet into the sky, offering a towering number of stairs to ascend in order to gain views of the tuff cone crater, the succulents in the botanical garden, and the spectacular ocean glistening beyond. Since the views along the road are quite astounding themselves, unless you have a week to explore this stretch of land—or it's Tuesday and you missed snorkeling in Hanauma Bay—you might skip this hike.

Just across from Koko Crater turnoff on the highway is Sandy Beach. This is *the* locals' beach, the kind of place where Hawaiians gather for weekend BBQs, bodysurfing, hang gliding, sunning themselves on the blond strands, and braving the treacherous waves. Don't bother swimming here unless you can tackle serious currents and crashing swells.

Two miles east of Hanauma Bay, there will likely be a bunch of cars and buses parking on the *makai* side of the road. Follow suit and wander down to Halona Blowhole lookout. A blowhole is a common occurrence on the islands and occurs when water surges through an underwater lava tunnel, groaning as it shoots upward to release a spout of water and wind that often reaches a staggering 30 feet. This blowhole is impressive if the tides are participating.

Just a hop, skip, and a jump away, you can hike out to the easternmost point of O'ahu: Makapu'u Point Lighthouse. Meander a mile down a fire road, opening unto the sea, where the 1909 lighthouse stands over the ocean. In summer, those with hiking shoes and a bit of adventure can trek down to tide pools (though check the tide charts in advance). In winter, don't even think of swimming; instead you come out here to watch the humpback whales put on an acrobatic show. In the distance, Turtle Island and Rabbit Island are off limits to humans as they are home to native seabirds. You'll have to hop back in the car and park on the other side of the point to access Makapu'u Beach Park. While this stretch of white sand might look appealing, it is the domain of locals who have been battling these rough waves since they were *keikis*. Swimming is dangerous. It's advisable to leave it to those who are familiar with the currents.

On the *mauka* side of the highway, Sea Life Park is an aging version of Sea World. It is all about fulfilling fantasy here—swim in a shark cage surrounded by baby hammerheads, frolic with dolphins, watch sea lions dance to Michael Jackson, or spot tropical fish in cloudy tanks—a fun choice if you have kiddos or deep pockets.

Back on the highway, soak in the views all the way to Waimanalo. With one traffic signal, this tight-knit agricultural community might not be doing backflips for your tourist dollars, but there are a few worthy destinations to put on your radar. After the raging seas of Sandy and Makapu'u, the 4-mile Waimanalo Beach Park is a welcome destination. The *keiki*-friendly waves and soft sand make for a fine extended beach day. It's especially pleasant with an organic plate lunch picnic and a smoothie from Sweet Home Waimanalo, or a container of spicy tacos, beans, and rice brought over from Serg's Mexican Kitchen. Surfers should head a mile north to Waimanalo Bay Beach Park, while kayakers and surfers populate the seas at Bellows Field Beach Park (though this beach is on a military site, so it's only open to the public on weekends and holidays). For those in the market for Hawaiian-made crafts, Naturally Hawaiian Gallery shows off the ocean-themed art of Patrick Ching as well as jewelry and keepsakes made on O'ahu.

If the remote Waimanalo is your choice for a quiet getaway, Hale Nalo offers Zen-themed suites and a second-floor "tree house" just a minute's walk from the sea. All accommodations are sparkling clean, with private bathrooms and kitchenettes. Children over 12 are allowed; however, the guesthouse is mainly geared toward mature travelers.

GO O'AHU CARD

Want to save on O'ahu's attractions? A Go O'ahu card offers one-, two-, three-, five-, and seven-day all-inclusive passes to over 30 O'ahu attractions, including everything from lu'aus to moped rentals. I found the one-day card to leave me wanting, so if you spring for one, opt for at least three days, which you can use over a two-week period.

From Waimanalo, cut inland on Highway 72 toward Kailua. The signs are helpful here, as the road often weaves through residential areas. Stay on Kailua Road until it reaches the heart of the Windward Coast—the charming seaside village of Kailua. Those who have spent time on O'ahu often forgo Waikiki's packaged hotels and opt instead to rent a house or condo in this quiet community, made popular as President Obama's choice vacation destination. I highly recommend you reserving a few days to explore this vacation town and its surrounding area.

The reason so many adore Kailua is her stunning beaches and laid-back vibe. The masses head to Kailua Beach Park, which might not have much sand left on high-tide days, but the grassy picnic area, fun breaks, and incredibly white sand and azure seas make this picturesque beach one of O'ahu's most attractive. From Kailua Beach Park, work those muscles and kayak to Flat Island seabird sanctuary. Alternatively, to access a less-popular beach, walk along the Kailua Road south to the exclusive Lanikai Beach, which is backed by Beverly Hills–style mansions and offers no parking to the masses. Both beaches are suffering from erosion, but the swimming and bodyboarding keep me coming back. Paddlers take note: From Lanikai you can kayak to the northern Mokulua Island, a seabird sanctuary. Surfers, on the other hand, should head to Kalama Beach Park, just north and west of town. You can hire kayaks, SUP boards, and snorkel gear at Kailua Sailboards and Kayaks. This outfit also leads kayak trips out to the surrounding bird sanctuary islands. Those on a budget will want to poke into the various board shops to find competitive deals on rentals. Scuba divers: Aaron's Dive Shop leads dive charters and tours of the extensive reef beyond the shore.

Kailua Beach

Central Kailua is a hub of activity, packed with eateries, boutiques, and outfitters, all wanting your hard-earned cash. For ages it seemed like Kailua would fall victim to being home to a collection of so-so restaurants. However, the upsurge of innovative chefs moving into Kailua has brought some downright delicious options to town. Lunches in Kailua run the gamut. Pick up grab-and-go hot food and sandwiches (as well as organic groceries) at Down to Earth Foods to enjoy at the beach throughout the day. Or if you are less of a planner, Kalapawai Market occupies a prime location near Kailua Beach and offers sandwiches and salads to adoring crowds. In town their casual sister restaurant, Kalapawai Café and Deli, serves gourmet comfort food for three meals daily. They also have a coffee shop on site for those in need of a caffeine fix. Dishes like Meyer lemon risotto and sweet potato ravioli are treats to be remembered. Dinner is a touch better than lunch, and reservations are recommended.

It's hard not to be smitten with Cactus Bistro, which uses local produce to craft Latin American cuisine paired with South American wines and spirits. I cannot get enough of the turkey chorizo tacos, the *kiawe* smoked Hamakua mushroom tacos, locally sourced Cuban sandwich, or the Malbec-braised *Kuahiwi* grass-fed beef short ribs. This lunch and dinner joint is one of Kailua's newest stars.

Crepes No Ka 'Oi delivers a fine Popeye's Power (which as you might expect is packed with leafy spinach), or a Lover's Delight (a fruity concoction topped with Nutella). For *furikake*-crusted tofu, garlic chicken and rice, and *kalua* pork with kale, Uahi Island Grill caters to those wanting healthful lunches and dinners. Finally, if you are around on a Thursday evening from 5 to 7:30, head over to Kailua Farmers' Market for plenty of local flavor, *ono grindz*, and abundant produce to populate your condo's kitchen.

Boutiques, antiques shops, and galleries congregate in downtown. Pop into Bookends, one of O'ahu's last bookstores, to grab a beach read. For a formerly loved aloha shirt, head over to Ali'i Antiques. It's hard not to want everything at Mu'umu'u Heaven, which features breezy women's island clothing, vintage mu'umu'us, and accessories. Another fun store for the ladies is Fighting Eel, a locally owned boutique ripe with well-crafted fashion basics. They often host truck shows with steep discounts. Global Village is the one-stop shop for crafty jewelry, island clothing, and gifts. For home décor and tropical souvenirs, don't miss Under a Hula Moon.

Kailua lacks those resorts found in Waikiki, and for most, this is the allure. However, to delight in Kailua's charms, you should probably rent a beach house or condo. Pat's Kailua Beach Properties can assist with finding the right vacation rental for your needs. When it comes to B&Bs, many residents rent out rooms in their houses, but are not allowed to put signs out front to advertise this fact, so book accommodations well in advance. There's a spacious studio apartment at Hula Breeze that comes with a kitchenette and access to the shared pool, washing machine, and dryer. Those on a budget will appreciate the simple wicker furnishings, the access to the pool, and the complimentary continental breakfast at Papaya Paradise.

The only full-service hotel in the Kailua area is Paradise Bay Resort. While it is a bit out of town near the military base, the resort features plenty of water sports activities, a pool, and boat tours to the reef to keep guests busy. Choose from waterfront cottages or spacious suites all with cooking facilities, simple furniture, private lanais, and Wi-Fi. There's a substantial resort fee, which "pays" for parking, breakfast, and access to the Friday-evening fire and knife show.

For those staying the night in Kailua, breakfasts are presided over by the infamous Boots and Kimo's Homestyle Kitchen. You'll wait ages for a table in the low-key dining room—so go really early before the tour buses arrive. The service can be shoddy, and the atmosphere is bland as can be. But those mac-nut pancakes make this gal giddy every time. Though they cater to those with a sweet tooth, you can find a decent sausage and eggs.

Complete with that homey feel I often associate with breakfast, Cinnamon's Restaurant delivers mouthwatering guava chiffon or red velvet pancakes as well as insanely big omelets packed with all types of sausages and meats you can imagine. Those looking to watch their waistlines can join the surfers at Lanikai Juice for fruit bowls topped with granola and coconut, and super-sweet smoothies. For a handful of piping-hot *malasadas* (which take 15 minutes to prepare), Agnes Portuguese Bake Shop lures its share of pastry lovers. Pair your sweet treats with a cappuccino from ChadLou's Coffee Shop or Morning Brew.

Local kids sell shave ice on the He'eia pier.

After your belly is full, take Kailua Road south to Oneawa Street. Turn onto Kaha Street and park at Kawai Nui Marsh. Once an ancient fishpond, today O'ahu's largest marsh is a home to seabirds. There's a walking path around the area, but those with limited time should skip this walking path for others farther along. I like to come here in the morning for a contemplative walk through nature.

DETOUR: THE PALI HIGHWAY

The emerald interior of O'ahu might not get as much press as the island's turquoise waters or haute cuisine, but that doesn't mean you shouldn't save some time to explore this hidden wonderland. This is a fine side trip for people splitting up this itinerary, as this road travels back to Honolulu (and into Waikiki); it is possible to continue to the North Shore on another day. From Highway 72 just before it hits Kailua, take Highway 61 (the Pali Highway) southwest.

Pali means "cliffs" in Hawaiian. And these cliffs drip with greenery and waterfalls so enchanting it seems little elves should inhabit the mountains. This region is not without its folklore. This highway has been built three times. Locals swear the area is haunted—especially Old Pali Highway (see below).

For your first site, take Uluoa Street left; turn right on Manu Aloha and then right on Manu O'o Street. Ulupo Heiau State Monument is laden with spirits, and while it's not much to look at today, it was once a temple. Check out the artist's drawing in front of the *heiau* of how this temple for human sacrifice might have looked when it was in all its glory.

For a quick and rewarding, although mosquito-infused, hike, off the highway turn left on A'uloa Road and veer left onto Maunawili Road. Park just before the road becomes restricted to public vehicles. Whether you choose to just experience the 2.5-mile Maunawili Falls Trail or connect to the 10-mile Maunawili Trail, you'll find yourself steeped in the jungle as you wander along the stream in this peaceful environment.

The road weaves through the Ko'olau Mountains and valley, leading you to the magnificent Nu'uanu Pali Lookout, which offers views beyond expectations. However, this is also the site of Hawai'i's storied last battle, when Kamehameha I "united" the islands by taking them by force. Rumor has it when workers were constructing the Old Pali Highway, they found hundreds of skulls just over the ridge—I told you the area was creepy.

To immerse yourself in O'ahu's haunted history, turn off onto Old Pali Highway, which is also called Nu'uanu Pali Drive. Travel through tunnels of banyans deep into the forest. Keep your eyes peeled for the resident ghosts said to haunt this area. You can hike in these haunted hills, by parking at the lookout and taking the paved fire road (there is a sign that says ROAD CLOSED, but no one pays attention—especially not the ghosts). Along the path you'll spot small waterfalls, graffiti, and maybe a spook or two.

Along Old Pali Highway, you can also access Jackass Ginger Pool and waterfall. Just before the first stone bridge, there is a small parking area; take the Judd Memorial Trail on this easy 1-mile round-trip hike. Though locals like to swim here, I cannot recommend it; leptospirosis bacteria are present in many of Hawai'i's freshwater pools.

The highway merges back with Pali Highway around Queen Emma's Summer Palace and then plunges into Honolulu. The palace, built in 1849, served as the royal retreat of King Kamehameha IV and his wife, Queen Emma. The lush surrounding gardens, Victorian and Hawaiian treasures, rare artifacts, and personal memorabilia of Hawai'i's royalty reward those who make the trek.

DETOUR: HO'OMANLUHIA BOTANICAL GARDEN

Just off H3 in Kane'ohe, Ho'omanluhia Botanical Garden is a 400-acre collection of rare and endangered plants from Hawai'i, Polynesia, Malaysia, Africa, and Southeast Asia. There are walking trails around the 32-acre artificial lake. You can also camp, should you so desire; just call in advance to see if there is space. Mosquitoes are in residence, so prepare your skin.

As you head out to explore the Windward Coast, know that there are two highways that travel through the community of Kane'ohe, and they connect farther up the coast. Kahekili Highway (63) is the inland road that delivers you to Valley of the Temples. This nondenominational cemetery houses the impressive Byodo-In Temple, built in 1968 to replicate a nearly 1,000-year old Kyoto temple. Upon entrance, it's impossible to miss the giant Buddha. The peacock-infested grounds are lovely to meditate in.

I prefer taking the coastal route, Kamehameha Highway (83), which connects with Highway 63 just after Valley of the Temples. For those uninterested in Buddhist temples, or hungry folks in the market for one of O'ahu's best plate lunches, take Highway 63 northwest from Kailua's Highway 630. You'll pass through Kane'ohe, which might occupy prime beachfront real estate, but this chilled-out beach town has not fallen into the tourist game. Even the languid Kane'ohe Bay, which stretches for 7 miles, lacks appeal—the silted waters are a bane for swimmers. However, at He'eia State Park, Holokai Kayak and Snorkel Adventure leads three-hour kayak and snorkel trips beyond the silted waters to O'ahu's barrier reef and Moku o Lo'e (aka the Coconut

This is how you'll spend your days on the Windward Coast.

Island). If kayaking isn't your cup of tea, you can poke around the park to spot the He'eia Fishpond, an ancient breeding ground for seafood. Cross over the highway to the pier, watch the local kids try to snag tropical fish with a piece of string and chewed-up beef jerky, and then order up the guava chicken plate lunch or the pork stew *lau lau* at He'eia Pier General Store and Deli. This funky take-out window reached international fame in the past few years as a market-fresh plate lunch joint with a lot of heart. These days, the focus is still on quality, but the owners are trying to lure back local fishermen and aren't as keen on using sustainable ingredients. On busy weekends, there are often a couple aunties and *keikis* selling shave ice on the pier.

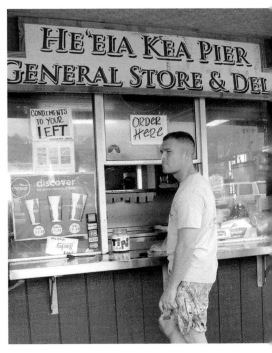

The popular He'eia Kea Pier General Store and Deli

After Kane'ohe's two highways merge, the road becomes two lanes and weaves in and out of the coast. Along the way, Sunshine Arts Gallery features handcrafted creations by O'ahu residents. For those interested in the art of poi, a traditional Hawaiian food made of pounded taro that is—to put it nicely—an acquired taste, Waiahole Poi Factory is the spot to sample the thick poi paste. They have very limited hours, so call in advance.

When the bay ends, you have entered Kualoa, once O'ahu's most sacred destination reserved for educating the next generation of royals. Today Kualua is a playground for outdoor lovers. Ground zero for water play and bird-watching is Kualoa Regional Park. The grassy park is graced by palm trees, which provide plenty of shade for picnickers. In the distance Mokoli'i Island, otherwise known as "Chinaman's Hat," houses seabirds; occasionally when the tide is low, fishermen make their way to its shores. The beach itself is safe for swimming for most of the year, but is to be avoided in summer when jellyfish hang around the shallows. Along the southern side of the white sand beach, there's a salt marsh, where you may spot endangered birds. If you are in a hurry to get to the North Shore, just take a quick stretch break here to snap a photo.

As you depart Ka'a'awa Valley descending into Ka'a'awa, the drive becomes the stuff of legend. The cliffs and sea merge together in a fierce act of devotion. And you, my

---

KUALOA RANCH

Just beyond Kualoa Regional Park is Kualoa Ranch & Activity Club. Outside the ranch are the ruins of missionary doctor Gerrit Judd's sugarcane mill. Here you can go horseback riding and arrange helicopter rides, ATV tours, snorkel trips to Secret Beach, or movie set bus tours. Set on 4,000 acres, the ranch itself is a worthy stop (it has been featured in its share of films). Aunty Pat's Café's buffet is a hearty spread of Hawaiian cuisine. For tours, call in advance—they generally sell out.

---

friend, get to sinew between the two. You can bypass Swanzy Beach Park, a favorite for those on the prowl for fish to fry and families hunting for soft waves. Across the street is a gas station and Uncle Bobo's (for plate lunches and shaved ice that I tend to skip, knowing shrimp trucks and decadent shaved ice are in my future). Around mile marker 27, keep your eyes peeled for Crouching Lion rock formation, an imposing mountain believed to have been a relative of Pele turned to stone. The formation was given its moniker by Westerners. Continuing on, Kahana Bay is a very kid-friendly beach with a sandy bottom and a handful of beachfront campsites that are tough to score. Surfers: There's a decent reef break on the Crouching Lion side of the bay.

Two miles north of Kahana, Punalu'u Beach Park's reef protects most of the shore from those typical pounding waves that make the region famous. Still, as is the case with all ocean destinations, don't let that get you too comfortable. There is a fierce current here as well. Near the beach, visit the internationally acclaimed Kim Taylor Reece Gallery to view thought-provoking black-and-white photos of the islands.

If your belly is talking in Hau'ula, look for the Shrimp Shack next door to the red Ching's Store. This colorful outfit hawks coconut, garlic, or fried shrimp, as well as a yummy Kona coffee atop vanilla ice cream. All is best enjoyed as a picnic at Hau'ula Beach Park.

Just a bit up the highway sits the community of La'ie, home to Brigham Young University Hawai'i. You may wonder what that giant structure is looming in the hills above town. That's a replica Mormon Temple, constructed in 1919. While many of you will (and should) bypass this area on your way to shrimp trucks and massive waves, those who are in the market to see a Disney-esque replica of Pacific Island villages—seven, to be exact—will want to bookmark time to explore the Mormon church's Polynesian Cultural Center. Tour buses come from Waikiki en masse in the late afternoon to tour the villages set on 42 landscaped acres, watch the afternoon canoe parade, and then stay into the evening for the lu'au and *Ha: Breath of Life* show, featuring BYUH students performing upbeat Pacific Islander music, fire dancing, and hula. The food at the lu'au is average (and those wanting a *mai tai* are out of luck, as there is no booze allowed); still, these performances, while not especially postcard-worthy, offer families a fun show.

Surfers should motor 0.5 mile south of the Polynesian Cultural Center to La'ie Beach Park, whose other moniker, Pounders Beach, is a hint at the effect of the wintertime waves. Other than that, I am not swooning much in town. However, if you need a fix, Hukilau Café is the local favorite for breakfast and plate lunch.

As you depart La'ie, keep an eye out just north of town for Malaekahana State Recreation Area—a stunning beach boasting year-round swimming (though always be on the lookout for currents), surfing, and windsurfing. In the distance, Moku'auia (Goat Island) houses nesting birds; in low tide you'll often see people braving the currents to reach the sandy shores. You can camp at Kalanai Point with a permit.

Two miles north of La'ie, Kahuku was once a sugar plantation community, as evidenced by the ramshackle houses lining the streets. This agricultural community is home to shrimp farms that source the popular shrimp trucks lining the road. Plates can be downright overpriced, and it is helpful to know that the trucks typically take off by 6 p.m. Favorites include Romy's Kahuku Prawns & Shrimp, Giovanni's Original White Shrimp Truck (probably the most popular of the lot), and Famous Kahuku Shrimp

KO'OLAU RIDGE HIKING TRAILS

Hikers with time on their hands have a wonderland to explore high in the hills over the Windward Coast. While Sacred Falls State Park remains closed because of dangerous conditions, you can still get those hiking boots dirty. Since this is the rainier side of the island, use caution when heading up. Never go hiking when there has been rain or the forecast calls for wet weather. Flash floods are common. Also, know that local hunters are on the march for feral pigs. So wear bright colors and talk loudly. One of the stars of the area is Hau'ula Loop Trail. Across from Hau'ula Beach Park, drive up Hau'ula Homestead Road. This 2.5-mile trail features an abundance of quiet, as well as a fine collection of native plants along the way.

One of Hawai'i's last remaining traditional land divisions, Kahana Valley features fertile soil from the mountains to the sea, and was once home to fields of taro that grew like wildfire in this wet region. The community of Kahana was a former fishing village, and as with many ancient villages, the introduction of foreign diseases, growth of sugarcane, and World War II jungle training took their toll on the area. Today you can explore Ahupua'a o Kahana State Park's lush hiking trails (again, avoid them if it has been raining). The easy mile-long Kapa'ele'ele Trail rewards the intrepid with a great view of the bay in the distance. Explore the various ancient sites scattered throughout the park as you descend toward the ancient Huila Fishpond in the bay.

Truck. Circle-the-island tours deposit tourists up here throughout the day, so expect long lines. If you aren't a fan of shrimp, Kahuku Superette is considered to have some of the freshest *poke* on the island.

And then you happen upon the North Shore. Characterized by a community spirit that surprises most first-timers, the North Shore houses families, salty surfer types, and those smitten with the laid-back vibe and close proximity to O'ahu's most beautiful stretch of sea. If you've been to the island before, I cannot recommend enough allowing yourself more than a short afternoon to explore this region. Though there is only one major resort, you can find vacation rentals and guesthouses surrounding the main community of Hale'iwa, a fantastically fun town dripping with color and sass.

Unless you've lived under a rock for your entire life, you've likely heard of the North Shore's infamous winter surf breaks. Waves peak at up to 50 feet in winter, drawing crowds of pro surfers and those eager to catch a glimpse of the physical prowess of the daring. Unless you have surfed major breaks before, do not attempt to swim in or surf those waves in winter. Come summer, the waves mellow out and the sea is the domain of swimmers and snorkelers.

Kawela—or, as it is better known, Turtle Bay—features lava rocks hugging pristine inlets of turquoise seas, some gentle enough for *keikis* and others housing massive waves. It's impossible to be up here and not ache to stop at the luxurious Turtle Bay Resort perched on the edge of Kuilima Cove, the preferred swimming and snorkeling area in

NORTH SHORE AGRI-TOURISM

Across from Romy's Shrimp Stand, Kahuku Farms offers a tractor-pulled tour of the fields Friday through Monday at 2 p.m. During the tour, you'll learn about traditional farming methods and get to sample their delicious fruit. If you don't make it for a tour, they have a small farm café with smoothies, salads, and sandwiches sourced from the soil that surrounds you, plus a shop hawking jams and other tasty treats alongside bath and beauty products reaped from the land.

Agri-Tours O'ahu leads educational tours of a variety of working farms throughout the island. Each day, the destinations vary, whether it be visiting Waialua Estate's coffee and chocolate farm, or a working chicken ranch, a taro field, or organic orchards. Learn about traditional Hawaiian farming practices and then gobble up a farm-fresh lunch afterward.

While Dole Plantation is no longer a working farm, those who visit can learn about the history of pineapples on O'ahu. Families stop here to break up the trip from Waikiki to the North Shore. Kids ride the Pineapple Express, a vintage-style train, and get lost in the 2-acre Pineapple Garden Maze. You can access the farm via H2 south of Hale'iwa.

winter. Walk the expanse of the resort along paths passing pounding surf and mellow coves fronted by white sand. If you'd like to stay awhile, the hotel offers cottages, condos, and traditional hotel rooms, most with views of the swells. Expect a lively pool area, horseback riding, hiking trails, tennis, golf, surf lessons from masters, a collection of fun lounges including Surfer, the Bar, and a spa that will ease those swimmer's muscles. The resort's restaurants are geared toward their upscale clientele, but it is hard not to be won over by the oceanfront Ola Restaurant; though overpriced, I like coming here for a cocktail and afternoon snack after a swim. The signature restaurant 21 Degrees North showcases all you'd expect: gorgeous views, pricey organic entrées featuring delicacies like Kona lobster, and crafty cocktails. Even if you are not staying here, it is worth some time to sample the high life.

Fresh produce is abundant on the North Shore.

Whisper the word *Waimea* to surfers and watch the glee wash over their eyes. This oasis of green hills boasts some of the world's best surf breaks, a river that slices through lush mountains dotted with native plants, and Waimea Falls. For the off-the-beaten path travelers, Waimea beckons you to unfold her layers and explore her inner reaches, all the while remembering that this is the domain of ancients who grew heaps of taro, passed on to the people who have chosen this fertile region as their home.

Like the rest of the North Shore, Waimea has her share of legendary surf spots, teeming with pro wave riders, many of whom own real estate here. At mile marker 9, Sunset Beach's 2 miles of white sand comprise a hotbed for surfers in winter, who come from across the globe to ride these 20-foot giants. In summer, you'll find plenty of swimmers and families teaching the littles to ride the waves.

Across from Sunset Beach Park School is the legendary 'Ehukai Beach Park—or, as you probably know it, Banzai Pipeline. This surfer's beach has a serious reputation for being *the* wintertime wave to catch to make a name for yourself in the big-wave surfing scene. These breaks are presided over by a tight-knit group of locals, adding to the fun of getting yourself pounded by the massive waves that crash onto a shallow reef. In winter I recommend that you venture out here to watch the surfers battle the waves; in summer, you are free to hop in yourself.

About 0.5 mile before you reach Waimea Bay you'll happen upon Pupukea Beach Park. The shell of white sand merges with the deep blue sea and lava rock to inspire poetry, among other things. Out in the ocean is Pupukea Marine Life Conservation District, whose lava caves are rich with sea life. Divers and kayakers should contact Hawai'i Eco Divers for information about tours to explore the caves and surrounding bays in summer. Closer to shore, this beach park is split into three mini parks. For *summertime* swimming and snorkeling to spot sea turtles, head to the southern beach, Three Tables. Also in summer, tide pool fans wearing sturdy water shoes will want to explore Old Quarry's shallows to try and spot super-fast crabs jutting between the lava rocks. Despite the ominous name, at the northern end of this beach across from the gas station, Shark's Cove is one of the North Shore's best snorkeling and diving areas in summer.

Continuing on, Waimea Bay features a symbiotic relationship between water so blue you don't believe it to be true, sand so white it seems Photoshopped, and a snaking river cutting its way through it all. In winter, the waves are so fierce, the invitation-only Quicksilver in Memory of Eddie Aikau surf competition is held here—though only when the waves are the perfect style and size (over 20 feet). In summer, unbelievably, the waves and currents almost disappear and the waters are back in the hands of snorkelers and swimmers.

Inland, the sacred Waimea Valley stands guard over this spectacular beach. This

Turtle Bay Resort

DETOUR: UP PUPUKEA ROAD

While everyone congregates on North Shore's beaches, it is possible to find solace up Pupukea Road. Travel uphill and continue for about 0.5 mile until you see the turnoff for Pu'u o Mahuka Heiau State Monument. At almost 2 acres, this is the largest sacred site on the island. Archaeologists believe this lava rock temple was constructed in the 1600s for sacrifices. Though today this *heiau* might look like a pile of rocks, the area holds sacred value for Hawaiians. Do not go inside or walk on the rocks, not even to take that picture of that sparkling bay below.

Back on Pupukea Road, continue traveling *mauka* for 2 miles until the road ends. Here you'll find Kaunala Loop Trail, a 4.5-mile path popular with hunters (wear bold colors and sing loudly) and mountain bikers that offers sweeping views of the sea. Officially the park is only open to the public on weekends and holidays. The whole trail takes just over two hours to hike, and I only advise trying when it has not been raining.

massive nature preserve illustrates O'ahu's cultural and ecological history without being overly cheesy. View thousands of types of plants protected by the abundantly wet hills at the gardens, endangered birds, and archaeological sites as well as replicas of *heiaus* and temples. One of the main reasons people come here is to stand in the shadows of the 40-foot Waimea Falls (you can swim in the pool, though not if you have any open cuts). The cultural center at the foot of the valley offers lei-making classes, hula instruction, a lu'au lunch, and live music on select days; you can also grab locally made crafts to take home. On Thursday evenings from 3 to 7, the Hale'iwa Farmers' Market takes over the main building and grassy

A guitarist at Hale'iwa Farmers' Market

lawn. Pro surfers and their families populate the lawn eating banana taro bread or *kalua* pork quesadillas, listening to live music. There are a handful of artists selling their wares here as well.

On any given day, you'll find food trucks roving in beach parking lots—though al-

THE PLACE FOR YOGA ON THE NORTH SHORE By Lilly Barels

When you need to flush out the lactic acid in your muscles from all that surfing and hiking, the North Shore Yoga Co-op is the place to do it. Daily classes offer a range of levels and styles of practice. Take part in a slow, restorative yin class after your long day in the sun or get there early for the packed, funky-flow sweat-a-thon with wild music and excited yogis. Visit the website for more information, including the current schedule: www.north shoreyoga.org.

legedly the government is cracking down and forcing them to move every three hours. Keep an eye out for Lui Buenos (near Waimea Bay) and Tacos Vicente (by Sunset Beach). Alternatively, Ted's Bakery's brick-and-mortar eatery is a one-of-a-kind North Shore experience. Breakfast sandwiches invite surfers, while plate lunches win the hearts of almost everyone who passes by. Don't skip the chocolate *haupia* or banana cream pies; trust me, afterward you'll want to buy the whole pie. If you'd like to make your own food for a picnic, there's a Foodland by Pupukea Beach.

The area doesn't have many traditional lodging options. Ke Iki Beach Bungalows offers one- and two-bedroom beachfront cottages decked out in floral interiors, with kitchens, lanais, Wi-Fi, and barbecues. Budget travelers will appreciate Kalani Hawai'i, near Sunset Beach. Whether you rent a house, a private room, or a dorm bed with shared bath, this attractive complex promises comfortable accommodations in a family-friendly community.

And then you arrive in Hale'iwa, the soul of O'ahu, characterized by colorful plantation houses lining the roads; surfers, artists, and healers in board shorts and flip-flops; and lines of tourists pouring into town throughout winter. Hale'iwa drew missionaries in the early 1800s to construct a riverfront schoolhouse and plant roots. Today it's all about waves. The North Shore Surf and Cultural Museum is ground zero to learn about the history of the adventurers who first braved these giant swells. View old surfboards

THE SURF BUS By Lilly Barels

The Surf Bus was created to share all things fun on the North Shore in one package, as visitors who ride commercial tour buses usually miss out due to short photo-op stops. The North Shore Activities Tour on The Surf Bus includes your choice of biking, snorkeling, SUPping, surfing, bodyboarding, swimming, and hiking to waterfalls. Call Leila Alli at 808-226-7299, website www.northshoresurfbus.com.

A food truck in Hale'iwa

and photos and even grab a few vintage souvenirs to hang around your bar at home. Don't bother knocking on the door when there is surf. Those wanting an extended stay in the area should book well in advance—though in summer I have had luck with last-minute accommodations through airbnb.com. There are no hotels in town.

Hale'iwa is not without its beaches. Hale'iwa Ali'i Beach Park boasts killer waves, known to barrel overhead. International surf competitions heat up here in winter—though in summer, you'll wonder how the North Shore could possibly be considered a surf destination as you watch locals ride stand-up paddleboards along the glassy sea. Hale'iwa Beach Park is the spot to swim, play a game of pickup soccer, and have a picnic. For those wanting to rent a board or take a lesson (which is advisable even if you have actually stood on a board elsewhere), ask around at Hale'iwa Ali'i. Outfitters line the beaches offering boards for hire and lessons throughout the year. Surf n Sea offers rentals, boards for purchase, and apparel, as well as surf, SUP lessons, and dive instruction. If you are in the market for an original surfboard crafted on the North Shore, Kimo Greene is one of the best shapers on the island.

To cater to the tour buses that descend upon Hale'iwa in winter, boutiques and galleries line the highway and fill the innards of North Shore Marketplace, a hotbed for boutiques, souvenirs, and fun stylish boutiques like Silver Moon Emporium. Hawaiian Island Creations hawks surf gear. Global Creations and Interiors is the place for those perfect pillows celebrating hibiscus flowers, or a choice pair of earrings to wear with a flimsy summer dress. The Growing Keiki caters to dressing the younger set in adorable surf gear and island-style dresses. When I am in the area, I never miss a chance to explore Hale'iwa Art Gallery's local paintings, photos and sculptures.

DETOUR: HIGHWAY 930'S DESOLATE STRANDS

As you leave Hale'iwa, you arrive in Waialua, a former sugarcane town that is now quite desolate. However, in town Waialua Sugar Mill is worth a bit of time. This fun collection of shops hawks everything from locally made soaps and chocolates to funky vintage furnishings. This is where you'll find Waialua Estate's chocolate and coffee (see the "North Shore Agri-Tourism" sidebar). Continue on through town to Mokuleia Beach, popular with sunbathers and summertime kayakers. Out this far, it seems the entire island has melted into oblivion. Highway 930 winds toward the eastern edge of Ka'ena Point (for more on this, see chapter 1) and passes unkempt white sand beaches known for rough seas. It is possible to hike all the way to the western shores of O'ahu along the trail. It's about 5 miles round trip, and the scenery is impressive, to say the least.

When it comes to filling your belly, Hale'iwa's food scene satisfies to those on the run, or those in the market to spend hours enjoying pitchers of beer with friends, old and new. Food trucks line the highway, the most notable of these being Macky's Sweet Shrimp Truck, which is much like those in Kahuku, but wisely parked in the North Shore's busiest town instead. The former food truck Opal Thai Food recently scored a brick-and-mortar location in Hale'iwa Shopping Center. Arguably O'ahu's best Thai food, this no-frills eatery might be off-putting to some as the owner comes over to help you decide

Orion Barels surfing a North Shore wave *Chris Hunt*

what to eat. Favorites include the crab fried rice and the spicy curries. But everything I've had is quite good. BYOB. Kua 'Aina Sandwich Shop is an institution up here. Known for heaping portions of meat, this crowded lunch spot keeps them coming back time and time again. I am not exactly smitten, but I am a fan of the *ahi*, or the avocado burgers.

Lively throughout the day and night, Luibueno's Mexican Seafood and Fish Market is *the* spot to go after dark. Colorful interiors, with giant pictures of Clint Eastwood and Elvis on the walls, house pro surfers, travelers, and families, who swear by the beer-battered fish tacos. The margaritas are huge, so don't get one of you are motoring back to Waikiki.

In an inlet by Hale'iwa Beach Park, Jameson's by the Sea offers one of Hale'iwa's only (slightly) upscale eateries. Complete with sunset views, pricey seafood dishes, and Ted's Bakery desserts, this is the spot for romance. In the same vein, Hale'iwa Joe's is one of those restaurants you imagine in a surfer town: close to the sea, boasting seafood fresh off the boats in the distance and a lively atmosphere ideal for sitting outside and drinking a cocktail. The food is hit or miss, but the *pupus* and sunset views bring me back.

In the morning, grab breakfast at Kono's, a local fave for pork-stuffed burritos (they have a veggie option as well) or biscuit sliders. Another breakfast ritual in the North Shore is Café Hale'iwa, where griddle fare and giant plates of eggs and meat prepare surfers and families for the day. For your caffeine buzz, Coffee Gallery delivers traditional coffees, lattes, and super-sweet blended drinks ideal for a post-beach day.

Highway 83 meets up with Farrington Highway as you exit Hale'iwa, leading you

---

NORTH SHORE SHAVE ICE

The North Shore might be known for its waves, but there is another infamous attraction up in these parts—shave ice. Brought over from Japan with migrants working in the sugarcane fields, this sweet treat has been a way to beat the heat since the 1700s. Hawai'i has placed its fingerprint on this super-sweet delicacy, by first lining the bottom of the paper cone with red beans and ice cream and then topping that with perfectly shaved ice drenched in all types of sweet syrup. Less is more in my book. And be sure to balance sweet with sour to allow you to reach the delectable ice cream near the bottom.

On the North Shore, M Matsumoto Grocery Store has been serving shave ice since 1951 to lines of devotees—and I mean *lines*; this historic store serves up to 1,000 cones a day! Just down the road, Aoki's serves a similar version out of a little red house, just with a shorter line (and sugar-free options). However, arguably the best shave ice in the state can be found closer to Honolulu in Mo'ili'ili at Waiola Shave Ice, which adds sweetened condensed milk and *mochi* to the fixin's. Brave the line that snakes down the block and you be the judge.

straight to Honolulu. There are a number of highways that slice through the island's innards. Frankly, I am usually less than inspired on most of these roads. The fastest is H2, which takes you past Dole Plantation (see the "North Shore Agri-Tourism" sidebar), and grants you access to Wahiawa Botanical Gardens, a charmer of an arboretum offering almost 30 miles of bamboo groves and shady native trees to rest beneath. If you are making the stop at the gardens, top off your day with a visit to Sunny Side Restaurant for peach-pear or chocolate cream pie. Or, if you are in the market for President Obama's favorite shave ice, in Mo'ili'ili stop at Waiola Shave Ice (see the sidebar). The highway winds back toward Honolulu, where you can join with chapter 1's itinerary onto the west side of the island.

IN THE AREA

ACCOMMODATIONS

Hale Nalo, 41-19 Kaulu St., Waimanalo. Clean, well-decorated rooms just a short walk from Waimanalo Beach. Call 808-744-8405. Website www.halenalo.com.

Hula Breeze, Kailua. Well-kept and comfortable studio with kitchenette, only 0.25 mile to the beach. Call 808-469-7623.

Kahala Hotel and Resort, 5000 Kahala Ave., Honolulu. A luxury resort on a white sand beach, just 10 minutes away from bustling Waikiki, offers just about every amenity known to travelers. Call 808-739-8888. Website www.kahalaresort.com.

Kalani Hawai'i, 59-222 Kamehameha Hwy., Hale'iwa. Private and secure lodging options on a beautifully landscaped property near the beach. Call 808-551-3382. Website www.kalanihawaii.com.

Ke Iki Beach Bungalows, 59-579 Ke Iki Rd., Hale'iwa. Quaint and clean beach cottages, centrally located by Foodland in the heart of the North Shore. Call 808-638-8829. Website www.keikibeach.com.

Paradise Bay Resort, 47-039 Lihikai Dr., Kaneohe. Secluded location, private cove, and simple rooms along the sea, though the resort fee is a slight annoyance. Call 808-239-5711. Website www.paradisebayresorthawaii.com.

Papaya Paradise, 395 Auwinala Rd., Kailua. This popular B&B in Kailua rents out its two units well in advance. Call 808-261-0316.

Pat's Kailua Beach Properties, 204 S. Kalaheo Ave., Kailua. One of the largest providers for vacation homes and cottages on the Windward side of the island. Call 262-4128 or 808-261-1653. Website www.patskailua.com.

Turtle Bay Resort, 57-091 Kamehameha Hwy., Kahuku. Beautiful accommodations overlooking the northernmost point of the island, offering a slew of restaurants, lounges, beaches, a pool, and a spa. Call 808-293-6000. Website www.turtlebayresort.com.

ATTRACTIONS AND RECREATION

Aaron's Dive Shop, 307 Hahani St., Kailua. Open year-round for dive trips and charters in Kailua and the surrounding area. Call 808-262-2333. Website www.aaronsdiveshop.com.

Ali'i Antiques, 21 Maluniu Ave., Kailua. A superb secondhand and antiques shop offering everything from Pyrex to aloha shirts. Call 808-261-1705. Website www.aliiantiques.com.

Bookends, 600 Kailua Rd., Kailua. Pick

up beach reads, maps, and souvenirs. Call 808-261-1996.

Dole Plantation, 64-1550 Kamehameha Hwy., Wahiawa. Learn about the rich agricultural history of the island in a fun atmosphere complete with a train and a botanical maze. Sample the pineapple soft serve. Call 808-621-8408. Website www.dole-plantation.com.

Dolphin Quest at Kahala Hotel and Resort, 5000 Kahala Ave., Honolulu. Train dolphins, swim with them, or just watch these spectacular creatures exist in close proximity to humans. Call 808-739 8918 or 808-739-8888. Website www.kahalaresort.com/activities/dolphin-quest-encounter.

Fighting Eel, 629 Kailua Rd., #130, Kailua. A cute boutique in the center of town. Call 808-738-9301. Website www.fightingeel.com.

Global Creations and Interiors, 66-079 Kamehameha Hwy., Hale'iwa. A unique beach art gallery, offering a host of colorful paintings. Call 808-637-1780.

Global Village, 539 Kailua Rd., Kailua. A fun local boutique with jewelry and crafts. Call 808-262-8183. Website www.globalvillagehawaii.com.

Growing Keiki, 66-051 Kamehameha Hwy., Hale'iwa. My favorite kids' store on the island. Call 808-637-4544. Website www.thegrowingkeiki.com.

Hale'iwa Art Gallery, 66-252 Kamehameha Hwy., Hale'iwa. Local art highlights nature. Call 808-637-3368. Website www.haleiwaartgallery.com.

Hawai'i Eco Divers and Kayak Tours, 61-101 Iliohu Pl., Hale'iwa. Rent gear or arrange a tour with these master guides. Call 808-499-9177. Website www.hawaiiecodivers.com.

Hawaiian Island Creations, 66-224 Kamehameha Hwy., Hale'iwa. A surf shop that sells clothing, boards, and more. Call 808-637-0991. Website www.hicsurf.com.

Holokai Kayak and Snorkel Adventure, 46-465 Kamehameha Hwy., Kaneohe. Head out to explore the outer reef of the Windward Coast. Call 808-235-6509. Website www.heeiastatepark.org.

Kailua Sailboards and Kayaks, 130 Kailua Rd., Kailua. Rent gear from this dependable outfitter. Call 808-262-2555. Website www.kailuasailboards.com.

Kim Taylor Reece Gallery, 53-866 Kamehameha Hwy., Punalu'u. Iconic paintings of the islands. Call 808-293-2000. Website www.kimtaylorreece.com.

Kimo Greene Surfboards, 50 Sand Island Access Rd., Honolulu. North Shore surfer Kimo Greene is one of the state's best board shapers. Call 808-778-5466. Website www.sandislandsurfboards.com.

Kualoa Regional Park, 49-479 Kamehameha Hwy., Kahalu'u. Call 808-237-8525.

Mormon Temple La'ie, 55-600 Naniloa Loop, La'ie. Call 808-293-2427.

Mu'umu'u Heaven, 767 Kailua Rd., Kailua. More than those Mrs. Roper–type dresses can be found at this Kailua boutique. Call 808-263-3366. Website www.muumuuheaven.com.

Naturally Hawaiian Gallery, 41-1025 Kalanianaole Hwy., Waimanalo. A charmed art gallery in the small Waimanalo community. Call 808-259-5354. Website www.patrickchingart.com.

North Shore Surf and Cultural Museum, in the North Shore Marketplace, 66-250 Kamehameha Hwy., #E2, Hale'iwa. Learn all there is to know about the North Shore's favorite sport—as long as there are no waves that day. Call 808-637-8888. Website www.northshoresurfmuseum.com.

North Shore Marketplace, 66-250 Kamehameha Hwy., D203, Hale'iwa. Call 808-637-4416.

Polynesian Cultural Center, 55-370 Kamehameha Hwy., La'ie. One of

O'ahu's biggest tourist attractions offers a dry lu'au, a canoe parade, and replica Polynesian villages to explore. Call 808-293-3333. Website www.polynesia.com.

Queen Emma's Summer Palace, 913 Pali Hwy., Honolulu. Get up here before 4 p.m. to tour this regal retreat for Hawaiian royals. This is where you can drool over posh furnishings, a hand-crafted piano, and luscious grounds, ripe with tropical flora. Call 808-595-3167. Website www.daughtersofhawaii.org.

Sea Life Park, 41-202 Kalanianaole Hwy., Waimanalo. Keikis love the playground overlooking the sea and the sea lion and dolphin shows, while adventurers line up for the chance to stand in an underwater cage surrounded by sharks. Call 808-259-2500. Websitewww.sealife parkhawaii.com.

Silver Moon Emporium, 66-250 Kamehameha Hwy., G170, Hale'iwa. Forgot a cute outfit to wear to dinner? Never fear, this boutique's got you covered. Call 808-637-7710. Website www.silvermoonhawaii.blogspot.com.

Spa at Kahala Hotel and Resort, 5000 Kahala Ave., Honolulu. Splurge on the Hula Hands treatment, a four-handed massage. Call 808-739-8888. Website www.kahalaresort.com/spa.

Spa Luana at Turtle Bay Resort, 57-091 Kamehameha Hwy., Kahuku. What's better than their chocolate coffee glaze skin treatment? Only an oceanfront massage. Call 808-293-6000. Website www.turtlebayresort.com.

Sunshine Arts Gallery, 47-653 Kamehameha Hwy., Kaneohe. Contemporary and vintage Hawaiian artwork. Call 808-239-2992. Website www.sunshinearts.net.

Surf n Sea, 62-595 Kamehameha Hwy., Hale'iwa. One of the North Shore's best dive and surf shops can set you up with gear and tours. Call 808-637-9887. Website www.surfnsea.com.

Under a Hula Moon, 572 Kailua Rd., Space 116, Kailua. Pacific home décor with style and a touch of sass. Call 808-261-4252. Website www.hulamoonhawaii.com.

Valley of the Temples, 47-200 Kahekili Hwy., Kaneohe. A string of Buddhist meditation temples and gardens. Call 808-239-8811. Website www.valley-of-the-temples.com.

Wahiawa Botanical Gardens, 1396 California Ave., Wahiawa. A lesser-known 27-acre botanical garden between the North Shore and Honolulu. Call 808-621-7321.

Waimea Valley, 59-864 Kamehameha Hwy., Hale'iwa. Home to a cultural center, an afternoon Polynesian feast, hiking trails to waterfalls, and a lively farmers' market on Thursday evening. Call 808-638-7766. Website www.waimeavalley.net.

DINING

21 Degrees North at Turtle Bay Resort, 57-091 Kamehameha Hwy., Kahuku. A breathtaking ocean view paired with crab-crusted sea bass and exotic cocktails makes this upscale restaurant worth the price. Call 808-293-6000. Website www.turtlebayresort.com.

Agnes Portuguese Bake Shop, 46 Hoolai St., Kailua. Fresh *malasadas* and pastries inspire those with a sweet tooth. Call 808-262-5367. Website www.agnesbakeshop.com.

Aoki's Shave Ice, 66-117 Kamehameha Hwy., Hale'iwa. This stop on the shave ice circuit also features a variety of homemade syrups with sugar-free options. Call 808-637-7017. Website www.aokishaveice.com.

Boots and Kimo's Homestyle Kitchen, 151 Hekili St., Kailua. Don't miss the pancakes with macadamia nut sauce. Call 808-263-7929.

Cactus Bistro, 767 Kailua Rd., Kailua. Open for lunch and dinner, offering Latin cuisine with a Hawaiian twist. Call

808-261-1000. Website www.cactus bistro.com.

Café Hale'iwa, 66-460 Kamehameha Hwy., Hale'iwa. Try the café egg sandwich or the Hawaiian sweet bread French toast. Open daily for breakfast and lunch (and Wed.–Sat. for dinner). Call 808-637-5516.

ChadLou's Coffee Shop, 45 Kihapai St., Kailua. Pretty latte art paired with pastries and waffles. Call 808-263-7930. Website www.chadlous.com.

Ching's Store, 53-360 Kamehameha Hwy., Hauula. Stock up on snacks like *poke, musubi,* and butter *mochi.* Call 808-237-7017.

Cinnamon's Restaurant, 315 Uluniu St., Kailua. Try the red velvet pancakes or eggs Benedict for breakfast. Call 808-261-8724. Website www.cinnamons808.com.

Coffee Gallery, 66-250 Kamehameha Hwy., C106, Hale'iwa. Delicious coffee and espresso drinks and creative pastries like maple bacon cinnamon rolls and blueberry cream cheese scones cater to surfers. Call 808-637-5355. Website www.roastmaster.com.

Crepes No Ka 'Oi, 131 Hekili St., #106, Kailua. Small café offering both sweet and savory crepes for reasonable prices. Call 808-263-4088. Website www.crepes nokaoi.com.

Down to Earth Foods Kailua, 201 Hamakua Dr., Kailua. Shop for organic groceries and visit the hot food and salad bar or sandwich/smoothie/fresh juice station. Call 808-262-3838. Website www.downtoearth.org.

Famous Kahuku Shrimp Truck, 56-580 Kamehameha Hwy., Kahuku. Shrimp, *mahi mahi,* or steak plates with rice and mac salad. Call 808-389-1173. Website www.hishrimp.com.

Foodland La'ie, 55-510 Kamehameha Hwy., La'ie. Purchase necessary groceries and supplies here—but no alcohol, due to Mormon influence. Call 808-293-4443.

Foodland Pupukea, 59-720 Kamehameha Hwy., Hale'iwa. A local hangout/grocery store; come to load up on supplies, or sip a coffee out front and people-watch. Call 808-638-8081. Website www.foodland.com.

Giovanni's Original White Shrimp Truck, 56-505 Kamehameha Hwy., Kahuku. The shrimp scampi is extra garlicky and delicious. Call 808-293-1839. Website www.giovannisshrimptruck.com.

Hale'iwa Farmers' Market, in Waimea Valley, 59-864 Kamehameha Hwy., Hale'iwa. Don't miss the fresh pesto pizza, warm portobello mushroom croissants, and homemade pasta stand while loading up on local produce. Call 808-388-9696. Website www.haleiwafarmers market.com/haleiwa.

Hale'iwa Joe's, 66-011 Kamehameha Hwy., Hale'iwa. Order a sandy snorkel cocktail and a bunch of *pupus* like the *kalbi* ribs, garlic mushrooms, and black and blue *ahi.* Call 808-637-8005. Website www.haleiwajoes.com.

He'eia Pier General Store and Deli, 46-499 Kamehameha Hwy., Kaneohe. Only open 9–3, Tue.–Sat. Order the guava chicken or hamburger steak plate lunch. Call 808-235-2192.

Hoku's at Kahala Hotel and Resort, 5000 Kahala Ave., Honolulu. Expensive beachside dining that highlights sustainable seafood and meat. Reservations recommended. Call 808-739-8888. Website www.kahalaresort.com.

Hukilau Café, 55-662 Wahinepee St., La'ie. Hawaiian plate lunch options like *loco moco* and *kalua* pork make La'ie's resident students return. Call 808-293-8616.

Jameson's by the Sea, 62-540 Kamehameha Hwy., Hale'iwa. While gazing at the beautiful view of the ocean and harbor, don't miss the dinner salad with their Gorgonzola house dressing, and the ice cream pie for dessert. Call 808-637-6272. Website www.jamesons hawaii.com.

Kahuku Superette, 56-505 Kamehameha Hwy., Kahuku. Some locals argue that the superette has, hands-down, the best *shoyu ahi poke* on the island. Call 808-293-9878.

Kailua Farmers' Market, 609 Kailua Rd., Kailua. Try the fried green tomatoes or *ono* pops and load up on organic produce. Call 808-522-7088.

Kalapawai Café and Deli, 750 Kailua Rd., Kailua. Grab-and-go salads and sandwiches, or enjoy your meal in the dining room with wine and coffee bars. Call 808-262-3354. Website www.kalapa waimarket.com.

Kalapawai Market, 306 S. Kalaheo Ave., Kailua. Load up your beach picnic basket with cold drinks and deli sandwiches. Call 808-262-4359. Website www.kalapawaimarket.com.

Kona Brewing Company, 7192 Kalanianaole Hwy., Hawai'i Kai. A fun atmosphere with winning brews, wings, and pizza. Call 808-394-5662. Website www.konabrewingco.com.

Kono's, 66-250 Kamehameha Hwy., Ste. G110, Hale'iwa. Known for breakfast burritos and creative lunch sandwich specials. Call 808-637-9211.

Kua 'Aina Sandwich Shop, 66-160 Kamehameha Hwy., Hale'iwa. Known for their half-pound and third-pound hamburgers as well as their *mahi mahi* with avo sandwich. Call 808-637-6067. Website www.kua-aina.com.

Lanikai Juice Kahala, 4346 Waialae Ave., Honolulu. Tropical smoothies, *acai* bowls, and fresh juices. Call 808-732-7200. Website www.lanikaijuice.com.

Lanikai Juice Kailua, in the Kailua Shopping Center, 600 Kailua Rd., Kailua. Tropical smoothies, *acai* bowls, and fresh juices. Call 808-262-2383. Website www.lanikaijuice.com.

Luibueno's Mexican Seafood & Fish Market, 66-165 Kamehameha Hwy., Hale'iwa. The beer-battered *mahi mahi* fish tacos are a must along with the calamari appetizer and homemade *churro* dessert. Call 808-637-7717. Website www.luibueno.com.

Macky's Sweet Shrimp Truck, 66-632 Kamehameha Hwy., Hale'iwa. Try the garlic butter or coconut shrimp plates. Call 808-780-1071.

Matsumoto Shave Ice, 66-087 Kamehameha Hwy., Hale'iwa. Shave ice mecca offering homemade tropical syrups with sugar-free options. Call 808-637-4827. Website www.matsumoto shaveice.com.

Moena Café, in the Koko Marina Shopping Center, 7192 Kalanianaole Hwy., Suite #D-101, Hawai'i Kai. Serves local ingredients for breakfast and lunch, including eggs Benedict and farm-fresh salads. Call 808-888-7716. Website www.moenacafe.com.

Morning Brew, 600 Kailua Rd., Kailua. Coffee and espresso bar also offers egg scrambles, veggie quesadillas, and *ahi* tuna skewers. Call 808-262-7770. Website www.morningbrewhawaii.com.

Ola Restaurant at Turtle Bay Resort, 57-091 Kamehameha Hwy., Kahuku. Fancy Hawaiian fusion cuisine with your toes in the sand. Call 808-293-0801. Website www.olaislife.com.

Olive Tree Café, 4614 Kilauea Ave., Honolulu. Try the *babaganoush*, hummus, and fresh fish *souvlaki*. Call 808-737-0303.

Opal Thai Food (by Long's Drugs) 66-460 Kamehameha Hwy., Hale'iwa. Authentic Thai dishes like spicy garlic chicken wings topped with fried basil and coconut noodles. Call 808-637-7950.

Plumeria House at Kahala Hotel and Resort, 5000 Kahala Ave., Honolulu. Open-air restaurant with all-day menus offering gluten-free French toast, the Kahala burger, and sunset *mai tais* as well as a large buffet for breakfast and dinner. Call 808-739-8888. Website www.kahalaresort.com.

Romy's Kahuku Prawns & Shrimp, 56-781 Kamehameha Hwy., Kahuku. Try the butter and garlic, or sweet and spicy shrimp plates. Call 808-232-2202. Website www.romyskahukuprawns.org.

Roy's Hawai'i Kai, 6600 Kalanianaole Hwy., Honolulu. Hawaiian fusion cuisine popular for celebratory dinners; don't miss the famous chocolate soufflé dessert. Reservations required. Call 808-396-7697. Website www.roysrestaurant.com.

Serg's Mexican Kitchen (two locations) 41-865 Kalanianaole Hwy., Waimanalo; 2740 E. Manoa Rd., Honolulu. Try the chicken *flautas*, *carne asada* burrito, and fresh salsa bar. Call 808-259-7374.

Shrimp Shack, 53-360 Kamehameha Hwy., Punalu'u. Variations on shrimp recipes please those looking for sustenance along the Windward Coast highway. Call 808-256-5589. Website www.shrimpshackoahu.com.

Sunny Side Restaurant, 1017 Kilani Ave., Wahiawa. Known islandwide for fresh-baked pies, but also serves homestyle breakfast and lunch daily. Call 808-621-7188

Surfer, the Bar at the Turtle Bay Resort, 57-091 Kamehameha Hwy., Kahuku. Lounge with a cocktail, listen to live music, and talk story with a professional surfer. Call 808-293-6000. Website www.turtlebayresort.com.

Sweet Home Waimanalo, 41-1025 Kalanianaole Hwy., Waimanalo. Nutritious, local ingredients used for seared fish tacos and poi bowls. Call 808-259-5737. Website www.sweethomewaimanalo.com.

Tacos Vicente Food Truck, location varies along the North Shore. Try the surf-and-turf burrito or tacos al pastor. Call for location 808-356-9111. Website www.tacosvicente.com.

Ted's Bakery, 59-024 Kamehameha Hwy., Hale'iwa. The bacon, egg, and cheese breakfast sandwiches on homemade rolls are beyond words. Also try the teriyaki beef plate lunch. And do not miss the chocolate *haupia* pie. Call 808-637-6067. Website www.tedsbakery.com.

Uahi Island Grill, 131 Hekili St., Kailua. Healthy, contemporary Hawaiian eatery with an knack for making local produce taste like heaven. Call 808-266-4646. Website www.uahiislandgrill.com.

Uncle Bobo's, 51-480 Kamehameha Hwy., Ka'a'awa. BBQ, chili fries, and shave ice, oh my! Call 808-237-1000. Website www.unclebobos.com.

Waiahole Poi Factory, 49-140 Kamehameha Hwy., Kaneohe. Traditional Hawaiian lu'au menu with fresh, hand-pounded poi. Call 808-239-2222. Website www.waiaholepoifactory.com.

Waiola Shave Ice, 2135 Waiola St., Honolulu. Traditional syrup flavors with add-ons like tapioca, condensed milk, and *mochi*. Call 808-949-2269.

Whole Foods at Kahala Mall, 4211 Waialae Ave., #2000, Honolulu. Stock up on local produce and organic groceries. Call 808-738-0820. Website www.wholefoodsmarket.com/stores/honolulu.

OTHER CONTACT INFORMATION

Hawai'i Visitors Bureau, 2270 Kalakaua Ave., Ste. 801, Honolulu. Call 877-525-OAHU (6248). Website www.gohawaii.com.

Kauaʻi's Hideaways Beach on the North Shore

3 Kaua'i's Ancient Wonders and Modern Luxuries

FROM KAPA'A TO THE NORTH SHORE

Estimated length: 38 miles

Estimated time: 1½ hours, or 3 leisurely days

Getting there: Most fly into Honolulu International Airport and connect into Lihu'e Airport on an inter-island flight via Hawaiian Airlines (www.hawaiianairlines .com), Go! (www.iflygo.com), and Island Air (www.islandair.com). However, many airlines, including Hawaiian Air (www.hawaiianairlines.com), United (www.united.com), American (www.aa.com), and Delta (www.delta.com), fly directly from the mainland, from most major California cities. Rental car offices outside the airport include Alamo (www.alamo.com), Budget (www.budget.com), Dollar (www.dollar.com), Hertz (www .hertz.com), National (www.national.com), and Thrifty (www.thrifty.com).

Getting around Kaua'i is fairly easy. H 50 circles the 70 miles of drivable land; however, it has numerous names and can get confusing. In Lihu'e, heading west, it is called H 50 (Kaumuali'i Highway). From Lihu'e, heading north, the highway is called H 56 (or Kuhio Highway). Getting from one end of the island to the other takes about an hour and a half. The average speed between towns is around 30 mph. In town, you can pretty much count on traffic; it is best to stay off the roads in this area 7–8 a.m. and 3–5 p.m. on weekdays.

Highlights: The North Shore's tropical scenery; chilling out on Hanalei Bay; exploring the Na Pali Coast; exploring native plants at Limahuli Gardens; eating fresh-caught fish at Kilauea Fish Market; surfing and swimming on the North Shore.

Verdant, yet bursting with shocks of red, pink, yellow, and even blue flowers, Kaua'i represents all that mainlanders imagine when jetting to the Pacific. Kaua'i is the fourth largest in the Hawaiian chain and is located just 100 miles northwest of O'ahu, yet this tropical isle feels continents away from the hustle of Honolulu. It's surrounded

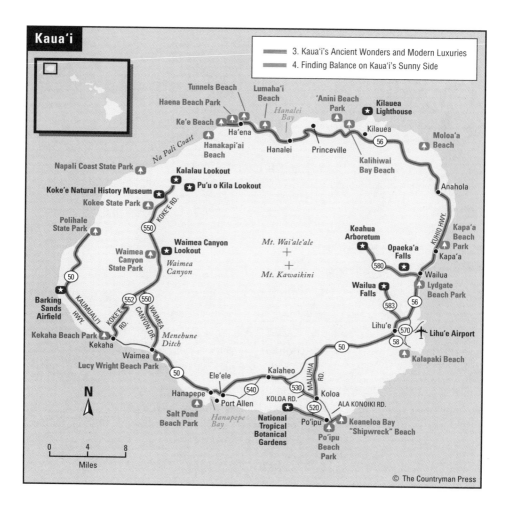

by turbulent reef breaks, and home to one of the rainiest places on the planet; only 5 percent of the island is accessible by car. Nature has done its part to ensure Kaua'i's isolation.

While in the past the treacherous seas made it nearly impossible for people to get on or off the island, now flights shuttle people in, bringing both environmental threats and economic joys. With modernization currently battling it out with Mother Nature, new changes occur daily. Big-box shopping centers, fancy condominium complexes, multi-million-dollar houses, and high-end resorts all challenge the simplicity of this fragile environment. The Hawaiian people, who have always lived hand-in-hand with nature, are now learning to deal with another set of dramatic changes in their homeland.

From the airport, take Highway 50 east through Lihu'e (for more on Lihu'e, see chapter 4), and take a peek into Kapaia Stitchery. This homegrown shop caters to quilters with an array of fabrics, as well as offering classes for those wanting to learn this sacred art. Passing two lava stone churches, Lihu'e First Church (1840) and Lihu'e United Church, detour *mauka* on Highway 583 and travel 4 miles to Wailua Falls. Kings once jumped off these twin 100-foot falls to prove their worth. Today, with half the water flow, this feat is too dangerous to attempt—though that doesn't mean some don't try. The hike here is way too slippery for you to bother.

This is where Highway 50 turns into Highway 56. On the left you'll see Ara's Sakana-ya Fish Market, the go-to spot on the island for fresh-caught local seafood (grab some to prepare in your condo) and yummy *poke*. Continue traveling northeast along the coast to reach Wailua, one of Kaua'i's most historically significant areas. Many of the ancient Kaua'i people settled along the Wailuanuiaho'ano, the great Wailua River basin, in the ancient kingdom Puna. Today the area is rich with condo complexes, funky restaurants, and a lively salt-of-the-earth community along the river.

Travel *makai* off the highway, following the signs for Lydgate Beach Park. Crafted with love by local families, this beach park shows off Kamalani Playground designed by local *keiki*, BBQ and picnic areas, sporting fields, and enclosed lava rock swimming areas, perfect for timid or young swimmers. There is a long walking path for a stroll or bike ride that leads to Kaha Lani, an oceanfront condo resort favored by longtime residents and in-the-know visitors looking for privacy, full kitchens, a pool, and access to the

A GUIDE TO DRIVING ON THE ISLANDS

Driving in Hawai'i, though it might appear easy, can be quite hazardous. There are numerous deadly crashes each year, and speeding is the main cause. Police officers are out in full force to catch speeders, people who aren't wearing their seat belts, or drunk drivers. Pay close attention to posted speed limit signs and no matter how much you like those free lu'au *mai tais*, make sure you always have a designated driver.

Here are some basic local driving customs to know.

❖ Don't honk your horn. In Hawai'i this is considered rude.

❖ Let faster drivers pass, when safe to do so.

❖ Don't tailgate.

❖ On one-lane bridges, make sure to stop at the white line to check if there is oncoming traffic. If no one is waiting at the line on the other side, you are free to drive. If the car in front of you is crossing (and no one is waiting), follow. However, if cars are waiting on the other side, yield to them. The general rule is if you are the fifth–seventh car, stop and let the people waiting on the other side go.

area's beaches, hikes, and restaurants. Most of the units are individually owned. Contact Rosemary Smith at Rosewood Properties to arrange accommodations.

Here you'll find the first of Wailua's seven *heiaus*. These were reserved exclusively for the use of *ali'i* and are now a National Historical Landmark. Frankly, most of these *heiaus* look like no more than a pile of rocks. However, all carry religious and spiritual power for the Kaua'i people and should be treated with the greatest respect (see the sidebar for guidelines to visiting a *heiau*). At the north end of Lydgate Park, Hikina Akala Heiau was a place of refuge for anyone who had broken a *kapu* (taboo). The wrongdoers could make offerings to the gods and, after a few days, resume their lives.

As you travel *mauka* on Highway 580 along the Wailua River, you can spot Malae

In ancient times, royals proved their strength by jumping off dangerous Wailua Falls.

The sacred Wailua River

Heiau, which anthropologists believe is the first recorded Menehune *heiau* because of the type of stonework, uncommon in other parts of Hawai'i. This is one of Kaua'i's largest *heiaus* with walls reaching up to 13 feet high. On your left, just past the boat launch, **Holoholoku** is the oldest known *heiau* not built by Menehune. Originally, this structure was constructed to honor the *ali'i* Mo'ikeha's marriage and be the space where his children would be born. In the *heiau* are two boulders, which constitute the **Pohaku Ho'ohanau Birthstone**. Royal women gave birth here, and all children born in this *heiau* became chiefs. After a birth, the umbilical cord was wrapped and wedged into the rock. The fate of the child depended on what happened to the cord. For example, if the cord

---

VISITING A *HEIAU*

A *heiau* is a temple built of rectangular lava rock, fit together so adeptly that many walls still stand today. They used to be filled with palm leaves, wood, grasses, and sacred objects. Though they may look like a pile of rocks to you, often overgrown by brush or seemingly forgotten, remember that these are religious sites, sacred to Hawaiians. They are fragile and cannot be replaced. So please honor the suggestions listed below.

❖ View the *heiau* from the exterior. Do not climb on or over the rock walls—they may collapse.

❖ Do not excavate, destroy, or alter any historic site on state land or you will be fined $10,000.

❖ Do not leave offerings or trash at a *heiau* structure. Coins, candles, incense, and similar items cause long-term damage.

---

was carelessly handled and rats ate it, the child would grow up to be a thief. Another known use for this *heiau* was as a place of human sacrifice to the gods. Just before Opaeka'a Falls, Poliahu Heiau was the home for ceremonial items. There was also a three-floor tower where the head priest prayed for advice from the gods.

As you weave up the road, on your right you have a fantastic view of Nounou "Sleeping Giant" Mountain. One legend says the giant Puni was sleeping when O'ahu warriors attacked. The Menehune threw rocks at him to wake him, but they bounced off his stomach and flew into the sea, scaring off the warriors. When the Menehune went to wake him the next day, they realized some rocks had gotten in his mouth; he had choked on them and died. Today it is possible to hike muddy trails into the jungle and up to the top of the 1,000-foot mountain; you can find a trailhead just past Opaeka'a Falls off Kuamo'o Road.

Just off the right side of the road, the 40-foot Opaeka'a Falls was once the site of a sacred ancient community. Now it is a stop on the tour bus circuit. The closest you can (and should) get is the gated path along the road. In 2006, two hikers died trying to access the falls. Please do not hike down here; this is *not* a trailhead and can be very dangerous.

From the other side of the road, you can get a great photo of the bucolic Wailua River State Park. The 12-mile Wailua

COCOA LOVERS UNITE!

Up in the Wailua hills, it is possible to arrange a guided tour and chocolate tasting at Steelgrass Farm. Three-hour tours are on the pricey side, but chocolate fans will appreciate the caffeinated glee of exploring the lovely 8-acre farm.

River begs to be explored, and fans of kayaks can have a heyday paddling up the river to a "secret" waterfall. Kayak Wailua leads 5-mile tours up the river to Secret Falls (you have to hike an additional muddy mile to access these falls). The adventure lasts about four or five hours, and they leave twice a day. If you'd prefer to have some freedom to explore the river yourself, hire a kayak through Outfitter's Kaua'i. Along the way, you can explore the riverfront Kamokila Hawaiian Village, a replica of a traditional ancient community, complete with a birthing stone—yes, ladies, that is where ancient ladies squatted to give birth—and lovely grounds along the river. You can also drive here by following the signs just past Opaeka'a Falls. Another site along the river is the rather run-down Fern Grotto, which you can take a boat trip to; however, your time is better spent at other gardens.

Kamokila Hawaiian Village

About a mile uphill, Kaua'i's Hindu Monastery sits like a dollop of gold atop the river. Hawai'i's most stunning monastery features over 450 acres of landscaped gardens tended to by fierce devotees of Shiva. Access the grounds and temples in the morning, and join a guided tour on select days (call for a reservation). However, if you want to view the world's largest single-pointed quartz crystal, weighing in at 700 pounds, you'll have to be a vegetarian—only those committed to not eating breathing beings can view the spectacle. This 50-million-year-old beauty is hidden in Kadavul Temple.

DETOUR: POKAHU-KANI "BELLSTONE" *HEIAU*

Just after mile marker 1 on Highway 580 is a dirt road heading back toward the ocean. Follow this road to the end; the Pokahu-kani "Bellstone" is 100 feet past the guardrail. This rock had many uses for ancient Kaua'i people. Because of the clear loud sound when struck, chiefs could communicate between *heiau*. One major function was to ring the bellstone when a royal woman gave birth.

Rosewood's yellow Victorian cottage

Farther up the road, Keahua Arboretum was once a sweet green space with swimming areas and abundant hiking trails. Today locals partake in unsavory activities, often making this green space an unsafe place to spend time. From here it is possible to access the Powerhouse Trail, a popular mountain biking road that leads to the North Shore, but take everything with you, as car break-ins are common.

Accommodations in the Kapa'a hills are abundant and relatively inexpensive. My favorite is Rosemary and Norbert Smith's Rosewood Inn, characterized by two impeccably designed yellow Victorian houses. Guests can stay in the B&B rooms, reserve one of the lovely cottages (with full kitchen and outdoor shower), or grab a bed in the bunkhouse, which boasts a shared kitchenette. Norbert's koi pond, organic fruit trees, and flowering plants show off his landscaping experience. Rosemary also runs Rosewood Kaua'i, a vacation rental agency.

Another choice lodging option is Mike and Martina Hough's Kaua'i Country Inn. Cheery Hawaiian-motif interiors, a hot tub, a yummy breakfast, complimentary kayaks, and spacious rooms are on the menu. Beatles fans will go gaga over Mike's museum, which includes memorabilia like original artwork and Brian Epstein's Mini Cooper.

Back where Highway 580 meets Highway 56, the dilapidated buildings to your left are the ruins of the famed Coco Palms. Since Hurricane 'Iniki destroyed this historic property, frequented by Elvis Presley during the filming of *Blue Hawaii*, there has been talk of developers bringing it back to its lustrous shine, though still to no avail. Instead, travel north on Highway 56 to grab a bite to eat. This area, combined with that of the neighboring community of Waipouli, offers some of the island's best budget eats, as well as one of Kaua'i's finest restaurants.

In the Kinipopo Shopping Village, breakfasts are best at Tutu's Soup Hale, where you can find a poi English muffin topped with organic eggs, or a sweet Dutch pancake. Lunches rely on hearty soups, organic salads, and fanciful sandwiches crafted with aloha. Another local favorite, Monico's Taqueria (probably Kaua'i's most authentic Mexican food) serves up a decent mole or fish taco. Over the years, establishments have come and gone in this center; hopefully Cakes by Kristen sticks around for a while so you can sample her creative cupcakes and decent cups of coffee. Another fun stop is Passion Bakery Café for fresh-baked loaves of bread, cookies, and pastries.

Across the street Mema Thai is the island's most dependable table for spicy curries, and traditional noodle dishes flavored with basil and sugar. In the rear of the strip mall, that little house in the back shaded by a canopy of trees is Caffee Coco. A popular night spot, Caffee Coco promotes healthy living with *ahi* rice bowls, veggie pastas, and tofu sandwiches, all served along a bubbling stream. In the evenings there is live music and an army of mosquitoes buzzing around the candlelit dining area. Next door, Kintaro packs the house for sushi and celebratory *teppanyaki* dinners. Reservations are highly recommended in the evenings.

In the same complex, Bambulei is a charming boutique to purchase something more than flip-flips and board shorts. They also have a selection of well-chosen vintage clothing. The nearby (albeit ailing) Coconut Marketplace houses Whaler's General Store, a decent stop for cheap shark tooth necklaces and Hawaiian books, as well as chocolate-covered mac nuts and water bottles. This outdoor mall has a battery of stores selling jewelry, T-shirts, and local music. There is a farmers' market on Tuesday and Thursday mornings, as well as free hula on Wednesday at 5 p.m. and Saturday at 1 p.m.

A TROPICAL PARADISE

Smith's Tropical Paradise's gardens feature peacocks, an Easter Island replica, a sweet pond hugged by tropical plants, and that particular calm associated with gardens. You'll hear many calling their evening lu'au Kaua'i's best. And while I may not entirely agree, I do think this is one of the most alluring options on the island, especially for the price. The food, drink, and energy devoted to a fun show make this a fun evening out for first-time visitors.

The marketplace also houses Eggbert's, a local fave for eggs and sausage, or massive omelets.

For those smitten with this stretch of coastline, Lae Nani offers spacious one- and two-bedroom units with upscale kitchens and a pool. Outrigger manages the majority of the units, but Rosewood also can score a couple of choice condos. The rocky peak at the ocean is Kukui Heiau, once a departure and arrival point for travelers. At night, fire torches (made of *kukui* nut trees) pointed out the way for canoes.

When it comes time for dinner, reserve a table at one of Kaua'i's best restaurants, Hukilau Lanai. Hidden in the Kaua'i Coast Resort at Beach Boy, the 5–6 p.m. happy-hour dinner is a great bargain, though I prefer to eat here after dark when the *tiki* torches are ablaze and the live music wafts in from the lounge. This is where the locals go for special occasions to splurge on fresh-caught seafood like *ahi poke* nachos, Kona Kampachi *ceviche*, or the Hukilau Grill, a trio of fish and risotto. A selling point is the wine menu of bottles costing $20 or less.

Just up the road, Waipouli houses a collection of unassuming strip malls packed with shoppers day and night. Whether you need to rent snorkel gear at Snorkel Bob's,

---

SOARING OVER KAUA'I

One of the most impressive ways to glimpse the whole of Kaua'i is by helicopter. These tours fly over waterfalls cascading down Mount Wai'ale'ale, the Na Pali Coast, and Manawaiopuna Falls (the waterfall in *Jurassic Park*, which you can only see by helicopter). Since the weather in Kaua'i changes by the hour, often helicopter tours will get canceled due to bad conditions. This is a good thing. If a pilot cancels your flight, it is for your safety. However, since rain brings rainbows and waterfalls, a bit of rain is okay, so don't get freaked out. To avoid having a canceled trip for your entire journey, book your tour early in your vacation, so you have time to reschedule. When selecting a tour company, don't be afraid to ask questions regarding the price versus the length of the tour (usually about an hour). Expect to pay more than $200 per person.

Blue Hawaiian Helicopters (www.bluehawaiian.com) takes to the skies in pricey (and comfortable) Eco-Star helicopters. Island Helicopters (www.islandhelicopters.com) has been flying since 1980. They are concerned with the ecological impact of tourism on Kaua'i, so the tours are set up to give you a better understanding of the ecology of the island. Jack Harter Helicopters (www.helicopters-kauai.com) is the longest-running helicopter tour on Kaua'i. Note that if you sit in the backseat of the open-window helicopter, bring a jacket—it gets cold. They offer 60- and 90-minute tours and pride themselves on employing pilots who know a vast amount about Kaua'i. Mauna Loa Helicopters (www.maunaloahelicopters.com) is the most popular outfitters on the island, so call well in advance to book a tour.

KAUA'I'S BEST FARMERS' MARKETS

This starfruit is sweet as can be.

At 3 p.m. on Wednesday, cars line the parking lot at Kapa'a New Park. A chant is sung and then the masses descend on the vendors, who sell everything from local honey to soursop, apple bananas to star fruit. For a market with even more flavor, if that's possible, head up north to Hanalei's Saturday market (at 9:30 a.m.), which also features a fun boho-hippie vibe and plenty of *keikis* running around the field.

stock up on organic groceries, smoothies, and hot food at Papaya's Natural Foods, or pop into Foodland to grab fixings for dinner, chances are you'll return to the area numerous times. If you have cash to burn, Marta's Boat hawks *keiki* and women's clothing, handcrafted jewelry, fun shirts, and crafts made by the owner's hubbie. Beyond the mini mall, the venerable Kaua'i Pasta is the go-to spot for heaping bowls of pesto pasta for lunch and dinner. Often the wait can be excruciating. Across the street, Outrigger Waipouli scooped up the last piece of oceanfront real estate in Kapa'a, much to locals' chagrin. However, this handsome condo-tel is the largest full-service accommodation in the area, offering full kitchens, washing machines in units, a saltwater river pool, and a sandy-bottomed hot tub.

Continuing on Highway 56, Kapa'a is like a breath of fresh air, complete with a walkable downtown inserted into historic buildings, a beach, the island's finest farmers' market, as well as Kaua'i's best coffee shop. You'll want to bookmark plenty of time in town. If you are interested in the history of this former sugar community, reserve a space at the Kapa'a Town Walking Tour.

At the northern end of town, Kapa'a Beach Park, backed by palm trees, makes a popular picnic area. There's a free public pool and a sporting field that often hosts festivals and events too. The paved walking path leads north from town to Kealia Beach Park (there are plans for this path to stretch to Lihu'e). This isn't the best beach in the world, but if you are in the area, it makes for a fine place to drink a coconut off snagged the aunty's truck parked along the highway.

Shoppers will delight in Kapa'a's boutiques. Start in Pono Market, a hole-in-the-wall hawking tasty *poke* and plate lunches, to grab Hawaiian snacks and affordable leis. As long as you can bypass the name, Hula Girl features breezy men's aloha shirts and women's island wear. It's hard not to want just about everything at the women's boutique The Root, where fashion is the name of the game. And if you want to bring home a ukulele, it's all about Larry's Music and Boutique. For surf gear and clothes, head over to Tamba Surf Shop, where the locals will instruct you on the best places to catch waves that day. Finally, on the *mauka* side of the street, just past the beach, Kaua'i Products Fair offers sarongs, jewelry, and handcrafted art. Peek in the back of the outdoor market to find Artists of Kaua'i, a gallery showcasing the work of seven locals. Also in the back of the marketplace, Small Town Coffee Company serves Kaua'i's best latte, as well as waffles, breakfast sandwiches, and pastries. They have an adjacent bookstore that also sells local art.

When it comes to eating, Kapa'a won't disappoint. From its perch atop the heart of Kapa'a, Olympic Café has the convivial vibe associated with college towns, massive plates of food and all. This open-air eatery offers three meals daily, plus a wild happy hour known for large plates of nachos and beer. Food is decent, though slightly over-priced. I favor breakfasts for *ahi* and eggs, or griddle fare, but lunchtime salads are also worth the splurge. The modest Ono Family Restaurant is open throughout the day, but the winning menu item is their mac nut pancakes topped with their signature coconut syrup (which you can purchase to bring back to your condo). Another breakfast option, Kountry Kitchen seems like it should be in Milwaukee rather than Kaua'i. The perky servers keep your coffee full as they serve up *kalua* pork scrambles or vegan egg dishes.

When it comes to lunch, next to Java Kai (a decent choice for a cup of joe), Mermaid's Café caters to yogis soaking up the sun as they sip smoothies and dive into *ahi nori* wraps. Though I've yet to visit Verde, local friends swear by the meaty tacos, mango margaritas, and *ahi* tostadas. To shop for picnic fixings or stock up your condo, Hoku Foods Natural Market hawks an array of pricey organic produce.

Dinners in Kapa'a are presided over by The Eastside, which offers a romantic set-

Trickster surfers at Kealia Beach

WHAT'S THE DEAL WITH ALL THOSE CHICKENS?

At first you might think they are cute—a novelty, even. You'll take pictures at the airport or up at Koke'e, or at the parking lot of your accommodation. But come 4 a.m., it'll be another story. The unfortunate reality of Kaua'i is that the chickens get up before you do. The positive side is that you never need an alarm clock.

No one knows exactly when chickens were introduced to Kaua'i, but we do know that Polynesian sailors had them aboard ships for food. After Hurricane 'Iniki destroyed many of the cages of captive birds, the chickens ran wild, breeding like crazy. Now no matter where you are staying—a Poipu condo or the St. Regis—chickens are a presence. So if you are a light sleeper, bring earplugs. And make sure to watch the roads when you drive. Recently a friend came to meet me at the beach and hit a chicken on the way. And in case you are wondering, those skinny fowls don't make good eating.

One of the island's maddening chickens

ting to enjoy *hulu huli* chicken and *hoisin* ribs. The chocolate cake keeps me coming back. Around the way, head to Sushi Bushido for a fun ambience paired with good sushi, live music, and a hopping bar. Order the "Kaua'i" or the "butter me up" rolls with some sake and enjoy the live reggae music.

After you've exhausted your stay in Kapa'a, travel north on Highway 56 to mile marker 10, where the walking path from Kapa'a ends. Kealia Beach caters to surfers, sunbathers, and picnickers. You'll probably want to swim laps elsewhere, though, as the sea is rough. I like to stop here while I wait for a massage appointment at Angeline's Mu'olaulani. This family-owned operation doesn't bother with the pomp and circumstance of resort spas; instead the *lomilomi* massage, complete with two therapists kneading your swimmer's muscles, is a simple affair, punctuated with ocean breezes and an outdoor shower afterward.

Up the street, locals call in their orders at Duane's Ono Char-burger, rather than waiting for ages at this modest take-out joint. It's all about the heaping burgers, the crispy fries, and the chickens roaming past the picnic tables. This is the only eatery in Anahola, save Moloa'a Sunrise Fruit Stand (at mile marker 16), which is a decent spot for a post-rubdown smoothie, or a rice bowl if you cannot wait to reach Kilauea.

Half a mile past mile marker 16, detour *makai* on Ko'olau Road. This pastoral landscape leads to a beach rarely seen by travelers. Turn onto Moloa'a Road and take it until

The quiet Moloaʻa Beach

it ends at Moloaʻa Beach. Look familiar? This beach was featured in *Gilligan's Island*. You'll quickly fall in love with the sloping white sands, the chilled-out vibe, and the lack of just about anyone—or anything—else. In summer, there is decent swimming at the northern edge.

Koʻolau Road continues north, meeting up with Highway 56 just before mile marker 20. And when you get back on the highway, you've officially reached the North Shore, arguably Kauaʻi's (and maybe even the state's) most beautiful region. Literally dripping with flora, where streets signs are covered with vines and waterfalls spray down mountainsides, this low-key area is a blend of crunchy granola types, gazillionaires (many celebrities own property here), and everyone in between. The North Shore easily lures visitors back, inviting them to stay longer each time, until often they just fail to ever leave.

NA 'AINA KAI BOTANICAL GARDENS

If you have cash to burn and you fancy manicured gardens, budget some time to explore the labor of love that is Na 'Aina Kai Botanical Gardens—a wonderland for nature lovers of all ages. Visitors can tour the facilities, hike to the beach, get lost in the thousands of Asian species of trees, or let the kiddos explore the children's gardens. The souvenir shop is a nice place to score something for the flower lovers in your life. Just after mile marker 21, turn *makai* on Waipala Road and look for the sign.

At mile marker 21, Kilauea is characterized by its slow pace, epic beaches, and views galore, not to mention the array of farms, community spirit, and one of the yummiest take-out joints on Kaua'i. Kilauea caters to those wanting to slow *waaaay* down. This is where I come to rent a house, read (or write) a book, and escape the hustle of the rest of the world, and considering this is about as far as you can get in the United States from the mainland, you will not be alone in your efforts. Look around and you'll see an effervescent community of yogis, farmers, renegades, and those touched with a Zen spirit.

Since it rains up here. A lot. The beaches in the area are not as dependable as those found elsewhere, though there are a couple you can hike to when the surf is low and the rocks aren't too slippery. Ask locals if conditions are right, and then for directions if all is a go. Too many people have been hurt, and even killed, hiking to Kaua'i's "secret" beaches for me to take responsibility for recommending these beach hikes.

Turn *makai* onto Kilauea Road, passing St. Sylvester's Catholic Church, an octagonal structure with a roof that looks like a rice hat. Inside check out the murals, painted by Jean Charlot, a famous island artist. Another church of interest, Christ Memorial Episcopal Church, (1941) is where Kolo Road meets Kilauea Road. The lava rock structure is surrounded by an attractive garden. Continue until the road

Along the road are plenty of honor-system flower stands.

ends to access Kilauea Point National Wildlife Reserve to see shearwaters, red-footed boobies, great frigates, and breeding Laysan albatrosses. Enter the lighthouse to get schooled about its clamshell lens (the world's largest spotlights up to 90 miles into the distance), peek at mating shorebirds, and marvel at the rough seas that surround this magnificent point. Often you'll see whales from your perch in winter as well as the Hawaiian state bird, the *nene* (though stay back, these critters can be fierce).

Closer to Highway 56 on Kilauea Road, you'll find some of the North Shore's best shopping, located in the 100-year-old Kong Lung Center, or across the street in Kilauea Plantation Center (though at press time, this center was slated to become a massive mall development). The Kong Lung Co gallery offers Asian-flavored art and furnishings. Grab Kaua'i-made soaps and candles at Island Soap and Candle Works, though the scent of this small shop is not for sensitive noses. Banana Patch Studios caters to those in the market for island tchotchkes to place on the mantelpiece. And the

A rainbow is a common sight on the North Shore.

From the Kilauea Point National Wildlife Preserve and lighthouse, you can view albatross nesting areas.

haute Cake Nouveau caters to modern women in the market for silk panties, rare jeweled earrings, and breezy apparel.

In Kong Lung, Kilauea Bakery and Pau Hana Pizza reels in devotees for their thick pizzas, sweet pastries, and heaping sandwiches. If you prefer a slightly upscale sit-down lunch or dinner, Lighthouse Bistro features live music in the evenings, colorful local artwork lining the walls, and heaping plates of affordable pasta. Across the street, Kilauea Fish Market is hidden behind the Plantation Center. This fish market sells not only fresh-caught *ahi* or *opakapaka*, but also tofu or *ahi* wraps packed with fresh veggies and savory sauces. Make time to sample one of Kauaʻi's superstar eateries. Their plate lunches and tacos are good, but the wraps win this gal over every time. If you need groceries, albeit pricey ones, Healthy Hut offers organic produce, natural cereals, canned goods, and snacks.

Off Highway 56, just a touch south of Kilauea Road, travel *mauka* on Kuawa Road to reach The Garden at Common Ground. A newer eating establishment, event center,

Kilauea Fish Market

and organic garden, this outdoor eatery pleases slow-food lovers with beautiful salads and sandwiches packed with locally grown organic veggies. They serve a decent *chai*, pretty good organic coffee, and wonderful desserts. I like to bring my kids here to run through the gardens while we wait (and at times it can take ages) for our food to arrive. For less pricey frothy beverages, Banana Joe's Fruitstand occupies a slab of land on the *mauka* side of the Highway 56's mile 24. If a banana smoothie sounds like it would hit the spot, this colorful shack has your name on it.

Staying in Kilauea is a treat. If you are okay without sleeping steps from the sea, but are looking for some romance, Aloha Sunrise and Sunset Cottages is situated on an organic farm. Catherine and Allen's private bungalows feature Hawaiian artwork, bark-cloth sofas, high-thread-count sheets, and all the organic fruit you can ingest. Families head over to Lee Roversal's North Country Farms. Lee runs the local CSA and seems to know everyone on the island. Her modest timbered cottages feel like a mountain getaway while being in the center of a tropical organic farm. Perks include a welcome breakfast basket, a kitchenette, tons of fruit, a lanai, and outdoor showers.

Just beyond Kilauea are two small communities housing decent beaches. Kalihiwai Bay Beach can be accessed from Highway 56; travel *makai* onto the southernmost Kalihiwai Road (there are two). This long sandy bay is ideal for summer swimming. Winter invites experienced surfers to battle the major swells. Farther north on Highway 56, you'll travel over Kalihiwai Bridge and weave onto 'Anini Road, then pass a surfboard stuck in the trees that reads SLOW DOWN. You've reached 'Anini Beach, a local favorite for its shallow entry into the sea; there aren't any waves, thanks to the reef that protects the shore. Windsurfers, stand-up paddlers, and *keikis* love this beach, and I've yet to meet a traveler who wasn't smitten with it as well. Shady grassy areas are ideal spots where you can picnic, camp, or hang out for hours, only taking a break to dive into the sea and swim with the schools of tropical fish. For my money, I'd find a vacation rental within waking distance of this beach and start plotting how to live here indefinitely.

If pricey condos and resorts hugging world-class golf courses sounds like the perfect vacation destination, the resort area of Princeville has your name on it. The Princeville area was once the sugar plantation of Kamehameha I's doctor and adviser Robert Wylie. He named the area for the king's son, Prince Albert, who came to visit the island just a couple of years before the small child died. Along the highway, Princeville Center is the commercial area of this planned community. Grab groceries at Foodland, sample super-sweet ice cream at Lappert's, or enjoy three meaty meals a day paired with brews, Bloody Marys, or spiked milk shakes at the surf-themed Paradise Bar and Grill. The center itself is an outdoor affair with kiosks hawking everything from sun cream to activities. There is a gas station, so if you are continuing north, fuel up.

You may be surprised that this resort area does not boast a wealth of sandy beaches—though there are a few notable swimming areas. Hike down steep cliffs to Hideaways Beach (park at Pali Ke Kua's property and walk down the paved path near building 1) for some of the North Shore's best snorkeling. Alternatively, park at St. Regis Princeville and follow the path to Pu'u Poa "Princeville" Beach, a stretch of white sand backed by Princeville's hulking resort and fronted by Bali Hai Mountain.

On the way to 'Anini Beach

Have you become smitten with the high life and want to stay awhile? The St. Regis Princeville is the splashiest resort on the North Shore. Opulent as a castle

The historic Hanalei Bridge

and occupying a prime perch atop Hanalei Bay, the former Princeville Resort has been spruced up to offer handsome accommodations facing the gardens or sea. Throw in a giant infinity pool (with a fun bar and grill attached), three hot tubs, and five restaurants, including the famed Kaua'i Grill presided over by Jean-Georges Vongerichten, the Tavern for comfort food by the golf course, and St. Regis Bar for evening music and fruity cocktails. Active types can take on the Makai or Prince Golf Course, swat balls at the tennis courts, or arrange a medicinal massage at Halele'a Spa. If you don't want to splurge on this luxury retreat, my secret is to come here for sunset cocktails and *pupus*—that way you can soak up the best this fanciful resort has to offer without obliterating your child's college tuition.

The remainder of Princeville is the domain of vacation rentals, many of which are extraordinary feats of posh architecture. Parrish Collection Kaua'i manages stellar units in many of the buildings. My favorite condo complexes include the Mauna Kai's A-framed huts perched on stilts over the jungle, Pali Ke Kua's oceanfront units (though these are highly coveted, so reserve well in advance), Pu'u Poa's spacious units featuring massive windows overlooking the expanse of the sea, and the shingled Sealodge's affordable, and smallish, units, which are perfect for families.

When it comes to eating in the resort area, there are a couple of fine-dining establishments in resorts and condos (namely Nanea and Infigo's), but I have had mixed experiences at both and recommend saving your money for Hanalei's restaurants instead.

HO'OPULAPULA HARAGUCHI RICE MILL TOUR

The only legal way to enter the Hanalei National Wildlife Refuge is by reserving a tour of Hawai'i's only remaining rice mill. The Haraguchi family constructed the mill in the 1880s. On the tour, you will learn about Hawai'i's agricultural and cultural history by viewing endangered native waterbirds, exploring the cultivation and uses of taro, plus, of course, wandering around the historic rice mill. Tours are intimate and led by Haraguchi family members.

FULL-DAY ADVENTURES

Adventurers often make Hanalei the base for kayaking down the Hanalei River or to the Na Pali Coast, diving at Tunnels Beach, deep-sea fishing, kite surfing, or embarking on a catamaran trip to spot dolphins and whales, to name a few activities. Kaua'i Island Experience does it all. Contact these guys in advance to set up some serious adrenaline thrills.

Another option is to book a summer trip with Captain Sundown Catamaran Kuuipo. This outfit prides itself as the only catamaran tour departing from Hanalei. They offer fishing, snorkeling, sunset cruises, and plenty of talking story from the Hawaiian native captains.

As the road descends from Princeville, you'll be granted picture-perfect views of Bali Hai or, as locals call it, Makana Mountain. Ancients once celebrated hula graduations from atop the peak by throwing fire into the sea. Men waited in canoes below to catch the burning spears as an act of love to the girls of their dreams, branding themselves with the flaming tips. From the Hanalei Lookout, you can see the taro fields, hugged by emerald mountains dripping with waterfalls. After taking some photos, descend into the valley and cross the 1912 Hanalei Bridge into Hanalei.

Hanalei has a whimsical effect on visitors. Beyond being the legendary home of Puff the Magic Dragon, this small town is what most envision when jetting off to Hawai'i. World-class surf, astounding snorkeling, calm waters for swimming, outstanding farm-to-table restaurants, a low-key vibe, a walkable commercial area, lush gardens, and some of the most challenging hiking in the world are just some of the draws. Staying up here for an extended amount of time is *highly* recommended.

The North Shore is about surf and, when the rain dries up, epic beach days. And there are few better places on the planet to catch a swell than at Hanalei Bay. To access the beach, travel *makai* on Aku Road and then turn right on Weke Road. This large crescent is fronted by mansions and miles of white sand, and offers shady grass areas for picnicking and a long fishing pier (often inhabited by *kupuna* strumming ukuleles at sunset). From the south, Black Pot hugs the pier and is the spot to learn to surf. There are often outfitters with rental boards and deals on lessons in the parking lot. Pavilion Beach draws picnickers and bodysurfers (keep an eye out for the large pavilion right by the parking lot). Surfers head to the north edge of the bay to Pine Trees. If this is your only day to explore Hanalei, be sure to come here at sunset, when the lighting is spectacular. Pat's Taqueria truck often parks near the pier during the day. To rent or purchase boards, including SUP and kayaks, Hanalei Surf Company does the job.

Many of Hanalei's buildings date back to the early 1900s. The most notable of these

Hanalei's taro fields

is the mission hall of the Waioli Huiia Church (1912)—the oldest surviving church on Kaua'i. Built to reflect the American Gothic architecture of New England, the shingled church has a belfry tower with an old mission bell. The green clapboard structure is still used by the public and has a fantastic choir at 10 a.m. on Sunday.

The commercial area of Hanalei envelops Highway 56, offering some chic shopping destinations for families, antiques lovers, and those wanting that tiny bikini. In the Hanalei Center (the former schoolhouse), on the *mauka* side of the road, don't miss a stop into Yellowfish Trading Co for Hawaiian antique furniture, fun jewelry, and one-of-a-kind gift ideas. On the south side of the center, Havaiki features ancient tribal artifacts, from weapons to jewelry, and is more like a museum than a store—though you can definitely purchase any of the art. If nothing else, check out the penis gourds.

Across the street is Ching Young Village Shops, an outdoor mall that acts as the town center when it is raining. There are plenty of souvenir shops to explore, as well as Kokonut Kids for the adorable little ones in your lives and Kaua'i Nut Roasters for yummy snacks ideal for long hikes. Ladies, head to Bikini Room for skimpy beach apparel, surfer threads at Hanalei Paddler, and whimsical cover-ups at The Root.

Waioli Huiia Church

Hanalei has no shortage of belly-filling options. Breakfasts fit for surfers and families are served up in Hanalei Wake Up Café or Hanalei Coffee Roasters. I like to grab picnic goods at Harvest Market for lunch. If you want someone to prepare your food for you, there's always Bubba's Burgers, or Neide's Salsa and Samba for Brazilian and Mexican fare—neither of which is postcard-worthy, but both offer reliable eats.

Dinners in Hanalei are another story. As if it jumped out of San Francisco, Bar Acuda Tapas and Wine offers Kaua'i's most urban dining experience, complete with mood lighting, big blue couches doubling as dining room chairs, a dazzling wine list, and perfectly prepared shared plates like *banderillas* or Marshall Farm honeycomb. Desserts like the lemon ricotta cheesecake are divine.

The family-friendly Hanalei Dolphin Restaurant and Sushi Bar occupies a prime perch along the river, where children play tag throughout the evening. Seafood dishes are pricey, catering to tourists who want to enjoy the nautical-themed interiors, tropical cocktails, and addictive seafood chowder. You can also pop in for lunch, when sushi fills the menu. Up the street, Hanalei Gourmet feels like the heart and soul of town, with rowdy clientele, live music, a slamming beer menu, murals along the walls, and tables way too close together. Join the locals for Dewey's Gorgonzola burger or mac nut fried chicken. This is also one of the North Shore's liveliest bars.

Emblematic of Hanalei, Postcards Café occupies an old clapboard house and offers slow-cooked organic dinners on select nights. Start with a biodynamic Merlot, then savor

Hanalei Pier

the seafood in peppered pineapple, pastas packed with locally grown veggies, or vegan carrot cake. Carnivores should note that there is no meat or poultry served, but chances are you'll appreciate a break from Hawai'i's love affair with pork and beef.

After dark, skip the lu'au and instead head over to Tahiti Nui, the oldest dive bar on the island. Known for luring celebrities, tourists, and locals, this hole-in-the-wall is *the* spot for a *mai tai*, some live music, short ribs, or a Kobe burger. This historic bar has held its head high since 1964, and today is the only North Shore watering hole open until 2 a.m.

Truth be told, I have never been impressed by Hanalei's lodging scene. Your money is better spent heading a bit farther north or south. However, if you really need to lay your head, budget travelers will appreciate Hanalei Inn's rustic retro theme (rumored to be favored by rocker David Lee Roth), the gardens, and the laid-back vibe near the beach.

As the road continues past Hanalei, the drive couldn't be more scenic as it slices through lush landscapes, over tiny bridges, and along the dazzling sea. Beyond mile marker 6, turn right into the dirt lot to find Lumaha'i Beach. This dramatic beach, dotted with lava rocks and treacherous currents, is too dangerous to swim in, but is the place where Mitzi Gaynor "washed that man right out of her hair" in *South Pacific*. Often people come here to sunbathe, take sunset walks, or wade in the green river spilling into the turquoise ocean. A mile farther you'll find pretty much the last services before you hit Haena. The Last Chance Store offers overpriced sunblock and water, while Red Hot Mama's is a decent stop for starved hikers and kayakers in the market for heaping burritos.

For a fun B&B experience, travel *mauka* on Alamihi Road to find Hale Ho'omaha B&B. At this stilt house in the lush Waihina area, just a short walk from Tunnels Beach, the Hawaiian-themed rooms feature private bathrooms and lanais, and are decked out with riches from owner's world travels. Throw in an ozonated hot tub, plenty of books and games, an aloha spirit, and a breakfast spread fit for *ali'i* and you'll see why this B&B lures repeat visitors like none other.

HAWAIIAN SLACK KEY GUITAR CONCERTS

If you happen to be in Hanalei on Friday at 4 p.m. or Sunday at 3 p.m., join Doug and Sandy McMaster at Hanalei Community Center for a slack key guitar concert.

On the *makai* side, Hanalei Colony Resort might seem out of place as the largest structure in the area, but there is nothing ostentatious about this recently renovated condo-tel, ideal for romance, family celebrations, or to escape just about everything. Unplugged, the resort offers no TVs or phones, but prides itself on its remote location to ease away the stresses of

Check into the low-key Hanalei Colony Resort.

daily life. Throw in private lanais ideal for watching the rain greet rainbows over the sea, fully equipped kitchens, plenty of space, games, and a pool. Take the beach walk to Tunnels, arrange a massage at the on-site spa, or enjoy a yummy Greek salad, live jazz, or hearty meat dishes at Mediterranean Gourmet (this oceanfront restaurant also has a stellar wine list). Na Pali Art Gallery and Coffee House makes a good pre-beach pit stop for coffee and bagels in the mornings, and is one of my choice shopping destinations for local artwork.

Just past mile marker 8, Makua "Tunnels" Beach is tough to access, so park at Haena Beach Park and walk south along the beach for 0.5 mile back toward Hanalei. This is one of the loveliest sunset-viewing beaches around, as well as the best snorkel and dive spot on the island. Surfers love this reef break in winter, but those without a lot of experience should steer clear of waters when the surf is up. Grab snorkel gear at Hanalei Surf Company. For information about dive trips, see chapter 4.

The next mile of driving is one of Kaua'i's most glorious roads: Slow down and inhale the beauty. At mile marker 9, Haena Beach Park is *not* for swimming, but you can surf and camp, and of course marvel at the beauty of this lush landscape. On the *mauka* side of the highway, Maniniholo Dry Cave was allegedly carved out by Menehune, looking for their missing fish. Bring a flashlight to travel deep into the mountain's cool interior.

Ancient farming methods on display at Limahuli Gardens

Just before you arrive at Ke'e Beach, Limahuli Garden seems to guard the *mauka* side of the highway. This 1,000-acre garden and preserve (part of the National Tropical Botanical Garden) blankets a tropical valley overlooking Hanalei Bay. Guests can take either a 2½-hour guided tour (well worth the money) or a 1½-hour self-guided tour (the garden offers an informational pamphlet to guide your walk). Wander through lava rock terraces rich with still-thriving taro and native plants, stopping occasionally to view a native plover, see whales spouting in the open sea, or just take in the giant mountainous peaks guarding the trees. Of all the gardens in Kaua'i, this one speaks of not only the biological history of the island, but also the cultural. This area was once the site of a sustainable *ahupua'a* (a model for a neighborhood): All the water flowing from the mountains irrigated the food, then was routed back to the original water source to continue the cycle. Noticeably, plants and food thrived here for the ancients. Make sure to have plenty of mosquito repellent with you. While in the garden, face the ocean near the *hala* tree at view spot 35 and look for the large rock on the edge of the eastern mountain. Legend has it that Pohaku was a rock determined to ascend the mountain, and the god Kane helped in exchange for the rock serving as guardian of the island. And it is believed that when Pohaku decides to leave its perch, Kaua'i's surrounding waters will rise and swallow the island.

Just after the gardens, a small lot on the *makai* side grants access to two wet caves. Hike up the 150-foot trail to access Waikanaloa Cave. Closer to Ke'e Beach, just off the road, is Waiokapala'e Wet Cave. Pele dug these ancient sea caves when she was looking for fire. Today you are not allowed to swim in them, but they are quite lovely to look at.

At the end of the highway, you reach Ke'e Beach. This white sand lagoon, tucked in a mountainous nook and protected by a rocky reef, is great for snorkeling, though you

---

THE LEGEND OF A FIERY GODDESS: PELE

Pele arrived on Ke'e Beach during a hula ceremony. Here she first laid eyes on Lohiau, king of Kaua'i, while he pounded a drum. She fell in love with him immediately. And it wasn't hard for this gorgeous woman to woo the king and get him to consent to live with her, but first she had to find a proper place to live, near fire. After searching for what seemed like ages, she found the perfect place—on the Big Island. She sent her younger sister Hiiaka to bring her lover to her, warning Hiiaka not to kiss Lohiau and that they must return within 40 days. Or else.

After a tough journey, Hiiaka arrived at Haena, where Lohiau's sister explained that Pele's lover had died. Hiiaka could see the spirit of her sister's lover soaring over the mountains and captured it in a flower. In an amazing feat, she worked the spirit back to his body and brought him back to life.

By this time, it had been more than 40 days, but Lohiau and Hiiaka were returning to Pele! Overjoyed, Hiiaka threw her arms around Lohiau and kissed him. Pele, the fiery goddess, shrieked until lava covered her lover, all the while cursing love and her sibling. Hiiaka and Pele's battle concluded with Hiiaka igniting Kilauea (the active volcano on the Big Island).

During the battle, Pele's brothers found Lohiau's body sticking out of the lava and brought him back to life once more. They took him back to Haena, where Hiiaka joined him in his house (Kaulu-o-paoa and Kaulu-o-laka Platforms on Ke'e Beach). They lived together in Haena until his mortal death.

A tangle of roots is the norm on the Kalalau Trail.

must be a decent swimmer, because the current is extremely strong in winter. Even if you do no more than get your feet wet, come here: This is the only beach that offers a glimpse of those sought-after views of the Na Pali Coast. Along the beach path, Kaulu-o-paoa and Kaulu-o-laka Platforms are now *heiaus*, standing as the former house of Hiiaka and Lohiau. Hula *halaus* leave offerings at these platforms.

The pictures you most often see associated with Kaua'i are of the Na Pali Coast State Park, a 6,175-acre natural wonder. Spiked verdant cliffs spill into the untouched Pacific. Streams, waterfalls, coffee and mango trees, and unequivocal views make this a hiker's paradise (and probably the best hiking spot in all of Hawai'i). The most popular is the Kalalau Trail, an 11-mile steep trek along the Na Pali cliffs with stops at rocky beaches, waterfalls, and spectacular view spots. This trail is not advisable soon after or during rain, when it is extremely slippery and steep. Please use caution when deciding to hike here. If you are hiking the Kalalau Trail, make sure to start before 8 a.m. to beat the crowds and the heat. Unless you are in amazing shape and have camping gear and supplies, do not try to hike the entire trail (22 miles round trip). You can get the idea of the beauty by hiking 4 miles round trip to Hanakapi'ai Beach or by adding another 4 miles round trip to get to Hanakapi'ai Falls. Another option for serious adventurers is to kayak the coast with Na Pali Kayak. Refer to chapter 4 for other ways to access this jaw-dropping coastline.

IN THE AREA

ACCOMMODATIONS

Aloha Sunrise and Sunset Cottages, 4899-A Waiakalua St., Kilauea. Two thoughtfully decorated cottages on a beautiful 7-acre estate. Call 888-828-

1008. Website www.kauaisunrise.com /sunset.

Hale Ho'o Maha B&B, 7083 Alamihi Rd., Hanalei. A quaint bed & breakfast with cute tropical fruit names for the rooms, a short walk to the beach. Call 808-826-7083. Website www.aloha.net /~hoomaha.

Hanalei Colony Resort, 5-7130 Kuhio Hwy., Haena. Oceanfront rooms with fully equipped kitchens and private lanais, resort-like amenities on site. Call 808-826-6235. Website www.hcr.com.

Hanalei Inn, 5-5468 Kuhio Hwy., Hanalei. A budget hotel located on a residential street, a short walk from the beach, with a simple outdoor space and small rooms. Call 808-826-9333. Website www.hanaleiinn.com.

Kaha Lani, 4460 Nehe Rd., Lihu'e. One- and two-bedroom oceanfront condos with fully equipped kitchens. Call 808-822-9331. Website www.castleresorts.com.

Kaua'i Country Inn Bed and Breakfast, 6440 Olohena Rd., Kapa'a. Four eclectic rooms with full breakfast, a hot tub, beach gear, and an on-site Beatles museum. Call 808-821-0207. Website www.kauaicountryinn.com.

Lae Nani, 410 Papaloa Rd., Kapa'a. Oceanfront condos with full kitchens, large lanais, a heated oceanfront pool, and tennis courts. Call 808-822-4938. Website www.laenanikauai.com.

North Country Farms, 4387 Kahili Makai St., Kilauea. Two tropical bed & breakfast cottages on an organic farm. Call 808-828-1513. Website www.north countryfarms.com.

Outrigger Waipouli, 4-820 Kuhio Hwy., Kapa'a. Handsome one- and two-bedroom condos on the beach with full-service hotel amenities. Call 808-823-1401. Website www.outriggerwaipoulibeach condo.com.

Pali Ke Kua, 5300 Ka Haku Rd., Princeville. All units operated by various owners and managers. Search online for units.

Ke'e Beach from the Kalalau Trail

Parrish Collection Kaua'i Vacation Rentals. Call 800-325-5701. Website www.parrishkauai.com.

Rosewood Inn/Rosewood Properties (Kaua'i Vacation Rentals), 872 Kamalu Rd., Kapa'a. A variety of accommodations ranging from studios and cottages to apartments and private homes (including the Rosewood Inn). Call Rosemary Smith 808-822-5216. Website www.rosewoodkauai.com.

St. Regis Princeville Resort, 5520 Ka Haku Rd., Princeville. Luxury resort featuring sophisticated hotel amenities overlooking Bali Hai Mountain and Hanalei Bay. Call 808-826-9644. Website www.stregisprinceville.com.

ATTRACTIONS AND RECREATION

Angeline's Mu'olaulani. Specializing in *lomilomi* massages. Call 808-822-3235. Website www.angelineslomikauai.com.

Banana Patch Studio, 2484 Keneke St., Kilauea. A great gallery chock-full of Hawaiiana, jewelry, and note cards. Call 808-828-6522. Website www.banana patchstudio.com.

Bambulei, 4-369 Kuhio Hwy., Kapa'a. A cute boutique with plenty of flavor. Call 808-823-8641. Website www.bambulei .com.

Bikini Room, 4489 Aku Rd., Hanalei. As the name suggests, come in to grab swimsuits. Call 808-826-9711. Website www.thebikiniroom.com.

Cake Nouveau in the Kong Lung Center, 2484 Keneke St 104, Kilauea. An almost urban boutique with a great collection of women's clothing and jewelry. Call 808-828-6412.

Captain Sundown Catamaran Kuuipo, The only snorkel tour to depart from Hanalei. Call 808-826-5585. Website www.captainsundown.com.

Ching Young Village Shops, 5-5190 Kuhio Hwy., Hanalei. Call 808-826-7222. Website www.chingyoungvillage.com.

Coconut Marketplace, 4-484 Kuhio Hwy., Kapa'a. Website www.coconut marketplace.com.

Halele'a Spa at St. Regis Princeville Resort, 5520 Ka Haku Rd., Princeville. Gorgeous treatment rooms and massages with exotic ingredients inspire. Call 808-826-9644. Website www.stregis princeville.com/spa.

Hanalei Paddler, 5-5161 Kuhio Hwy., Hanalei. Great outdoor adventurer's shop that carries decent clothing and sandals. Call 808-826-8797.

Hanalei Surf Company, 5-5161 Kuhio Hwy., Hanalei. Boards, gear, and rentals. They also have a "backdoor" shop around the corner, hawking much of the same gear. Call 808-826-9000. Website www.hanaleisurf.com.

Havaiki, 5-5161 Kuhio Highway G, Hanalei. A gallery of Polynesian artifacts. Call 808-826-7606. Website www .havaikiart.com.

Hindu Monastery and Kadavul Temple, 107 Kaholalele Rd., Kapa'a. Abundant gardens and meditation spaces in the Kapa'a hills. Call for a tour reservation. Call 808-822-3012. Website www .himalayanacademy.com.

Ho'opulapula Haraguchi Rice Mill Tour, 5-5070 Kuhio Hwy., Princeville. Reserve a space on their tours and lunches. Call 808-651-3399. Website www.haraguchiricemill.org.

Hula Girl, 4-1340 Kuhio Hwy., Kapa'a. A breezy island-style boutique for men and women. Call 808-822-1950. Website www.ilovehulagirl.com.

Island Soap and Candle Works in the Kong Lung Center, 2474 Keneke St., Kilauea. Handmade soaps and candles with serious aromas. Call 808-828-1955.

Kamokila Hawaiian Village, 5443 Kuamoo Rd., Kapa'a. Tour a replica Hawaiian village, or rent a canoe or

KOOLAU THE LEPER

The Chinese brought leprosy to the islands in 1840. Once people were known to have contracted the disease, they were carted to Kalaupapa on Moloka'i. Many lepers, not wanting to leave their beloved Kaua'i, hid in the Kalalau Valley. Jack London immortalized the most famous hero of this time in his true story *Koolau the Leper*.

After Koolau contracted the disease, he said he would go to Kalaupapa, but only if his wife and son could go too. The authorities said no. In revolt, he took his family to the valley and swore never to be taken alive. Authorities came into the valley to take him to the colony, but Koolau killed a sheriff. Then a larger group of police and soldiers set into this rainy forest to round up all of the lepers hiding here. This time Koolau killed three sheriffs and ended a serious attempt to capture him.

He and his family stayed in the Kalalau Valley for years, getting supplies from friends who considered him a hero. Unfortunately, during this time, his son contracted leprosy and died in 1896. Koolau died soon after. His wife then returned to the South Shore and remarried. But Koolau became a symbol of resistance to the way leprosy was treated on Hawai'i.

kayak. Call 808-823-0559. Website www.villagekauai.com.

Kapa'a Town Walking Tour. Reservations required. Call 808-245-3373. Website www.kkbedbath.com/walkingtour/rackcard.html.

Kapaia Stitchery, 3-3551 Kuhio Hwy., Lihu'e. The island's best place to score fabric and quilts. Call 808-245-2281. Website www.kapaia-stitchery.com.

Kaua'i Island Experience. Adventure outfitter that can gear you up for almost any activity you imagine. Call 808-346-3094. Website www.kauaiexperience.com.

Kaua'i Products Fair, 4-1621 Kuhio Hwy., Kapa'a. An outdoor marketplace. Call 808-246-0988. Website www.thekauaiproductsfair.com.

Kayak Wailua, 4565 Haleilio Rd., Kapa'a. Rent kayaks to paddle down the Wailua River. Call 808-822-3388. Website www.kayakwailua.com.

Kilauea Plantation Center, 4270 Kilauea Rd., Kilauea. Call 808-828-1111.

Kilauea Point National Wildlife Reserve, 3500 Kilauea Rd., Kilauea. Tour the lighthouse and learn about nesting seabirds. This is a great place to view whales. Call 808-828-1413. Website www.fws.gov/kilaueapoint.

Kinipopo Shopping Village, 4-356 Kuhio Hwy., Wailua-Anahola. Call 808-766-7016. Website www.kinipopovillage.com.

Kokonut Kids in the Ching Young Village Shops, 5-5190 Kuhio Hwy., Hanalei. A cute shop for *keikis* with pricey clothing to make you wish you could rock that little dress. Call 808-826-0353. Website www.kokonutkidskauai.com.

Kong Lung Center, 2484 Keneke St., Kilauea. Call 808-828-1822. Website www.konglungkauai.com.

Kong Lung Trading Co in the Kong Lung Center, 2490 Keneke St., Kilauea. Upscale Asian décor for those with cash jumping out of their wallets. Call 808-828-1822. Website www.konglung.com.

Larry's Music and Boutique, 4-1310 Kuhio Hwy., Kapa'a. Shop for instruments and music. Call 808-652-9999. Website www.kamoaukes.com.

Lihu'e First Church, 4320 Nawiliwili Rd., Lihu'e. Call 808-245-2274.

Lihu'e United Church, 4340 Nawiliwili Rd., Lihu'e. Call 808-245-6253.

Limahuli Garden, 5-8291 Kuhio Hwy., Haena. Possibly the state's best garden, showcasing native plants, *heiaus*, and edibles. Call 808-826-1053. Website www.ntbg.org/gardens/limahuli.php.

Makai Golf Course at St. Regis Princeville Resort, 4080 Lei O Papa Rd., Princeville. Call 808-826-1912. Website www.makaigolf.com.

Marta's Boat, 4-770 Kuhio Hwy., Kapa'a. A funky boutique showcasing women's clothing and local art. Call 808-822-3926. Website www.martasboat.com.

Na 'Aina Kai Botanical Gardens, 4101 Wailapa Rd., Kilauea. A labor of love, this botanical garden offers tours for all types of visitors. Call 808-828-0525. Website www.naainakai.org.

Na Pali Kayak, 5-5075 Kuhio Hwy., Hanalei. Rent kayaks to paddle the Na Pali Coast. Call 808-826-6900. Website www.napalikayak.com.

Prince Golf Course at St. Regis Princeville Resort, 4080 Lei O Papa Rd., Princeville. Call 808-826-1912. Website www.makaigolf.com.

Princeville Center, 5-4280 Kuhio Hwy., Princeville. Call 808-826-1133. Website www.princevillecenter.com.

Saint Sylvester's Catholic Church, 2390 Kolo Rd., Kilauea. Call 808-828-2818.

Smith's Tropical Paradise Gardens and Lu'au, 174 Wailua Rd., Kapa'a. A lively evening lu'au, with a buried pig, plenty of kitsch, and ample grounds to wander around. Call 808-821-6895. Website www.smithskauai.com.

Snorkel Bob's, 4-734 Kuhio Hwy., Kapa'a. Rent snorkel gear. Call 808-823-9433. Website www.snorkelbob.com.

Spa at the Hanalei Colony Resort, 5-7130 Kuhio Hwy., Haena. Arrange a massage after a long day of hiking. Call 808-826-6235. Website www.hcr.com/spa.

Steelgrass Chocolate Farm Tour, 5730 Olohena Rd., Kapa'a. Three-hour tours of this coffee and chocolate farm. Call 808-821-1857. Website www.steelgrass.org/chocolate.

Tamba Surf Shop, 4-1543 Kuhio Hwy., Kapa'a. Buy clothing, rent boards, and purchase your own surfboards to take home. Call 808-823-6942. Website www.tambasurfcompany.com.

The Root (two locations), 4489 Aku Rd., Hanalei; 4-1435 Kuhio Hwy., Kapa'a. (Hanalei) 808-826-2575; (Kapa'a) 808-823-1277.

Waioli Huiia Church, 5-5393A Kuhio Hwy., Hanalei. A historic North Shore church that sits in the shadows of the lush mountains. Call 808-826-6253. Website www.hanaleichurch.org.

Whaler's General Store in the Coconut Marketplace, 4-484 Kuhio Hwy., Kapa'a. Call 808-822-9921.

Yellowfish Trading Co., 5-5161 Kuhio Hwy., Hanalei. Possibly the sweetest boutique/antiques shop on the island. Call 808-826-1227.

DINING

Ara's Sakana-ya Fish Market, 3-4301 Kuhio Hwy., Lihu'e. Known for spicy *poke* on rice, or fresh fish. Call 808-245-1707.

Banana Joe's Fruitstand, 5-2719 Kuhio Hwy., Kilauea. Tropical smoothies and local produce on the road to the North Shore. Call 808-828-1092. Website www.bananajoekauai.com.

Bar Acuda Tapas and Wine, 5-5161 Kuhio Hwy., Hanalei. A fusion of sustainable small plates accompanied by a well-thought-out wine list. Reservations recommended. Call 808-826-7081. Website www.restaurantbaracuda.com.

Bubba's Burgers, 5-5161 Kuhio Hwy., Hanalei. Juicy burgers, french fries, and a vanilla milk shake, served with sass. Call 808-826-7839. Website www.bubba burger.com/bb-hanalei.html.

Caffe Coco, 4-369 Kuhio Hwy., Kapa'a. Organic, healthy Hawaiian fusion fare with vegetarian, vegan, and gluten-free options like *ahi* with brown rice. Live music on select nights. Call 808-821-0066. Website www.caffecocokauai.com.

Cakes by Kristen in the Kinipopo Shopping Village, 4-356 Kuhio Hwy., Wailua-Anahola. In a strip mall, coffee and desserts by master bakers. Call 808-823-1210. Website www.cakesbykristin .com.

Duane's Ono Char-burger, 4-4350 Kuhio Hwy., Anahola. Be sure to order onion rings with your burger, as well as the killer milk shakes. Call 808-822-9181.

Eggbert's in the Coconut Market-place, 4-484 Kuhio Hwy., Kapa'a. Omelets and macadamia nut pancakes with coconut syrup lure repeat visitors. Call 808-822-3787.

Farmers' Market in the Coconut Marketplace, 4-484 Kuhio Hwy., Kapa'a. Tuesday and Thursday 9 a.m.–noon. Gather tropical fruits, baked breads, and locally made arts and crafts. Website www.coconutmarketplace.com.

Foodland at Princeville Center, 5-4280 Kuhio Hwy., Unit G-101, Princeville. Call 808-826-9880. Website www.princevillecenter.com.

Hanalei Coffee Roasters, 5-5813 C Kuhio Hwy., Hanalei. People watch from the lanai as you drink your coffee and enjoy pastries. Call 808-826-6717. Website www.hanaleicoffeeandtea.com.

Hanalei Dolphin Restaurant and Sushi Bar, 5-5016 Kuhio Hwy., Hanalei. Super-fresh sushi and hot sake make for a pricey but delicious feast. North Shore's most popular place to have dinner. Call 808-826-6113. Website www .hanaleidolphin.com/hanalei-sushi -lounge.htm.

Hanalei Gourmet, 5-5161 Kuhio Hwy., Hanalei. Fish-and-chips and live music—need I say more? Call 808-826-2524. Website www.hanaleigourmet.com.

Hanalei Wake Up Café, 5-5144 H 560, Hanalei. Yummy omelets, pancakes, and macadamia nut cinnamon rolls. Call 808-826-5551. Website www.hanalei wakeupcafe.com.

Harvest Market, 5-5161 Kuhio Hwy., Hanalei. Grab your produce and groceries, and a sandwich from the deli for a beach picnic. Call 808-826-0089. Website www.harvestmarkethanalei.com.

Healthy Hut, 4270 Kilauea Rd., Kilauea. Organic groceries to stock your vacation rental. Call 808-828-6626.

Hoku Foods Natural Market, 4585 Lehua St., Kapa'a. Fresh, local, and organic produce, bulk goods, and raw foods. Call 808-821-1500. Website www .hokufoods.com.

Hukilau Lanai, 520 Aleka Loop, Kapa'a. The menu offers a variety of tastes from BBQ ribs and *poke* nachos to several fresh island catches. Reservations recommended. Call 808- 822-0600. Website www.hukilaukauai.com.

Java Kai, 4-1384 Kuhio Hwy., Kapa'a. Coffees, smoothies, fresh juice, and pastries, plus free Wi-Fi and a happening center-of-town vibe. Call 808-823-6887. Website www.javakaihawaii.com.

Kaua'i Grill at St. Regis Princeville Resort, 5520 Ka Haku Rd., Princeville. An elegant restaurant featuring a gorgeous tasting menu with seasonal items like *mahi mahi* with a nut and seed skin. Views are spectacular. Reservations required. Call 808-826-2250. Website www .kauaigrill.com/.

Kaua'i Nut Roasters in the Ching Young Village Shops, 5-5190 Kuhio

Hwy., Hanalei. Call 808-826-7415. Website www.kauainutroasters.com.

Kaua'i Pasta, 4-939 Kuhio Hwy., Lihu'e. The best Italian food on Kaua'i; try the gorgonzola stuffed dates, or garlic herb steak with gouda mac n cheese. Call 808-822-7447. Website www.kauaipasta.com

Kilauea Bakery and Pau Hana Pizza in the Kong Lung Center, 2484 Keneke St., Kilauea. Pizza is the main attraction, but don't miss the homemade soups and fresh baked goodies. Call 808-828-2020.

Kilauea Fish Market, 4270 Kilauea Rd., Kilauea. Sample the famous ahi wrap or the ono tacos. Call 808-828-6244.

Kintaro, 4-370 Kuhio Hwy., Kapa'a. Fresh sushi, teppanyaki tables, and a hopping bar cluttered with locals drinking the Purple Haze or Kryptonite sake cocktails. Reservations recommended. Call 808-822-3341.

Kountry Kitchen, 1485 Kuhio Hwy., Kapa'a. Enormous pancakes and omelets served for breakfast. Lunches are just as massive, but not as tasty. Call 808-822-3511.

Lappert's at Princeville Center, 5-4280 Kuhio Hwy., unit G-111, Princeville. Satisfy your sweet tooth with ice cream. Call 808-826-7393. Website www.princevillecenter.com.

Lighthouse Bistro in the Kong Lung Center, 2484 Keneke St., Kilauea. Pastas like the pesto with chicken shine. As do the fresh seafood and meats. Live music in the evenings. Reservations recommended. Call 808-828-0480.

Mediterranean Gourmet at the Hanalei Colony Resort, 5-7130 Kuhio Hwy., Haena. Oceanfront dining featuring diverse flavors ranging from France to Greece to Lebanon, a fine wine list and live jazz. Call 808-826-9875. Website www.kauaimedgourmet.com.

Mema Thai, 4-369 Kuhio Highway A2, Kapa'a. Reasonably priced Thai food, offering the traditional staples you'll find at most Thai eateries. Call 808-823-0899.

Mermaid's Café, 4-1384 Kuhio Highway B1, Kapa'a. Wraps and rice bowls, smoothies and fruit juices please yogis. Call 808-821-2026. Website www.mermaidskauai.com.

Moloa'a Sunrise Fruit Stand, 6011 Koolau Rd., Anahola. Organic fruit stand with smoothies and sandwiches. Call 808-822-1441.

Monico's Taqueria in the Kinipopo Shopping Village, 4-356 Kuhio Hwy., Wailua-Anahola. Authentic Mexican food like carnitas and seafood enchiladas in a colorful dining room. Call 808-822-4300. Website www.monicostaqueria.com.

Na Pali Art Gallery and Coffee House, 5 Kuhio Hwy., Hanalei. Buy a fancy coffee drink and purchase some designer jewelry, or Hawaiian art. Call 808-826-1844. Website www.napaligallery.com.

Neide's Salsa and Samba, 5-5161 Kuhio Highway #105, Hanalei. Enjoy Brazilian and Mexican dishes on the lanai as the rain tumbles down and the bird serenade you. Call 808-826-1851.

Olympic Café, 4-1387 Kuhio Hwy., Kapa'a. Kalua pork, fresh fish tacos, and Pacifico on draft served in an open air dining room. Open for three meals daily. Call 808-822-5825

Ono Family Restaurant, 4-1292 Kuhio Hwy., Kapa'a. Try the mac nut pancakes or French toast special for breakfast; lunches are less inspired. Call 808-822-1710.

Papaya's Natural Foods, 4-831 Kuhio Highway #330, Kapa'a. Stock up on organic groceries or visit the café and order fresh juice and taro burgers. Call 808-823-0190. Website www.papayasnaturalfoods.com.

Paradise Bar and Grill at Princeville Center, 5-4280 Kuhio Hwy., unit A-101,

Princeville. Casual surfer-style restaurant with omelets for breakfast, fresh local produce in salads for lunch, and tasty steaks for dinner. Call 808-826-1775. Website www.princevillecenter.com.

Pat's Taqueria, Hanalei Pier, Hanalei. Order the fish tacos or ask for the pork quesadilla (it's not on the menu!). Open from 12-3pm.

Passion Bakery Café in the Kinipopo Shopping Village, 4-356 Kuhio Hwy., Wailua-Anahola. Try the mac nut sticky bun or passion fruit cream cheese French toast muffin. Call 808-821-0060.

Pono Market, 4-1300 Kuhio Hwy., Kapa'a. Plate lunches to go, poke, leis, and Hawaiian snacks. Call 808-822-4581.

Postcards Café, 5-5075 Kuhio Hwy., Ste A, Hanalei. Enjoy fresh seafood and natural cuisine in a small house on the southern end of Hanalei. This is slow food folks. Reservations required. Call 808-826-1191. Website www.postcards cafe.com.

Red Hot Mama's, 5-6607 Kuhio Hwy., Hanalei. The last place to grind before the end of the road, so fuel up on a carnitas burrito or tofu veggie tacos with brown rice. Call 808-826-7266.

Small Town Coffee Company and Bookstore, 4-1613 Kuhio Hwy., Kapa'a. Tasty breakfast items like waffles and eggs accompanied by latte art. Call 808-821-1604. Website www.smalltowncoffee .com.

St. Regis Bar at St. Regis Princeville Resort, 5520 Ka Haku Rd., Princeville. Fancy cocktails accompanied by nightly live music by local artists. Call 808-826-9644. Website www.stregisprinceville .com.

Sushi Bushido, 4504 Kukui St., Kapa'a. Creative sushi rolls with live music on Friday night, and funky artwork decorating the joint. Call 808-822-0664. Website www.sushibushido.com.

Tahiti Nui, 5-5134 Kuhio Hwy., Hanalei. One of the last authentic tiki bars. Come in for a mai tai…or three. Call 808-826-6277. Website www.thenui.com.

The Eastside, 4-1380 Kuhio Hwy., Kapa'a. Reserve a table in advance to experience Kaua'i romance at this foodie haven. Meat eaters: Don't pass up the rib eye, bathed in a delicate jus. Call 808-823-9500. Website www.theeastside kauai.com.

The Garden at Common Ground, 4900 Kuawa Rd., Kilauea. This organic farm churns out delicious acai pancakes, or baked salmon with fresh veggies from their gardens. Call 808-828-1041. Website www.cgkauai.net/the-garden.

The Tavern at St. Regis Princeville Resort Golf Club, 5-3900 Kuhio Hwy., Princeville. Chef Roy Yamaguchi's new digs at the St. Regis golf course offers a killer mai tai and buttermilk fried chicken that melts in your mouth. Call 808-826-8700. Website www.tavernbyroy .com.

Tutu's Soup Hale in the Kinipopo Shopping Village (behind Kaua'i Water Ski and Surf Company), 4-356 Kuhio Hwy., Wailua-Anahola. Come in for hearty breakfasts and earth-conscious salads and sandwiches. Call 808-639-6312. Website www.tutusouphale.com.

Verde (in the Kapa'a Shopping Center), 4-1101 Kuhio Hwy., Ste. A-3, Kapa'a. Ahi tacos, margaritas, and veggie enchiladas are all the rage at this Kapa'a hot spot. Call 808-821-1400. Website www.verde hawaii.com.

OTHER CONTACT INFORMATION

Kaua'i Visitors Bureau. Website www.gohawaii.com.

From any South or West Shore beach, views of the sunset are divine.

4 Finding Balance on Kaua'i's Sunny Side

FROM LIHU'E TO POLIHALE

Estimated length: 68 miles

Estimated time: 2½ hours, or 4 leisurely days

Getting there: From Lihu'e Airport, take Highway 50 west (also called Kaumuali'i Highway). Getting from Lihu'e to Poipu takes about half an hour. To access Waimea Canyon State Park, you'll need another couple of hours each way to brave Waimea Canyon Drive's 13-mile mountain road.

Highlights: Exploring the Na Pali Coast; swooping over the island's uninhabited interior in a helicopter; Waimea Canyon State Park; Poipu's sunny shores; hiking through the Garden Isle's tropical botanical wonderlands; watching the sunset at Polihale Beach.

Most people arrive on Kaua'i with images of exquisite Polynesian women placing leis around their necks while muscled men wearing grass wraps serenade them with ukuleles. Though this still happens at lu'aus and resorts, this is not modern Kaua'i. Despite people deeply engrossed with the natural beauty around them, it can often be difficult to find the actual culture of the isle. This is not the place for happening nightlife or huge music festivals. Most traditional architecture has disappeared, and now Kaua'i is home to mini malls ands big-box stores. Locals dress similar to people in Southern California or Florida and drive in the same cars, listening to similar music. When you look close enough, however, you find a unique potpourri culture unlike anywhere else in the world; here aloha is a way of life, not just a word.

Arriving in Lihu'e automatically eases you into Kaua'i's slow pace, but if you need a bit of assistance, hop onto H 51 south for just under a mile and turn right on Rice Street, then left on Kress Street. Hidden in an old plantation building, squeaky door and all, is Hamura Saimin Stand, owned and operated by the Aikos since the 1950s. Join the government officials (wearing aloha shirts, of course), construction workers, and tourists on the 35 low stools to slurp up piping-hot bowls of *saimin*. Order the special, which adds more meat to the bowl. Afterward, scoop up the remaining slices of their *lilliko'i* pie before it sells out.

A block north on Rice Street, make a dutiful stop into the Kaua'i Museum to learn about the cultural, historical, and geological history of the island. Housed in a former library constructed in 1924, the museum lets you explore replica canoes and vintage photos, and gain insight into the role of volcanoes and coral on the island. The gift shop is a must, offering some of the finest crafts money can buy. If you are here for King Kamehameha Day or May Day (which is Lei Day in Hawai'i), this site hosts fun parties.

Take Rice Street south until it ends at Nawiliwili Harbor and the adjacent Kalapaki Beach. Mostly a cruise ship hub, this area tends to be overlooked by all but locals and ship passengers without a day trip planned. Kalapaki Beach is one of the East Shore's best surf breaks in winter and offers a grassy area to relax, coupled with a handful of fine eateries ideal for cocktails and sunset viewing. If the swells are up, rent gear at Kalapaki Beach Boys.

Those with cash to burn can pick up top-notch surf clothing and boards at Kama'aina Surf and Sport—they also give surf lessons. Tropic Isle Music and Gifts sports ukuleles and Hawaiian tunes to bring home. There are other open-air shops scattered around the Harbor Mall. And if you've forgotten some essentials, back in the center of Lihu'e, Kukui Grove Shopping Center on Rice and Kaumuali'i Highway offers the island's largest collection of shops, as well as restaurants and a movie theater.

When it comes to dining, the harbor shelters overpriced resort-style restaurants alongside beach shacks serving shave ice. Duke's Kaua'i is known for that sand-in-your-toes afternoon *mai tai*, live music, and pricey seafood dishes served myriad ways. Occupying a prime perch overlooking the bay, Café Portofino delights local omnivores with pastas packed with fresh veggies (a rarity on Kaua'i), hunks of meat, and savory seafood dishes paired with fine Italian wines and sophisticated live music.

If you have limited time on the island and want to be centrally based, the century-old Kaua'i Inn is this local's choice for affordable accommodations. Rooms are decked

DETOUR: GROVE FARM HOMESTEAD

Explore the 1864 plantation owned by G. N. Wilcox, the son of Lucy and Abner Wilcox, who created one of the most lucrative sugar plantations on Kaua'i. Tour this living museum to view the working farm, the three houses from the 1800s through the early 1900s, the largest collection of Hawaiiana books on the island, and unusual artifacts like an original shave ice maker. Since this is one of the oldest sugar plantations left on the island, the entire property is rich with history, from the train tracks that guard the front entrance to the *kamani* tree in front of the main house.

Nawiliwili Harbor's Kalapaki Beach

out with recycled wood floors, kitchenettes, and tropical-themed interiors, plus there's a pool, BBQs, a simple breakfast, and nice views of the surrounding mountains and Mene-hune Fishpond (see the sidebar). Closer to the sea is the artsy Garden Island Inn Hotel with 21 rooms, complete with kitchenettes and interiors crafted by local painter Camille Fontaine.

In the morning, just off Rice Street, enjoy fluffy pancakes at the historic Tip Top Café. Join locals who occupy the vinyl booths talking story as they eat *loco moco*, Portuguese sausage and eggs, or waffles. Alternatively, if it's Sunday, take the highway east of Lihu'e for a mile to Kilohana Plantation, another Wilcox property, to enjoy a brunch like none other at Gaylord's. Aside from being housed in a glorious historic plantation home, set in manicured grounds that beg to be explored, the restaurant is one of Kaua'i's finest. Though expensive, the brunch is my favorite meal offered; its buffet infuses the entire property with that celebratory all-you-can-eat spirit. Island-themed lunches and dinners are tasty as well, relying on traditional Caesar salads, thick cuts of meat, and tropical fruit desserts. Also on the property, you can take a horse-and-carriage ride, hop

MENEHUNE AND THEIR LEGACY

You may hear whisperings of miniature people who inhabited the islands prior to Westerners. Supposedly these Menehune were such amazing builders that they could construct an entire *heiau* (a sacred temple) overnight. The most famous of these is Alekoko "Menehune" Fishpond, along Hulemalu Road, just around the corner from Kaua'i Inn. As the little people were constructing this waterway under the orders of Chief Alekoko, they instructed the royals not to look while they were working. Intrigued, the chief and his sister peeked, and the Menehune immediately dropped their stones, cleaned their bloody hands in the water, and contaminated this picturesque fishpond forever.

Menehune Fishpond

aboard a historic train, get looped at the evening lu'au, or shop at the galleries that showcase Hawaiian artwork and crafts, jewelry and pottery.

Continue west on Highway 50 for 7 miles and follow the signs toward Poipu and Koloa. Turn *makai* onto Maluhia Road and pass beneath a mile-long Eucalyptus Tree Tunnel. The trees were brought from Australia by sugar barons to stabilize the soil and now provide a bit of cool shade and menthol aromas to the South Shore. Koloa is where the island's first sugar mills flourished. Many of Kaua'i's most historic buildings, mostly places of worship, can be found in this small community. The Japanese heritage of the sugar mill workers is evident in the Koloa Hongwanji Mission (1910) and the Koloa Jodo Mission (1910), which were built by Japanese woodworkers. On the way from Koloa to Poipu, you cannot miss the striking Koloa Church (1859). Next door you'll find the lava rock exterior of Koloa Union Church and the Koloa Missionary Church. Finally, Kaua'i's oldest Catholic church, St. Raphael's Catholic Church (1856), is located just outside of town. To get to St. Raphael's, take Weliweli Road to Hapa Road (turn right) and drive until the pavement ends. To learn more about Koloa's rich history, pop into the Koloa History Center, where volunteers offer walking tours.

In town, you can rent snorkel gear or purchase your own at Snorkel Bob's. Progressive Expressions is the go-to spot for surf gear, clothing, and rentals. Fathom Five Divers leads snorkel and dive boat trips to explore some of the island's most interesting underwater regions, including Ni'ihau, so pop in if you want to view the island's wealth of underwater treasures. Pohaku T's T-shirts and gift items have all been crafted by Kaua'i residents. If you have a bit of time, Larry's Music offers free ukulele lessons before you purchase your instrument.

There are a handful of restaurants in Koloa that aren't inspired. However, that doesn't mean food (or drinks) is scarce. Cap off your day of shopping by sampling Koloa Rum or Pinot Grigio at the Wine Shop. Then grab some of the island's best *poke* or the area's cheapest plate lunch at Koloa Fish Market. You can also find teri chicken with a mean mac salad at Sueoka's Store.

Take Poipu Road south and suddenly it seems the entire landscape has morphed into upscale resorts, high-end condos, and touristy restaurants. You've officially entered Poipu. Without a town center, Poipu relies on mini malls and resorts to cater to the money-eyed travelers who flock to the island's sunniest destination. It's hard not to fancy this vacation paradise, especially once you hit up the beaches with their Technicolor reefs abundant with sea life, white sand, and water so clear you can see your toes. Poipu-area beaches get crowded. There are many safe locations for kids and inexperienced swimmers, plus the sun shines almost year-round, so it's no wonder.

Where Ho'owili Road meets Pe'e Road, Poipu Beach Park is one of Kaua'i's best-developed beach parks. At this expansive area that also includes the beach at the Sheraton, visitors join ranks with the monk seals and whales, dolphins and turtles often seen from shore. You'll find an enclosed lagoon for children to play, access to the open sea for snorkelers, surfers, and bodyboarders, a lifeguard, a playground, a grassy area for barbecues, showers, and toilets. On the eastern edge of Poipu Beach, Brennecke Beach is a popular surf- and boogie board location; the waves can be rough, however, especially in winter. Since the beach is so small, surfboards are not allowed near the shore.

At the eastern end of the Grand Hyatt Resort, take Poipu Road to Ainako Road to access Keaneloa Bay "Shipwrecks" Beach. Though this is not a swimming beach, it is

KAUA'I'S LOVE–HATE RELATIONSHIP WITH RAIN

Hidden in the heart of the island, Mount Wai'ale'ale is one of the wettest places on earth, receiving an average of 450 inches of rain a year. Considering Seattle gets an annual 36 inches of rain, you can imagine the effect of all that water. Occasionally it will find its way down to the coast and cause flooding—as it did in 2006, when it rained for 40 days straight, causing a dam to break and a number of deaths.

That being said, there is a popular phrase you will hear repeated on the islands—*You can't get rainbows without the rain.* Embracing Hawai'i's rainy side is like tolerating your lover's affinity with fantasy football. In general the south and west sides of the island are dry and offer plenty of sunny beach days, while the north is more tropical, but wet.

KOLOA PLANTATION DAYS

This nine-day festival on Kauaʻi's South Shore celebrates the rich sugar industry history of Koloa. The July festival offers free family-oriented sports events such as tennis, softball, rodeo, and sailing canoe races. You'll also find historic walks, block parties, a craft fair, Polynesian dancing, watercolor workshops, entertainment, and, as is the case with all Kauaʻi festivals, a slew of food. Call 808-822-0734. Website www.koloaplantationdays.com.

---

a decent sandy spot to hang out in the shadows of the Grand Hyatt (and use their services). Bodyboarders and boogie boarders favor the eastern end of the beach. Locals jump off the giant sandstone cliff, but it is pretty dangerous, so use extreme caution. This right and left reef break offers a consistent, hollow ride of up to 300 meters on a good day. Waves can get big—up to 16 feet. Few people surf here; those who do are experienced locals. Occasionally this rough beach mellows out and offers a rare glimpse of petroglyphs carved into the sandstone, though they're usually buried beneath the sand. Keep walking east along the beach, and hopefully you'll be one of the lucky ones to spot this ancient site.

For another stunning beach, pass the Hyatt and drive down the 2-mile unpaved (and very bumpy) Poipu Road, turn right on Mahaʻulepu Road, and continue until it ends. The land leading up to Mahaʻulepu Beach is privately owned, yet this beach is a sacred site for Hawaiians, so people are allowed to visit it during the day (the gates lock between 7 p.m. and 7 a.m.). Please show respect for this land, as the owners can choose to close it to the public anytime, which would be a shame because this is one of the most beautiful beaches on the South Shore. *Mahaʻulepu* literally means "falling together." This name refers to a land-and-sea battle in the 1300s when King Kalaunuio-Hua tried to become ruler of all the Hawaiian Islands. He failed, which is partially why this area is so sacred—it represents the strength of the Kauaʻi people. There is a dune trail to get to this expansive white sand beach with turquoise water. Though there is a swimming spot with an enclosed lagoon, be careful: The currents get very strong and there are no lifeguards. Not recommended for inexperienced swimmers.

The western beaches of this resort area are off Lawaʻi Road. Prince Kuhio Beach is across from Prince Kuhio Park on Lawaʻi Road, and is a decent snorkel and dive spot, with an awkward entrance into the water: You have to walk over a variety of sharp coral. In the summer, there is a decent surf swell at Acid Drop (on the far right side of the beach). Across the street in the park, Hoʻai Heiau can be found in this monument to Prince Kuhio, Hawaiʻi's first delegate to the US Congress. The fishpond and house platform near the statue constitute the *heiau*. In March on Prince Kuhio Day, people bring flowers and celebrate the life of this famous Hawaiian leader.

The sacred sands of Maha'ulepu Beach

Next to Beach House Restaurant on Lawa'i Road, this area has many names (Lawa'i Beach, Beach House, *Keiki*, or Baby Beach), but since it is next to its restaurant namesake, the Beach House moniker seems to have stuck. The rocky bottom makes this an uncomfortable swimming beach, but sunbathers and families love the sandy area (when the tide hasn't swallowed the sand). Surfers populate the water during the winter swells at PK's (Prince Kuhio's), where you should look for southeast swells and northeast winds.

PICKING UP SHELLS

For those of you who haven't seen the *Brady Bunch* in Hawai'i special, you might not know the curse of the shells. On the record, it is illegal to take any shells from a Hawai'i beach. But even deeper, folklore shows that if you remove shells from beaches, you will be cursed. Since precious shells are important to the biodiversity of the land, and there are few of them left, please do not take any with you. If you really want a Hawaiian shell, buy one from a shop. The history of this curse goes back to the days of Pele, the fire goddess. Ancient Hawaiians believed that to take lava rock from the island would anger the fiery goddess who would then place a curse on the wrongdoer. Hawaiians still take this bit of folklore very seriously.

Near the end of Lawa'i Road, on the *makai* side, there's a parking lot with tents selling souvenirs. At the fence to the eastern edge of the lot, there's a great view of Spouting Horn. Water shoots through a submerged lava tube 25 to 60 feet into the air (depending on surf conditions—high tide is best), creating a sound like a large groan right before it spouts. You will see locals fishing near the gap, and often tourists, thinking it is safe, walk all the way to the lip of the rock and get buffeted by the power of the sea. Ancients used to believe a sea monster lived beneath the tube and sucked people into the sea whenever they got too close to the edge. Try to keep this wisdom in mind when tempted to head down there.

Across the road is National Tropical Botanical Gardens (NTBG) visitors center, set in a 1920s plantation home that acts as a shop and information point for all three of the association's Kaua'i gardens. Check in here for tours to the McBryde and the Allerton Gardens. Reserve well in advance for the 2½-hour guided tour of Allerton Garden. Legend has it that O'ahu's Queen Emma came to Kaua'i to mourn the death of her young son and husband; she created this retreat from the exotic flowers and rare trees brought by visitors. And now the lasting effects of her love affair with bougainvillea are evident in the winter, when the mountain's walls are draped with the fuchsia. Take a tram into the Lawa'i Valley floor, visit a remote beach, and explore the artistic garden, complete with sculptures, bamboo forests, and the astounding Moreton Bay fig trees.

Guided tours of Allerton include a visit to the McBryde Garden. However, those with limited time or short attention spans can take a quick tram ride into the valley from NTBG headquarters and enjoy a self-guided tour of McBryde's 250-acre gardens. Pay special notice to the ancient Canoe Garden, which showcases the Polynesian plants that the ancients brought with them to the island. As you meander down the stream, you will see palms, a variety of flowering trees, orchids, *heliconias*, coffee plants, Maidenhair Falls, chocolate and ginger plants, and the world's largest native Hawaiian plant garden.

Spouting Horn

There are two main outdoor shopping areas in Poipu. **The Shops at Kukui'ula** was constructed in the early 2000s and inspires with Kaua'i-made furnishings and jewelry at **Halele'a Gallery**, or designer clothing and haute bracelets at **palm palm**. **Galerie 103** sells international art and affordable prints that you'll be eager to bring home. **Red Koi Collection** offers the perfect place to score decorative *koa* wood bowls.

Closer to Poipu Beach, **Poipu Shopping Village** has been a mainstay in the community for years, inviting visitors to sit in the shade of the banyan trees and watch **free hula shows** on Monday and Wednesday at 5 p.m. Shoppers delight in the array of gifts and souvenirs on hand. **Cariloha** features merchandise made entirely of bamboo. **Honolua Surf Co.** and their sister shop **Honolua Wahine** are my go-to destination for surfer clothing and sandals. Parents will find it hard not to swoon over the *keiki* gear in **Sand Kids**.

Foodies rejoice in Poipu's dining scene—though you will need a chunk of change to fully appreciate the abundance. Breakfasts are presided over by **Joe's on the Green**, a reasonably priced favorite on **Kiahuna Golf Club**'s greens. Known for its lively alfresco atmosphere, sports on the TVs, and a pretty darn tasty *loco moco*, Joe's won't disappoint.

You'll probably want to sample every meal offered at Jim Moffat's **Living Foods**

National Tropical Botanical Garden's Allerton Garden

The huge roots of the National Tropical Botanical Garden's Moreton fig trees

Market and Café in the Shops at Kukui'ula. Stellar espresso drinks and pineapple brioche French toast make diners drool in the morning. Lunches and dinners are a potpourri of organic specialty items like paninis or lobster potpies. They also sell one of the island's best selections of biodynamic wines, organic produce and meats, and smoothies.

For casual lunches in Poipu Shopping Village, head to **Puka Dog**. This hole-in-the-wall serves any kind of hot dog, sausage, or veggie dog you can (or cannot) imagine. How can you pass up throwing mango relish and *liliko'i* mustard atop a wiener? Their lemonade is the best in town. Top off your meal at **Papalani Gelato**. Seriously, folks, this is Hawai'i's best scoop of deliciousness.

Free hula performance at Poipu Shopping Village

For a no-frills lunch, try Savage Shrimp. These guys used to hawk their garlic shrimp in a truck. Now this brick-and-mortar restaurant is in the fancy Shops at Kukui'ula, but they still merely grill, marinate, and offer their sweet and spicy shrimp atop Styrofoam plates. Also in the mall, Tortilla Grill offers a lively vibe (complete with yummy mango margaritas) to enjoy quesadillas, salads, and *carne asada* throughout the day. The fish tacos are the way to go. On select evenings you'll find live music or DJs spinning tunes to inspire the young and beautiful to boogie the night away.

Hidden in the Moir Gardens at the Kiahuna Plantation Resort, Plantation Gardens Restaurant and Bar invites you to sit on the wraparound porch and begin your adventure gazing at the dazzling collection of succulents in the gardens as you sip a cucumber *mojito*. Hawaiian-style entrées are easily shared. Winning options include seafood *lau lau* or the trio sampler, wrapped in a *ti* leaf and grilled on *kiawe* wood. Save room for the cheesecake.

Though it is now open for lunch as well, the Beach House Restaurant is that iconic tropical vacation dinner destination ablaze with *tiki* torches. There is no better place to watch the sunset fade into the sea with a cocktail in hand, a shared plate like the crab-cakes or watermelon salad, and then a gorgeous (but *sooo* expensive) wasabi-crusted fresh catch entrée. Save room (and cash) for dessert, where chocolate reigns supreme. Budget hunters: Come here for *pupus* and cocktails at sunset rather than splurging on dinner.

Maui farm-to-table chef Peter Merriman has extended his empire to offer two restaurants in the Shops at Kukui'ula. The casual Merriman's Downstairs Cafe features outdoor seating, a scrumptious Kobe burger, gourmet pizzas (they are half price at happy hour!), and doughnuts that are off the charts. Upstairs, Merriman's Fish House caters to evening diners in the market for plates like *ono* with a lemon caper sauce. The chocolate purse dessert is worth a visit in itself. Reservations are highly recommended.

Josselin's Tapas Bar and Grill is Poipu's after-dark hot spot. Josselin's is known for its small plates, which are to be shared with the table. Favorites include the *ahi* belly with *unagi* vinaigrette, and the 36-hour pork belly. The sangria cart offers three different types to sample. Another fun evening stop is **Keoki's Paradise**. Slightly Disney-esque inside, filled with greenery and that particular jovial character of holiday bars, Keoki's is known for *pupus*, pricey entrées, huge cocktails, and a chocolate dessert that four people can fill up on.

My favorite sunset spot (and the best place to boogie off those *mai tais*) is at **Sheraton's Rumfire**. Watch the sunset with *pupus* from your oceanfront perch, then grab dinner elsewhere and return for fun themed dance parties. For those wanting a more subdued atmosphere, the Grand Hyatt's **Stevenson's Library** might make you want a stiff martini and some olives as you discuss the rising stock prices, or you can sit back and enjoy the live music that occurs in the evenings.

If you'd like to rent a condo, know that each complex might have a variety of people managing and renting individual units. This means that quality can vary. Always ask to see photos of the units you are interested in. On the island, **Parrish Collections Kaua'i** manages some of the nicest units as well as some jaw-dropping vacation villas. Condo complexes worth looking into include **Makahuena**'s oceanfront condos; **Poipu Kapili**'s community of units surrounding a grassy lawn punctuated with a pool; the affordable **Waikomo Stream Villas**, hugged by tropical landscaping adored by birds; and **Whaler's Cove** (a wildly popular oceanfront luxury complex that fills up six months in advance).

POIPU LU'AUS

Chances are if you've seen one lu'au, you've seen them all. Geared toward tourists who want an all-inclusive experience of dinner, drinks, and entertainment, lu'aus are surely energetic feats (and entertaining to boot), but they are expensive. If you are in the market, Poipu has two worthy options. **Grand Hyatt Tihatu Lu'au** is the largest lu'au on the island. What makes this an experience is the show—maybe the best on Kaua'i. This big production, with great costumes and dancers, and lots of drums, is fun for kids and people who want a *show*. And worth the price of admission is the chance to watch the fire knife dancer, who is the best I have ever seen.

Sheraton Surf to Sunset Oceanfront Lu'au is the only lu'au on the beach. This outfit hawks better food than most and puts on an entertaining show (mostly this is because of the hysterically cheeseball MC). A highlight is the dinner musicians, who are easy on the ears. FYI: If you aren't interested in paying for the food and drinks, you can walk on the beach and get a free show.

Offering something for most budgets, Poipu Plantation Resort resides in an almost 80-year-old plantation house. You can reserve B&B rooms (which include a full tropical breakfast), or condos and cottages with kitchens and separate bedrooms. All come with minimalist Hawaiian décor and breezy lanais. The location across from the sea is another plus, as are the friendly staff. Also in the area is the new Koa Kea Hotel and Resort. Gathering inspiration from the island, rooms feature *koa* wood, earth tones, and private lanais. Though I've yet to experience this resort, friends who have stayed here have been pleased with the on-site Red Salt Restaurant and The Spa's body treatments with local ingredients, not to mention the pool and great location near the Shops at Kukui'ula.

From the open-air lobby that spills out onto 52 acres of tropical grounds overlooking the sunny ocean to the understated rooms decked out in *koa* wood and marble sinks, Grand Hyatt Kaua'i provides luxury seekers with plenty to write home about. The saltwater pools, waterslide, and hot tubs are open 24 hours a day. Add to the mix seven restaurants and six lounges, including the romantic Tidepools Restaurant, a sensory treat set atop the pond, lit by candles and offering privacy throughout the thatched-roof structure to enjoy coconut lobster cappuccino, seared *opah* in a vanilla hollandaise, and the chocolate peanut butter cake. The resort also houses its share of shops, a lu'au (see the sidebar), and the award-winning Anara Spa—even if you aren't staying at this mega-resort, budget an afternoon for a massage treatment. Your muscles will thank you. The hotel is associated with the oceanfront Poipu Bay Golf Course, designed by Robert Trent Jones Jr. and home to the PGA Grand Slam of Golf.

Grand Hyatt Kaua'i's Tidepools Restaurant

To the south, the neighboring community of Lawa'i houses the wonderful Marjorie's Kaua'i Inn, located above the National Tropical Botanical Garden, with sweeping views of the jungle, rainbows, and a wide variety of birds. No expense has been spared in adding lovely little touches around this B&B, including a saltwater lap pool overlooking the valley, a Jacuzzi, lovely garden art, and a valley facing Bali hut, perfect for morning coffee or afternoon wine and cheese. Many travelers inhale a breath of fresh air when they arrive at Marjorie's; some rarely abandon the giant lanai. Three rooms, all on the ground floor, have a full bath, kitchenette, mountain views, queen beds, artistic furnishings (no country décor within miles), and flat-screen TVs. Continental breakfast includes fruit off their trees, pastries, and coffee.

Farther along on Highway 50, you reach the small community of Kalaheo. Most will pass through on their way to more photogenic locales. However, the area offers more bang for your buck in the accommodations department. Owners Lucy and Terry Ryan lovingly crafted the Bamboo Jungle House into a tropical retreat by offering a lava rock Jacuzzi and lap pool, an orchid garden, and wide private lanais. Plus Lucy and Terry's kind, yet distant demeanors allows for the privacy you might have been searching for by staying away from the crowds. Just a few miles away from those famous Poipu beaches, this B&B offers three smallish rooms with mosquito-net-draped beds and high ceilings. Lucy supplies earplugs for the roosters, in-room flowers, and local bath products. All of the hot water in this B&B is solar powered.

On the *makai* side of the highway is Kalaheo Café and Coffee Co.—a ray of sunlight after Poipu's polished restaurant scene. On the way to Koke'e State Park, fuel up on pastries, breakfast sandwiches, and big cups of coffee; lunches and dinners feature organic greens paired with garlic cilantro fries, or a decadent grilled Reuben.

If you want to know where Kaua'i's native Hawaiians live, head to the West Shore. This area is dry and dusty with that iconic Kaua'i red dirt, and none of the tourist infrastructure of Poipu—and for many that is a refreshing change. Four miles west of Kalaheo are the unassuming twin towns of Numila and 'Ele'ele, neither of which is hankering for your tourist dollars—except for the Kaua'i Coffee Company plantation, on the *makai* side of the highway, where you're invited to take a self-guided tour of the plantation and sample all the coffee you can imbibe before deciding which blend to lug back home.

Marjorie's Kaua'i Inn's meditative grounds

As you reach 'Ele'ele, you'll see the turnoff for the Port Allen Boat Harbor. On the *makai* side of the road is the locally favored Grinds Café. I tend to skip this breakfast and lunch joint, but if your belly needs satisfying, the *loco moco* and teri

---

THE BEST DEAL IN TOWN

Golfers on a budget shouldn't bother with the pricey Poipu greens. Instead head to Kukuiolono Golf Course, where fees are a tenth of those in resort areas. Built in 1929 and donated to the state by Walter McBryde, this course is one of the best-kept secrets on the island, with low rates and stellar views of lush Japanese Gardens (which is where King Kamehameha's son Walter is buried), the ocean, and lava rock gardens. Since it is first come, first served, get here early.

---

burger are winners. In the same complex is the Port Allen Marine Center, ground zero for Na Pali Coast trips, which generally last about four hours. It is possible to go on out a boat trip and then head up to Koke'e on the same day, but this is a big dose of adventure. Instead budget one major outing per day so as to have some downtime on the sunny West Shore beaches in the afternoon.

The following are all respectable outfitters, offering versions of the same Na Pali Coast experience, depending on your level of adventure seeking. All provide food and beverages. Blue Dolphin Charters offers catamaran tours to the Na Pali Coast and occasionally to Ni'ihau, with snorkeling, scuba diving, and a slide off the back of the boat. They also lead sunset cruises. Captain Andy's Sailing Adventures' sunset and snorkel tours on sailboats, and raft expeditions to the Na Pali Coast, are specialties. Holo Holo Charters explore the cliffs and Ni'ihau via the 61-foot catamaran. Liko Kaua'i Cruises is owned by native Hawaiians and delivers snorkel cruises to the Na Pali Coast—often traveling farther along the coast than any other West Shore tour company. They are one of the only companies to allow pregnant women and young children on their cruises. Na Pali Riders is one of the cheapest ways to see the Na Pali Coastline. Guests go out on this outfitter's rigid-hull rafts (with no shade) for snorkeling, whale-watching, or sea cave tours. Bubbles Below Scuba Charters offers dive trips to the South and West Shores, and the Lehua Crater near Ni'ihau (in the summer only). They recommend that you

HANAPEPE FRIDAY NIGHT ART NIGHT

Friday evenings Hanapepe comes alive with artists and musicians. Galleries swing open their doors, often offering wine to tourists who pop in to view their sculptures, paintings, and furnishings. The street party occurs 6–9 p.m. Participating galleries include Arius Hopman Gallery's photography studio, Banana Patch Studio's island-themed paintings, Dawn Traina Gallery's tribute to all things Hawai'i, and Kaua'i Fine Arts for antique maps.

dive with them once before going out to Ni'ihau, since the trip is rough. Once a week, they also take divers out to the Na Pali Coast Mana Crack dive (a sunken barrier reef).

At the next junction off Highway 50, you reach historic Hanapepe, a slice of the Wild West. Travel *mauka* on Hanapepe Road to access this former native Hawaiian community, now Kaua'i's art hub, packed with galleries. While the Aloha Theater represents the art nouveau era, most of the 1920–1930s buildings are noted for their large display windows, false-front parapets, and the pent roofs or awnings at their front elevation. Today you'll find galleries (see the sidebar) occupying the historic buildings as well as one of Kaua'i's last booksellers: Talk Story Bookstore. Wander across the Hanapepe Swinging Bridge, which was constructed for people to carry water into town. The bridge swings over the river (often getting a little too creaky and swingy when more than one person is on it) and was reconstructed after Hurricane 'Iniki blew the original away.

Most agree that the food on the West Shore is mediocre at best; however, the appearance of Mele's Kusina food truck now lures foodies from Poipu wanting plate lunch, fish tacos, and fried ice cream that won't break the bank. Auntie Mele parks near the bridge in Hanapepe on weekdays from about 10 a.m. to 2:30 p.m. and stays until 8:30 p.m. on Fridays. The pulled pork plate lunch draws repeat visitors.

As long as you can overlook the eyesore of a drive (pass the 17-mile marker and take Lele Road *makai*) to Salt Pond Beach Park, you'll be greeted with one of the most consistently sunny stretches of shore, complete with an enclosed rock pool for *keikis*, monk seals, and one of the finest windsurf sites on the island. The grassy area offers plenty of shade and BBQ areas, and in summer months you can watch the native Hawaiians harvest salt from the ponds.

Surfers should take the highway west to mile marker 21 to find Pakala "Infinities." Beach access is on the south side of the road near the sticker-covered guardrail. Pass through the gate and walk about 5 minutes on the dirt path; the break is on the left. Expert surfers found Pakala and nicknamed it Infinities because the ride seems to last forever. This left reef-breaking world-class wave is for all levels. You can get up to a 500-meter ride. Little annoyances are the rocky bottom, and territorial locals.

A NOTE ABOUT THE OCEAN

Hawai'i's ocean is very choppy, especially in winter. Often your boat tour will get canceled or rescheduled. This is for your safety. If you are visiting in winter, take note that some outfitters still go out in choppy weather; it is advisable to take precautions against seasickness—a very common happening on tours. Because of the tumultuous seas, many companies do not allow young children or pregnant women.

NI'IHAU: THE FORBIDDEN ISLE

Nothing creates intrigue like hearing a place is off limits. Ni'ihau, 17 miles away from Kaua'i, a tabletop plateau that can sometimes be seen in the distance from the West Shore in Koke'e, is just that—an illusive and forbidden land.

In ancient times, it was believed that Ni'ihau was the afterbirth of Kaua'i. And it was here that Captain Cook brought enough trouble to complicate life in the whole chain of islands. Leaving goats and syphilis on what he termed Yam Island, Cook changed both the ecological face of the island as well as the health of its people. After the goats ate the native plants and the people became ill, these 70 square miles became an arid dry land, physically, metaphorically, and now literally (there is no alcohol allowed on the isle).

In 1864 the native Hawaiians, descendants of those who survived the syphilis epidemic, were not pleased when, in an effort to keep the affluent Scottish widow Eliza Sinclair and her family in Hawai'i, King Kamehameha sold Ni'ihau to them for $10,000. Unfortunately for her (but luckily for us), the king had first attempted to sell her the marshy (and undeveloped) Waikiki, but she turned it down for what then seemed like an abundant remote island to herself. However, that year had brought Ni'ihau unusual rains. When the Sinclairs realized that they had actually bought a desert-like island with poor soil and angry inhabitants, they had to reevaluate.

Eliza Sinclair brought sheep to Ni'ihau, started a still-working sheep ranch, and hired the indigenous people to work there. Today over 200 people live in the shadow of Ni'ihau's highest point—the 1,281-foot Pani'au, which is made of limestone and sand dunes. Here, interestingly, in the shadow of the rainiest place in the world, sits the driest place in Hawai'i—it often rains less than an inch a year. Yet there are three lakes (including the biggest in the Hawaiian chain). Unfortunately, they tend to dry up and turn into red mudflats each year.

The majority of the population lives in the community of Pu'uwai. This is the only island where Hawaiian is the primary language (though children learn English in grade school). Rumor has it this is the only place where some full-blooded Hawaiians still exist. For work, the residents farm and create shell necklaces and craftwork that sells for big bucks on Kaua'i. Unfortunately, the economy is suffering from droughts and a lessening of ranch activities. There is talk of a bigger military presence on the island to subsidize the economy, and maybe a high-end resort. But as of now, the land and its people are a pristine example of life without outside influence.

Motoring west on Highway 50 gets you to historic Waimea Town. Typically visitors pass through on the way to Waimea Canyon, briefly pausing to honor the destination where Captain James Cook and his crew docked his ships, bringing weaponry and syphilis to the native Hawaiians, who, believing he was the god Lono returning on a floating island, canoed out to the ships with an abundance of fresh food (and an array of excitable women). These days the locals may not be as welcoming, but the aloha spirit lives on in this western town. The West Kaua'i Technology and Visitors Center offers free historic walking tours of Waimea at 9:30 a.m. on Monday (reservations required). Also by reservation, on most Fridays local aunties teach lei- and poi-making classes.

If you prepare to do your own walking tour of Waimea, on Huakai Road, you'll find the oldest building in town: the New England–style Gullick-Rowell House (1829), located near the entrance to the hospital. Back on Kaumuali'i Highway, if you head east toward town, pass the Old Sugar Mill on the right; two blocks from there is the art deco Waimea Theater (1938), which still shows movies. Continue east past the Hawaiian Church (1865), which has had a congregation since 1820, and find the Yamase and Masuda Buildings (1919), and the Collectibles and Fine Junque Antique Store (1890) across the street. Wander toward the center of town to check out the Electric Power Company Building (1907) and the First Hawaiian Bank's (1929) facade-style structure. In the center of town at Hofgaard Park stands Captain Cook's Monument. Finally, on the hill above town on Haina Road is the oldest church in town, the United Church of Christ (1859).

Across from the Waimea River on the northern park of Waimea Town, Lucy Wright Beach Park is where Captain Cook first stepped on Hawaiian soil. Yet residents named it for Lucy Wright, a popular community member who died in 1931. Since the river empties into the ocean, the water is a bit murky. On weekends, people picnic at this 5-acre beach park, kids play on the playground, sporting events take place on the grassy field, and plenty of people hit the waves. Swimming and surf are only good when the water is clear. The sand can get hot since it is a mixture of lava rock and sediment from the river.

For a little glimpse into ancient history, take Menehune Road *mauka*; when you see the swinging bridge, look left to view the Menehune Ditch. This ditch is a brilliant pre-

WAIMEA TOWN CELEBRATION

This two-day event brings over 10,000 people to the town of Waimea to celebrate the rich history of this area. Presented by the West Kaua'i Technology and Visitors Center, this event is held on the Friday and Saturday following the President's Day weekend in February. The oldest festival on the island presents live music from local musicians, ukulele and ice-cream-eating contests, and tons of food and drink. Plus there is an outrigger canoe race, a "Fun Run," softball tournaments, and cowboy events. Local nonprofits and schools hold fund-raisers here, and you are likely to get to sample some excellent local-style food. As is the case at most Hawaiian events, later in the day the party is likely to get rowdy.

MONK SEAL ETIQUETTE

Chances are you will see a Hawaiian monk seal at a local beach. Though they are endangered species, because Kaua'i is the only Hawaiian island to ban Jet Skis and other loud watercraft, visits from these majestic animals are frequent. To ensure their protection, please help make the beach a place they will want to return to by following these simple guidelines.

❖ Stay 100 feet away and inland from a monk seal in the water, on the sand, or on the rocks. Often lifeguards will rope off the area around them; do not enter the roped-off area.

❖ Do not come between a mother and her pup. Monk seals can become aggressive.

❖ Seals come out of the water to rest, so please remain quiet in their presence.

❖ Don't feed the seals.

❖ Do not use a flash when taking pictures.

A beached monk seal

❖ Keep children away from these animals, as they can be aggressive.

Fines for harassing monk seals are steep (at least $25,000 and jail time). If you observe any monk seal disturbances, please call the state monk seal hotline: 808-983-5715.

---

contact engineering feat: a stone aqueduct made of rocks smoothed and squared into a tight wall for water to flow through. It is said to have stretched up to 25 miles inland. Now most of the ditch is covered by road, but you can still see a 2-foot section. Interestingly, the ditch still irrigates taro patches below.

Shoppers should pop into Kaua'i Granola to grab sweet breakfast cereal to decorate their yogurt. For kitschy souvenirs, the West Kaua'i Craft Fair is near the entrance to the Old Sugar Mill. While not winning awards for creativity, the crew at Red Dirt Shirts use Kaua'i's annoyingly persistent dirt (which is a nightmare to try to clean) to dye T-shirts with snarky sayings scrawled across the fronts. Even if you are not a fan of liliko'i (or, as mainlanders call it, passion fruit), Aunty Liliko'i Passion Fruit Products can be a useful stop to grab locally made edibles like her yummy fruit-infused mustard.

When it comes to eating, don't expect gourmet creations. Breakfasts are fast and filling at Obsessions Café, favoring all types of meat alongside eggs. Along the highway, both Island Taco (get the wasabi ahi taco) and Shrimp Station (for sweet coconut shrimp plates) are popular with the lunch crowd. Locals might not tell you, but I'll spill the beans: Go to Ishihara Market for *bentos*, plate lunches, and oh-so-fresh *poke*. A touch more upscale, the historic Wrangler's Steakhouse flavors their steaks with a *paniolo* vibe, offering up that country spirit in a historic building. Wait for a table on the wraparound porch, peruse the gift shop, and, if you are here at midday, order the affordable plantation lunch, served in a tin and packed with tempura and teriyaki. When you are ready for Kaua'i's best shave ice, JoJo's Anuenue Shave Ice and Treats, a spin-off of the original JoJo's on the highway, features mac nut ice cream beneath a layer of sweet tropical ice and topped with *haupia* cream. It's to die for.

When you are ready for beers, Waimea Plantation Cottage's Grove Café is the place to be. The highlight of the experience is the beer selection, brewed in house, best enjoyed on the porch gazing up toward Koke'e State Park (even better after an epic hike—see below). While not likely to be your favorite meal, the pork sliders and sweet potato fries, or the *ahi poke*, are the surefire treats.

Adventurers like to base themselves in Waimea for easy access to the state park, the epic surf, and the dependable sun. Budget seekers and those wanting to rent their own cottage should consider Waimea Inn, in the center of town just steps from the ocean. What used to be the church house now feels like a renovated plantation. There are four spacious rooms, a suite, and three cottages decorated in modern furnishings. A shared large lanai, overlooking the trees and few houses on the street, is the perfect place to read a book and unwind.

Waimea Plantation Cottages occupies 27 acres of banyan-tree-covered lawns along a quiet beach. Here you'll find 59 stand-alone cottages, from studios to five-bedroom units, all built between 1880 and 1940; you might easily conjure the image of sug-

Waimea Town's Plantation Church

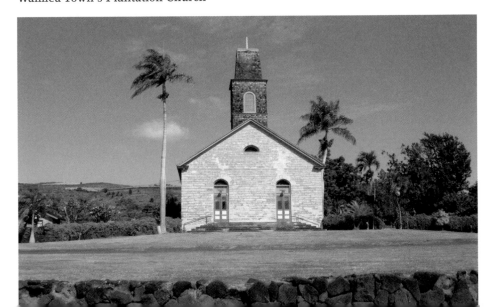

arcane workers relaxing on lanais after a long day in the fields. Or maybe this will feel more like grown-up summer camp, with flashlights on your room key; children play on the wide expanses of lawn, people ride around in golf carts, couples sit on rocking chairs or hammocks reading, families sing around bonfires, local *kapuna* sing to guests, and the evening is best spent on the micro-brewery's deck, sipping house-brewed beer. Cottages have fully renovated kitchens, cable TVs, fresh orchids, DVD players, and private lanais. There is no AC in the rooms, but fans and trade winds keep them fairly cool, though it can get warm in summer. Guests have access to the black sand beach and the pool, shuffle-board, the on-site spa, volleyball courts, and Ping-Pong tables.

Gas up, then grab food and drink before you take Highway 550 (also known as Waimea Canyon Drive) *mauka* from Waimea. Since you are heading to Kaua'i's most interesting geological region (Waimea Canyon and Koke'e State Park), you'll want to make sure that conditions are ideal for your plans—that means no rain in the forecast for hikers, and those wanting those magazine-worthy photos of Kalalau will want to head up here as early as possible. This very windy road weaves through a dazzling number of native trees, including *koa* and *ohi'a*.

Waimea Canyon State Park starts about 6 miles from Waimea, and you'll get your best views of the 13-mile-long, 2,500-foot-deep gaping hole lovingly dubbed the "Grand Canyon of the Pacific" by Mark Twain at mile marker 10's lookout. Unique from the Grand Canyon of Arizona, this four-million-year old lava rock offers Christmas-like color

RUSSIANS—IN KAUA'I?

In 1804 Georg Schaeffer, a German doctor traveling with Russians who was attempting to help the Russians set up a colony on the island, healed Kaumuali'i and his wife from their ills. In return, he was enlisted as the co-monarch of Kaua'i. On the sly, he and Kaumuali'i had dreams of conquering the other Hawaiian Islands. But what a sweet deal Schaeffer got! For arranging exclusive trade rights for Russia with Kaua'i, getting permission to make factories, and promising to protect the island from intruders, Schaeffer received land and unheard-of power. He constructed Fort Elizabeth, a lava rock fort on the banks of the Waimea River. He renamed Kaua'i places with Russian monikers; even the chiefs got Russian names. He started growing tobacco, cotton, melons, and vineyards. Kaumuali'i even gave Schaeffer the valley of Hanalei *and* its 30 families.

This little cross-cultural affair lasted until 1817, when the Americans, wanting trade rights and power of their own, spread rumors about Schaeffer; they then said the United States and Russia were at war. Soon the fickle nature of even the most isolated humans appeared. Schaeffer was forced to leave. All the Hawaiian names were changed back. Forts fell. And the Russians were all but forgotten—except for the remains of Fort Elizabeth that you can still see today.

Waimea Canyon in all its glory

schemes, with the plentiful Waipo'o Falls spilling over the green and red horizontal cliffs. As the road continues inland, there are overlooks offering jaw-dropping views of the canyon every mile or so. Hikers can descend into the canyon on a variety of trails—though be sure to head up here early and bring plenty of hydration. At mile marker 9 the Iliau Nature Loop is a quick path with excellent views. For something more strenuous, the 5-mile round-trip Kukui Trail forks off Iliau Nature Loop, descending 2,000 feet into the canyon.

Continue onto Koke'e Road. If it's clear, bypass Koke'e State Park's Koke'e Museum for the moment to reach Kalalau Overlook, at mile marker 18. This elusive view

The Kalalau Lookout's stunning view of the Na Pali Coast *Oliver Reyes*

spot often gets fogged in before noon. Below, the Na Pali cliffs yawn into an array of blue, green, brown, and red that cannot be matched anywhere else. This vista might just be your screensaver forever. There's a peaceful 4-mile round-trip hike to Pu'u o Kila Lookout (or you may drive on Koke'e Road until it ends). this lookout is where you can find Pihea Trail, which offers a steep and slippery mile walk to Pihea Lookout (this is where the birders get all giddy—some of the earth's last honeycreepers can be found here). From here, athletic birders should continue for 1.5 miles to Alaka'i Swamp (if you have a four-wheel-drive vehicle, you can access this trail off Camp 10–Mohihi Road, just before Koke'e Museum). The construction of the wooden boardwalk has made the muddy walk more accessible for the masses to view some of the remaining native Kaua'i birds and trees. However, even with the wooden walkway, thigh-high mud is not uncommon here. Wear sturdy shoes and clothes you don't mind getting dirty. Understand that this bridge helps and hurts, by displacing native fragile plants but also protecting the ground from invasive seeds and feet. Try to clean the bottoms of your shoes *before* heading out onto the trail.

Koke'e Natural History Museum, a 60-year-old nonprofit museum, has an interesting exhibit showcasing native birds and plants, an intense exhibit focusing on weather patterns on the island, including a visual display about Hurricane 'Iniki, and artifacts of ancient Hawaiian culture. If you haven't made it to the Kaua'i Museum, it offers interesting glimpse into how native Hawaiians used to cook, hunt, and create art. The museum staff are very knowledgeable about the park. You can get detailed trail maps here, which I recommend for those planning longer hikes. Plus they have an extensive book and craft shop. The nonprofit hand of the organization also works to reduce the impact of invasive plant and animal species in this fragile environment.

Tent campers with a state park permit can set up shop across the meadow from the museum, where you'll find picnic tables and toilets. If you get a permit from the State Division of Forestry and Wildlife, you can camp in more rustic areas deeper into the park. For years there has been talk of opening a resort up in the area. As of now, if you want a roof over your head, there are very rustic cabins available. These include up to four beds, a woodstove, showers, and bathrooms. It gets cold up here, so bring jackets. Koke'e Lodge serves forgettable food and drinks that you will appreciate after a long hike.

Travel back down Koke'e Road for 13 miles to sea level to reach Kekaha. Mostly occupied by military families, this quiet community offers Kaua'i's longest beach. The 15-mile-long Kekaha Beach Park is a surfer's dream: Epic waves crash onto the white sand, while only a handful of people come to this sunny stretch of shore. Only experienced swimmers and surfers need bother.

Romance seekers breathe a sigh of relief upon entering the tasteful tropical-themed B&B Hale Puka'ana, which means "house of the Hawaiian sunset." Lovingly constructed by Patrick and Jules McLean, the three suites, located across the street from the ocean, feature stunning Travertine-tiled baths, cherry and bamboo floors, and sophisti-

Polihale State Park

cated décor without being stuffy. Enjoy the outdoor bar, full breakfast, private entrance, tropical fruit smoothie welcome, beachfront yoga classes, and low-key ambience.

About an hour before sunset, hop back on Highway 50, and continue traveling west. Turn left on the dirt road 200 yards past the Missile Facility and hold your breath as you bounce over 4 rough miles of unpaved road to reach Polihale State Park. The white sand stretches for 15 miles, butting up to the edge of the Na Pali Coast and meeting up with Kekaha Beach Park. Here you'll find rolling sand dunes, favored by locals in trucks and dune buggies, and clear blue seas. You can camp here with a permit. Experienced surfers ride waves here, but the current is very strong and not recommended for beginners or even bodyboarders. However, if the sand gets too hot, Queen's Pond, a reef-protected swimming area, is a nice place to get wet. This is the perfect destination to bring a picnic and watch the sunset. Note that driving out to Polihale Beach means that you are officially breaking your rental car contract. If you really want to go out here, make sure to rent a four-wheel drive. The one time I drove out here in a regular car, we almost cracked the axle. It is a tough journey, no doubt.

While out here, you can view one of the oldest and most sacred *heiau* on Kaua'i. This four-terraced structure once measured almost 100 feet; it was paved and built when the god Ku fell in love with Chief Polihale's daughter. When the chief refused to give Ku his daughter's hand, Ku took the shape of a black dog and started killing people. Chief Polihale prayed to Kane and Kanaloa, who arrived as birds to defeat the canine. This *heiau* became the lovers' first Hawaiian home. Today this beach is one of the most romantic places to watch the sunset and marvel at nature's bounty.

IN THE AREA

ACCOMMODATIONS

Bamboo Jungle House, 3829 Waha Rd., Kalaheo. A stay at this bed & breakfast includes your choice of one of the tropical-themed rooms, complimentary fresh juices, and a breakfast with local coffee. Call 808-332-5515.

Garden Island Inn Hotel, 3445 Wilcox Rd., Lihu'e. The 21 newly renovated rooms at this inn feature kitchenettes, flat-screen TVs, and complimentary beach gear. Call 808-245-7227. Website www.gardenislandinn.com.

Grand Hyatt Kaua'i Resort and Spa, 1571 Poipu Rd., Koloa. Kaua'i's most posh resort lures discerning travelers with a gorgeous spa, plenty of upscale restaurants, and an amazing pool area. Call 808-742-1234. Website www.kauai.hyatt.com.

Hale Puka'ana, 8240A Elepaio Rd., Kekaha. Expect luxurious accommodations and romantic views of the ocean at this classic Hawaiian B&B. The owners, Patrick and Jules, provide all the necessities for your stay on Kaua'i, including a CD mix (radio signals can be weak in Kekaha). Call 808-652-6852. Website www.kekahakauaisunset.com.

Kaua'i Inn, 2430 Hulemalu Rd., Lihu'e. This plantation-style inn is located on 3 acres of tropical land where the Nawili-wili Bay meets the Huleia River. Choose the soaking tub suite if you want views of the Haupu Mountains and Nawiliwili Bay while relaxing in a two-person tub.

Call 800-808-2330. Website www.kauai
inn.com.

Kiahuna Plantation Resort, 2253
Poipu Rd., Koloa. The buildings that
make up this resort are scattered over a
35-acre garden. A special children's program that runs daily for $55–70 makes
this resort a nice option for families with
some extra cash to spend. Call 808-742-
1698. Website www.outrigger.com.

Ko'a Kea Hotel and Resort, 2251
Poipu Rd., Koloa. The 121 rooms in this
boutique, oceanfront hotel are decorated
with colors inspired by the sea. Call 808-
828-8888. Website www.koakea.com.

Makahuena's, 1661 Pe'e Rd., Koloa.
Every condo is oceanfront with a full
kitchen, washer and dryer, and private
lanai. Call 808-742-2482. Website www
.castleresorts.com.

Marjorie's Kaua'i Inn, 3307-D Hailima
Rd., Lawai. Each of the three modern-
style rooms has its own private deck and
mini kitchen. Call 800-717-8838. Website
www.marjorieskauaiinn.com.

Parrish Collections Kaua'i, 3176
Poipu Rd., Koloa. This rental outfit offers
numerous options on the North Shore,
South Shore, and west side. For a kick,
look online at their jaw-dropping villas.
Call 800-325-5701. Website www.parrish
kauai.com.

Poipu Kapili, 2221 Kapili Rd., Koloa.
The oceanfront condo rentals at this resort feature well-equipped kitchens, private lanais, and cable TV. Some also
include washer and dryer units. Call
808-742-6449. Website www.poipukapili
.com.

Poipu Plantation Resort, 1792 Pe'e
Rd., Koloa. The convenient location
(Brennecke's Beach is only a short walk
away) and numerous housing options
(choose from bed & breakfast suite, cozy
cottage, and luxurious oceanfront
condo) make this resort an attractive option. Call 808-742-6757. Website www
.poipubeach.com.

Sheraton Kaua'i Resort, 2440 Hoonani Rd., Poipu. The recent $16 million
renovation included the addition of
three fire pits, an expanded multi-level
pool, and eight private cabanas. Call
866-716-8209. Website www.sheraton
-kauai.com.

Waikomo Stream Villas, 2721 Poipu
Rd., Poipu. These 800- to 900-square-
foot apartments surrounded by lush gardens feature a pool, lanais, and loft
areas. Call 800-325-5701. Website www
.parrishkauai.com.

Waimea Inn, 4469 Halepule Rd.,
Waimea. This Craftsman-style home was
once the residence of the pastor of the
Waimea Japanese Christian Church. Its
four suites are located steps away from
the ocean. Call 808-338-0031. Website
www.innwaimea.com.

Waimea Plantation Cottages, 9400
Kaumuali'i Hwy., Waimea. These seaside
historic cottages are nestled within a 27-
acre coconut grove. Call 877-997-6667.
Website www.waimeacottages.com.

Whaler's Cove, 2640 Puuholo Rd.,
Poipu. The luxury condo rentals at this
Poipu Beach resort provide gorgeous
views of the Pacific Ocean. Call 800-225-
2683. Website www.whalerscoveresort
.com.

ATTRACTIONS AND RECREATION

Allerton Garden, 4425 Lawa'i Rd.,
Poipu. View towering rain forest trees,
numerous fountains and pools, miniature waterfalls, and a grove of bamboo
trees while on a tour of this tropical garden. Call 808-742-2623. Website www
.ntbg.org.

Anara Spa, in the Grand Hyatt, 1571
Poipu Rd., Koloa. This spa includes lava
rock showers, a giant lap pool, an outdoor aerobic area, and an array of spa
treatments, including treatments for
teens and tweens. Call 808-742-1234.
Website www.anaraspa.com.

Arius Hopman Gallery, 3840C Hanapepe Rd., Hanapepe. Hopman specializes in watercolors and photography. Call 808-335-0227. Website www.hopman art.com.

Banana Patch Studio, 3865 Hanapepe Rd., Hanapepe. Shop for ceramic tiles, pottery, fine art, and gifts. Call 808-335-5944. Website www.bananapatchstudio .com.

Blue Dolphin Charters, 4353 Waialo Rd., 'Ele'ele. This company offers catamaran tours of the Na Pali Coast and Ni'ihau. They guarantee that you will see dolphins on morning tours, or the tour is free. Call 808-335-5553. Website www.bluedolphinkauai.com.

Bubbles Below Scuba Charters, P.O. Box 157, 'Ele'ele. Observe 350-pound turtles, sharks, and shrimp while on your dive tour. Twilight and night dives are also available. Call 808-332-7333. Website www.bubblesbelowkauai.com.

Captain Andy's Sailing Adventures, 4353 Waialo Rd., Suite 1A-2A, 'Ele'ele. They also offer snorkeling and whale-watching. Call 800-535-0830. Website www.napali.com.

Cariloha Bamboo, 2360 Kiahuna Plantation Dr., Poipu. Every piece of merchandise in this store, from bath towels to polo shirts, is made from bamboo. Call 808-742-5220.

Collectibles and Fine Junque Antique Store, 9821 Kaumuali'i Hwy., Waimea. Vintage clothing, beautiful antiques, and plenty of tchotchkes. Call 808-338-9855.

Dawn Traina Gallery, 3840-B Hanapepe Rd., Hanapepe. Traina specializes in images of Hawaiian people engaged in cultural activities. Call 808-335-3993.

Fathom Five Divers, 3450 Poipu Rd., Poipu. For over 25 years, this tour operation has taken divers to South and North Shore locations in six-person boats. Their philosophy is to take you to where you want to dive, rather than tell you where to go. Call 808-742-6991. Website www.fathomfive.com.

Fort Elizabeth, mile marker 22, Kaumaulii Hwy., Waimea. This National Historic Landmark was built in the 19th century.

Galerie 103, 2829 Ala Kalanikaumaka St., Koloa. Shop at this store for artwork by internationally acclaimed artists as well as local Kaua'i ones. Call 808-742-0103. Website www.galerie103.com.

Grove Farm Homestead, 4050 Nawiliwili Rd., Lihu'e. Enjoy the two-hour guided tour of this former sugar plantation. Call 808-245-3202. Website www .grovefarm.org.

Halele'a Gallery, 2829 Ala Kalanikaumaka St., Koloa. A chic boutique that features original artwork, *koa* furniture, and handmade items. Call 808-742-9525. Website www.haleleagallery.com.

Harbor Mall, 3501 Rice St., Lihu'e. There is an array of boutiques, specialty shops, and spas in addition to five restaurants at this mall near Kalapaki Beach. Call 808-245-6255. Website www.harbormall.net.

Holo Holo Charters, 4353 Waialo Rd., Ste. 5A, 'Ele'ele. These guys take guests out on a 61-foot catamaran to the Na Pali Coast and Ni'ihau. Their sunset cruises are perfect for couples. Call 808-335-0815. Website www.holoholo charters.com.

Honolua Surf Co. and Honolua Wahine, 2360 Kiahuna Plantation Dr., Poipu. A board-sport lifestyle shop. Call 808-742-7567.

Kalapaki Beach Boys, 3610 Rice St., Lihu'e. With gear for surfing, paddling, sailing, kayaking, snorkeling, canoe paddling, and bodyboarding, this rental shop is sure to offer exactly what you need. Call 808-246-9661. Website www .kauaibeachboys.com.

Kama'aina Surf and Sport, 3486 Rice St., Lihu'e. This sport shop carries numerous brands from Knockout Hawai'i to Body Glove. They also offer surf and paddle lessons. Call 808-241-5229. Website www.ksshawaii.com.

Kaua'i Coffee Company, 870 Halewili Rd., Kalaheo. Take some time to explore the visitors center, participate in a coffee tasting where you can sample favorites like the fruity Kaua'i Blue Mountain coffee, or go on a walking tour of the coffee plantation. Tours are available at 10, 1, and 3. Call 800-545-8605. Website www.kauaicoffee.com.

Kaua'i Fine Arts, 3905 Hanapepe Rd., Hanapepe. Look for *tiki* carvings, shark tooth weapons, and paintings. Call 808-335-3778.

Kaua'i Museum, 4428 Rice St., Lihu'e. Explore the museum's collection of Hawaiian saddles, missionary-style furniture, china table settings, stone tools, and art. Call 808-245-6931. Website www.kauaimuseum.org.

Kiahuna Golf Club, 2545 Kiahuna Plantation Dr., Poipu. This course has a range of tees from junior to expert, many with views of the ocean and Mount Kahili. Call 808-742-9595. Website www.kiahunagolf.com.

Kilohana Plantation, 3-2087 Kaumuali'i Hwy., Lihu'e. Ride the train, hike in the rain forest, and enjoy a gourmet picnic at this sugarcane plantation. Check out the Koloa Rum Company's tasting room and mansion, also on the property. Call 808-245-5608. Website www.kilohanakauai.com.

Koke'e Natural History Museum, Koke'e State Park, P.O. Box 100, Kekaha. Offers bird-watching opportunities, nature trails, and views of Waipo'o Falls. Open daily 10–4. Call 808-335-9975. Website www.kokee.org.

Koloa Church, 3269 Poipu Rd., Koloa. Call 808-742-9956.

Koloa History Center. The history center displays photographs and artifacts about Koloa's history and sugar plantations. Call 808-245-7238. Website www.oldkoloa.com.

Koloa Hongwanji Mission, 5521 Koloa Rd., Koloa.

Koloa Jodo Mission, 3480 Waikomo Rd., Koloa. This Buddhist temple has been around since 1910. Call 808-742-0457. Website www.koloajodo.com.

Koloa Missionary Church, 3370 Poipu Rd., Koloa. Call 808-742-6777. Website www.koloamc.org.

Koloa Union Church, 3289 Poipu Rd., Koloa. Call 808-742-6622.

Kukui Grove Shopping Center, 3-2600 Kaumuali'i Hwy., Lihu'e. A collection of stores and restaurants. Visit on Monday for an open-air market that features local handicrafts, fresh fruit, and shave ice. Call 808-245-7784. Website www.kukuigrovecenter.com.

Kukuiolono Golf Course, 854 Pu'u Rd., Kalaheo. This nine-hole layout offers a beautiful view of Kaua'i's South Shore. Call 808-332-9151.

Larry's Music, 5330 Koloa Rd., Ste. 1, Koloa. Check out the fabulous assortment of ukuleles. Call 808-742-1500.

Liko Kaua'i Cruises, 4516 Alawai Rd., Waimea. This cruise company offers the opportunity to view sea caves, waterfalls, and miles of white sand beaches. Equipment and instruction are provided for those who want to snorkel. Call 808-338-0333. Website www.liko-kauai.com.

McBryde Garden, 4425 Lawa'i Rd., Poipu. The garden includes a distinct variety of micro-environments. Check out the chocolate, ginger, and allspice plants near Maidenhair Falls. Call 808-742-2623. Website www.ntbg.org.

Na Pali Riders, P.O. Box 1082, Kalaheo. See the sights in a durable, inflatable raft, which provides excellent opportunities for snorkeling and exploring sea caves, waterfalls, and shallow inlets. Call 808-742-6331. Website www.napaliriders.com.

National Tropical Botanical Gardens Visitors Center, 4425 Lawaʻi Rd., Poipu. A restored 1920s plantation cottage serves as visitors center for the gardens. Inside you will find a gift shop, small exhibits, and the check-in point for tours of the McBryde Garden and Allerton Garden. Call 808-742-2623. Website www.ntbg.org.

palm palm, 2829 Ala Kalanikaumaka St., Koloa. Shop here for handmade fine jewelry, etched glass, and women's handbags. Call 808-741-1131. Website www.palmpalmkauai.com.

Progressive Expressions, 5420 Koloa Rd., Koloa. Now owned by the Hanalei Surf Company, the first surf shop on the South Shore still carries a sense of history and authenticity in its surfboarding shaping and designs. They sell and rent boards, gear, and clothing. Call 808-826-9000.

Pohaku T's, 3430 Poipu Rd., Koloa. Shop for locally designed T-shirts and clothing for the entire family. Call 808-742-7500. Website www.pohaku.com.

Poipu Bay Golf Course, Ainako St., Koloa. This course, designed by Robert Trent Jones Jr., isn't home to the PGA Grand Slam of Golf for nothing. It's situated on 210 acres of oceanfront rolling greens, with an array of tropical plants and ancient Hawaiian sites along the course—no wonder the greats play here. Call 800-858-6300. Website www.poipu baygolf.com.

Poipu Shopping Village, 2360 Kiahuna Plantation Dr., Poipu. Besides the shopping and dining options, this shopping center offers free entertainment including Tahitian dance shows, fire knife dancing, and live drumming. Call 808-742-2831. Website www.poipushopping village.com.

Polihale State Park, off Kaumualiʻi Hwy., Hwy. 50, Waimea. A historical state beach park. Call 808-587-0400.

Red Dirt Shirts, 4350 Waialo Rd., ʻEleʻele. Choose from T-shirts, sweatshirts, and polo shirts dyed with the iron-rich native dirt that gives clothing a red hue. Call 800-717-3478. Website www.dirtshirt.com.

Red Koi Collection, 2829 Ala Kalanikaumaka St., Koloa. Check out the sculptures, paintings, wood carvings, and textiles at this elegant art stop. Call 808-742-2778. Website www.redkoihawaii.com.

Sand Kids, 2360 Kiahuna Plantation Dr., Poipu. A children's shop with a variety of clothing, games, and toys. Call 808-742-2288.

The Shops at Kukuiʻula, 2829 Ala Kalanikaumaka St., Koloa. This mall features a variety of local stores and surf shops, cafés and restaurants, and a gourmet farmers' market on Wednesday 4–6 p.m. Call 808-742-9545. Website www.kukuiula.com.

Snorkel Bob's, 3236 Poipu Rd., Koloa. This Hawaiian chain of stores rents snorkel gear and can direct you to the best seasonal snorkeling spots. Snorkel Bob's also arranges kayak tours. Call 800-262-7725. Website www.snorkelbob.com.

The Spa, inside Koa Kea Hotel and Resort, 2251 Poipu Rd., Koloa. Choose a treatment that utilizes natural, local ingredients such as red Kauaʻi clay, guava, and seaweed. Call 808-828-8888. Website www.koakea.com.

St. Raphael's Catholic Church, 3011 Hapa Rd., Koloa. Call 808-742-1955.

Talk Story Bookstore, 3785 Hanapepe Rd., Hanapepe. A bookstore with a large selection of secondhand, new, and out-of-print books. Call 808-335-6469. Website www.talkstorybookstore.com.

Tropic Isle Music and Gifts, 3416 Rice St., Lihuʻe. A one-stop shop for Hawaiian jewelry, clothing, and musical instruments. Call 808-245-8700. Website www.tropicislemusic.com.

Waimea Canyon State Park, 11.1 miles north of Kekaha on Kokeʻe Rd.

The rim of the canyon overlooks the deep, colorful gorge of Waimea Canyon. Call 808-274-3444. Website www.hawaii stateparks.org.

Waimea Theater, 9691 Kaumuali'i Hwy., Waimea. This historic movie theater still shows movies. Call 808-338-0282. Website www.waimeatheater.com.

West Kaua'i Craft Fair, in Waimea Town. Check out live music and local food every Saturday and Sunday.

West Kaua'i Technology and Visitors Center, 9565 Kaumuali'i Hwy., Waimea Town. Features exhibits and programs reflecting the ethnic diversity of the community. Check out the lei-making and poi-making demonstrations or head off on a historic walking tour on Monday. Call 808-338-1332. Website www.wkbpa.org.

Yamase Building, at the corner of Moana Rd. and Kaumaulii Hwy., Waimea. This building was designed by Seiichi Yamase, an itinerant Japanese temple architect, in 1921.

DINING

Aunty Liliko'i Passion Fruit Products, 9875 Waimea Rd., Waimea. Try the award-winning Passion Fruit Wasabi Mustard or sample some of the passion-fruit-scented personal care products available. Call 808-338-1296. Website www.auntylilikoi.com.

Beach House Restaurant, 5022 Lawai Rd., Koloa. Enjoy Pacific Rim cuisine that takes advantage of locally sourced ingredients. Reservations recommended. Call 808-742-1424. Website www.the -beach-house.com.

Café Portofino, 3481 Hoolaulea Way, Lihu'e. A romantic restaurant that serves classic Italian dinners such as *osso buco*, the house specialty, and seafood *diavolo*. Reservations recommended. Call 808-245-2121. Website www.cafeportofino.com.

Duke's Kaua'i, 3610 Rice St., Lihu'e. Stop by 4–6 p.m. daily for Aloha Hour's appetizers and drink specials, or enjoy fresh fish tacos on Taco Tuesday. Call 808-246-9599. Website www.dukeskauai.com.

Gaylord's, 3-2087 Kaumuali'i Hwy., Lihu'e. Try the ranch-style Kilohana burger, fresh fish tacos, and *hoisin*-glazed spare ribs. Don't forget banana cream pie for dessert! Call 808-245-5608. Website www.gaylordskauai.com.

Grinds Café, 4469 Waialo Rd., 'Ele'ele. Breakfast is served all day alongside pizza, burgers, and salads at lunchtime. Call 808-335-6027. Website www.grinds cafe.net.

Grove Café, 9400 Kaumuali'i Hwy., Waimea. This restaurant specializes in fruity cocktails and house-brewed beer. Enjoy pub fare with a multi-ethnic twist. Call 808-338-9733. Website www.waimea -plantation.com.

Hamura Saimin Stand, 2956 Kress St., Lihu'e. Polish off a hearty, steaming bowl of *saimin* at this famous restaurant that stays open until midnight on Friday and Saturday. Call 808-245-3271.

Ishihara Market, 9890 Kahakai Rd., Ste. A, Waimea. Arrive early for the best selection of *bentos*. Call 808-338-9915.

Island Taco, 9643 Kaumuali'i Hwy., Waimea. This taco stop is open 11–5 daily. Choose from its menu of tacos, burritos, and quesadillas. Call 808-338-9895. Website www.islandfishtaco.com.

JoJo's Anuenue Shave Ice and Treats, 9726 Hwy. 50, Waimea. Fruity flavors like coconut, watermelon, passion fruit, and mango are the favorites at this ice cream parlor.

Joe's on the Green, 2545 Kiahuna Plantation Dr., Poipu Beach. Classic breakfast fare is served 7–11:30 a.m., with early-bird specials available. Call 808-742-9696. Website www.joesonthe green.com.

Josselin's Tapas Bar and Grill, 2829 Ala Kalanikaumaka, Poipu. Try one of the signature sangrias served tableside.

Flavors include *lychee*, mango, and passion fruit. Pair your sangria with an assortment of tapas made with local ingredients. Call 808-742-7117. Website www.josselins.com.

Kalaheo Café and Coffee Co., 2-2560 Kaumuali'i Hwy., Kalaheo. Famous for their breakfast menu that includes a Hawaiian sweetbread French toast topped with pineapple and macadamia nuts. You'll appreciate the cilantro garlic fries served on the side with most sandwiches and burgers. Call 808-332-5858. Website www.kalaheo.com.

Kaua'i Granola, 9633 Kaumuali'i Hwy., Waimea. Samples abound at this store, so you can taste before you buy. Try granola in island flavors like piña colada orguava crunch, or buy a box of chocolate-dipped macaroons. Call 808-338-0221. Website www.kauaigranola.com.

Keoki's Paradise, 2360 Kiahuna Plantation Dr., Koloa. Enjoy *pupus* and cocktails at the Bamboo Bar, or combine your choice of appetizer, entrée, and dessert for $22 from the chef's Sunset Menu. Call 808-742-7534. Website www.keokis paradise.com.

Koke'e Lodge, Koke'e State Park, mile marker 15, Waimea. Grab a quick breakfast or lunch at this stop inside Koke'e State Park. Call 808-335-6061. Website www.thelodgeatkokee.net.

Koloa Fish Market, 5482 Koloa Rd., Koloa. This lunch place is only open until 6 p.m. on most days, so make sure you get there early! They provide a full deli counter with numerous options as well as pre-made *bento* boxes for those on the run. The daily specials come with rice, tossed greens, and homemade macaroni salad. Call 808-742-6199.

Living Foods Market and Café, in the Kukui'ula Village, 2829 Ala Kalanikauamaka, Koloa. Offering the island's largest selection of organic, sustainable, and locally grown produce, the café serves crepes, paninis, pizzettas, and

agua fresca. Call 808-742-2323. Website www.livingfoodskauai.com.

Mele's Kusina, 3864 Hanapepe Rd., Hanapepe. This food truck offers fish tacos, seafood plates, and fried ice cream at a decent price. Call 808-651-0778.

Merriman's Downstairs Café, 2829 Ala Kalanikaumaka St., Koloa. Try the mouthwatering Kobe beef burger served with a side of hand-cut fries dipped in chipotle ketchup. Call 808-742-2857. Website www.merrimanshawaii.com.

Merriman's Fish House, 2829 Ala Kalanikaumaka St., Koloa. Enjoy fresh-caught seafood such as *mahi mahi* and poached lobster, or enjoy selections from the raw bar including *ahi* tuna and Keahole lobster. Call 808-742-8385. Website www.merrimanshawaii.com.

Obsessions Café, 9875 Waimea Rd., Waimea. This café is known for its filling breakfasts as well as its sandwiches. Call 808-338-1110.

Papalani Gelato, 2360 Kiahuna Plantation Rd., Poipu. Enjoy gelato with a Hawaiian twist: Mango, coconut, macadamia nut, *lychee*, and papaya star in these icy confections. Call 808-742-2663. Website www.papalanigelato.com.

Plantation Gardens Restaurant and Bar, 2253 Poipu Rd., Koloa. The menu at this upscale restaurant reflects the cuisine of Old Plantation Hawai'i with dishes such as shrimp *ceviche*, house-made barbecue *kalua* pork *manapuas*, and seafood *lau lau*. Call 808-742-2121. Website www.pgrestaurant.com.

Puka Dog, 2360 Kiahuna Plantation Dr., Koloa. What happens when you take a bun-sized loaf of bread, stuff it with grilled Polish sausage, and smother it with sauces like sweet Maui onion relish or spicy garlic pepper cheese? You get the Puka Dog, a uniquely Hawaiian treat. Call 808-332-5239. Website www .pukadog.com.

Red Salt Restaurant, 2251 Poipu Rd., Koloa. An oceanfront setting with large picture windows combined with upscale seafood selections such as vanilla-bean-seared *mahi mahi* give this restaurant its sophisticated flair. Call 808-742-4288. Website www.koakea.com.

Savage Shrimp, 2829 Ala Kalanikaumaka, Poipu. Love shrimp? Enjoy it any way you can imagine at this restaurant where you can have shrimp scampi, shrimp curry, coconut shrimp, and shrimp tacos all in one sitting. Call 808-742-9611. Website www.savageshrimp .com.

Rumfire, at Sheraton Kaua'i, 2440 Hoonani Rd., Poipu. Ocean views delight at this lively bar and restaurant. Call 808-742-4RUM. Website www.rumfirekauai .com.

Shrimp Station, 9652 Kaumuali'i Hwy., Waimea. Choose from a wide variety of shrimp dishes, from Cajun and Thai shrimp to shrimp tacos and shrimp burgers (similar to a crabcake). Call 808-338-1242. Website www.shrimpstation .com.

Stevenson's Library, in the Grand Hyatt, 1571 Poipu Rd., Koloa. Take a seat at the 27-foot handcrafted *koa* wood bar and enjoy the extensive collection of Cognac and Port served alongside fresh sushi. Call 808-240-6456. Website www .kauai.hyatt.com.

Sueoka's Store, 5392 Koloa Rd., Koloa. This snack shop and grocery store offers fresh fruits and vegetables, meat and seafood, and a wide variety of Asian grocery products in addition to local-style plate lunches. Call 808-742-1112. Website www.sueokastore.com.

Tidepools Restaurant, 1571 Poipu Rd., Koloa. The koi pond complements the romantic atmosphere at this restaurant where the entrées feature local seafood and fresh produce. Call 808-240-6456. Website www.kauai.hyatt.com.

Tip Top Café, 3173 Akahi St., Lihu'e. A comfy, casual café best known for its fluffy pancakes loaded with macadamia nuts, bananas, and pineapple. Call 808-245-2333.

Tortilla Republic Grill + Margarita Bar, 2829 Ala Kalanikaumaka St., Koloa. Fish tacos, margaritas, and guacamole made tableside are the highlights at this trendy Mexican restaurant. Call 808-742-8884. Website www.tortillarepublic .com.

The Wine Shop, 5470 Koloa Rd., Koloa. This shop offers a wide variety of wine and prepackaged gourmet foods. While at the shop, ask for list of partner restaurants in the area that will waive the corkage fee and allow you to bring your own bottle for dinner, provided it was purchased at The Wine Shop. Call 808-742-7305. Website www.thewine shopkauai.com.

Wrangler's Steakhouse, 9852 Kaumuali'i Hwy., Waimea. Enjoy rib eye and an all-you-can-eat salad bar at this casual, cowboy-themed steakhouse. Call 808-338-1218.

OTHER CONTACT INFORMATION

Kaua'i Chamber of Commerce. Call 808-245-7363. Website www.kauai chamber.org.

Kaua'i Visitors Bureau. Call 800-262-1400. Website www.kauai-hawaii.com.

Keikis frollic on Kawili Beach.

5 Moloka'i's Unearthed Charms

Estimated length: 90 miles
Estimated time: 4 days

Getting there: Most visitors arrive via the Maui-Moloka'i ferry (www.molokai-ferry.com) from Maui. This rough ride takes about an hour and a half, and frankly, while an attractive option, is not recommended. The trip across the channel turns even the toughest Hawaiians green. Trips occur twice daily Monday through Saturday, and once a day on Sunday. Alternatively, Moloka'i Airport receives inter-island flights from Maui, Honolulu, and Lana'i on Island Air (www.islandair.com), Go! (www.iflygo.com), Mokulele (www.mokulele.com), and Hawaiian Airlines (www.hawaiianairlines.com). The airport is a dinky affair, and you half expect Tattoo from *Fantasy Island* to be standing on the tarmac. Even more attractive is when your baggage is wheeled to a bench next to the Alamo car rental desk (www.alamo.com) for you to grab at will.

Getting around the island is fairly easy, as there is one main highway that travels from the east to the west; strangely, however, it changes names in Kaunakakai from Highway 450 to Highway 460.

Highlights: Untapped beauty sans crowds; a breathtaking mule ride to Kalaupapa; friendly locals; diving at the only great barrier reef in Hawai'i; the Halawa Valley; and an inspiring serenade by local *kupuna* elders.

There are no resorts boasting spas and fine dining—heck, if you can find a *mai tai* with an umbrella—or, better yet, a restaurant open past 8 p.m.—you've scored. Despite its address in one of the world's most visited archipelagoes, despite the stunning 95 miles of coastline, the only great barrier reef in Hawai'i, and world-class hikes, Moloka'i doesn't lure in tourists. You'll find one hotel and a couple of condos, along with a handful of places to eat that are, I am afraid to report, mediocre at best. But Moloka'i holds a charm unlike any other Hawaiian destination. As one local said on my last visit, "Moloka'i is what O'ahu was before Pan Am arrived." And that, my friends, is one big reason to pack your bags.

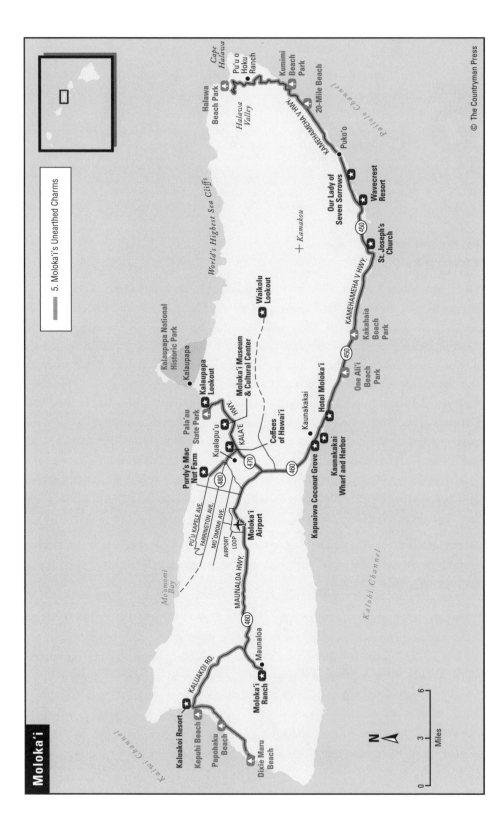

Moloka'i

5. Moloka'i's Unearthed Charms

Kalohi Channel

Pailolo Channel

Kalaupapa Channel

Cape Halawa

Pu'u o Hoku Ranch

Kumimi Beach Park

Halawa Beach Park

20-Mile Beach

Halawa Valley

KAMEHAMEHA HWY.

Puko'o

Wavecrest Resort

Our Lady of Seven Sorrows

450

St. Joseph's Church

Kamakou

KAMEHAMEHA V HWY.

World's Highest Sea Cliffs

Kakahaia Beach Park

450

Waikolu Lookout

One Ali'i Beach Park

Kalaupapa National Historic Park

Kalaupapa

Kalaupapa Lookout

Moloka'i Museum & Cultural Center

Pala'au State Park

KALA'E HWY.

Coffees of Hawai'i

Hotel Moloka'i

Kaunakakai

Kualapu'u

470

Purdy's Mac Nut Farm

480

460

Kaunakakai Wharf and Harbor

Kapuaiwa Coconut Grove

PU'U KAPELE AVE.

FARRINGTON AVE.

MO'OMOMI AVE.

AIRPORT LOOP

Moloka'i Airport

Mo'omomi Bay

MAUNALOA HWY.

460

Maunaloa

Moloka'i Ranch

KALUAKOI RD.

Kaluakoi Resort

Kepuhi Beach

Papohaku Beach

Dixie Maru Beach

Kaiwi Channel

N

0   3   6

Miles

© The Countryman Press

Overlooked by most, Moloka'i invites visitors to look beyond its dusty appearance, overpriced stores, and relatively few offerings by way of tourist services. Here you have to get out and talk to a local, ask questions, cook someone dinner instead of expecting to be catered to. Your money may buy you a boat trip to the Pali coast or a fancy beach house for a week, but your kindness will get you invited on a hike to explore the *kuhio* grove or dance hula with the *kupuna heiau*, or grant you access to find the one of the most sacred places in the whole state. It is not about driving down uncharted roads here hoping to stumble upon a hidden gem. Rather, people come here to understand Hawaiian culture and history, and relax without crowds.

From Moloka'i Airport, take Highway 460 east; about 5 miles down the road, you pass Church Row. Across the street, Kapua'iwa Coconut Grove was planted for King Kamehameha V, and while it does make for a fine photo stop, be cautious: Many main-landers have been knocked out cold by falling coconuts. Continue for another 3 miles until you reach the island's only city, if you can call it that, Kaunakakai.

Moloka'i's main drag boasts a handful of commercial offerings, a couple of historic buildings, and no stoplights. Yet despite its lack of services, visitors and locals find themselves revisiting town throughout the day. My first stop is always to Kalele Bookstore and Divine Expressions, for a free coffee and plenty of talking story from Auntie Teri, a Moloka'i transplant. Her small bookshop features an interesting collection of spiritual titles, Hawaiiana, and Moloka'i art. She also will "Post-a-Nut" for you—which basically means that you pick out a coconut, decorate it, and then mail it to someone back home. The trick is to pick out a smallish one without much water inside, as the postage can get ridiculously expensive (last time I partook, I paid $30 a nut!). Teri also acts as the de facto visitors center, offering maps and travel advice.

Water lovers and the adventurous should pop into Moloka'i Fish and Dive. Owners Tim and Susan Forsberg school visitors on the best dive sites on the 28-mile-long great barrier reef to spot blue holes, whales, rays, butterfly fish, parrot-fish, wrasses, trumpetfish, white-tipped reef sharks, hammerheads, turtles, uni-cornfish, and many more. They also can tailor whale-watching cruises, kayak adventures, fishing trips, and guided water-fall hikes. Outdoor adventurers might want to hire bikes, helmets, and locks at Moloka'i Bicycle.

Post a nut in Moloka'i.

A MOLOKA'I SECRET FOR FOODIES

Foodies rarely have reason to rejoice on Moloka'i, but local salt queen Nancy Gove aims to change that with her Pacifica Hawai'i Salt. Gove harvests and crafts gourmet sea salts for gourmands to add to their pantries. Call in advance to arrange an hour tour of the salt-making facilities and sample smoked salts. Call 808-553-8484. Website www.pacificahawaii.com.

If you are renting a condo or house, there are two markets in town, which vary in price, popularity, and offerings. Health food fans crowd the aisles in Outpost Natural Foods, which is overpriced, but does have organic produce and dairy products. Most, however, will join the crowds at Friendly's Market. If you want fresh-caught seafood, there's a fisherman who parks in front of Friendly's in the late morning with a truck full of fish. The aunties often bring their massive avocados, mangoes, and tasty apple bananas into town to sell, even on non-farmers'-market days, so keep an eye out. Speaking of which, the Saturday-morning farmers' market is *the* weekly event in Moloka'i, so try to plan your visit accordingly. Those of you used to sprawling markets awash with fresh fruits and veggies may not be blown away, but the freshly made snacks and breads, tropical fruits, and interesting collection of Hawaiiana make for a fun glimpse into local culture.

In a strip mall just as you enter town are Moloka'i Burger and Moloka'i Pizza Café (which offers heaping pizzas and pastas as well as a few arcade games while you wait). If

Kaunakakai aunties line the road selling their produce.

plate lunch is calling your name, Moloka'i Drive-In offers Hawai'i-sized meat dishes alongside mac salad and rice for diners to eat on the go. Maka's Corner is also known for its plate lunches, burgers, and *saimin* served to adoring locals. Kanemitsu Bakery and Restaurant is a Moloka'i institution. Visitors and locals line up after dark in an alley for their "midnight bread run." The onion-and-cheese bread is legendary. The restaurant lacks in the charm department (it's hot, the tablecloths are sticky, and the service is so-so), but the eggs with rice and Portuguese sausage, or the pancakes, do the trick for breakfast. Rawlin's Chevron is the choice for gas, milk, TVs, and just about anything else you'll need.

After grabbing a bite to eat and groceries, continue traveling east on Highway 460. About a mile down the road is Kaunakakai Wharf and Harbor, where you can catch the ferry to and from Lahaina. This is also the departure point for diving, snorkeling, whale-watching, and fishing trips.

Highway 460 turns into Highway 450. Continue for another mile and change, and on the right is Hotel Moloka'i. Beyond retro, the A-framed wood huts populate an oceanfront stretch of land and are decked out in 1970s décor, including sandpaper walls with petroglyphs of surfers, geckos, turtles, and suns. Rooms can get hot, with no AC, but the screen doors leading to private lanais and lofty ceilings help inspire the breeze. Rooms also feature green-tiled

Hotel Moloka'i

rock sinks with turtle motifs, flat-panel TVs with cable, and kitchenettes in some rooms. The grounds are serene, with enchanting flowers, views of the sea from the hammocks, a pool, and a lively concert of birds that belt out good morning to the sun an hour or so before dawn. Additional perks include spa services, Wi-Fi, continental breakfast, an activities desk, and the acclaimed Hula Shores restaurant. The last time I was on the island, the restaurant had recently burned down and was in the process of a major overhaul. At press time, hotel staff said they had plans for the alfresco dining room to feature locally sourced produce, seafood, and meats for breakfast, lunch, and dinner with

WANT GOURMET FOOD? HIRE A LOCAL CHEF.

Don Hill earned his chops in the armed forces, learning how to sling meals for hundreds of hungry servicemen and -women, and then turned to restaurant kitchens. Today visitors to Moloka'i can hire him—for a meal, for a week—to craft his memorable creations, to teach cooking classes, or both. When I was last on the island, he gave my five-year-old a knife skills class, taught me how to select and slice *ahi* sashimi, and then whipped up a traditional Hawaiian meal of the freshest *poke* paired with *lomilomi*, rice, *kalua* pork, and cheesecake. Call 808-553-5804.

views of the ocean. There is also a lively bar, especially on Friday evenings when Na Kupuna performs (see the sidebar).

In the morning, those in decent shape will want to drive past Kaunakakai on Highway 460. Turn right on Highway 470 and continue for 10 miles up the winding road to Moloka'i's top attraction: a mule ride or hike down the north sea cliffs to Kaluapapa Peninsula, the former leper colony. In the 1800s, King Kamehameha banished all lepers to this remote colony at the foot of the world's highest sea cliffs. Today, while there are a handful of residents left, those in good health (and over 16 years old) may visit, but only with a permit and a guide. If you opt for the mule ride (which most visitors do), don't expect some regal jaunt atop a mule—the 3-mile trail down the cliffs (or *pali*) is steep, with 26 switchbacks and 1,400 stairs. By mule, it takes 45 minutes to get down the trail and an hour up. Hikers can also descend the steep cliffs (the trip downhill lasts about 1½ hours—so bring snacks, water, and lots of energy). Once you arrive, everyone must explore the village with Damien Tours (if you are with Moloka'i Mule Ride, your transport includes the payment for the tour as well as lunch). These tours of the village are 3½ hours by bus.

On the tour, you'll learn about Father Damien, the Belgian priest who gave up everything to care for the leprosy patients sequestered in the colony. Before his arrival, life was bleak in the colony, but he inspired the residents to build houses, plant trees, and take pride in their community. He contracted the disease and died there, only to be granted sainthood. On the tour, you will visit the settlement, the visitors center, Kalawao, and St. Philomena Church (built in 1872). Keep your eyes on the stunning views of the Pali Coast and Kahiwa Waterfall. The only other way to peep at the area is via boat or kayak trip, or

NA KUPUNA

There is no need to bother with expensive lu'aus when you can experience the real deal here on Moloka'i. Friday night at the Hula Shores, a collection of *kupunas* (elders) strum ukuleles and sing Hawaiian tunes from a thick playlist. They don't face the audience of locals, time-share owners, and weekenders; instead they sit facing one another around a long card table laughing, sipping wine and beer, and, as leader Lono says, "playing to keep their brains active." A few *kupuna* hula dancers join the show,

A round of applause for the *kapunas*

a local music legend in board shorts jams for a few tunes, kids chase each other, and the wind blows the palms and sea behind them.

Kalaupapa Peninsula from above

flying in a hired plane (which you can do via Pacific Wings). Note that this adventure will leave you exhausted (emotionally and physically).

If you are not game for the trek down to Kalaupapa, you can still catch glimpses of the colony and the Pali Coast from the Pala'au State Park. Shaded by ironwood and eucalyptus trees, this cool and misty park offers a leisurely meander past the Kalaupapa Overlook to Kauleonanahoa (better known as the Phallic Stone, or, as my sons call it, Penis Rock). Locals believe that women who bring offerings and stay the night at the foot of this iconic rock will become pregnant.

On the way back down Highway 470, if it is before 2 p.m., the Moloka'i Museum offers a minimal glimpse into Moloka'i's cultural history. This restored sugar mill was built in 1878. Near the foot of the hills along Highway 470 is one of Moloka'i's best restaurants, Kualapu'u Cookhouse. A casual affair with a patio and a colorful interior filled with kitsch décor, this cookhouse serves lumberjack portions of plate lunches, pancakes, and burgers. Another worthy stop in the area is Coffees of Hawai'i. This coffee plantation offers fine coffee drinks, breakfast fare, and sandwiches. And the Plantation Store offers an impressive collection of souvenirs, art, and books on the island. On Sunday afternoon, local musicians perform on the lanai. Next door take a peek into the newly built Moloka'i Arts Center, which offers an array of art classes, including lei and jewelry making.

In the central part of the island, Purdy's Mac Nut Farm takes about half an hour. Take Highway 490 two miles west of Kualapu'u. Turn right on Lihi Pali Avenue and continue for 0.3 mile. Park on the side of the road and go on up the driveway. The owners encourage self-guided tours of the farm and offer macadamia nut samples. You likely won't leave without purchasing a couple of pounds of these snackable treats.

Known as "Penis Rock," this sacred spot is believed to bring fertility to women who sleep here.

Kids and adults rejoice when they enter Ho'olehua Post Office and find baskets of coconuts for them to decorate and send back home. It's called "Post-a-Nut" and has become an institution here on Moloka'i.

Just past Kaunakakai on Highway 460, Paddler's Inn offers American- and Hawaiian-style cuisine like ribs and salads paired with beers and well drinks. Locals tend to hang out here after dark, so if you are looking for some nightly entertainment, this is one of the main contenders with jazz musicians, Hawaiian tunes, sports on the TVs, and a healthy collection of spirits.

Wake up and motor out to Moloka'i's dry side to explore some of Hawai'i's most remote beaches. This region has been trying to define itself since the 1800s, when King Kamehameha created Moloka'i Ranch, hoping to cash in on so much barren land. He soon learned, like those eager moneymakers that followed, that not much flourished in this dry, red dirt. For a minute, pineapples grew like weeds out here, then farmers herded cattle (unfortunately, the bovines came down with TB), and then a resort tried to flourish and failed.

Today the arid western side is known for its beaches. Bring a picnic and plenty of water and take Highway 460 west to turn right on Kaluakoi Road. The entire journey is 23 miles. Here you'll reach a collection of beaches worthy of sending home a coconut

DETOUR: MO'OMONI BEACH

Another reason to hire a four-wheel-drive vehicle is to make a trip out to the windswept Mo'omomi Beach. Take Farrington Avenue west, past Highway 480, where the road becomes unpaved. Continue for 2.5 miles until you see the picnic pavilion. The ecology here is fragile, and the ocean is rough, so stay on paths as you view the sand dunes. The Nature Conservancy offers guided tours of the area to teach visitors about the endangered birds and monk seals that call the beach home: www.nature.org.

DETOUR: KAMAKOU PRESERVE

Armed with a four-wheel-drive vehicle (or a Nature Conservancy guide, 808-553-5236; www.nature.org), nature lovers can explore the Kamakou Preserve. This untamed wilderness houses over 200 native plants and rare Hawaiian birds, and the rain forest provides views of Moloka'i's unexplored interior. The turnoff to the trailhead from Highway 460 is between mile markers 3 and 4. Continue on the unpaved road for 5.5 miles where the Moloka'i Forest Reserve begins. This area is rich with ironwood and eucalyptus trees. Continue for 2.5 miles past the Sandalwood Pit, where royals forced commoners to carry the valuable sandalwood on their backs to the harbor for export. Travel 1 more mile and arrive at the Waikolu Lookout at the start of the Kamakou Preserve. On a clear moment, the view of the valley, waterfalls, and ocean will blow your mind. Go early for the best chance of clear weather. Hikers can wander for a mile to reach the Pepe'opae Trail, which weaves past *ohi'a lehua* trees and the bog's miniature forest, then opens onto a jaw-dropping view. The whole hike is 4 miles and can be wet and muddy.

about. To the north on Kaluakoi Road is a former resort community of Kaluakoi. The main condo complex out here is Paniolo Hale; however, there is nothing else out here— no services, no gas stations, nada. If that appeals, contact Moloka'i Vacation Rentals to learn about the condos and houses they rent on the west side. The beaches that surround Paniolo Hale include Make Horse Beach (which is lovely, but not swimmable) and Kawakiu Beach (a favorite for strong swimmers in summer).

To the south take Kaluakoi Road and travel south on Puhakuloa Road to find the gorgeous but incredibly dangerous Papokahu Beach, a white sand beauty with an undertow not braved by the fiercest locals, who camp under the *kiawe* trees to celebrate family events. Six miles south is Dixie Maru Beach, popular with families, local surfers, and snorkelers. The *kiawe* trees drop sharp thorns, so keep your sandals on when not in the water. You can hike along the sea for 3 miles to find even quieter beaches at La'au Point (there are signs telling you to turn back, but those were

A mellow sunset on Moloka'i

Papokahu Beach looks stunning, but the current is quite dangerous.

geared toward the developers that locals thwarted from creating a luxury resort on these shores).

Back up at Highway 460, turn right toward Maunaloa, a former plantation town and failed resort community. There's not much here, save Maunaloa General Store, an overpriced grocery boasting a freezer packed with ice cream treats. The main reason to trek out here is to visit Big Wind Kite Factory. Owners Jonathan and Daphne Socher sell a staggering number of kites, both in stock and custom designed. They also offer lessons to newbie fliers. If you get a chance to chat up the owners, ask about hikes to Kaana, the birthplace of hula and the royal coconut grove.

On the way back to Kaunakakai on Highway 460, travel for 6 miles and then turn left onto Hua Ai Road. Continue for less than a mile until you find Kumu Farms, an organic farm that features a fine collection of produce, grass-fed beef, handcrafted pasta, and a winning pesto. Grab as much produce as you can afford—Manu's apple bananas are quite tasty.

If you'd like to treat yourself to a lei, 2.5 miles before Kaunakakai on Highway 460 is Moloka'i Plumerias. The orchard smells so sweet that you may want to dive into the flowers. Here you can pick up leis or flowers, or just soak in the aroma before heading back to your room to cook a fresh-off-the-farm dinner.

In the morning, hop in the car and travel east on Highway 450 to take in Moloka'i's most scenic drive. This 27-mile road hugs the sea, weaving among palms, vines, modest houses, and beaches that beg to be explored. There are no gas stations east of Kaunakakai, so fill up before heading out. As you drive along the southern side of the island, you may spot lava rock walls in the sea—these are ancient fishponds. Caretakers have been working to restore these ancient farming sites and welcome visitors. Mervin Dudoit, the caretaker at Ali'i Fishpond, just 0.5 mile south of Hotel Moloka'i, is especially informative.

At mile marker 6, Kakahai'a Beach Park offers a grassy strip for a picnic. The waters here are murky because of runoff, but if you are traveling with someone who needs to stretch their legs, you can try to spot the Hawaiian stilt in the Kakahai'a National Wildlife Refuge on the *mauka* side of the highway.

At the 10-mile marker sits the sweet St. Joseph's Church, constructed in 1876 by Father Damien. On May 10, St. Damien's Feast Day, locals march from this church to Father Damien's Our Lady of Seven Sorrows, which is 4 miles to the east, and was constructed in 1874.

Between the two churches, after mile marker 13 is Wavecrest Resort. This condo complex offers spacious units with kitchens, lanais, and views of the sea. Units have been individually decorated by the owners and can be hit or miss, so view photos before booking. Year-round residents populate the pool and the library lounge. Try to score a room in building A; these have the best views of the sea.

At mile marker 16, you'll find the community of Puko'o, which used to be Moloka'i's main city. Today it's all about *da grindz* and the beach. Grab a plate lunch of teriyaki or *katsu* and a smoothie at Mana'e Goods and Grindz; you'll probably want to stock up on water and snacks as well, as this is the only stop in these parts. Across the road, 16-Mile Beach is known for its mellow surf and easy swimming for the *keikis*. FYI: Watch out for chickens and lazy dogs napping on the road.

The 18-mile marker houses Dunbar Beachfront Cottages, which rents out two modest two-bedroom houses complete with kitchens, lanais, washers and dryers, and Wi-Fi. The remote location beckons romance seekers or a smallish group wanting some privacy.

Ask any local where to swim on the east side and they'll point you to 20-Mile Beach (aka Murphy's Beach), conveniently located at the 20-mile marker. Here you can swim

An example of an ancient fishpond

and snorkel, if you can brave the collection of rocks around the shore. Local *keikis* and surfers hang out at Rock Point and Sandy Beach, both a mile up the road. If I were you, however, I'd hold off for Halawa Valley to get your beach fix.

As you near mile marker 22, the road grows narrower. Slow down and be a courteous driver. Much of the rest of the one-lane drive sinews along a cliff, making this white-knuckled driver nervous (for more on driving in Hawai'i, see chapter 3). The views are lovely, especially around the 24-mile marker, where you'll see Mokuho'oniki, a sanctuary for seabirds like *iwa* and frigatebirds.

Pu'u o Hoku Ranch appears at the top of the hill. This organic farm/retreat center/collection of vacation rentals is ideal for those who truly want to unplug and seep in the sounds of Moloka'i. Houses are tastefully decorated, and can be stocked with the ranch's produce and beef for a fee.

You'll be rewarded for your efforts around the 25-mile marker, where travelers are offered a view of the majestic Halawa Valley and the Pacific beyond. The valley was the first community on the island until the houses and the taro fields were wiped out by a tidal wave in 1946. A flash flood in 1964 added to the misery. Today hard-core Halawa Valley locals still call the area home and are working to bring the taro fields back. The valley offers more by way of exploring than most have time for; however, it is possible to re-

Halawa Valley

A historic church in Halawa Valley

ally indulge in the area if you plan ahead. Moa'ula Falls and Hipuapua Falls cascade down the mountain as if guarding this lush valley. You can hike the 2-mile trail to the waterfalls, and—if you have no open cuts—swim in the pools below. But you must get a permit or hike in with a guide. You can arrange a guided hike with Moloka'i Fish and Dive, or from just about any local wanting to make a few bucks.

The valley gapes toward the sea and offers two popular beach parks known for their good surf (though only expert surfers should brave the waves in winter) and summer swimming. The smaller Kamaalaea Beach will make you wonder how this lovely cove stays so deserted and pristine. The larger Kawili Beach lures surfers, families, and swimmers, and is the launching point for kayak trips to the Pali Coast (contact Moloka'i Fish and Dive). This is the end of the road for Moloka'i, and it sure feels like you've stumbled upon a slice of nirvana.

IN THE AREA

ACCOMMODATIONS

Dunbar Beachfront Cottages, 9940 Kamehameha V Hwy. (Hwy. 450), Kaunakakai. Two private, secluded beachfront vacation rentals on the sand. Call 808-558-8153. Website www.molokai-beachfront-cottages.com.

Hotel Moloka'i, 1300 Kamehameha V Hwy. (Hwy. 450), Kaunakakai. Simple oceanfront resort with friendly staff, pool, restaurant, and continental breakfast. Call 808-553-5347. Website www.hotelmolokai.com.

Moloka'i Vacation Rentals. A variety of short- or long-term accommodations available. Call 800-367-2984. Website www.molokai-vacation-rental.net.

Pu'u O Hoku Ranch, mile marker 25, Kaunakakai. Rustic, 1930s ranch-style accommodations on a cattle ranch, ideal for those wanting to get off the grid. Call 808-558-8109. Website www.puuohoku.com.

Wavecrest Resort, 7142 Kamehameha V Hwy. (Hwy. 450), Kaunakakai. Oceanfront condo complex with one- and two-bedroom units. Call 509-393-3410. Website www.molokaioceanfront.com.

ATTRACTIONS AND RECREATION

Ali'i Fishpond, Kamehameha V Hwy. (Hwy. 450) east of Kaunakakai at mile marker 4. An example of traditional fishing methods.

Big Wind Kite Factory, 120 Mauna Loa Hwy., Maunaloa. Buy a kite, custom-order one, or get a lesson on how to fly these megaliths. Call 808-552-2364. Website www.bigwindkites.com.

Damien Tours. You need to pay to explore Kalaupapa. Call 808-567-6171. Website www.fatherdamientours.com.

Ho'olehua Post Office, 69-2 Puupeelua Ave., Ho'olehua. Mail a coconut to your friends back home. Call 808-567-6144.

Kakahai'a National Wildlife Refuge. Website www.fws.gov/kakahaia.

Kalaupapa National Historical Park. One of Hawai'i's most important historic sites. You can hike here, take a mule ride, or fly, but no matter how you arrive, you need to arrange a tour of this former leper colony. Call 808-567-6802. Website www.nps.gov/kala/index.htm.

Kalele Bookstore and Divine Expressions, 64 Ala Malama Ave., Kaunakakai. The unofficial visitors bureau, with local crafts and books, and plenty of aloha. Call 808-553-5112. Website www.molokaispirit.com.

Kumu Farms, 9 Huaai Rd., Kualapu'u. An organic farm with a slew of produce to prepare in your condo. Call 808-351-3326. Website www.kumufarms.com.

Moloka'i Arts Center, 1630 Farrington Ave. (Hwy. 470), Kualapu'u (located at the Coffees of Hawai'i Plantation). Take an art class, or see what locals are painting. Call 808-567-9696. Website www.molokaiartscenter.com.

Moloka'i Bicycle, 80 Mohala St., Kaunakakai. Rent a two-wheeler to pedal around the isle. Call 808-553-3931. Website www.bikehawaii.com/molokaibicycle.

Moloka'i Fish and Dive, 61 Ala Malama Ave., Kaunakakai. *The* spot to arrange boat trips or kayak adventures, or to grab a souvenir. Call 808-553-5926. Website www.molokaifishanddive.com.

Moloka'i Mule Ride. Ride a mule down to Kalaupapa. It's trying, but worth your time. Call 808-567-6088 or 800-567-7550. Website www.muleride.com.

Moloka'i Museum and Cultural Center. A small collection of artifacts. Call 808-567-6436.

Moloka'i Plumerias, 1342 Mauna Loa Hwy., Kaunakakai. Grab flower leis from this sweet flower farm. Call 808-553-3391. Website http://molokaiplumerias.com.

Pacific Wings. Flights into Kalaupapa are expensive, but they save you the painful bottom from sitting on a donkey half the day. Call 888-575-4546. Website www.pacificwings.com.

Purdy's Macadamia Nut Farm, 4 Lihi Pali Ave., Ho'olehua. Explore this local mac nut farm. Call 808-567-6601. Website www.molokai-aloha.com/macnuts.

DINING

Coffees of Hawai'i—Moloka'i Plantation, Café and Espresso Bar, 1630 Farrington Ave. (off Hwy. 470),

Kualapu'u. Home of the mocha mama and a yummy breakfast or lunch; live music on Sunday afternoon. There's a sophisticated gift shop on site as well. Call 808-567-9490. Website www.coffees ofhawaii.com.

Farmers' Market, Ala Malama St., Kaunakakai. Saturday 8–noon. Find organic produce as well as locally made crafts and keepsakes.

Friendly's Market, 90 Ala Malama St., Kaunakakai. Full-service market with fresh local produce. Call 808-553-5595.

Hula Shores Restaurant at Hotel Moloka'i, 1300 Kamehameha V Hwy., Kaunakakai. On the water, full bar, live music on Friday and Spam fried rice—what else could you ask for? Call 808-553-5347. Website www.hotelmolokai .com.

Kanemitsu Bakery and Coffee Shop, 79 Ala Malama St., Kaunakakai. Get your fresh-baked sweet bread and cinnamon rolls early in the morning or eat a greasy, stick-to-your-ribs breakfast or lunch at the restaurant (closes early). Call 808-553-5855.

Kualapu'u Cookhouse, Hwy. 470 and Ulwao St., Kualapu'u. Large portions of Hawaiian-style local favorites and traditional American fare. Call 808-567-9655.

Maka's Corner, 35 Mohala St., Kaunakakai. Try the *kalbi* ribs or the *katsu* plate lunch. Call 808-553-8058.

Mana'e Goods and Grindz, *mauka* (mountain) side of Hwy. 450 E., Kaunakakai. Hawaiian plate lunch, smoothies, and snacks, *the* only spot to stop for lunch on the east side. Call 808-558-8498.

Maunaloa General Store, 200 Mauna Loa Hwy., Maunaloa. The only grocery store on the west side of the island. Call 808-552-2346.

Moloka'i Burger, 20 W. Kamehameha V Hwy., Kaunakakai. Get your burger-and-fries fix or enjoy Mexican Tuesday. Call 808-553-3533.

Heaping portions of *loco moco* at Kualuapu'u Cookhouse

Moloka'i Drive Inn, 15 Kamoi St., Kaunakakai. Local-style fast food. Cash only. Call 808-553-5655.

Moloka'i Pizza Cafe, 15 Kaunakakai Pl., Kaunakakai. Friendly, cash-only pizza parlor with arcade games, pastas, and salads. Call 808-553-3288.

Outpost Natural Foods, 70 Makaena Pl., Kaunakakai. Organic produce and vegetarian items available. Call 808-553-3377.

Paddler's Inn, 10 Mohala St., Kaunakakai. Hawaiian and American food with happy-hour specials. Open for breakfast, lunch, and dinner. Call 808-553-3300. Website www.molokaipaddlers inn.com.

Rawlin's Chevron, 20 Mauna Loa Hwy., Kaunakakai. Good for hot and cold snacks as well as sundries and toiletries. Call 808-553-3214.

OTHER CONTACT INFORMATION

Alamo Rent A Car, Bldg. #2 Airport Loop, Hoolehua. Call 888-826-6893.

Moloka'i Visitors Bureau. Website www.gohawaii.com.

Sweetheart Rock

6 Spooks, Spirits, and Rejuvenation on Lana'i

Estimated length: 141 miles

Estimated time: 6 hours, or 3–4 leisurely days

Getting there: Mokulele (www.mokulele.com), Go! Airlines (www.iflygo.com), and Island Air (www.islandair.com) all fly into Lana'i Airport from Honolulu International Airport and Kahului Airport. Alternatively, if you are already on Maui, Expeditions Ferry offers five trips (which are just over an hour) to Lana'i's harbor from Lahaina Harbor. Ferry rides can be extremely rocky, so it is advised to travel early in the morning, and bring along some Dramamine, especially if you have a weak stomach.

When you arrive in Lana'i, the Four Seasons shuttle charges a nominal fee (this is waived for guests of the hotels) to deliver you to the hotels, or into Lana'i City. Dollar Rent A Car (www.dollar.com) is located in Lana'i City, just a couple of blocks from Hotel Lana'i, and rents four-by-four Jeeps at exorbitant rates. Most people hire a car for a day or two to explore the outer reaches of the island and then use the Four Seasons shuttle to travel among their hotel, the harbor, Lana'i City, and Manele Bay.

Highlights: Sacred *heiaus*, a ghost town, alpine conifer trees, Manele Bay, rugged beaches packed with nesting sea turtles, and luxurious resorts.

L ana'i defies most expectations about Hawai'i. Sure, there are luxurious resorts, two in fact (and at press time, another on the way), both owned and operated by Four Seasons Resorts, and of course you can expect to find glorious beaches—actually there is really only one that is easily accessed by mere mortals, or rather, those on the prowl for soft adventures. However, the allure of Lana'i reaches beyond that bikini and *mai tai*, and into a storied beginning rich with ghosts, weaponry, and innovation.

Since Pacific Islanders began inhabiting the Hawaiian Islands, it was thought that Lana'i was haunted by evil, man-eating spirits. As with all legends, stories vary, but my favorite tale is how Hawaiians believed that only sorcerers, ghouls, and goblins lived on the rocky mountains of Hawai'i's sixth largest isle. One day Prince Kaulalaau, son of the

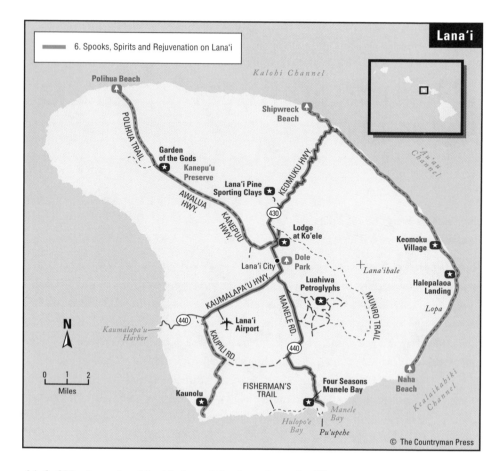

chief of Maui, was banished to Lana'i for the crime of pulling up Maui's breadfruit trees. It was thought he would not survive, but rumor has it that the tricky prince outwitted the spirits, driving them from the island and pulling up all the breadfruit trees on Lana'i as well. From across the ocean, the chief saw his son's glowing fire night after night, imagined his son's courage battling the ghosts, and let him take control of the haunted isle. In Lana'i's earliest marketing campaign, the prince encouraged people from other islands to inhabit the isolated Lana'i, claiming the ghostly spirits had been exorcised.

It was a matter of time before Lana'i, conquered by Kamehameha the Great, became a part of the Kingdom of Hawai'i. In 1778 Kalaniopu'u, the king of the Big Island, invaded Lana'i and killed almost all of the isle's 4,000 residents. Their spirits are believed to wander the island today, congregating in the forests along the Munro Trail—how's that for spooky?

After a relatively long run as a part of the monarchy, Lana'i's history took a strange twist in 1922, when James Dole arrived, purchased the island, and started his pineapple plantation. Word got out that there was work to be had and migrants from around the Pacific arrived to slave away in the fields, making Lana'i one of the game changers in the world of pineapples. Though Lana'i has been out of the agricultural game for many years, it is still considered the "Pineapple Island." And while Lana'i is a member of the state of Hawai'i and the county of Maui, it is the only privately owned Hawaiian Island. In 2012 Larry Ellison bought 98 percent of the island for hundreds of millions, claiming that he would retain the low-key feel and community spirit of the island, and more recently announcing that he would be researching green energy along her shores. At press time, he had purchased Island Air, added a larger runway to the airport, and started bulldozing to build an eco-resort named Club Lana'i on Lopa Beach.

Today Lana'i offers a unique, almost alpine charm. Dotted with Cook pines, the topography looks like it belongs in the High Sierra, not the South Pacific. Lana'i City, the only town, boasts no traffic lights, no malls, no chain stores, and relatively few palm trees. The locals offer a brand of country kindness more akin to the Midwest than Hawai'i, which may be why the ghostly spirits seem to still enjoy the isle. Since the island is only 13 miles wide and 18 miles long, with views of surrounding Moloka'i, Maui, and Kaho'olawe, it seems simple to explore the entire isle in a day. However, there is only one paved road leading out of town (from the Lodge at Koele to Four Seasons Manele Bay). The other roads require off-road vehicles, alternating among rocky paths, sandy lanes, and trails better traversed in a go-cart than a car.

Most travelers begin and end their journey in Lana'i City, which occupies the term *city* very loosely. The heart of the island is Dole Park, an endearing square of grass with a playground, a community center, and a maze of Cook pines. Much occurs here, from playdates to picnics, teenage antics to taking care of the elderly, so while it may not seem like a spot worth more than a bathroom break at most, if you settle in for a spell, you'll start to gauge who's who in town.

Of the three hotels on the island, two are in Lana'i City. On the modest side (and by my family's account, home to some creepy paranormal activity), Hotel Lana'i offers plantation-style accommodations across the street from Dole Park. The herb-lined garden leads guests into the yellow plantation house, where the friendly staff serve continental breakfast. Breezy rooms might lack a TV and offer tight bathrooms, but the Hawaiian quilts, thatched rugs, and local art showcase an attention to detail

Lana'i's Cook pines are a common sight throughout the island.

Hotel Lana'i's interiors

uncommon in many budget accommodations. The hotel's on-site Lana'i Grille (the Lana'i outpost of Bev Gannon's Maui empire) occupies a chunk of the lobby area and is wise choice for dinner—if you are on the island longer than a few days, you'll likely return more than once. Gannon's *ahi poke* tacos with goat cheese and the catch of the day bathed in pecans inspire.

For one of the most worthy splurges in the state, save up for a few nights (or at least pop over for the nightly music in the lounge, a round of golf, or a meal) at Four Seasons Lodge at Koele. This plantation-style building is where Hawaiians vacation when they want a cool breeze, scrumptious gardens, and the *ali'i* treatment. While some visitors claim to have seen a ghost of a buck romping around in the forest above the property, the draw for most is the calming of the spirit. Family friendly rooms provide plenty of technological amenities as well as plush beds, spacious baths, and private patios. The hotel features two restaurants: The upscale Dining Room serves farm-fresh cuisine like Keahole lobster with whipped Yukon gold potatoes, *haricot verts*, and lobster emulsion, paired with a winning wine list; the more casual Terrace Restaurant serves three meals daily, including a tantalizing duck leg confit with white bean ragout. The hotel also offers a small pool, a spa, a world-class golf course, a game room, and free shuttle service throughout the island. Guests of the resort are allowed full access to the services at Manele Bay.

In town, join the locals for breakfast at Blue Ginger Café, a mellow diner serving sweet pastries, *loco moco*, or *saimin*. Alternatively, grab a latte and a bagel at Coffee Works, a former O'ahu café now run out of a plantation-style house with a patio that begs visitors to read the newspaper and stay awhile.

Take an hour to visit the Lana'i Culture and Heritage Center and explore the artifacts from Lana'i's storied past. View archaeological findings and plantation-era documents as friendly

Four Seasons The Lodge at Koele

volunteers offer a rich patchwork of stories—be sure to take some time to ask about the haunted history of the island.

If the ghost stories gave you the creeps, head over to Lana'i Pine and Sporting Clays to practice your archery on the 3-D archery range. This outfit also rents horses, offers a charmed horse-drawn carriage ride around town, and leads a wild go-cart trip along the haunted 7-mile Munro Trail. Alternatively, if you'd prefer to go ghost hunting by foot, hike the Munro Trail, which ascends an exhilarating 3,366 feet to the peak Lana'i'hale. From

Take in a round of archery while on Lana'i.

up here, try to spot the O'ahu, Moloka'i, Maui, Kaho'olawe, and the Big Island. The trail is named for George Munro, a naturalist from New Zealand who noticed that island's first Norfolk Island pine made excellent use of the Lana'i fog, so he planted the pine trees across the island, bringing cooler weather and more rain to the inland reaches of Lana'i.

Locals call a walk around town the "Dole Stroll." And while you won't find the chic boutiques of Lahaina or Waikiki, you can stumble upon some cute shops like Dis and Dat Shop, characterized by a colorful little vehicle in the lawn and stacks of art, jewelry, and curiosities. The Local Gentry features men's and women's clothing plus a healthy collection of slippers, sarongs, socks, and bath products; and the inspiring Mike Carroll Gallery showcases oil paintings, many of which are inspired by the island.

If you are looking for a dependable place to grab a bite to eat, in addition to the above-mentioned restaurants, put Pele's Other Garden on your list. This popular pizzeria and deli, with a healthy beer selection, an outdoor patio, and a colorful interior, offers live music on select nights. Sandwiches are pricey, but the servings are large enough to stretch over two meals. You may also want to pop into Café 565 for a plate lunch of chicken *katsu*, a burger, or a hefty salad. The service is slow, so don't arrive too hungry.

Take the shuttle to Manele Bay for an afternoon of relaxing on Hulopoe Beach, Lana'i's most stunning strand. Whether you relax in the shade, frolic in the waves, or go tide pooling, this beach has the potential to become your favorite Hawaiian swimming spot, maybe of all time.

Dis and Dat Shop along the Dole Stroll

Hulopoe Beach

Before the sun begins to set, take a walk southeast for about 10 minutes on the sandy path to the picturesque Pu'u Pehe, Sweetheart Rock. This legendary site is seeped in lore. Locals say that the Lana'i warrior Makakehau became smitten with the Maui maiden Pehe; whenever he saw her, he began to cry. One day he took her to his island and hid her in a sea cave below the Manele cliffs. On a particularly stormy day, he found his maiden had drowned. Makakehau held her in his arms and climbed the 80-foot cliffs to bury his beloved. Grief stricken, he plummeting into the pounding surf below, where today, if you listen closely, you may hear his wails. For those less enamored with mythology, instead keep an eye out for spinner dolphins and sharks.

Perched atop Hulopoe Beach is Lana'i's award-winning beach resort, Four Seasons Manele Bay. When most imagine an island oasis, they picture this luxury spread of oceanfront lodging dripping with amenities. Jet setters pay the big bucks for nonsmoking rooms with private lanais, overlooking the landscaped grounds or the sea, marble bathrooms, local artwork, free Wi-Fi, and fine linens atop plush beds. Throw in an epic pool and hot tub with views of the ocean, four restaurants and bars, a lively children's playroom, art tours, tennis courts, golf courses, and a fitness center, and you begin to understand why travelers save up for this resort. Guests also are allowed full use of the services at Lodge at Koele. If you don't want to splurge on a room, the decadent spa might be more of what your body needs. Book a treatment like the Ki Pola Ho'olu, a cooling *ti* wrap paired with a *lomilomi* massage in the oceanfront *hale*.

Afterward, enjoy a fanciful meal at one of the Four Seasons' signature restaurants. The hotel upgraded its dining options in early 2013, adding Nobu Lana'i (which offers a poolside sushi bar as well as internationally acclaimed chef Nobu Matsuhisa's classic takes on Japanese cuisine). Another new addition, One Forty offers steak and seafood dishes with spectacular ocean views. Cap off the night with a cocktail at Hale Ahe Ahe Lounge.

Wake up early the next morning, pick up your rental car, and grab a picnic lunch at Lana'i Ohana Poke Market, a hole-in-the-wall where you can score a heaping spicy *ahi* bowl with rice, seaweed, and macaroni salad for a reasonable price. If that doesn't inspire, there are two grocery stores on the island, Richard's and the Pine Island Markets. Or if it happens to be Saturday morning, the local farmers' market takes over Dole Park, so join the locals who line up for fresh fruit, locally made jams, and homemade food before heading out on your off-road adventure. Be sure you have a full tank of gas and plenty of food and water, because where you are going there are no services.

From Dole Park drive north on Keomuku Highway, turn left on Kanepu'u Highway, and continue toward Awalua Highway. You'll pass through a couple of cattle gates, and the road will become dusty dirt. You'll end up on Polihua Trail and then travel for 4 miles of bumps through the Kanepu'u Preserve, housing Hawaiian native trees. Watch out for deer—they spring out of nowhere and have caused many accidents. Continue a bit more until the trees disappear and you stumble upon Garden of the Gods or, as locals call it, Keahiakawelo—red boulders offering views of Moloka'i and Maui. The boulders are the result of thousands of years of erosion, yet my favorite ancient tale says these rocks house the spirits of ancient Hawaiian warriors. Whether or not you believe science or legend, this otherworldly sight will have you snapping photos before hopping back in the car.

Continue north on Polihua Trail, which weaves down the hill for 6 miles of switchbacks and stunning vistas of the archipelago, to Polihua Beach, popular with nesting green sea turtles and, in winter, humpback whales. Getting to this beach is tricky, as you have to drive through beach sand. Ask the staff at the rental car office to mark on your map how far it is safe to drive—they will likely instruct you to park at the DOLLAR RENT A CAR sign and walk the rest of the way. Though the 2 miles of white sand mixing with azure water is lovely, this beach is not safe for swimming. Kamikaze surfers sojourn here to ride the infamous waves, not for the faint of heart.

Four Seasons Manele Bay

Garden of the Gods

Backtrack to Keomoku Road and travel north (away from Lana'i City) over 8 miles of sharp turns and lovely views. At the end of the road, kick the four-wheel drive into gear and get ready for a rough ride. Turn left for 1.5 miles of thick beach sand until you either can drive no more, or reach Kaiolohia, commonly known as Shipwreck Beach. This area is known for its current and shallow reef, and the 8-mile beach has been the culprit in many wrecks (hence the name), including the World War II Liberty Ship you can see today. Park in the large clearing, where you will find good snorkeling, protected swimming, and many green sea turtles. Just past the SHIPWRECK sign, you can hike 100 yards to the Kukui Point petroglyphs. Continue for 6 miles along the remote beach and you'll pass a slew of boat remains until you reach another WWII tanker wrecked on the rocks.

When you've had your fill of the ghostly remains of hulls and anchors, head back to Keomoku Road and travel southeast on the bumpy road. Less than a mile from the end of the paved road you'll find Maunalei, the site of a former *heiau*. When the Maunalei Sugar Company used the stones of this former sacred site to build a fence, stories say the spirits urged salt water into the wells and brought sickness to the work crew, ending their reign on this isle.

Continue for 6 miles on this very pockmarked road to Lana'i's ghost town, Keomoku. The short-lived sugar plantation is now no more than ruins under a blanket of flora. A wander through the semi-reconstructed Ka Lanakila Malamalama Church might offer a glimpse at a spook from another era, but you'll more likely be creating insect ghosts as you swat at those hungry mosquitoes.

Two miles down the road you'll pass Halepalaoa Landing, home to a small cemetery for Japanese sugarcane workers from the late 1800s. Walk out on the pier in winter to spot whales breaching, or unpack your lunch to enjoy on the shady and deserted Halepalaoa Beach, just southeast of the pier.

Continue for another 4 miles and you reach Naha Beach—the end of the road. Local fishermen dive here, but don't be fooled: The sea is rough and should only be braved by *very experienced* swimmers. This is a lovely and quiet destination, and those interested in the remains of ancient culture will appreciate the ancient fishponds, just offshore. Expect to be driving for at least an hour each way to reach Naha, and budget your time so you are not negotiating the roads after dark. You should not attempt to turn around on beach access roads; instead, use the main road.

Early the next morning, contact Trilogy Lana'i Ocean Sports to schedule a dive, snorkel, or scuba trip at the world-class Cathedrals. Try to get into the sea early, before the crowds from Maui arrive. The reef is one of the best and least-crowded dive spots on the islands.

For another creepy excursion, travel back toward Lana'i City on Manele Road. Two miles before you reach town, notice a small cluster of trees on your right and turn on the dirt road; continue for a mile until you see a house and a gate. Turn left onto the dirt road and look for the stone marker and turnout: Here you'll find the strangely quiet Luahiwa Petroglyphs, Lana'i's largest collection of stone carvings. While you may not see the spirits here, you will surely feel their presence.

Your last bit of ghost hunting requires you to drive on Manele Road back toward Lana'i City until you reach Kaumalapa'u Highway (Highway 440). Drive west 0.5 mile past Lana'i Airport and bear left on a rough gravel road to the sea. Find the stone marker that explains the history of Kaunolu and take the interpretive trail to the ruins of the ancient fishing village (double-check with Dollar how far you should drive on this road).

One of Lana'i's hidden North Shore beaches

This once thriving village was destroyed by missionary-transmitted disease and today houses an abundant collection of ruins, including Halulu Heiau, Lanaʻi's *puʻuhonua*— a place of refuge for criminals to be absolved from their sins. The break in the wall, known as Kahekili's Jump, is where professional cliff divers compete for the world title. Under no circumstances should you jump, or this ghost stories chapter may have to include your story as well.

Cap off your visit to Lanaʻi by living it up. Most consider Lanaʻi a luxurious retreat to escape the world. If teeing off relaxes your spirit, treat yourself to a round of golf at the Lodge at Koele. Or schedule a massage treatment at the Manele Bay Spa to ease those muscles and bring your body and mind to a peaceful state. Splurge on an ocean-front dinner and a sunset *mai tai* at one of Manele Bay's restaurants before preparing to jet back home.

IN THE AREA

ACCOMMODATIONS

Four Seasons Lodge at Koele, 1 Keomuku Hwy., Lanaʻi City. A plantation-style abyss in the highlands of Lanaʻi, with two restaurants, a lounge, live entertainment, a spa, a world-class golf course, and unsurpassed service. Call 808-565-4000. Website www.fourseasons.com/koele.

Four Seasons Manele Bay, 1 Manele Rd., Lanaʻi City. Perched atop the Pacific, with sophisticated rooms, a sprawling pool, three restaurants, two bars, a children's area, a divine spa, and a world-class art collection, this hotel is Lanaʻi's most luxurious resort. Call 808-565-2000. Website www.fourseasons/manele bay.com.

Hotel Lanaʻi, 828 Lanaʻi Ave., Lanaʻi City. Charming Hawaiian-style rooms, with free continental breakfast and an on-site restaurant, steps from Dole Square. This sweet B&B caters to travelers on a budget. Call 808-565-7211. Website www.hotellanai.com.

ATTRACTIONS AND RECREATION

Dis and Dat Shop, 418 8th St., Lanaʻi City. Cute trinkets, crafts, and jewelry, many of which were made on the island. Call 808-565-9170. Website www.disanddatshop.com.

Expeditions: Maui-Lanaʻi Ferry, 658 Front St., Ste. 127, Lahaina. Service between Maui and Lanaʻi, five times a day, seven days a week. The ferry provides an opportunity to spot whales between December and May. Call 808-661-3756. Website www.go-lanai.com.

Lanaʻi Art Center, 339 7th St., Lanaʻi City. Center offers classes and studio time. Visiting Artist Workshops and gallery featuring local artists' work at reasonable prices. Call 808-565-7503. Website www.lanaiart.org.

Lanaʻi Culture and Heritage Center, 730 Lanaʻi Ave., Lanaʻi City. Learn about the rich history of the island at this small museum and cultural center. Call 808-565-7177. Website www.lanaichc.org.

Lanaʻi Pine and Sporting Clays. Offers shooting and archery classes and courses as well as horseback riding, ATV treks, and carriage rides through town. Call 808-563-9385. Website www.lanaigrandadventures.com.

Local Gentry, 363 7th St., Lanaʻi City. Cute boutique near Dole Park. Call 808-565-9130.

Mike Carroll Gallery, 443 7th St., Lana'i City. Check out Carroll's paintings of the islands. Call 808-565-7122. Website www.mikecarrollgallery.com.

Spa at The Lodge at Koele, 1 Keomoku Hwy., Lana'i City. Specialized massage treatments in a low-key atmosphere. Call 808-565-4000. Website www.fourseasons.com/koele/spa.

Spa at Manele Bay, 1 Manele Bay Rd., Lana'i City. The choice spa on the island for tropical-smelling crèmes lathered on the skin. Massages and facials are the road to relaxation. Call 808-565-2000. Website www.fourseasons.com/manele bay/spa.

Trilogy Ocean Sports. This is the only full service dive operation on the island of Lana'i, offering scuba, snorkeling and snuba tours daily. Call 808-874-5649. Website www.scubalanai.com.

DINING AND DRINKING

Blue Ginger Café, 409 7th St., Lana'i City. A friendly café that locals love, known for its banana pancakes and *saimin* (island-style chicken noodle soup). Call 808-565-6363. Website www.bluegingercafelanai.com.

Café 565, 408 8th St., Lana'i City. This casual restaurant serves pizza, subs, and local fare, including a fine Kula veggie sandwich on picnic tables. Call 808-565-6622.

Coffee Works, 604 Ilima Ave., Lana'i City. Hawai'i's oldest coffeehouse offers espresso drinks and pastries for breakfast and lunch. Call 808-565-6962. Website www.coffeeworkshawaii.com.

Dining Room at Four Seasons Lodge at Koele, 1 Keomuku Hwy., Lana'i City. Upscale farm-to-table eatery promises to feed the senses with an array of meats and produce grown nearby. Reservations required. Alternatively, dine at the more casual Terrace Restaurant for quality farm-fresh cuisine day and night. Call 808-565-4000. Website www.fourseasons.com/koele.

Lana'i City Grille, 828 B2 Lana'i Ave., Lana'i City. Bev Gannon's simple eatery slings a ridiculously good catch of the day bathed in pecans. Closed on Tuesday. Reservations are recommended. Call 808-565-7211. Website www.hotel lanai.com/grille.html.

Lana'i Ohana Poke Market, 834 A Gay St., Lana'i City. The island's best selection of fresh *poke*, ideal for a picnic lunch. Call 808-559-6265.

Nobu Lana'i, Four Seasons Manele Bay, 1 Manele Rd., Lana'i City. Stellar Japanese cuisine by world-class chef Nobu Matsuhisa. Dine poolside or in the upscale dining room, with views of Manele Bay. Reservations recommended. Call 808-565-2000. Website www.fourseasons/manelebay.com.

One Forty, Four Seasons Manele Bay, 1 Manele Rd., Lana'i City. Steaks, seafood, and ocean views are on the menu at this posh restaurant. Reservations recommended. Call 808-565-2000. Website www.fourseasons/manelebay.com.

Pele's Other Garden Deli, 811 Houston St., Lana'i City. A self-described New York deli and bistro...Lana'i style. Yummy chicken Parmesan, flatbread pizza, beer, and cheesecake. There is music on Wednesday evening. Cash only. Call 808-565-7211. Website www.peles othergarden.com.

Pine Island Market, Ltd., 356 8th St., Lana'i City. Call 808-565-6488.

Richard's Market, 434 8th St., Lana'i City. Call 808-565-3780.

OTHER CONTACT INFORMATION

Lana'i Visitors and Convention Bureau, 431 7th St., Ste. A, Lana'i City. Call 808-565-7600. Website www.gohawaii.com/lanai.

FRUIT

Pineapple 1 for $3 or 2 for $5 Money IN BOX

1-FOR 3" OR 2-FOR 5"

A fruit stand along a Maui backroad

7 *Maui No Ka Oi*
CENTRAL AND WEST MAUI'S SUPERSTAR ATTRACTIONS

Estimated length: 94 miles
Estimated time: 3–5 days

Getting there: Maui's main arrival port is via Kahului International Airport. Most major airlines, including Hawaiian Air (www.hawaiianairlines.com), United (www .united.com), American (www.aa.com), and Delta (www.delta.com), fly here from the mainland, with direct flights from most major California cities, Las Vegas, Phoenix, and New York's JFK Airport. Inter-island flights are available via Hawaiian Airlines (www.hawaiianairlines.com), Go! (www.iflygo.com), and Island Air (www.islandair.com). Thrifty (www.thrifty.com), Avis (www.avis.com), Enterprise (www.enterprise.com), and Budget (www.budget.com) have car rental desks at the airport. For those arriving into Lahaina Harbor from Moloka'i and Lana'i, Enterprise, Avis, and Hertz also have nearby car rental offices and can pick you up from the harbor.

Getting around the central, west, and south parts of the island is fairly easy, as long as you can handle traffic. Take Highway 32 west from Kahului to Wailuku. Travel south on Highway 30 (which becomes Highway 310 for a spell and then switches back to Highway 30) to Kihei and follow South Kihei Road, which veers into Okolani Drive and then Wailea Alanui Drive, finally becoming Makena Road as you arrive near the southernmost tip of this itinerary. Zip back up Highway 31 north to Highway 30 west and circle through Lahaina and the west side of the island. Around Kapalua, the road becomes Kahekili Highway, which twists and turns its way back to Wailuku.

Highlights: Lahaina's restaurants; snorkeling in Napili and Honolua Bays; diving at Molokini Crater; watching the sunset at Makena Beach; hiking in 'Iao Valley State Park; sampling freshly roasted coffee straight off the farm.

"Maui no ka oi" began as a battle cry against Big Island warriors as they conquered the Valley Isle, adding it to King Kamehameha's kingdom. Today you'll hear locals wear this saying as a badge of honor, translating the ancient call into "Maui

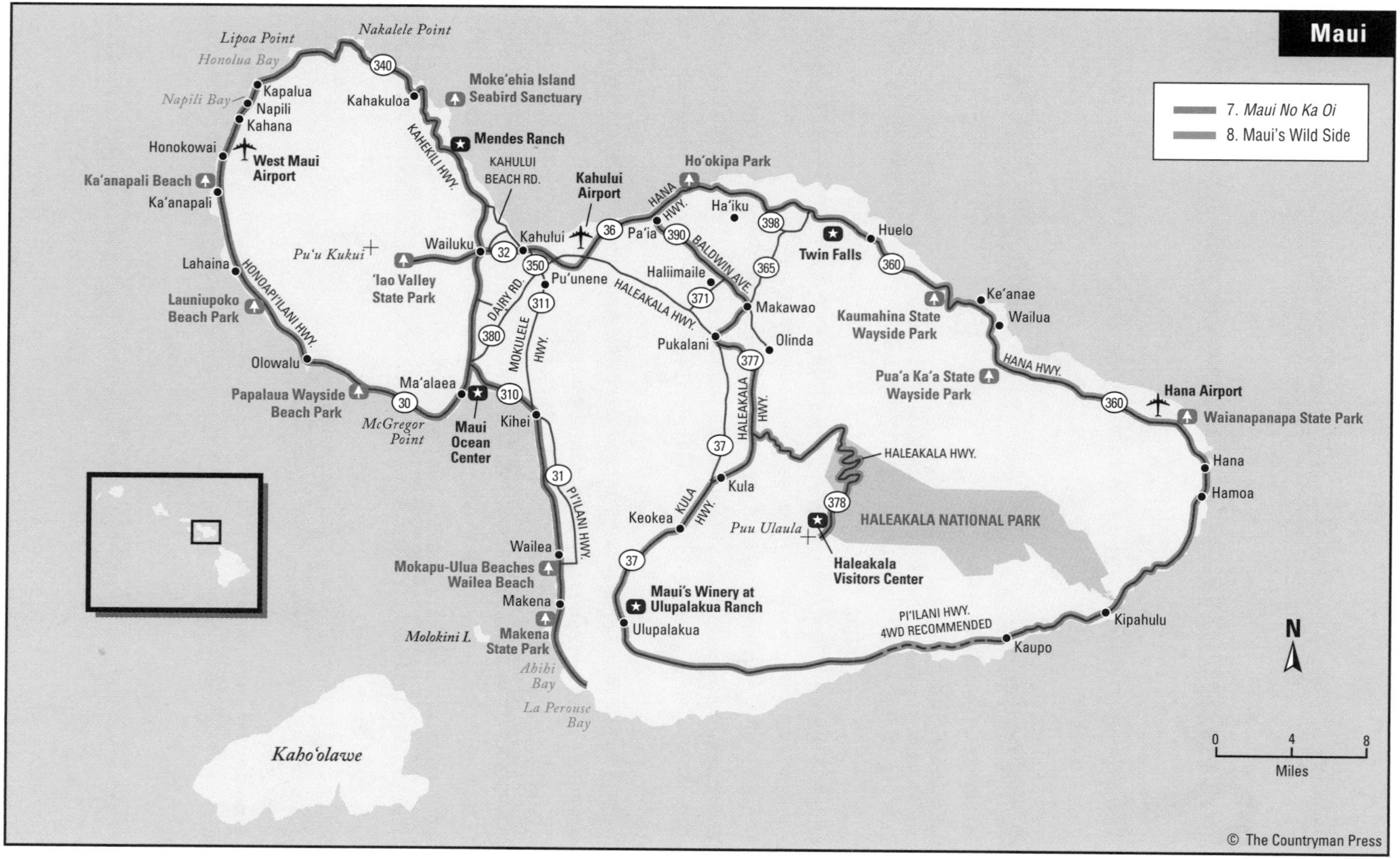

Maui

7. *Maui No Ka Oi*
8. *Maui's Wild Side*

N

0   4   8
Miles

© The Countryman Press

Nakalele Point

Lipoa Point

Honolua Bay

Napili Bay

Kapalua
Napili
Kahana
Honokowai
Ka'anapali Beach
Ka'anapali

340

Kahakuloa

KAHEKILI HWY.

Moke'ehia Island
Seabird Sanctuary

Mendes Ranch

KAHULUI
BEACH RD.

West Maui
Airport

Pu'u Kukui

'Iao Valley
State Park

HONOAPI'ILANI HWY.

Lahaina

Launiupoko
Beach Park

Olowalu

Papalaua Wayside
Beach Park

McGregor
Point

Ma'alaea

Maui
Ocean
Center

30

Wailuku

Waihe'e

32

DAIRY RD.

380

Kahului

Kahului
Airport

350

311

MOKULELE HWY.

310

Kihei

PI'ILANI HWY.

31

Mokapu-Ulua Beaches
Wailea Beach

Wailea

Makena

Makena
State Park

Molokini I.

Ahihi
Bay

La Perouse
Bay

Maui's Winery at
Ulupalakua Ranch

Ulupalakua

37

Keokea

Kula

KULA HWY.

37

HALEAKALA HWY.

377

Pukalani

Halimaile

HALEAKALA HWY.

HANA HWY.

36

Pa'ia

390

Ha'iku

371

Makawao

Olinda

Ho'okipa Park

Twin Falls

365

398

Huelo

360

BALDWIN AVE.

Kaumahina State
Wayside Park

Pua'a Ka'a State
Wayside Park

378

Haleakala
Visitors Center

Pu'u Ulaula

HALEAKALA NATIONAL PARK

HALEAKALA HWY.

PI'ILANI HWY.
4WD RECOMMENDED

Kaupo

Kipahulu

Waianapanapa State Park

Hana

Hamoa

Hana Airport

360

HANA HWY.

Wailua

Ke'anae

Kaho'olawe

is the best." Many travelers agree. Beloved by sun worshippers, scuba divers, foodies, outdoor adventurers, and luxury travelers, Maui's populous west side delivers a land of plenty. The Valley Isle's western shores boast the largest and most accessible sandy beaches in Hawai'i. Hikers relish the unexplored West Maui Mountains. Diving fanatics talk story of spinner dolphins and humpback whales. Sunsets over neighboring islands Moloka'i, Lana'i, Molokini, and Kaho'olawe are the stuff of legends. And those who want access to full-service resort communities should look no farther than Ka'anapali and Kihei—which despite the heaps of resorts and condos still manage to feel more like small towns than metropolises.

Maui's other nickname, the Valley Isle, refers to Central Maui's former sugarcane fields that stretch languidly between the island's two dormant volcanoes: Haleakala and the West Maui Mountains' Pu'u Kukui. These days you'll still see the remains of a thriving sugar industry, but the sugar barons are long gone. Central Maui houses two of Maui's largest communities—Wailuku and Kahului—and while the distance between them is a mere 5 miles, getting between the two can take up to half an hour in rush hour.

Considered less than inspiring by most, Kahului is where you may shop for groceries, hit up the mall or the swap meet, and windsurf. The industrial look and the traffic hide the beauty of Maui's crossroads, where east meets west, airliners rumble onto the island, and cruise ships drop their anchors. However, Kahului's natural abundance stands its ground amid development. Right after arrival, head west on Highway 32 to Kahului Harbor—the port for cargo vessels and cruise ships. Hidden here is Hoaloha Park, an oceanfront grassy area ideal for a picnic of freshly caught fish sizzled to perfection in a coat of panko, or served as a tangy *poke* from the beloved Cynnamon's food truck. At the western edge of the harbor, the free Maui Nui Botanical Gardens showcases native Hawaiian plants and begs to be meandered through.

Many of Kahului's restaurants are hidden in strip malls centered on or around Highways 36 and 32. The most notable table to grab Hawaiian comfort food is Da Kitchen Café, known for gigantic portions of Spam *musubi, loco moco*, and teriyaki. Another fun stop is Wow Wee Maui's Kava Bar and Grill,

> ## MAUI'S VINTAGE STEALS
>
> On Saturday morning head to Kahului for the huge Maui Swap Meet (310 W. Ka'ahumanu Ave., Kahului). This is *the* place to score Hawaiiana, aloha shirts, banana bread, and fresh produce for dirt-cheap prices.

which has a hidden sushi bar inside and a lively drinking area serving up the ancient kava root beverage that some say carries a whopper of a buzz. Hidden in Maui Mall, Tasaka Guri Guri Shop offers a sweet strawberry-and-pineapple confection sure to

---

GRADE A FOODIE FARE

Maui College's culinary program is famous statewide. The students run two eateries during the school year: a food court that serves yummy farm-to-table cuisine, and the multi-coursed Class Act for a surprisingly up-scale locally sourced sit-down meal atop white tablecloths (make reservations for this seasonal restaurant).

---

satisfy your dessert cravings. For your caffeine fix, nothing beats Maui Coffee Roasters' vanilla mac nut brews.

Neighboring Wailuku is what some might call the "real" Maui, housing the government, historic buildings, and many of the island's residents. While Wailuku doesn't necessarily earn its chops as a tourist destination, it is a central location for those not married to staying on the beach–especially if you can score a room at Old Wailuku Inn at Ulupono, a 1920s charmer of a mansion decked out in antiques, with gourmet breakfasts and free Wi-Fi.

History buffs can spend an hour exploring buildings listed on the National Register of Historic Places. Many were constructed by Maui's own architect C. W. Dickey, including Wailuku Library. The Bailey House Museum (a lava-and-wood home, built in 1833) houses an impressive collection of Hawaiian artifacts as well as The Duke's Surfboard, a hefty redwood longboard favored by Hawaiian surf legend Duke Kahanamoku, who brought Hawai'i's surf scene into the limelight. If you just want a photo op of a well-constructed building, it doesn't get much better than Ka'ahumanu Church, a tribute to King Kamehameha's favorite wife (of his 21!), who spearheaded a mass conversion to

Wailuku Union Church

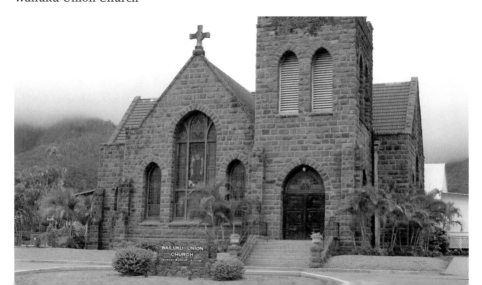

MAUI'S CULTURAL HUB!

After dark, Kahului's Maui Arts and Cultural Center promises live music on most nights. Plan to be in the area for the ukulele jams on the third Thursday of the month—or any of the annual events like June's slack key guitar festival and October's ukulele fest—and you're in for a treat. Check the local papers for evening performances.

Christianity on Maui. In town, the 1928 art deco 'Iao Theater hosts community theater productions of Broadway shows in the evenings.

Strung between the abandoned storefronts and pawnshops, Main Street Bistro, the brainchild of chef Tom Selman, serves comfort food items like blackened chicken and shrimp pasta salad or slow-cooked ribs all sourced from Maui ingredients. If you'd prefer more casual fare, the locally sourced sandwiches and pastries at the Wailuku Coffee Company are worth your dollars. Their coffee and espresso drinks hit the spot, especially after a hike.

On North Market, Native Intelligence sells *koa* wood bowls and instruments favored by discerning souvenir hunters. Antiques lovers might appreciate the Asian-style furnishings and kimonos at Brown Kobayashi. Those in the market for vintage aloha shirts and dashboard hula dolls straight out of the 1950s should pop into Bird of Paradise Unique Antiques.

When you catch a break in the rain, drive up 'Iao Valley Road as it weaves into the lush West Maui Mountains. This region was once considered so sacred that only

A surfer offers a shaka sign, a common greeting on the islands, to her friend.

A SECRET TREAT

For your Haleakala or Hana drive, get to the historic Home Maid Bakery's outlet between 5 and 10 a.m. (late risers can hit them up on the way back, from 4 to 10 p.m.). Score freshly baked doughnuts, crispy *manju*, shave ice, *mochi*, or fluffy taro dinner rolls that melt in your mouth.

Kepaniwai Park and Heritage Gardens

royalty could explore the mountains. Today you can strap on those hiking boots and bring along your Canon, and about 2 miles from Wailuku is Kepaniwai Park and Heritage Gardens. This free park is dedicated to Hawai'i's varied ethnic residents, with thatched *hales*, a Japanese temple, a Chinese pagoda, a Portuguese villa, as well as BBQs and picnic tables lining the stream that are very popular with locals on weekends.

The end of 'Iao Valley Road deposits you unto 'Iao Valley State Park, home to Maui's crowning beauty—'Iao Needle. Like O'ahu's Diamond Head, the trail up to see the needle is on the tour group circuit, those of the "I climbed [insert tourist destination] and survived" variety. That being said, the lush rain forest delivers a universe awash in green, with rocks jutting above the luscious stream below. There are a few trails off the parking lot. Most are mellow, and all offer spectacular photo opportunities. Though you will see locals diving off the bridge into the stream, I cannot recommend this feat. Also note that parking is free up here. Last time I visited, a guy in a very official-looking shirt was collecting a parking fee—just call me a sucker for knowing this park is free and still forking over the $5, duh!

When the beach and sun calls, take Highway 30 south to Highway 310 toward Kihei, passing the 3-mile-long Ma'alaea Beach, which spills into Kealia Beach (at the 6-mile marker of Highway 311), and then Kealia Pond National Wildlife Refuge and Boardwalk (bird-watchers will appreciate the slew of waterfowl found in this salt pond). Both beaches get very windy in the afternoons, making swimming and beachcombing unpleasant, but if you happen to be a windsurfer, these waters beg you to jump in. The best surf spot around here (especially in summer) is Ma'alaea Pipeline, located just south of the harbor.

Continue south on Highway 310 toward Kihei, a congested 7-mile stretch of condos, sunny beaches, lively restaurants and bars, and affordable hotels that is by no means off the beaten path. Traffic crawls along South Kihei Road. Besides budget hunting, many like to stay in the area for the dependable sun and the central location offering easy access to Maui's attractions. If you are fed up with Kihei's traffic, zip up to Highway 31, which stretches from Kahului/Wailuku area to the southern tip of Maui. There has been talk of connecting Kula with Kihei, but if it happens, it likely won't come to pass until my toddler is on his way to college.

Most adore Kihei for its beaches, which accommodate all levels of surfers and bodyboarders, *keikis*, lap swimmers, snorkelers, and those who just want to bronze their skin until it's crunchy. From the north, Kalepolepo Beach Park houses Humpback Whale National Marine Sanctuary headquarters, offering visitors a chance to learn about the whale-infested Pacific Ocean. Families bring the little *keikis* out to play in the protected waters of the ancient Koʻieʻie Fishpond—the lava rock walls shelter the small set from waves.

Farther south is the beloved Kalama Park, which not only provides Kihei's busiest ball fields, a beachfront playground, bathrooms, and a grassy shade area, but also is *the* place in Kihei to learn to surf. Heaps of bronzed surfers lead children and nervous-looking adults toward the toenail-sized waves that crash onto a collection of jagged rocks. Sounds fun, huh? Frankly, from one surfer to another, the crowds of people learning how to paddle out, then find a wave, stand, and crash with ease makes learning to surf here frustrating and kind of unsafe. That being said, Maui Beach Boys runs a professional lesson—my five-year-old was catching and riding waves by the time his two-hour class ended. This beach is also popular with SUP riders.

'Iao Needle

At Kaiʻau Place off South Kihei Road is Charley Young Beach. Popular with sunbathers, dog walkers, musicians, and bodyboarders, this small sandy enclave is your best chance of finding solitude in Kihei. The next set of beaches, Kamaʻole I, II, and III, are separated by rocks, but make up the most popular beaches in Kihei. Kam I, as locals call it, has a fine grassy area for picnickers and a volleyball court. Kam II beckons the masses to view the sunset. Kam III is the choice for swimming and often-murky snorkeling. All of the beaches offer services and fine bodyboarding. Kihei's last sandy area, Keawakapu Beach, stretches languidly to

Learning to surf in Kihei

Wailea. Here you can snorkel, whale-watch, swim, and watch spectacular sunsets. You can access the beach by traveling *makai* on East Lipoa Road and parking on the unpaved dirt lot.

Seems every truck parked along South Kihei Road hires kayaks, stand-up paddleboards, surfboards, and snorkel gear as well as offering some type of lesson, boat trip, or guided adventure. Shop around to find a deal to fit your budget. I've had good experiences with the following dependable folks: Big Kahuna Adventures, South Pacific Kayaks, Snorkel Bob's, and Maui Dive Shop.

If you'd like to bring a piece of Kihei home, Pi'ilani Village has a Borders Express bookshop, an ABC Store (the perfect place for those kitschy souvenirs and reasonably priced bottles of water), and a huge Safeway. To bring home a Hawaiian quilt, head over to Maui Quilt Shop at Azeka Shopping Center; this center is also home to countless boutiques. Kalama Village is a covered outdoor market where you can peruse a host of cheesy Hawaiiana, Tahitian pearls, and ukuleles.

Kihei is known as condo row, and those savvy web surfers out there can find extraordinary deals online. Most condo complexes offer individually owned units that are decorated in their own style—be it tropical chic, awash in wicker, or cluttered with doilies and kitschy antiques—and are also managed by various rental agencies. It can be exhausting just finding the right property for you. If you prefer to do your own sleuthing, www.vrbo.com has the largest collection of rental properties on the island. Always ask to see photos of the specific property before committing your dollars. Choice complexes are plentiful and include the ocean-view one-bedroom units at Punahoa, the quiet condos at Keawakapu Beach's Mana Kai Maui, and the 15-acre grounds playing host to the expansive Kamaole Sands.

Eight smallish wooden cottages dot a grassy swath of land inhabited by hammocks at Nonalani Cottages. Affordable accommodations feature cable TVs, kitchens, and enough room for a family—though quarters would be considered snug in most circles. Another option for those wanting to play house without being on Kihei's main drag is to book a studio or cottage at Hale Huanani. Tastefully decorated in Hawaiian breezy style, the spacious accommodations feature kitchenettes, flat-screen TVs, BBQs, and all the beach gear you'll need. Plus the hosts serve a decent continental breakfast daily.

If you're content without your own kitchen, you might find Maui Coast Hotel to be the best option in town. While not plush by any means, this dependable full-service hotel features friendly staff, shuttle service, Wi-Fi, a poolside restaurant with live music, and simple rooms with ACs, lanais, and local art along the walls. You can often find deals online, though most will find the resort fee unnecessarily pricey.

Finally, Two Mermaids on Maui B&B delivers fun beach-themed rooms, with blue walls and tropical décor, private baths, and comfy beds. Guests can use the BBQs and in-room guitars, enjoy breakfast by the pool, relax on the landscaped grounds, or talk story with the friendly hosts. If you looking to get hitched, Juddee performs weddings and commitment ceremonies.

While other parts of Maui boast haute cuisine and farm-to-table eateries, Kihei prides itself on its laid-back and affordable eats. From the north, the Grateful Dead–themed Stella Blues is located in a strip mall, with an effusive staff that serve hearty meals from morning until late when live music draws out the night owls. Don't miss the house-made granola and yummy French toast for early risers. Lunch and dinner can be hit or miss.

The most popular spot for breakfast is Kihei Caffe. Across the street from the beach, stand in line at this hole-in-the-wall and order at the counter. This greasy spoon specializes in huge breakfasts, favored by locals who adore the sweet treats and eggs served up on the outdoor patio.

No one will tell you about 808 Bistro, not because it's not good, but because no one wants the word to get out about this sweet spot, hidden in the back of a strip mall. Serving three meals daily, this alfresco café delivers a killer short rib potpie and a banana bread French toast that defy expectations. The same crew also run the awesome 808 Deli around the corner, which promises to satisfy the craving for creatively crafted sandwiches atop fresh bread.

Talk to enough locals and you may hear murmurings of a fish market that serves addictive *ahi poke*: Eskimo Candy Seafood Market and Deli. In addition to the *poke* bowls, you can find fried shrimp, fish tacos, and seafood chowder. Also highlighting the bounty of the sea, Koiso Sushi Bar offers creative sushi. They have only 16 seats, all of which are in demand every night, so reserve a table in advance. Another choice table for dinner is Cuatro. Enjoy spicy tuna nachos for appetizers, then get ready for fresh seafood served in a variety of styles—Mexican, Asian, Mediterranean, or Hawaiian, get it, cuatro?—and paired with fine wines. Reservations are highly recommended.

After dark, Kihei is the place to be—especially in the "Triangle"—aka Kalama Village—where it seems the entire island descends to sip libations and get their groove on. Life's a Beach is a fun bar and restaurant with live music and decent pub grub. On the newer side is the martini bar Ambrosia, which is popular with the LA crowd who dress to the nines and bob their heads to electronica, slurping up the strong cocktails from the vintage absinthe fountain. South Shore Tiki Bar draws those wanting that South Pacific atmosphere and has a small dance floor that gets packed early.

In the morning, take South Kihei Road south (it becomes Okolani Drive and then Wailea Alanui Drive). Suddenly it seems there are golf courses and haute hotels everywhere. Wailea is where the über-rich come to play, known for its four-star resorts, pricey golf courses, and upscale dining. Many might skip Wailea on their way to Makena, and though most of the businesses cater to those willing to spend $50 for an entrée, Wailea's beauty—especially her swimmable beaches—is unsurpassed.

Each major hotel houses a stunning crescent of sand that, like all beaches on the island, is open to the public. Sunsets are spectacular, and paired with fancy cocktails from an even fancier resort can make for the ideal vacation memory. Alternatively, joggers and walkers appreciate the 13-mile Wailea Beach Path that connects the beaches to one another, allowing you to beach-hop all day. Just north of Wailea Marriott Hotel is the parking area for Wailea's two most gorgeous beaches—Ulua and Mokapu. In the morning, snorkelers swim out to the coral-infested waters searching for yellow tangs and green turtles. In the afternoon, bodyboarders play in the waves and sunbathers populate the golden strands.

Between Grand Wailea and Four Seasons Resort Maui is the gorgeous Wailea Beach. Look around for celebrities on those resort chaise lounges, or just prop up those sunglasses and pretend to be famous as you chill out on one of Maui's loveliest beaches. Bring snorkel gear if you are here early enough as the reef runs south to Fairmont Kea Lani's Polo Beach, which, it is redundant to say, is also quite beautiful. After the resorts, on Makena Alanui Road you'll find Po'olenalena Beach, a choice destination for swimmers.

If you are over the beach, pro golfers rave about Wailea Golf Club, not only making it tough to score a tee time, but also helping to raise the price of a round of golf. That being said, most Hawaiian golf courses, including the three courses at Wailea Golf Club, offer twilight rates. If they are not golfing or sunbathing, the jet setters that populate Wailea take up court at Wailea Tennis Club, which boasts 11 courts, rentals, and lessons.

The high life wouldn't be so snazzy without a place to jazz up the wardrobe, and like all good resort destinations Wailea's got a doozy: The Shops at Wailea is an outdoor mall featuring high-end shops like Prada as well as local stores like Honolua Surf Company, ABC Store, and Aloha Shirt Museum and Boutique. Also in the mall is the South Shore's best coffee shop: Honolulu Coffee Company. The mall also hosts music events on Wednesday evening. In addition to shopping, you can grab a bite to eat in the mall. If you want something more than a resort buffet, Longhi's serves up the best French toast in Wailea, and also specializes in Mediterranean-style lunches and dinners like lobster cannelloni, as well as offering fine beers and cocktails to enjoy at the bar or on the patio. (FYI: There is another Longhi's in Lahaina, but it is not as dependable as this one.)

Outside of the resorts, travel to Wailea Gateway Center to Pita Paradise Wailea (there is another location in Kihei's Kalama Village). This Greek eatery specializes in hearty meats sandwiched in—you guessed it—pita, as well as freshly caught seafood (reeled in by the owner)

Dinner at Fairmont Kea Lani's Ko restaurant is not only delicious, but also beautiful.

atop salads and in those warm pockets of Middle Eastern–style dough.

A yummy addition to Wailea's dining scene is Maui celebrity chef Bev Gannon's Gannon's Restaurant and Red Bar at Wailea's Golf Club's Gold and Emerald Courses Clubhouse. It's open for three meals daily, and you don't have to dig golf to enjoy an ocean-view table along Wailea's choice greens. Items like *loco moco* with grass-fed beef and the Big Kahuna Omelette featuring *kalua* pork and Portuguese sausage delight early risers. For dinner don't miss the *miso*-glazed Kona *kampachi* or the Moroccan-spiced lamb rack.

Local celebrity Peter Merriman's Monkeypod Kitchen is a family-friendly eatery complete with lively décor, surf championships on TV, creative cocktails, outstanding beers, and fine locally harvested cuisine. Serving everything from flatbread pizzas to sashimi, heaping burgers to cheesecakes the size of my kindergartner's head, this popular eatery took the pulse of south Maui and delivered a winning remedy to Wailea's mass-produced fine-dining scene.

That being said, if you have money for a romantic oceanfront dinner, complete with *tiki* torches and fantastic service, look no farther than Wailea's resorts. Worth the splurge is Fairmont Kea Lani's Ko. Renovated in 2012, this expensive eatery backs a picturesque pool and pays tribute to the immigrants who worked in Hawai'i's sugarcane fields. Offerings include spicy tuna tempura, fern shoot salad, a gorgeous mac-nut-crusted *waloo*, and an intelligent kids' menu. Creative desserts include a fun take on shave ice and house-made gelato.

If the luxe life has your name on it, pony up your credit card and prepare to be wowed. Hands-down the most legendary resort on this side of the island is Four Seasons Maui. Besides the plush quarters catering to your every need—who doesn't need a marble soaking tub, an iPhone cleaner, or a concierge to fetch you sunscreen?—this resort boasts three pools, including an adults-only one with a swim-up bar, a lobby lounge

Body boarders gearing up at Makena Beach

with nightly Hawaiian tunes, oceanfront massage *hales*, a kids' club, and three restaurants, including the oceanfront Ferraro's Bar e Restaurant (a remarkable dining establishment that showcases meats and seafood cooked over a *kiawe* wood grill).

Fairmont Kea Lani caters to those wanting to wallow in luxury. The all-suite hotel stretches across 17 acres of tropical gardens leading to the sea. The spacious suites offer private bedrooms, lanais, and more technological amenities than you will likely need on vacation. Throw in a kids' club, an activities desk to rent water sports gear, cultural activities like canoe rides and hula lessons, a huge pool, the Spa Kea Lani's array of over 50 body treatments and facial remedies, and a staggering five restaurants. This resort might cost an arm and a leg, but you're sure to leave relaxed, refreshed, and ready to work for another 10 years to afford to return.

The stately Grand Wailea lounges across 40 acres, boasting one of Maui's largest hotels. Expect plush rooms with divine linens and private lanais, a world-class art collection, snorkeling, windsurfing and scuba instruction, and a collection of boutiques like Tiffany and Co. The six restaurants offer high-end and casual options and include the posh Humuhumunukunukuapua'a (a tribute to Hawai'i's state fish). Unwind after a long day of snorkeling with sea turtles at Spa Grande. Families appreciate the kids' club Camp Grande, teen activities like spa treatments, as well as the nine pools connected by a river (yes, grown-ups, there is an additional adults-only pool with The Grotto, a popular swim-up bar).

All the hotels offer nightly entertainment, including luʻaus should you go that route (though I don't enthusiastically recommend any on this side of the island). In addition to those listed above, Mulligan's on the Blue features live music, decent beers, and sports on the TV.

While many of us may drool at the excess studding Wailea's shores, locals bypass the upscale community and continue south to Makena—where hippies, nudists, surfers, divers, and residents come to frolic in the sea at some of Maui's best beaches. To access Makena, continue south from Wailea Alanui Drive as it becomes Makena Alanui Drive. The only real services out here are at Makena Beach and Golf Resort. Renovated in 2012, rooms offer fine views of the passing humpbacks from your private lanai, free Wi-Fi, and comfortable quarters geared toward in-the-know travelers. The hotel boasts its own 18-hole sea-to-mountain golf course, tennis courts fit for pros, the Makena Kai Day Spa, two pools, mini golf, bike rentals, yoga classes, plus snorkel and scuba lessons. The five restaurants have been fine-tuned to honor Maui's fresh produce and seafood. The hotel occupies a prime location at Maluʻuaka Beach (often called "Turtle Beach")—one of Maui's most underrated attractions—and is well worth a stop whether you are staying here or not.

Farther south, Makena State Park is divided between two areas. Big Beach will make most draw in their breaths at the spectacular views of the offshore islands, the insanely blue ocean water gulping up the white sand, and the daring feats performed by kamikaze surfers, bodyboarders, and boogie boarders braving these hefty waves. It is not safe for most of us to swim here. I have seen tough dudes battered around by these waves on so many occasions that it makes my head hurt just thinking about it. To get to Little Beach, travel north over the trail from Big Beach. This also-spectacular blend of sand and water is home to Maui's most renowned nude beach. More often than not, you'll find a couple of random BBQ, shave ice, and coconut trucks parked in the state park lot.

The more adventurous will want to continue south past Makena State Park for 3 miles through Ahini Kinaʻu Natural Area Reserve. Pass a rugged lava rock coastline, proof that Maui too was the result of lava flow—this one occurred in 1790. You'll see cars lined up on the road. Follow the paths to the sea and get ready to see some of Maui's astounding coastal snorkeling. Reef sharks, turtles, and tropical fish inhabit the coral around here.

The last stop on the road is La Perouse Bay—a former community taken down by the lava flow you just drove through. This windy point at the southern edge of Maui might

Maui Ocean Center aquarium houses a host of tropical fish and mammals.

inspire a *Titanic*-style holler or a mere gulp of fresh air as the spinner dolphins put on a show. You can hike the Kings Highway Trail from the sand at La Perouse Bay and travel over lava rock for a few miles. Alternatively, you can hitch a ride up the lava flow on a horse at Makena Stables.

When you've had your fill of the southern lip of Maui, zip north on Highway 31 for 20 miles to reach Ma'alaea. Most won't stay long in Ma'alaea. However, this elbow of land between Kihei and Lahaina houses Maui Ocean Center, an aquarium with schools of tropical fish, a stunning shark tank, and touch pools that makes *keikis* giggle. I like to score crafts, books, and toys at their store.

KAHO'OLAWE—HAWAI'I'S DESERTED ISLE

A shell of land off the western edge of Maui, Kaho'olawe wasn't always barren, but it has always been the neglected little sister of this archipelago. Maybe because of its close proximity to Maui, or maybe because ancient legend says that goddesses had a fight so massive that no one wanted to step foot on the land afterward, Kaho'olawe missed its chance at the lush tropical wonderland of its siblings and became first a penal colony, and later the site of US government bomb testing. These bombs destroyed the land. Like all good optimists, Hawaiians have begun working to reestablish a relationship with the island. And while we cannot gain entry to the island without prior authorization, it is possible to volunteer with the Kaho'olawe Island Reserve Commission (www.kahoolawe.hawaii.gov) to assist with large-scale restoration work.

TAKE A COFFEE TOUR ON MAUI'S WEST SIDE

While Kona's Big Island gets all the hoopla for growing Hawai'i's most coveted coffee beans, a little organic farm quietly awaits its day to shine. Piliani Kope Farm, the brainchild of mainlanders Greg and Susy Stille, is by nature a coffee farm, but if you ask Greg on one of his educational forays into the art and craft of sustainable farming in Hawai'i, he'll say that more than anything, he is reestablishing a relationship with the earth. The tours can be brief, or include a roasting lesson and lunch, but whatever you pay for, you'll get to sample the organic beans, hear the inspiring tales of these coffee growers' nascent beginnings, and get to trench through the 2-acre coffee field. Call 808-661-5479. Website www.pilianikopefarm.com.

Ma'alaea also acts as the departure point for snorkel and dive trips to nearby Molokini, a crescent of land just offshore. Though Molokini is now overrun with daily visitors, you can bet on spotting your share of tropical fish while poking around the reef. The eco-friendly Pacific Whale Foundation offers naturalist-led snorkel trips, and is also the guiding light in whale-watching cruises. This outfit has been educating locals and tourists about Hawai'i's aquatic life for over 30 years. From November to April humpback whales populate the waters around Maui to breed, give birth, and frolic in the warm waters. Book a morning trip for your best chance to get up close with the giant mammals. And never fear: If you are here in summer, you may still spot sperm or pilot whales (to name a few), as they travel past Hawai'i year-round. For all boat trips, reserve your space early in your visit so that you have time to reschedule should rough weather cancel your journey.

Most snorkel and whale-watching cruises offer snacks aboard the ship, but if you are starving afterward, Waterfront Restaurant's alfresco dining highlights freshly caught seafood, Caesar salads made at your table, and hunks of steak. While not snazzy, this waterfront eatery has been a choice destination for celebratory dinners since it opened over 20 years ago.

As you travel north on Highway 30, you pass Papalaua Point, which offers a good vantage point to spot passing humpbacks in winter. Continue on past Papalaua Wayside Beach Park and Ukumehame Beach Park, and around mile marker 15 is the village of Olowalu, where you *must* make time for a visit to Leoda's Kitchen and Pie Shop. As if it jumped straight out of Northern California's Wine Country, this outfit serves delectable house-made pies sourced from local farms—I'm talking coconut crème that tastes like the coconut just got cracked open—plus savory potpies, sandwiches, and salads.

At mile marker 18, travel *makai* at the stoplight to hit Launiupoko Beach Park. Many *grommets* have learned to surf here, while *keikis* play in the enclosed rock pool.

The famous Lahaina banyan tree is the focal point of the community.

Bring a sandwich from Leoda's to enjoy on a shady picnic table. For those of you who crave a less touristy Lahaina experience (you're 3 miles away physically, but this residential community feels worlds away from the bustle), book a room at **Ho'oilo House B&B**. This six-room ecologically minded inn features Balinese furnishings, private outdoor showers, a pool, and continental breakfast.

Arriving in **Lahaina** can be dizzying, to say the least. Gone are the sugarcane-covered mountains and the quiet rocky shores, and in their place is a bustling, lively town that will make some giddy and others horrified by the sheer number of activity desks lining Front and Hotel Streets; by the lines of tour boats along the shore; by the hordes, and I mean hordes, of tourists walking aimlessly past the historic buildings now populated with boutiques and kitschy souvenir shops. Lahaina's storied place in Hawaiian history reflects the nature of this community today. Ancient chiefs gathered in what was then called Lele to hold royal court. And when Kamehameha conquered most of the islands, and "unified" them, Lahaina was his capital. The missionaries that followed agreed that Lahaina's dependable sun and easy access to neighboring islands made for a great base. Whalers soon followed, favoring the boisterous watering holes—an institution still to be enjoyed in Lahaina—with sugarcane workers and then ultimately us, the tourists, on their heels.

In Lahaina, there is much to love. For every cheesy tourist trap eatery, you'll find a dining room to please the palate. For every activity in your reach from the harbor (from submarine rides to booze cruises) there's a host of thoughtful outfitters willing to guide you to experience resident humpback whales or out-of-the-way diving spots. Don't sneer too hard at Lahaina: She's just an old gal trying her best to please everyone, and not doing too bad a job.

History buffs appreciate the 1.5-mile self-guided walking tour of Lahaina's historic buildings—all of which have appropriate signage, so you know those pile of rocks have ancient significance. With time to rest and snack, plan about two hours of walking. Even if you can't be bothered with stories of the past, you cannot help but be taken with Banyan Tree Square at Front and Hotel Streets. This massive banyan lures tree climbers of all ages to marvel in the sheer abundance of her shade—over an acre! Most days you'll also find artists and musicians chilling under (or on) the branches. On the harbor side of the square, Old Lahaina Courthouse, built in 1859, houses Lahaina Art Society's gallery in the former jail, and the educational Lahaina Heritage Museum— grab a handy walking map Lahaina from the visitors center. Also off the square is the Baldwin House, constructed in 1834 by missionary Dwight Baldwin. This coral-and-stone house is the oldest Western-style building in Lahaina. Next door the Masters Reading Room was sort of a boys' club where captains kept their eyes peeled for va-grants.

Back at the square, turn right onto Front Street to find Holy Innocents' Episcopal Church. The summer home of Queen Lili'uokalani now houses an artful blend of reli-gious and Hawaiian artifacts, including an interesting Hawaiian Madonna picture. Far-ther down Front Street are the ruins of Hale Piula, the thwarted beginnings of Lahaina's royal palace—you gotta love a king who preferred to sleep in a thatched-roof hut. Behind

Lahaina's promenade

DETOUR: LAHAINALUNA SCHOOL

Just outside of town, take Lahainaluna Road *mauka* for 2 miles and find the oldest secondary school in America's western states, Lahainaluna School—now a public high school. It's notable for housing the printing press responsible for Hawai'i's first newspaper. Hale Pa'i, next door, showcases a small museum and a restored example of the primitive methods used to mass-produce newspapers and Bibles in the early 1900s.

---

the ruins is Kamehameha Iki Park, where you may see local woodcutters carving outrigger canoes, or you may spot homeless people resting. Cut through Malu'uluolele Park, a former home to a kingly burial chamber, and explore Waine'e Church and its cemetery, which is the final resting place for Queen Ke'opuolani. Peep into Hale Pa'ahao, the former jail, which looks much as it did when convicts constructed it in the mid-1800s.

Along the harbor you'll find the Library Grounds, which, as the name suggests, surround the library. The area was home to Lahaina's first taro field, the Brick Palace (a former Western-style lookout point, now no more than stones laid out to look more like a ball court than anything else), and the legendary Hauola Stone—this chair-shaped rock was once where queens gave birth to their royal offspring. Many thought this rock had healing powers. Look for it by the lava rocks just above the water. Lastly, to the south, check out the picturesque Lahaina Lighthouse.

Farther north on Front Street is Wo Hing Museum, which dates back to 1912 and presents Chinese cultural artifacts, including a dancing lion costume, plenty of photos of old Lahaina, and a shrine. There's a cookhouse out back and a theater. Continue north to Lahaina Center, and in the mall parking lot you'll find Hale Kahiko, a replica of a traditional Hawaiian village complete with thatched huts.

Lahaina beaches aren't the best for swimming and are packed with boats heading out to explore the underwater world. Outfitters offer every tour or water sports adventure you can dream of, so those of you on a budget should shop around. My favorites include Trilogy Ex-

FERRIES TO MOLOKA'I AND LANA'I

If you'd like to travel to Moloka'i or Lanai via ferry, book your ticket in advance. Expeditions Ferry shuttles travelers for 90 minutes on the rough waters to Lana'i. To travel to Moloka'i, *Moloka'i Princess* leaves one or two times daily. Both rides are very rough and not recommended for those with queasy stomachs. For more on this, see chapters 5 and 6.

cursions (for snorkel trips to Lana'i). Diver friends recommend Extended Horizon Scuba's eco-friendly tours to pretty much every worthy spot between Maui and Lana'i's famed Cathedrals. Reefdancer is a half-submerged glass-bottomed boat ideal for those too timid or too young to snorkel; Atlantis Submarine submerges tentative swimmers deep underwater in a safe environment.

Just north of Kamehameha Iki Park, Lahaina Breakwall offers gentle waves. Surf schools populate the waters here—most promising that you'll stand and ride a wave after two hours, or you'll get your money back. Splurge for private instruction for the best bang for your buck. Most of the instructors are quite good. I've heard that Nancy Emerson's School of Surfing and Goofy Foot Surf School produce plenty of new surfers.

If you are hunting for souvenirs, Lahaina is ground zero for everything from worldly art to grass skirts. Peruse the boutiques at the Cannery Mall; the Lahaina outpost of Maui Hands delivers Hawaiian crafts; alternatively, Hale Zen Home Décor and More will have you redecorating your house with their Balinese interiors.

For a decent breakfast, Sunrise Café might be a hole-in-the-wall, but it sure pleases those looking for French toast paired with Portuguese sausage or *kalua* pork. The food takes forever to come out, so if you are really hungry, go elsewhere. The beachfront Betty's Beach Café is pricey—you're paying for those views, my friend—but satisfies with scrambles, waffles, and a cuppa joe. If you pop in at dinnertime, a local's dirty little secret is that you can watch *Feast at Lele* from your table.

On weekends, brunch at Mala Ocean Tavern is a wise choice for fresh seafood, *loco moco*, and fluffy pancakes. Later in the day, this oceanfront restaurant, owned by Mark and Judy Ellman, features gorgeous presentations of mac and cheese with mushrooms and Maytag blue cheese, as well as the Balinese-spiced locally caught fish atop organic brown rice. Those on a budget appreciate the *tiki*-torch-lit happy hour's selection of cocktails, *ahi* burgers, and Mark's legendary Caesar salad. They also operate Mala Wailea and Honu Seafood and Pizza.

Ask around, and many will say if you have one meal to eat in Lahaina, you should head to Aloha Mixed Plate's shaded patio with views of the sea. You can't beat the coconut prawns, the teriyaki chicken, or the *kalua* pork; nor should you pass up the macaroni salad. Cocktails are abundant and enliven the joint, especially during happy hour or when Old Lahaina Lu'au's music starts up next door and the prices are halved.

Chef James McDonald's fingerprint is cemented on the Hawai'i food scene, with four restaurants and more on the way, plus his own farm (O'o Farms; see chapter 8). His west side dynasty makes it reasonable—and necessary—to experience at least one of his eateries. The family-friendly Pacific'O offers a tempting O'o Salad, sourced from his Upcountry farm, the leaning tower of tofu, and the banana pineapple *lumpia*. The more upscale, almost urban experience, complete with waterfront seating, a risotto bar featuring

---

FAB FESTIVALS IN LAHAINA

Lahaina loves a party, from its Friday Art Night, complete with live music and craftspeople selling their wares, to the lively Fourth of July and Halloween festivities. Don't miss March's Ocean Arts Festival, when a whole weekend is devoted to music, whales, art, and food. In late April, locals throw a raucous banyan tree birthday for an entire weekend. No matter where you are for King Kamehameha Day, there's a party—well, Lahaina's June party is like no other. Expect a parade, food, and plenty of fun.

---

locally caught seafood, O'o Farm beets, grass-fed beef lounging on top of the perfectly prepared rice, a soup that will keep you reminiscing long after you return home, and a dessert menu that will make you rekindle your love affair with chocolate, I'o Restaurant is a prime choice for a romantic dinner. McDonald also presides over the *Feast at Lele*, a three-hour dinner show fronting the sea that tells the story of Pacific Islanders and their relationship to Hawai'i. For all three dining experiences, make a reservation far in advance.

Lahaina Grill is dinnertime institution in Maui. Pricey and loud, with intuitive and friendly servers, you'll feel like you've found the most happening place on the island. New American–style dinners feature favorites like cake walk (a collection of seafood cakes), filet mignon, *opakapaka* with risotto, and luscious desserts like the triple berry pie. Bring your credit card—this one will cost you a bundle. Reservations highly recommended.

Above all the fancy meals I've had in Lahaina, if I had one meal to eat in all of Maui County, I'd head up into an industrial park and wait in the hot parking lot for a coveted table at Star Noodle. The brainchild of chef Sheldon Simeon, this funky, friendly Asian eatery promises house-pulled noodles in a host of broths, steamed buns, *miso* salmon, *hapa* ramen, and fried *saimin*, to name a few. Trust the servers and get whatever they instruct you to order.

Those with a sweet tooth will appreciate Ululani's Hawaiian Shave Ice's sweet cold treats. Another worthy stop is Ono Gelato Company for locally made gelato. As for your caffeine fix, while there are a number of coffee shops in Lahaina, I'm always left wanting that perfectly crafted caffeine fix. You are better off heading up to MauiGrown Coffee, or Piliani Kope, grabbing a bag of freshly roasted beans and making your own brew at your hotel or condo.

After dark, when the upscale crowd wants to dance, they head to Timba, above Pacific'O, to lounge with a cocktail as the ocean breezes by, groove to electronica, and be seen by the beautiful people of Lahaina. Another fun destination, especially for sports fans and

Ka'anapali Beach is a prime wedding location.

those wanting to find some fun live music, is Lulu's Lahaina Surf Club and Grill; while the food won't register on the Richter scale for anything special, the lively atmosphere packs a punch. I am not the biggest fan of the food at Lahaina Coolers, but this lively bar packs them in late at night.

If you opt for one lu'au in all of Hawai'i, don't miss Old Lahaina Lu'au. Book over a month in advance for this feast of the senses, with fantastic music, live hula, a glorious collection of Hawaiian cuisine ranging from *kalua* pork to *poke*, and the ideal dash of aloha needed to ensure you leave the lu'au just a bit tipsy and enthusiastic. Another fun night out is 'Ulalena. Occupying the Maui Theater, this energetic show tells the history of Hawai'i through acrobatics, music, and wild costumes.

The hotel options in Lahaina are surprisingly slim. On the north side of Banyan Tree

Square is Best Western Pioneer Inn, once *the* place to stay in town and a historic building worth a peek. Today this harborfront hotel offers whaling-themed rooms, an on-site Grill and Bar restaurant, and a prime address in the heart of West Maui's nightlife. There's a pool, and parking is nearby.

If you're searching for a romantic place to stay, book one of the 19 rooms at Plantation Inn. This property features modern amenities like flat-panel TVs alongside Victorian furniture and Hawaiian quilts. The on-site Gerard's Restaurant offers guests a gourmet poolside breakfasts like croque monsieur and French toast. Feel like the inner circle as the tourists from the beach descend on the restaurant for romantically lit French dinners boasting chilled cucumber soup with Surfing Goat Dairy cheese, or a heavenly duck confit. Guests of the hotel also receive access to the oceanfront Ka'anapali Beach Hotel's services.

It's hard not to appreciate the humble Lahaina Inn. Built in 1938, the 12 small rooms promise dark wooden antique beds, Hawaiian art, lanais, and reasonably priced rooms (by Hawai'i standards). The hotel sits atop Lahaina Grill, but never fear—it's not too loud. Splurge for a suite, for a bit more extra room. Guests have access to the services at Royal Lahaina Resort, which, despite the name, is on Ka'anapali Beach. Just north of Lahaina, Guest House B&B offers tropical-themed rooms with private hot tubs, lanais, and flat-panel TVs, plus a pool, complimentary beach gear, and friendly hosts. Travelers who want to be close to the sea, though, should look elsewhere.

If you have a penchant for sandy beaches, travel north on Highway 30. Two miles from town is Wahikuli Wayside Park, fine for snorkeling in the morning, but not worth lingering for long. Just before you hit Ka'anapali, Hanaka'o'o Beach Park appears, stretching out her golden sands and fine swimming opportunities. With a lifeguard, full services, and abundant sand, this beach pleases families, surfers, snorkelers, sunbathers, and swimmers.

And then, with a blink, you've arrived in the famous Ka'anapali Beach resort area. By no means a hidden gem, this community boasts five luxury hotels, six condo complexes, overpriced eating and shopping, and one of Hawai'i's most user-friendly beaches.

This is where you'll be swallowed up by that vacation spirit, complete with *mai tais* on lanais as the sun sets over the sea, and local guitarists strumming their evening serenades, endless days of sun, and spending lots of your dollars.

The 3-mile Ka'anapali Beach is about showing off your tan, your boogie boarding skills, and your surf abilities.

Lahaina's oldest hotel, Pioneer Inn

Rain brings rainbows.

Snorkelers who are strong swimmers should trek out to the turtle-infested waters just beyond Black Rock. In addition to Lahaina's water sports outfitters (many of which have desks in the area as well), in Ka'anapali you can arrange almost any activity from zip-lining to hiking, coffee roasting to parasailing, through the major hotels.

If you are passing through the area for the day, all roads seem to lead to Whalers Village, with 50 shops, a museum, plenty of restaurants, and many of the outfitters hawking activities. Start with a visit to Whalers Village Museum. This informative museum documents the whaling history of the region with photos and artifacts. On the way out, you may look at the full-sized sperm whale skeleton at the entrance of the mall with new interest. Favorites include Honolua Surf Company, the enchanting toys at Maui Toy Works, the beach-themed gifts at Sand People, and the maps and prints at Lahaina Printsellers.

On the beach side of the mall, you'll find two lively (albeit overpriced) dining options. My first choice is Hula Grill. It's all you'd expect from a resort-style eatery—a barefoot bar, fantastic cocktails, live music in the afternoons, and deliciously sweet seafood. The other prime oceanfront choice is Leilani's on the Beach. Downstairs is the casual bar and grill serving burgers and salads, while upstairs relies on its spectacular sunset views to lure in those with cash to spend on hunks of steak and seafood fit for *ali'i*. For my money, I prefer happy hour, paired with live music and *pupus*. There's a food court in the mall with Chinese food, pizza, and frozen yogurt that always leaves me wanting, as well as another high-end eatery that seems to keep changing hands.

Closer to Highway 30, CJ's Deli and Diner serves a fine burger in a simple dining room just off the golf course. You can also score sandwiches packed with deli meats shipped from New York. While I find their menu ambitious—eggplant Parmesan, chicken long rice, Danish meatballs—the more traditional stabs at comfort food are well prepared. Grab a Hana Box Lunch for the drive for those early outings.

'Aina Gourmet Market lures foodies to the outskirts of Ka'anapali.

For those of you who have an affinity for chain resorts, there's a Hyatt Regency Maui Resort and Spa at the southern edge of the beach, with a lovely spa, pools, a couple of decent restaurants—Japengo and Sonz Maui at Swan Court—aging rooms with views of the ocean, and the fun Drums of the Pacific Lu'au. Another dependable brand is the 23-acre Sheraton Maui at Pu'u Keka'a (or Black Rock). Even if you don't stay in this sprawling property, you'll want to check out the daring (though some might call them stupid) divers who leap off Black Rock, a lava rock that so magnificently juts up from the seafloor. The Spa of Black Rock is a great place to get those swimmer's muscles turned to Jell-O.

The most interesting property on this stretch of sand is Ka'anapali Beach Hotel. Sure, rooms are in need of some TLC, but the grassy grounds dotted with pools, lounge chairs, shade, and artifacts from Hawai'i's past make up for what you lose in splashy interiors. Plus, Maui's most Hawaiian hotel also provides plenty of cultural activities, three restaurants, an outdoor *tiki* lounge, nightly hula shows, and a spa.

A host of condo complexes offer luxury at all costs, plenty of space for those looking to stay awhile, pools, and fully equipped kitchens. It's hard not to be pleased with the newish one-bedroom condos at Ka'anapali Ali'i, which are quite spacious and provide upscale amenities like high-thread-count sheets and views of the coast. The venerable The Whaler at Ka'anapali has been offering lovely condos and hotel rooms in twin towers since this resort area began booming.

If Ka'anapali is a nice place to visit, but you'd prefer to stay by a more low-key beach, continue north for 0.5 mile on Highway 30 and turn left onto Lower Honoapi'ilani Road to find Honua Kai Resort. With a green pedigree, the spacious suites provide gourmet kitchen appliances and private lanais. Throw in a large infinity pool surrounded by rocks and palms, a gorgeous beach, and a kids' club that will make parents want to sign up for themselves. The hotel houses one of the most exciting new eateries to arrive on Maui in a long time: 'Aina Gourmet Market, another offering from chef James McDonald's crew of devotees. While it's ridiculously overpriced, urbanites will feel at home with the selection of organic wines, healthy snacks, lovingly crafted smoothies, sandwiches and salads, and gourmet coffee all sourced from within 100 miles of the market. The hotel's other restaurant, Duke's Beach House, is one of those Hawai'i mainstays for seafood, yummy burgers, and salads, plus it's one of the best beachfront bars on Maui.

Continuing north on Lower Honoapi'ilani Road, the area morphs into the funky Honokowai, which is rich with low-rise (and affordable by comparison with its affluent neighbors) condo complexes and reasonably priced eateries. The heart of the community is Honokowai Beach Park, a grassy field with a playground and picnic area. Unfortunately the waters are not ideal for swimming.

Most Ka'anapali resort dwellers bypass the restaurants in this funky area. Don't make that mistake. Breakfasts are legendary at the art-filled Java Jazz & Soup Nutz, where pancakes reign supreme and the coffee is piping hot. Lunches and dinners feature salads and grilled meats. Those wanting a quick bite will appreciate Fish Market Maui for *poke*, seafood sandwiches, *ahi* burgers, and sushi. You can also purchase fresh-caught fish to grill at your condo. Honokowai Okazuya is an expensive (cash only) take-out joint that serves Korean, Hawaiian, Japanese, Italian…the list goes on. Why all the hype? Order the lemon caper *ono* plate lunch and see for yourself. Lastly, for those wanting an organic quick hot lunch, or smoothies packed with sweet fruit, Farmers Market

Napili Bay is so alluring, you'll never want to leave.

Deli has your number—they also sell groceries, though the prices will make you a little queasy. On Monday, Wednesday, and Friday morning, there's a small farmers' market out front.

You won't see any signs advertising your entry into Kahana, save the gazillion-dollar homes lining the beach. Though this exclusive neighborhood doesn't offer much for tourists, the industrial Maui Brewing Company is home to a scrumptious coconut porter. This spacious ode to hops and *grindz* packs 'em in day and night for eco-friendly pub grub like nachos and burgers. If you'd rather enjoy a coffee, a small treat, or a grab-and-go breakfast or lunch, head to Hawaiian Village Coffee.

Farther north, you won't find a beach more idyllic than Napili Bay: a crescent of heaven, with a sandy bottom and a glassy turquoise sea ideal for snorkeling, swimming, and stand-up paddle boarding. While heaps of condos snuggle up to this shell of a beach, crowding the sand and sea with tourists, it is impossible not to fall in love with this picturesque bay. Maybe seven days a year does the bay see waves; at all other times, you can float in the warm waters with the angelfish. There's an activities center in Napili Kai Beach Resort, renting all sorts of gear, as well as selling fun beach snacks like popcorn and smoothies. If you're feeling industrious, though, you might want to look in the lost-and-found; often people leave behind the beach toys they purchase, and you may find a raft or ball sitting around.

Speaking of Napili Kai Resort, this newly renovated mainstay on this bay hands a dash of luxury to travelers wanting to stay in A-framed Polynesian-style rooms, no taller than a palm tree, spread across 11 acres. This is the Hawai'i you dream about: Family-friendly condos feature gourmet kitchens, Polynesian interiors, and giant windows framing the sea. Throw in four pools, a putting green, Wi-Fi in the lobby, and cultural activities daily, and you see why the masses sojourn return here annually.

The resort's oceanfront Sea House Restaurant is known for its creative presentations of locally sourced cuisine. Breakfasts offer specialties like the crater pancakes and the Moloka'i sweet potato frittata, while lunch and dinner feature the fresh catch bathed in mac nuts or atop a rich salad of *edamame*, brown rice, and papaya. A wall of plants on one side and a wall of windows facing Napili Bay make this an attractive choice for romance, while the outdoor seating (with $30 early-bird specials as well as *pupu* specials in the afternoon) make a reasonable option for families.

Though most units in the area offer kitchens, you may want a break from slaving over the stove. At the pool in Napili Shores, you'll find Gazebo Restaurant—literally a gazebo perched atop Napili Bay's "Turtle Town." The lines are epic, so go before you are starving. The aloha served up in this greasy spoon, the convivial atmosphere in the lines, and the pancakes are worth the wait. Up in Napili Plaza you'll find Maui Tacos, The Coffee Store, and Baan Thai restaurant. You'll also find Napili Market, which offers most of the goods you'll need to stock your condo, but more appealing is the tantalizing *poke* bar. In the complex is a **Boss Frog's Dive and Surf Shop** for rentals and take-home gear.

And then you reach **Kapalua**, by some accounts Maui's most luxurious destination, known for postcard-worthy beaches, the island's best diving, snorkeling, and world-class golf. Though it all seems like a manicured festival up here, this region features a handful of underrated destinations well worth exploring.

The prime attraction up here is the beach. Starting from the south is the sister bay to Napili, **Kapalua Beach**: a haven for snorkelers, sunbathers, and swimmers wanting a less crowded experience. Families populate the mellow waters, which rarely see waves. To get here from the parking lot of Napili Kai Beach Resort, take the stairs on the far right side through the tunnel to the beach. The beach's most amazing attribute might be **Merriman's Kapalua**, an oceanfront eatery offering upscale romantic dinners showcasing Maui produce. I recommend heading here for happy-hour sunset cocktails.

Honolua Bay is one of Maui's most pristine snorkel areas.

From Kapalua Beach, walk the Coastal Trail for just less than 2 miles to access Oneloa Beach, a 0.5-mile stretch of white sand with pretty mellow swimming in summer, but crazy riptides in winter that will likely keep you out of the sea. This beach can also be accessed from Ironwood Lane next to Kapalua Bay Golf Course—though the lot gets packed, so go early. As you continue on the Coastal Trail, you'll pass nesting birds and ancient burial grounds to reach Dragon's Teeth: lava rock spikes jutting up from Makaluaopuna Point. Be careful in this sacred spot; the rocks are slippery and should not be climbed. By car, you can reach the point from the end of Lower Honoapi'ilani Road. You'll have to walk about 10 minutes from the golf course. The Coastal Trail ends at D. T. Fleming Beach Park, one of those beaches that you imagine when thinking of Hawai'i: a shady collection of ironwood trees, with local painters re-creating the waves crashing against the white sand. To access this beach by car, find mile marker 31 and travel *makai*.

Just north of mile marker 32 there is a small parking area and stairs that lead to Slaughterhouse Beach. If the name itself doesn't frighten you away, this bay, along with its sibling Honolua Bay, make up the Honolua Makulei'a Bay Marine Life Conservation District and boast some of the best snorkeling and surfing in Maui. Slaughterhouse Beach offers fine swimming, bodyboarding, and snorkeling; from the parking area, you can often see spinner dolphins playing in the waves. Half a mile past mile marker 32 is small parking area with access to Honolua Bay. Most often you'll arrive here via a snorkel or dive boat, like those of Kapalua Dive Company. If you are driving, however, know that Honolua Bay is one of the top surf spots in the world. In winter, the waves are massive and parking is nearly impossible. Plus, locals get very territorial here. In summer, snorkeling is impressive, though you'll have to battle a rocky shore to get into those abundant waters. If nothing else, the views of the bay from above are breathtaking. You may even notice schools of fish dancing below.

After all that hiking and golfing and beachcombing and snorkeling, you are sure to be hungry. It's hard to top Honolua Store. Not really because the food is astounding, but rather because there is something quite attractive about this gourmet market, with hot and cold food selections, in a historic plantation house with seating on the wraparound porch. The Hawai'i chain Sansai Seafood Restaurant and Sushi Bar requires you to secure a reservation well in advance for dinners. The creative rolls, teriyaki, and sake draw resort dwellers. I have a soft spot for their crab ramen. If you are a slacker about reservations like me, you can line up for a seat at the sushi bar—but get here early or you'll be waiting for ages.

Kapalua offers two types of accommodations. Kapalua Villas decorate the golf greens, becoming impossible to get during January's PGA Tour, and offer 600 spacious one- to three-bedroom condos ideal for families. However, the real destination up here is Ritz Carlton Kapalua. The tropical-themed rooms offer enviable marble tubs and down comforters. The resort features its share of restaurants (there are six!), a pool, a glorious beach, a spa, tennis courts, and access to the golf courses that surround the property. While you are splurging, it's worth upgrading to an ocean-view club-level room, where you get plenty of extra perks for your buck. Families love Jean-Michel Cousteau's Ambassadors of the Environment program, which leads *keikis* into nature, as well as offering guided hikes and whale-watching cruises for grown-ups. As with most resort restaurants, eating is expensive.

Beyond Kapalua is Kahekili Highway—though it's not a highway by any stretch of the imagination, more like a strip of one-lane paved road framed by rock on one side and sheer cliff drops on the other. If you are like me, this 20-mile road from Kapalua to Wailuku is a white-knuckle journey that promises to inspire poetry at the stupendous beauty around every heart-pounding curve. I cannot recommend you brave this road if you like driving fast, or if it has been raining. The slower you go, the more you'll find to adore. Most sections require you to slow to a meager 5 miles an hour to make those blind curves, and if you happen upon another car, one of you, most likely *you*, will be taking this road in reverse until you come upon a turnout. It's treacherous, and terrifying, and worth every second of the two hours. Furthermore, when you get out of the car to explore the various sights along the road, be very careful: Many spots open out to a cliff with a deathly drop below. The drive is most picturesque and safe from Kapalua to Wailuku. Remember as you turn those blind corners to honk your horn to communicate to oncoming traffic that you are on the way.

At mile marker 34 is Punalau Beach, not recommended for swimming, but the tree-lined sandy shore is a nice place for some peace and quiet. Farther along at mile marker 38, Nakalele Point is home to a light station, arches, a rocky coastline, and Nakalele Blowhole. There's a labyrinth on the cliff, and views of the passing whales are tough to top.

Around mile marker 42, the markers switch and it becomes mile marker 16—don't ask why, just go with it. Just before mile marker 16 are the ocean baths, which you may hear brave folks talking about bathing in as the rough surf pounds the lava rock all around. While a great story to tell your grandkids, I cannot recommend that you get in the waters here without a local guide who knows the moods of the tides and waves. It can be slippery—even worse, the waves can carry you out of your chilled-out bath and into the rough seas beyond. While up here check out Pohaku Kani, a bellstone with ancient ceremonious significance that today is nothing more than rock that sometimes makes a bell sound.

It's impossible to miss Kakakuloa Head, a volcanic rock that reaches high over the sea, and sight of the spectacular cliff diving escapades of ancients—don't try it, it's totally not safe. From your perch as you curve around a bend, you'll spot Kakakuloa village below. This isolated town doesn't offer services other than a few stands geared toward the tourists who traipse through town on the way to Wailuku. You'll find a shave ice stand here, and Julia's—a green shack hawking some of the finest banana bread in Hawai'i.

Beyond Kakakuloa at mile marker 14 is Kaukini Gallery, showcasing local artists—over 100 of them! At mile marker 10 is Turnbull Studios and Sculpture Garden, another lovely window into Maui's impact on local artists. At mile marker 7 is Mendes Ranch, an outfitter willing to guide you and your clan on two-hour horseback rides through the dense forest. If you'd prefer to do the walking, take the Waihe'e Ridge Trail, a 5-mile journey through the trees, with views of the coast. To access the trail, from mile marker 7, travel *mauka* until you see the NA ALA HELE sign. Join native birds in exploring the trees that blanket the West Maui Mountains. After your hike, you'll be deposited back into Wailuku and can use chapter 8 to explore the Hana Highway and Upcountry.

IN THE AREA

ACCOMMODATIONS

Best Western Pioneer Inn, 658 Wharf St., Lahaina. Centrally located historic hotel with a mediocre restaurant. Call 808-661-3636. Website www.pioneerinn-maui.com.

Fairmont Kea Lani, 4100 Wailea Alanui Dr., Wailea. Luxurious oceanfront suites with a world-class spa, restaurants, a pool, and golf course. Call 808-875-4100. Website www.fairmont.com/kea-lani-maui.

Four Seasons Resort Maui, 3900 Wailea Alanui Dr., Wailea. Five-star resort popular with A-listers that provides luxury at every turn. Call 808-874-8000. Website www.fourseasons.com/maui.

Grand Wailea, 3850 Wailea Alanui Dr., Wailea. An exquisite Waldorf Astoria resort. Call 808-875-1234. Website www.grandwailea.com.

Guest House B&B, 1620 Ainakea Rd., Lahaina. Tropical rooms between Lahaina and Ka'anapali Beach feature breakfast, friendly hosts, a pool, and mini fridges. Call 808-661-8085. Website www.mauiguesthouse.com.

Hale Huanani Bed and Breakfast, 808 Kupulau Dr., Kihei. These two studios and a cottage include breakfast, BBQs, and friendly hosts who seem to have thought of everything. Call 877-423-6284. Website www.halehuananibandb.com.

Honua Kai Resort and Spa, 130 Kai Malina Pkwy., Ka'anapali. A green condo complex with full-service kitchens, an infinity pool, two restaurants, and luxurious amenities. Call 808-662-2800. Website www.honuakai.com.

Ho'oilo House B&B, 138 Awaiku St., Lahaina. Upscale B&B catering to discerning travelers with a pool, outdoor showers, gorgeous breakfast spreads, and an eco-friendly atmosphere. Call 808-667-6669. Website www.hooilohouse.com.

Hyatt Regency Maui Resort and Spa, 200 Nohea Kai Dr., Lahaina. Beachfront resort with beautiful grounds, a host of restaurants, a spa, and a lu'au. Call 808-661-1234. Website www.hyattregencymaui.com.

Ka'anapali Ali'i, 50 Nohea Kai Dr., Lahaina. Condo complex in the heart of Ka'anapali Beach. Call 866-664-6410. Website www.kaanapalialii.com.

Kahana Village, 4531 Lower Honoapi'ilani Rd., Lahaina. Two- and three-bedroom oceanfront condos in luxe Kahana. Call 808-669-5111. Website www.kahanavillage.com.

Kamaole Sands, 2695 S. Kihei Rd., Kihei. Condos with full kitchens and a great location in Kihei. Call 808-874-8700. Website www.kamaolesands.com.

Kapalua Villas, 500 Office Rd., Lahaina. Condos include kitchens and lanais with ocean views along the golf course. Call 808-667-4204. Website www.kapaluavillasmaui.com.

Lahaina Inn, 127 Lahainaluna Rd., Lahaina. Plantation-style rooms offer extra space with rocking chairs on the lanais. Call 808-661-0577. Website www.lahaina inn.com.

Makena Beach and Golf Resort, 5400 Makena Alanui, Wailea-Makena. Secluded beachfront resort with a spa, golf, and restaurants on a turtle-infested beach. Call 808-874-1111. Website www.makenaresortmaui.com.

Mana Kai Maui, 2960 S. Kihei Rd., Kihei. One- and two-bedroom oceanfront condos and hotel-style units in Kihei. Call 808-879-1561. Website www.manakaimaui.com.

Maui Coast Hotel, 2259 S. Kihei Rd., Kihei. Centrally located hotel in the heart of Kihei. The main full-service option in town offers a restaurant, pool, concierge, airport shuttle, and business center. Call 808-874-6284. Website www.mauicoasthotel.com.

Napili Kai Beach Resort, 5900 Lower Honoapi'ilani Rd., Lahaina. Full-service resort on Napili Bay, with a restaurant, cultural activities, and one-bedroom condos with kitchens. Call 808-669-6271. Website www.napilikai.com.

Nonalani Cottages, 455 S. Kihei Rd., Kihei. Cozy cottages with bay or garden views in the center of Kihei. Call 808-879-2497. Website www.nonalani cottages.com.

Old Wailuku Inn at Ulupono, 2199 Kahookele St., Wailuku. A historic Wailuku bed & breakfast boasting yummy breakfasts and landscaped grounds. Call 808-244-5897. Website www.mauiinn.com.

Plantation Inn, 174 Lahainaluna Rd., Lahaina. A tranquil inn catering to romance seekers, with an upscale restaurant and pool. Call 808-667-9225. Website www.theplantationinn.com.

Punahoa, 2142 Iliili Rd., Kihei. Beachfront condos in Kihei with small kitchens. Call 800-564-4380. Website www.punahoabeach.com.

Ritz Carlton Kapalua, 1 Ritz Carlton Dr., Kapalua. It doesn't get more posh than this upscale golf resort on the northwest tip of Maui. Call 808-669-6200. Website www.ritzcarlton.com.

Sheraton Maui Resort and Spa, 2605 Ka'anapali Pkwy., Ka'anapali. Sprawling oceanfront resort with pools, restaurants, a spa, and a fitness center. Call 808-661-0031. Website www.sheraton-maui.com.

The Whaler at Ka'anapali, 2481 Ka'anapali Pkwy., Lahaina. Old-school condo complex in Ka'anapali caters to repeat visitors. Call 808-661-6000. Website www.whalerkaanapali.com.

Two Mermaids on Maui B&B, 2840 Umalu Pl., Kihei. South Maui's nicest B&B turns on the charm with tropical décor and friendly hosts. Three-night minimum. Breakfast included. Call 808-874-8687. Website www.twomermaids.com.

ATTRACTIONS AND RECREATION

Aloha Shirt Museum and Boutique, 3750 Wailea Alanui Dr., Kihei. As the name suggests, this is a dependable destination to purchase an aloha shirt. Call 808-875-1308. Website www.the-aloha-shirt-museum.com.

Atlantis Submarines, 658 Wharf St., Lahaina. Dive beneath the sea in a submarine. Call 808-667-2224. Website www.atlantisadventures.com/maui.

Bailey House Museum, 2375A Main St., Wailuku. Plenty of artifacts to inspire the historian in the clan. Closed Sunday. Call 808-244-3326. Website www.maui museum.org.

Baldwin House, 120 Dickenson St., Lahaina. Tour this 1834 missionary abode daily 10–4. Call 808-661-3262. Website www.lahainarestoration.org.

Big Kahuna Adventures, 1913 S. Kihei Rd., Kihei. Surf lessons and kayak tours. Call 808-875-6395. Website www.big kahunaadventures.com.

Bird of Paradise Unique Antiques, 56 N. Market St., Wailuku. Kitschy and vintage finds in this cluttered shop. Call 808-242-7699.

Brown Kobayashi, 38 N. Market St., Wailuku. Asian antiques are on display, and go for hundreds of dollars. Call 808-242-0804.

Cannery Mall, 1221 Honoapi'ilani Hwy., Lahaina. Call 808-661-5304. Website www.lahainacannery.com.

Extended Horizons Scuba, 94 Kupuohi St., #A1, Lahaina. Scuba charter boats to Lana'i's and Maui's best dive sites. Call 808-667-0611. Website www.extendedhorizons.com.

Goofy Foot Surf School, 505 Front St., #123, Lahaina. Board rentals and lessons. Call 808-244-9283. Website www.goofyfootsurfschool.com.

Hale Kahiko, 900 Front St., Lahaina. A replica ancient Hawaiian village. Call 808-667-9216.

Hale Pa'ahao Prison, 187 Prison St., Lahaina. This is where the leaders sent those rowdy whalers when they'd gone too far. Call 808-667-1985. Website www.lahainarestoration.org.

Hale Zen Home Décor and More, 180 Dickenson St., Lahaina. Lovely home décor with a Balinese influence. Call 808-661-4802. Website www.halezen.com.

Holy Innocents' Episcopal Church, 561 Front St., Lahaina. A 1927 open-air house of worship. Call 808-661-4202. Website www.holyimaui.org.

Humpback Whale National Marine Sanctuary, 726 S. Kihei Rd., Kihei. Learn about these migratory visitors that populate the waters just beyond the coast. Call 808-879-2818.

'Iao Theater, 68 N. Market St., Wailuku. Historic art deco theater hosts events in the evenings. Website www.mauion stage.com.

Ka'ahumanu Church, 103 S. High St., Wailuku. A historic church in the heart of Wailuku. Call 808-244-5189.

Kapalua Bay Golf Course, 2000 Plantation Club Dr., Kapalua. Call 877-527-2582. Website www.golfatkapalua.com.

Kapalua Dive Company, 1 Bay Dr., Lahaina. Offers snorkel and dive trips to the area's best locations. Call 808-669-3448. Website www.kapaluadive.com.

Kaukini Gallery, mile marker 14, Kahekili Hwy., Wailuku. Local art along the Kahekili Highway. Call 808-244-3371. Website www.kaukinigallery.com.

Lahaina Art Society's Gallery, 648 Wharf St., #103, Lahaina. Gorgeous contributions to the art world. Call 808-661-0111. Website www.lahaina-arts.com /galleries.

Lahaina Heritage Museum, 648 Wharf St., Lahaina. A simple museum showcasing the history of Lahaina. Call 808-661-3262. Website www.lahaina restoration.org.

Makena Stables, 8299 Makena Rd., Kihei. Horseback rides from La Perouse Bay up along the mountains, with great views of the ocean. Call 808-879-0244. Website www.makenastables.com.

Maui Arts and Cultural Center, 1 Cameron Way, Kahului. Maui's cultural hot spot. Call 808-242-2787. Website www.mauiarts.org.

Maui Beach Boys. Surf lessons by masters. Call 808-283-7114. Website www.mauibeachboys.com.

Maui Dive Shop, Kamaole Shopping Center, 2463 S. Kihei Rd., #A-15, Kihei. Leads tours, charters, and lessons to explore Molokini and beyond. Call 808-879-1533. Website www.mauidiveshop.com.

Maui Hands, 612 Front St., Lahaina. Local crafts and artwork. Call 808-667-9898. Website www.mauihands.com.

Maui Nui Botanical Gardens, 150 Kanaloa Ave., Kahului. A free tropical garden highlighting native plants. Call 808-249-2798. Website www.mnbg.org.

Maui Ocean Center, 192 Maalaea Rd., Maalaea. One of the state's best aquariums features sharks, rays, tropical fish, and touch pools. Call 808-270-7000. Website www.mauioceancenter.com.

Maui Quilt Shop at Azeka Shopping Center, 1280 S. Kihei Rd., Kihei. An array of quilts for sale. Call 808-874-8050. Website www.mauiquiltshop.com.

Maui Swap Meet, 310 W. Ka'ahumanu Ave., Kahului. *The* place to score cheap souvenirs and tropical produce. Call 808-244-3100. Website www.maui exposition.com.

Mendes Ranch, 3530 Kahekili Hwy., Wailuku. Horseback rides through the tropical jungles above Wailuku. Call 808-244-7320. Website www.mendesranch.com.

Nancy Emerson's School of Surfing, 505 Front St., #201, Lahaina. Stand on a board, or get your money back. Call 808-244-7873. Website www.mauisurfclinics.com.

Native Intelligence, 1980 Main St., #2, Wailuku. Great boutique for lady's apparel. Call 808-249-2421. Website www.native-intel.com.

Pacific Whale Foundation, 300 Maalaea Boat Harbor Rd., Wailuku. Maui's best snorkel and whale-watching trips. Call 808-249-8811. Website www.pacificwhale.org.

Pi'ilani Village, 225 Piikea Ave., Kihei. Call 808-874-5151.

Reefdancer. Lahaina glass-bottomed boat tours, perfect for families. Call 808-667-2133. Website www.mauiglass bottomboat.com.

Snorkel Bob's Lahaina (three locations), 1217 Front St., Lahaina; 3350 Lower Honoapi'ilani Rd., Honokowai; Azeka Place 2, 1279 S. Kihei Rd., #310, Kihei. Rent gear, or buy masks and fins to bring home. Website www.snorkel-bob.com.

South Pacific Kayaks. Kayak rentals and trips in Kihei. Call 808-875-4848. Website www.southpacifickayaks.com.

Spa at Fairmont Kea Lani, 4100 Wailea Alanui Dr., Wailea. Maui's premiere spa for massage treatments using materials sourced from the island. Call 808-875-2229. Website www.fairmont.com /kea-lani-maui/activities-services/spa.

Spa of Black Rock at the Sheraton Maui, 2605 Ka'anapali Pkwy., Lahaina. Ka'anapali Beach spa offering delectable massages and facials. Call 808-667-9577. Website www.blackrockspa.com.

The Shops at Wailea, 3750 Wailea Alanui Dr., Wailea. Call 808-891-6770. Website www.theshopsatwailea.com.

Trilogy Excursions (two locations), 180 Lahainaluna Rd., Lahaina; 2525 Ka'anapali Pkwy., Ka'anapali. Informative snorkel trips to Lana'i and Molokini. Call 808-874-5649. Website www.sail trilogy.com.

Turnbull Studios and Sculpture Garden, 5030 Kahekili Hwy., Wailuku. Call 808-244-0101. Website www.turnbull studios.org.

Ulalena at the Maui Theater, 878 Front St., Lahaina. A fun evening show ideal for those interested in Polynesian history. Call 808-856-7900. Website www.ulalena.com.

Wailea Golf Club, 100 Wailea Golf Club Dr., Kihei. Call 888-328-6284. Website www.waileagolf.com.

Wailea Tennis Club, 131 Wailea Ike Pl., Kihei. Call 808-879-1958. Website www.waileatennis.com.

Waine'e Church and Cemetery, 535 Waine'e St., Lahaina. Website www .lahainarestoration.org.

Whalers Village, 2435 Ka'anapali Pkwy., Lahaina. Phone 808-661-4567. Website www.whalersvillage.com.

Whalers Village Museum, 2435 Ka'anapali Pkwy., Lahaina. Educational and entertaining glimpse into the whaling history of Lahaina and the region. Call 808-661-5992. Website www.whalersvillage.com/museum.

Wo Hing Museum, 858 Front St., Lahaina. Gain insight into Maui's rich Chinese history. Call 808-661-5553. Website www.lahainarestoration.org.

DINING

808 Bistro, 2511 S. Kihei Rd., Kihei. Breakfast treats like whale pie and banana bread French toast top the lists of return visitors. Lunches and dinners are less inspired. Call 808-879-8008. Website www.808bistro.com.

808 Deli, 2511 S. Kihei Rd., Kihei. Enormous sandwiches like chicken pesto or veggie-licious delight beachgoers looking for picnic grub. Call 808-879-1111. Website www.808deli.net.

'Aina Gourmet Market, Honua Kai Resort, 130 Kai Malina Pkwy., Lahaina. Organic breakfast sandwiches, lunch and dinner salads, and paninis, sourced from within 100 miles. Stellar coffee bar. Call 808-662-2832. Website www.aina gourmet.com.

Aloha Mixed Plate, 1285 Front St., Lahaina. Try *kalbi* ribs and Chinese black bean *chow fun*, or sit at the bar and sip fruity libations. Call 808-661-3322. Website www.alohamixedplate.com.

Ambrosia, 1913 S. Kihei Rd., Kihei. High-end martinis favored by upscale travelers, and the absinthe bar isn't so shoddy either. Call 808-891-1011. Website www.ambrosiamaui.com.

Betty's Beach Café, 505 Front St., Lahaina. Pancakes and coffee along the sea bring me back to Betty's, though they are open for lunch and dinner. Call 808-662-0300. Website www.bettysbeach cafe.com.

CJ's Deli and Diner, 2580 Kekaa Dr., #120, Lahaina. Three comforting meals daily with faves like meat loaf, BBQ ribs, and coconut prawns. Call 808-667-0968. Website www.cjsmaui.com.

Cuatro, 1881 S. Kihei Rd., Kihei. Tastes from around the globe like Asian grilled steak, or Mauiterranean grilled fish, paired with artful cocktails. Reservations recommended. Call 808-879-1110. Website www.cuatromaui.com.

Cynnamon's, parked on Kahului Beach Rd., Kahului. *Poke* fresh to order, *panko* fried fish, *teri ahi* all come with two scoops of rice and pickled veggies. Call 808-280-8384.

Da Kitchen Café, 425 Koloa St., Kahului. Hawaiian-style BBQ and local-style grinds like *loco moco*, fish-and-chips, and fried Spam *musubi*. Call 808-871-7782. Website www.da-kitchen.com.

Duke's Beach House, 130 Kai Malina Pkwy., Lahaina. Cocktails with umbrellas, sashimi, burgers, seafood, and music on the beach. Call 808-662-2900. Website www.dukesmaui.com.

Eskimo Candy Seafood Market and Deli, 2665 Wai Wai Pl., Kihei. It's all about *poke* rice bowls—get here early before they sell out. Call 808-879-5686. Website www.eskimocandy.com.

Farmers Market Deli, 3636 Lower Honoapi'ilani Rd., Lahaina. *Acai* bowls, fresh-squeezed organic juice, and a farmers' market on select days.

Feast at Lele, 505 Front St., Lahaina. Creative lu'au food taken up a notch with alcohol, beautiful views, and an incredible performance. Worth the splurge. Reservations required. Call 808-667-5353. Website www.feastatlele.com.

Fish Market Maui, 3600 Lower Honoapi'ilani Rd., Lahaina. Fresh seafood counter and restaurant to sat-

MAUI NO KA OI ❖ 225

isfy your cravings for *mahi mahi* plates and *ahi* bowls. Call 808-665-9895. Website www.fishmarketmaui.com.

Gannon's Restaurant and Red Bar, 100 Wailea Golf Club Dr., Wailea-Makena. Farm-to-table comfort food served on the Wailea greens. Breakfasts are my favorite. Reservations recommended. Call 808-875-8080. Website www.gannonsrestaurant.com/the-red-bar.

Gazebo Restaurant, 5315 Lower Honoapi'ilani Rd., Lahaina. A favorite for pancakes perched on the tip of Napili Bay. Waits are *looong.* Call 808-669-5621.

Gerard's Restaurant, 174 Lahainaluna Rd., Lahaina. Gorgeous French cuisine made for romance and fans of *foie gras.* Dinner reservations a must. Call 808-661-8939. Website www.gerardsmaui.com.

Hawaiian Village Coffee, 4405 Honoapi'ilani Hwy., Lahaina. Cappuccino and breakfast sandwiches please surfers. Call 808-665-1114. Website www.hawaiianvillagecoffee.com.

Home Maid Bakery, 1005 Lower Main St., Wailuku. This bakery has limited hours that often are well suited for that early-morning drive up to Haleakala or Hana. Call 808-244-7015. Website www.homemaidbakery.com.

Honokowai Okazuya, 3600 Lower Honoapi'ilani Rd., Lahaina. While seeming to have an identity crisis with the array of food types offered, this local favorite prepares just about everything with style. Call 808-665-0512.

Honolua Store, 502 Office Rd., Lahaina. Sandwiches, salads, pizza, and burgers served in a historic plantation house. People watch as you eat outside on the picnic tables. Call 808-665-9105.

Honolulu Coffee Company, 3750 Wailea Alanui Dr., #25-EW, Wailea. Let the full, sweet aroma speak for itself. Call 808-875-6630. Website www.honolulucoffee.com.

Honu Seafood and Pizza, 1295 Front St., Lahaina. Gourmet pizzas in a colorful atmosphere with a spectacular ocean view. Call 808-667-9390. Website www.honumaui.com.

Hula Grill, 2435 Ka'anapali Pkwy., Ka'anapali. Attractive ambience at both the barefoot bar and the dining room for live music, fruity cocktails, and *pupus* like *kalua* pork potstickers. Call 808-667-6636. Website www.hulagrillkaanapali.com.

I'o Restaurant, 505 Front St., Lahaina. Waterfront dining with local ingredients inhabiting the risotto or fresh-caught seafood offerings. Reservations recommended. Call 808-661-8422. Website www.iomaui.com.

Java Café, 1279 S. Kihei Rd., Kihei. Decent coffee and free Wi-Fi bring me back. Call 808-214-6095. Website www.javacafemaui.com.

Java Jazz & Soup Nutz, 3350 Lower Honoapi'ilani Rd., Lahaina. A gallery, coffee shop, and restaurant, with smoothies, live jazz, and 30 types of beers. Call 808-667-0787. Website www.javajazz.net.

Kihei Caffe, 1945 S. Kihei Rd., Kihei. Breakfast items like pancakes and French toast as well as local favorites like *loco moco* draw crowds. Call 808-879-2230.

Ko at Fairmont Kea Lani, 4100 Wailea Alanui Dr., Wailea. Poolside dining with live music features items like lobster tempura and rib eye with Moloka'i sweet potato. Reservations required. Call 808-875-4100. Website www.fairmont.com/kea-lani-maui/dining/ko.

Koiso Sushi Bar, 2395 S. Kihei Rd., Kihei. Small (and always busy) Japanese restaurant, so make a reservation beforehand. Call 808-875-8258.

Lahaina Coolers, 180 Dickenson St., #107, Lahaina. Three TVs by the bar promote a lively environment for beers or a meal. Call 808-661-7082. Website www.lahainacoolers.com.

Lahaina Grill, 127 Lahainaluna Rd., Lahaina. Reserve in advance to enjoy the seared *ahi* and the triple berry pie at this upscale mainstay in Lahaina's dining scene. Call 808-667-5117. Website www.lahainagrill.com.

Leilani's on the Beach, 2435 Ka'anapali Pkwy., Lahaina. Try the spicy tuna tower *pupu* and a sunset cocktail. Call 808-661-4495. Website www.leilanis.com.

Leoda's Kitchen and Pie Shop, 820 Olowalu Village Rd., Lahaina. Potpies, banana crème pies, and coffees sourced from nearby farms. Call 808-662-3600. Website www.leodas.com.

Life's a Beach, 1913 S. Kihei Rd., Kihei. Live music on Friday night, fun cocktails, and bar grinds. Call 808-891-8010. Website www.mauibars.com.

Longhi's Wailea, 3750 Wailea Alanui Dr., Wailea. While pastas, fresh seafood, and steaks inhabit lunch and dinner menus, breakfasts rule the roost at this Wailea eatery. Call 808-891-8883. Website www.longhis.com.

Lulu's Lahaina Surf Club and Grill, 1221 Honoapi'ilani Hwy., Lahaina. While food is hit or miss, it is all about the bar. Call 808-661-0808. Website www.lulus lahaina.com.

Main Street Bistro, 2051 Main St., Wailuku. Mother's roast beef sandwich and onion rings with smoky ketchup make this a popular choice for the work crowd. Call 808-244-6816. Website www.msbmaui.com.

Mala Ocean Tavern, 1307 Front St., Lahaina. Local greens for salads and wild seafood entrées make this tavern carbon-footprint conscious. Weekend brunches are in demand. Reservations recommended. Call 808-667-9394. Website www.malaoceantavern.com.

Mala Wailea, 3700 Wailea Alanui Dr., Wailea. Griddle breakfasts, bountiful salads for lunch, and beautiful, artistic entrées for dinner ranging from seafood to burgers. Call 808-875-9394. Website www.malawailea.com.

Maui Brewing Company, 4405 Honoapi'ilani Hwy., Lahaina. A green brewery with a great selection of hoppy beverages and pub grub. Call 808-669-3474. Website www.mauibrewingco.com.

Maui Coffee Roasters, 444 Hana Hwy., Kahului. Enjoy 100 percent pure Kona coffee and a breakfast pastry or lunch sandwich wrap before heading out to Hana. Call 808-877-2877. Website www.mauicoffeeroasters.com.

Maui College's Culinary Program Food Court and Class Act, 310 Ka'ahumanu Ave., Kahului. Be a guinea pig for the culinary school chefs at their food court, or in the Class Act exhibition kitchen, which offers ocean views and locally grown produce in an array of creative ways. Call 808-984-3225 or 808-984-3280. Website www.mauiculinary-campusdining.com.

MauiGrown Coffee, 277 Lahainaluna Rd., Lahaina. Call 808-661-2728. Website www.mauigrowncoffee.com.

Merriman's Kapalua, 1 Bay Club Place, Lahaina. Enjoy chef's nightly specials based on available fresh local produce and seafood. Reservations recommended. Call 808-669-6400. Website www.merrimanshawaii.com.

Monkeypod Kitchen, 10 Wailea Ike Dr., #201, Kihei. Seasonal cocktails, flatbread pizza, and an innovative seafood menu draw families and foodies. Call 808-891-2322. Website www.monkeypodkitchen.com.

Mulligan's on the Blue, 100 Kaukahi St., Kihei. Irish bar and restaurant on Wailea Old Blue golf course. Call 808-874-1131. Website www.mulligansonthe blue.com.

Old Lahaina Lu'au, 1251 Front St., Lahaina. A lu'au never tasted so good. With live music and free-flowing *mai tais*, you'll have to reserve your spot at least a month in advance for a place at this popular table. Call 808-667-1998. Website www.oldlahainaluau.com.

Ono Gelato Company, 815 Front St., Lahaina. Try the mac nut coffee gelato or the mango. Call 808-495-0203. Website www.onogelatocompany.com.

Pacific'O, 505 Front St., #114, Lahaina. Get a table along the beach and try a range of creatively prepared vegetarian dishes sourced from Upcountry paired with fresh *ono*. Call 808-667-4341. Website www.pacificomaui.com.

Pita Paradise Wailea, 34 Wailea Alanui Dr., Wailea. Greek bistro favored by surfers. Call 808-879-7177. Website www.pitaparadisehawaii.com.

Sansai Seafood Restaurant and Sushi Bar Kapalua, 600 Office Rd., Lahaina. Wildly popular; reserve a table at least two weeks out to sample the *panko*-crusted *ahi* sashimi and the shrimp dynamite. There's another location in Kihei that is not as dependable, but it is still worth a visit. Call 808-669-6286. Website www.sanseihawaii.com.

Sea House Restaurant, 5900 Lower Honoapi'ilani Rd., Lahaina. Lovely oceanfront dining featuring creative menu items throughout the day and evening, relying on organic produce and whatever local fishermen brought in that morning. Call 808-669-1500. Website www.seahousemaui.com.

South Shore Tiki Bar, 1913 S. Kihei Rd., Kihei. Party it up with live music, outdoor seating, and pizza. Call 808-874-6444. Website www.southshoretikilounge.com.

Star Noodle, 286 Kupuohi St., Lahaina. Sticky sweet buns and bowls of original noodle creations at this funky industrial eatery above Lahaina. Waits can feel like ages. Call 808-667-5400. Website www.starnoodle.com.

Stella Blues, 1279 S. Kihei Rd., Ste. B 201, Kihei. Dead-head-themed eatery serves big portions of American-style cuisine from morning to night. The bar features live music on select nights. Call 808-874-3779. Website www.stellablues.com.

Sunrise Café, 693 Front St., Lahaina. Cash only and long waits, but delicious breakfast and brunch satisfy most Lahaina visitors. Call 808-661-8558.

Tasaka Guri Guri Shop at the Maui Mall, 70 E. Ka'ahumanu Ave., Ste. C13, Kahului. Try the delicious ice-cream-meets-shave-ice concoction after a wander through Maui Mall. Call 808-871-4513.

Timba, 505 Front St., Ste. 212, Lahaina. Crowded dance floor and full bar with ocean views. Call 808-661-9873.

Ululani's Hawaiian Shave Ice, 819 Front St., Lahaina. Homemade tropical syrups drench these icy treats. Call 360-606-2745. Website www.ululanisshaveice.com.

Wailuku Coffee Company, 26 N. Market St., Wailuku. Enjoy coffee, breakfast sandwiches, salads, or pizza. Call 808-495-0259. Website www.wailukucoffeeco.com.

Waterfront Restaurant, 300 Maalaea Rd., Maalaea. Enjoy fresh seafood and beautiful views without the pretension of the resort-area eateries. Call 808-244-9028. Website www.waterfrontrestaurant.net.

Wow Wee Maui's Kava Bar and Grill, 333 Dairy Rd., Kahului. Sushi, hamburgers, and fresh-cut fries paired with a kava tea lure locals. Call 808-871-1414.

OTHER CONTACT INFORMATION

Expeditions Ferry, 658 Front St., Lahaina. Call 808-661-3756. Website www.go-lanai.com.

Maui Visitors Bureau. Website www.gohawaii.com.

Moloka'i Princess. Call 866-307-6524. Website www.molokaiferry.com/ferry.html.

The road to Hana

8 Maui's Wild Side
THE HANA COAST AND UPCOUNTRY

Estimated length: 139 miles

Estimated time: 8 hours, or 5 leisurely days

Getting there: From Kahului's International Airport, take Highway 36 east through Pa'ia. Just after Ha'iku, the road is called Highway 360 all the way to Hana, and then it switches names (again) to Highway 330; then Pi'ilani Highway (or Highway 31). This is basically the same road with new mile markers. As the highway veers Upcountry, it becomes Kula Highway (or Highway 37) and later Haleakala Highway, which deposits you back in Kahului. I've given specific driving directions throughout the chapter should you feel confused. For detailed flight and car rental information, view chapter 8. You might want to rent a four-wheel drive for this itinerary.

Highlights: The superlative road to Hana; exploring Maui's dormant Haleakala volcano; a foodie feast in Upcountry; the bohemian Pa'ia town; windsurfing at Ho'okipa Beach.

The Hawaiian demi-god Maui is said to be responsible for the creation of the Hawaiian Islands by casting a spell over the sea with his magical fishhook. This ambitious young man was disappointed when instead of creating a new continent he merely generated this small archipelago. If Maui were alive today, one would imagine he might find pride in his homeland, most especially his namesake island, which consistently wins hearts and awards for being one of the world's most beloved island paradises.

East Maui owns some of the state's loveliest beaches and hikes, as well as innovative restaurants and resorts. Yet most visitors spend the majority of their trip on the sparkling (and crowded) western shores, opting only for a day trip to experience Maui's Wild Side attractions like Hana Highway and Haleakala. While this itinerary can be braved in a day, I recommend that you devote a few days to exploring this enchanting region.

After descending Haleakala, bikers congregate in Pa'ia.

From Kahului Airport, travel east on Highway 36 for 7 miles to the small North Shore town of Pa'ia, Maui's funkiest town, long favored by transients, hippies, and artists. It wasn't always like this. In Maui's early days, plantation workers lived in the wooden shacks lining Baldwin Avenue. Today Pa'ia is changing hats once again: It's gaining a reputation as the closest town to Maui's largest surf break and finest windsurfing beach, not to mention host to innovative restaurants, galleries, and an upscale boutique hotel. Since most motor through Pa'ia on their way to and from Hana, or on a bike trip from Haleakala, try to time your visit either around 11 a.m. or in the later afternoon, when Pa'ia's colorful residents can be spotted roaming the streets and the restaurants are comparatively mellow. Pa'ia deserves some time, so plan to explore this eclectic community for a day or two. Also note that parking is tough to come by. There is a small lot on the *mauka* side of the road just before the town.

The impressive Pa'ia Inn works to escort guests into an oasis of beach chic. Rooms are on the petite side, offering flat-panel TVs and Wi-Fi along with AC and plush bedding. Asian antiques and Avi Kiriaty's artwork line the walls of this 1920s structure, while tropical color schemes populate bedding and shared spaces. The covered outdoor eating area acts as a hub for visitors to enjoy coffee and breakfast (for a fee). The property weaves from Hana Highway to Pa'ia Bay, with a private grassy barbecue area (at press time it was gaining a *tiki* bar) that opens to a series of white sand beaches.

Pa'ia Inn's stylish rooms

Next to the hotel, occupying the rear of a driveway and obscured by plants, is Pa'ia Bay Coffee, a sweet spot for espresso drinks, pastries, and sandwiches, Wi-Fi, and great tunes throughout the day. Along Hana Highway, Ono Gelato specializes in creamy mac nut and coconut flavors. The new Johnny B's Burgers serves up locally farmed beef burgers and spicy volcano fries on picnic tables alongside the highway. At the town's most bustling corner, Pa'ia Fish Market prides itself on serving that day's fresh catch in a taco, atop a salad, sandwiched between two hunks of bread, or sidling up to some veggies; make friends with locals and tourists at the shared picnic tables. Foodie friends swear by Flatbread Company, saying it pleases families craving good-for-the-earth pizzas made from organic ingredients and nitrate-free pepperoni, though I've yet had the chance to sample their goods. Finally, if you prefer a beach picnic, Mana Foods offers freshly made sandwiches, pre-made organic salads, and groceries.

Known for its galleries and fun shops, this town is tough to pass through without purchasing a souvenir—or 10! Alice in Hulaland hawks fun clothes for the whole family and island gifts like hula-skirted bottle cap openers. Art lovers must stop in Maui Crafts Guild, a cooperative gallery

Pa'ia Fish Market

for locals to showcase their pottery and jewelry. Maui Girl is *the* spot to purchase bikinis, while Maui Hands offers heaps of original paintings, leis, and woodworking pieces. Hana Highway Surf sells artistically crafted boards as well as cute surf clothing. If you want to rent surf or windsurfing gear, Hi Tech Surf Sports can hook you up.

Windsurfers love Maui's North Shore.

Pa'ia's North Shore beaches are known for their massive waves (the big waves at "Jaws" requires brave souls to be driven out on Jet Skis) and fantastic windsurfing. These two elements mean that the beaches can be windy and tough on the *keikis*. If you want to brave the surf

A county worker cleaning up a coconut palm.

(and the windsurfing) of champions, at mile marker 9 on Hana Highway is the picturesque Ho'okipa Beach.

Closer to Pa'ia (at mile marker 6 off Hana Highway), Baldwin Beach Park provides pockets of calm seas, especially in summer; the white sand, the sometimes rowdy collection of locals, and the great bodyboarding make this a fun place to experience the North Shore. If you have kiddos, at mile marker 5 on Hana Highway turn toward the water on Nonohe Place and then left at Kealakai Place to find Baby Beach, a protected swimming area, idea for the younger set (there are no services here).

After dark, Pa'ia town loves Charley's, a watering hole that occasionally houses live music. Milagros offers great people-watching, decent beers, and some fine grub for that afternoon cocktail and *pupu* for tourists. However, most agree the place to be in the evenings is at an oceanfront table at Mama's Fish House, the North Shore's finest restaurant located on the western edge of Ho'okipa Beach, 2 miles east of Pa'ia town. Watch the sunset and sip a *mai tai*. Then as the *tiki* torches light up and the stars twinkle above, enjoy staples like a lobster-and-crab-stuffed *mahi mahi*. If the romance of Mama's reels you in, Inn at Mama's is a collection of beachy 1970s-style cottages decked out in island furnishings for a big price tag.

Past Ho'okipa Beach the road begins its path toward Hana, a mere 45 miles away, but a trip that will likely take two to four hours each way. It is not that the road is that rough—it is paved, and two lanes for the majority of the way—but that it ribbons along a cliff atop the wild Pacific with waterfalls literally dripping from the mountains. To call the drive spectacular would not do it justice, so take it slow, pull over to let locals pass by, and always stop at the correct turnoffs to snap photos. Also note that gas is way cheaper in Pa'ia than Hana (I can see your smirk from here; yes, it can get even pricier), so fill up before leaving town.

At mile marker 16, turn right and head up Ha'iku Road to the off-the-beaten-path community that might even make Pa'ia seem conservative. Most will find little of inter-

IS SWIMMING IN WATERFALLS SAFE?

To fulfill the fantasy of a tropical vacation, some might just need to swim in a pool with a waterfall crashing behind. While this can be idyllic, use your best judgment beforehand, as Hawai'i's freshwater pools are known to carry leptospirosis. Only swim in pools that you see others swimming in, and *never* jump from rocks into these pools. Also, be sure you have no open cuts when going into these freshwater pools.

Swim beneath a waterfall on Maui's lush east side.

est up here, especially since the pineapple and sugar industries dried up. Yet the historic old town and the quiet country charm might make you want to stay awhile. Aside from a handful of vacation rentals, the affordable Ha'iku Plantation Inn draws repeat visitors. Rooms blend tropical stylishness with a dash of B&B girliness without feeling overdone, offering private baths and free Wi-Fi as well as access to 2 acres of landscaping, a hot tub, and breakfast.

In town you'll find Haleakala Bike Company, ground zero for bike tours down the volcano (for more on that, see Haleakala National Park). A handful of restaurants seem to change hands often enough, but the reliable Colleen's at the Cannery lures locals in for pizzas and pastas alongside fresh seafood; and Hana Hou Café is a mainstay with plate lunches ordered at the counter, and decent sushi paired with live music on some nights.

Hana Highway starts being called Highway 360 just after Ha'iku, and the mile markers begin at zero again. At mile marker 2, if you are itching to stretch your legs and spot a waterfall, or two, stop at the wide parking lot marked by a fruit stand. Twin Falls draws its share of tourists who hike about 10 minutes up the trail to the first waterfall and then continue along the path to reach the second. Many locals and tourists swim in the first

HOW TO KNOW WHERE TO STOP ON THE DRIVE...

Along the Hana Highway, it seems every direction you turn there's a waterfall. Many guidebooks offer ways to experience every one of them, often at the expense of your time, cleanliness, and safety. I have chosen to only include hikes to waterfalls that are safe and accessible via public land. I find that after a while you begin to get waterfall apathy, so I have including the most dramatic vistas that you just cannot miss.

The Hana Highway is filled with one-lane bridges like these.

falls, but I find them too muddy and crowded. There are much nicer falls for swimming and viewing later on in the drive.

At mile marker 5, note the collection of colorful mailboxes on the *makai* side. Drive down the road to the off-the-grid community of Huelo. Though it's rainy and a bit too remote for most first-timers to Maui, deals on vacation rentals can be found in this hamlet. A favorite for repeat visitors, Huelo Point Lookout offers a fanciful collection of cottages and luxurious houses with private hot tubs and access to a communal pool and organic produce. In the middle of "town" (and I use this term loosely) is Kaulanapueo Church, constructed in 1853 of coral blocks. Back up along the highway, Huelo Lookout fruit stand offers organic smoothies and crepes straight off the farm with views of the sea below.

After Huelo the road enters the Ko'olau Forest Reserve and the drive morphs into the stuff of legend with one-lane bridges and vines dripping down the mountains. At mile marker 9, you can immerse yourself in the forest at Waikamoi Ridge Trail, a mile-long interpretive trail that is both muddy and lush. You can also picnic here or use the restrooms.

If it has been raining, at mile marker 10 Waikamoi Falls provides an icy pool for swimming beneath its dramatic ribbon of water. Otherwise continue on; just beyond mile marker 10 is Garden of Eden Arboretum. For those who prefer a tamer, more manicured tropical experience, fork over some cash to wander the trails to Puohokamoa Falls. Frankly, I tend to skip this stop—I mean, isn't everything along the drive spectacular enough? Garden lovers, however, will be giddy about this tropical wonderland. At mile

DETOUR: HONOMANU BAY

For those with four-wheel-drive vehicles and an adventurous spirit, brave the rough road down to Honomanu Bay just after mile marker 14. This black sand beach is not for swimmers—though kids love to play in the stream that empties into the sea. Experienced surfers ride the waves in winter, but currents and rocks make it challenging and unadvisable.

marker 12's free Kaumahina State Wayside Park you'll find a grassy area to relax, reasonably clean toilets, and a fine view of the coast.

At mile marker 17, pat yourself on the back because you've reached the halfway point to Hana. The free Ke'anae Arboretum celebrates the medicinal uses of Hawai'i's plants as well as being a breeding ground for mosquitoes. Just past the arboretum on the *makai* side is the road to Ke'anae, a small rainy township housing one of the remaining Hawaiian coastal communities. The centerpiece of the village is Ke'anae Congregational Church, a coral-and-lava-rock building constructed in 1860. Just after the church, Ke'anae Landing Fruit Stand lures locals and tourists with legendary banana bread. Farther along, Ke'anae Beach's black sand might look inviting, but lava rock makes swimming nearly impossible.

Back up on Hana Highway is the creatively named Halfway to Hana fruit stand—a tempting choice for tasty banana bread. Between mile markers 19 and 25, you'll crane your neck upward to see more consecutive waterfalls than you ever imagined lived in symphony together. Three Bears Falls is 0.5 mile past mile marker 19 and offers fine view of a gusher. Pua'a Ka'a State Wayside Park is 0.5 mile beyond mile marker 22 and offers waterfall pools as well as bathrooms; many consider this the most worthy stop on the drive, especially since Dave's banana bread can usually be purchased from the rear of a flatbed truck. At the 24-mile marker, Hanawi Falls makes a nice photo op that will make your Facebook friends jealous.

At mile marker 25, Nahiku seems an explosion of activity. Really, the Nahiki Marketplace is the commercial center for this seaside community down the road. Snack on *kalua* pig tacos at Up in Smoke and then peruse the colorful collection of local art and handmade jewelry while you are stretching your legs. Food trucks often stop up here during "rush hour."

At mile marker 32 on the *makai* side, Waianapanapa State Park provides ad-

Outstanding homemade banana bread can be found along the highway to Hana.

DETOUR: 'ULA'INO ROAD

One of the most overlooked experiences on this drive pops up after mile marker 31 at 'Ula'ino Road. Most don't budget enough time to truly explore this vast region and miss these historic sites, and frankly, unless you are staying out here, you won't have time either. Travel down the hill to arrive at Ka'eleku Caverns, a vast system of lava caves worth spelunking with Maui Cave Adventures. As in all lava tubes, the climate can be chilly and downright uncomfortable.

Another postcard-worthy stop is Kahanu Gardens, a 294-acre botanical garden with Hawai'i's largest temple and a rich collection of rare and medicinal plants. The garden path passes Pi'ilanihale Heiau, the state's largest sacred site. No one knows exactly what this *heiau* was used for in ancient times, though most agree that it must have been a very spiritual site to be so large. While it might look like a line of lava rocks (and an impressively large one at that), this is a very sacred spot to native people. Please use respect when visiting.

venturers with a black sand beach, not quite ideal for swimming. Snorkeling here can be exciting and challenging, so use caution, especially in winter. You can explore the lava caves, or take the fantastic 3-mile trail all the way to Hana Bay. This park offers modest cabins and tent camping, though you need a permit in advance (see the camping sidebar). If you are lucky, you might be here on one of the few days out of the year that the waters turn a bright shade of red. Local lore says the reason is that an ancient princess was killed here; the red is her blood seeping from the lava rock. Scientists, on the other hand, say it is because red shrimp escape from cracks in the lava, giving off the illusion that the water is as rosy as Snow White's lips.

It is possible to arrive in Hana and wonder what all the fuss is about. In this slow farm town, cows outnumber the native Hawaiians and *haoles* who call this small community home. It is easy to start waxing philosophical about it being about the journey not the destination, yet arriving at Hana rewards travelers who opt to stay awhile (though most don't) with abundantly lush nature and the chance to slow *waaaay* down.

There are a host of vacation rentals in the area, including the oceanfront Hana Kai Maui, which rents airy studio and one-bedroom condos. Budget seekers who don't expect to spend much time indoors might appreciate Joe's Place, which offers cheap rooms with both shared and private bathrooms.

However, if you can afford the splurge, the plushest hotel between here and Ka'anapali Beach is Travaasa Hana. This former cottage-land evokes an unpretentious feel even though travelers hand over a jaw-dropping amount of cash to stay the night. An adult section offers romantic rooms with views of the sea, while the spacious family cottages hug a meadow ideal for a game of pickup soccer. Simplicity is on the menu of the earth-toned rooms, which are intentionally devoid of TVs and Wi-Fi, yet luxurious touches like coffee grinders paired with ceramic mugs and private patios please discerning travelers. All feature large tubs, walk-in separate tiled showers, and natural bath products made on Maui. The hotel offers an array of cultural activities—lei-making and ukulele classes, glider flights, horseback riding—as well as a world-class spa, two pools, and a fitness facility. The on-site gallery showcases impressive paintings and sculptures.

The hotel operates two restaurants. The main dining room is awash with the vibrant art of Kim McDonald (who, at press time, was opening a gallery in Pa'ia) and offers pricey cattle- and sea-inspired cuisine. On Thursday night, the Paniolo Lounge features Hawaiian music and hula—get here at 5:30 to order *pupus* off the lunch menu, which is way cheaper than the dinner prices. Up the street, the hotel's casual Hana Ranch Restaurant serves overpriced cowboy-inspired food like ribs and chicken as well as cocktails.

There are not too many other notable dining choices. The fish tacos at Braddah Hutts BBQ are a decent lunch option. Thai Food by Pranee has set up camp under a tarp across from the baseball field. The ladies serve a couple of scoops of rice, noodles, and curry dishes alongside a tasty papaya salad. Instead of dining under the tarp, which is hot and popular with mosquitoes, opt to have a picnic at the ballpark where former minor-league baseball team the San Francisco Seals used to have spring training.

Chances are if you are in Hana for a minute, you'll pop into Hasegawa General Store, where frozen sandwiches, kitschy souvenirs, and items like machetes go for big prices. Established in 1910, the store burned down in 1990 and has since been rebuilt to mirror the original—tin roof and all. Just up the street, Hana Cultural Center makes a good starting point to learn about the cultural history of the area through a fine collec-

WHERE'D THAT ALOHA SPIRIT GO?

For the most part, you can expect a healthy dose of aloha for your efforts to reach Hana. However, this is not always the case. Many local Hawaiians are not jazzed on the influx of tourism, and are known to treat visitors rudely—especially here in Hana. The two times I have been treated disrespectfully in all my time on Hawai'i occurred in Hana. I like to look at it like this: Hawai'i has been colonized for a long time, and there are local people who aren't keen on this fact. If I have to be on the receiving end of stink eye to experience paradise, I'll take one for the team. When the aloha spirit disappears, remember your manners and be a good ambassador for the rest of us travelers. And if all else fails, hit up the bar, where you can pay for a shot of kindness.

Hamoa Beach

tion of Hawaiian artifacts. The store also pleases those looking for crafty items like quilts to take home.

Truth be told, Hana's charms are about nature. Hana Bay Beach Park acts as the town center and is the place to be to experience the real Hana, especially on weekends when everyone comes out to picnic, surf (on the northern edge of the bay), and watch kids frolic in the waves. Red Sand Beach, popular with photographers and nudists, is down a path from the community center, and while this beach is not for swimming, the rosy sand against the azure waters can be a selling point for why you braved Hana Highway. Those who prefer land to the sea should take the 3-mile hike up Lyon's Hill (just inland off Travaasa's grounds) to the large Fagan's Cross—it is especially magical to descend at sunset, but bring a flashlight for the return trip.

I'd argue that the main reason to splurge on a hotel in Hana is to experience all that lies beyond the town. This region is especially delicious before the daytrippers arrive—so get up early. Just before mile marker 50, turn *makai* to Haneo'o Road. You'll pass Koki Beach, a surf spot, and 'Alau Island, a seabird sanctuary, to arrive at Hamoa Beach, a perfect crescent of sand washed by blindingly clear water that is adored by surfers, swimmers, children, and beachcombers.

Back on the highway about 10 miles beyond Hana, pull into the Kipahulu Ranger Station, fork over the parking fee (which is also good for entrance to Haleakala, since this is also a part of the national park), and get ready to be blown away. 'Ohe'o Gulch, known by most mainlanders as the Seven Sacred Pools (though they are stunning, they are not sacred), is a collection of seven waterfalls that plunge into one another, creating pools that beg to be swum in. Around noon these pools get very busy, so come early. And use caution. Every year there are news reports about another collection of tourists who were swept away by flash floods, or who ended up as a shark's dinner in the rough seas below. You can hike up Pipiwai Trail for 1.5 miles to reach a couple of secluded pools through a dwarfing bamboo forest. If you choose to camp in the park, you may want to follow the lead of Georgia O'Keeffe, who painted these pools on her historic visit to this rugged coastline—bring some art supplies.

A mile beyond the pools is the hippie and artist community of Kipahulu, where at Palapala Ho'omau Congregational Church you'll stumble upon Charles Lindbergh's grave—when Lindbergh learned he had terminal cancer, he opted to return to the land he loved to die in Maui. He is buried behind the church.

Across the street, grab your own organic tropical fruit, coffee, and spices at Ono Organic Farms, where farmers offer a tour and tastings of the goods. Between mile markers 40 and 41, Laulima Farms allows customers to hop on a bike and power the juicer to make your own organic smoothies—however, you still have to pay for your pedaling. If you plan to be in Kipahulu on a Sunday evening, ask around for directions to Café Attitude, an organic vegetarian diner and artists' salon. While you won't likely see Hana residents Weird Al Yankovic and Woody Harrelson, you can peep the ways in which this wild feast of nature inspires.

The Seven Sacred Pools

To continue on from here toward the rear end of Haleakala and Upcountry, you are likely violating your rental car agreement. If you are still reading, know that besides a couple of blind one-lane turns, and a 4-mile stretch of unpaved road that does occasionally get washed out (ask about road conditions at Hana's gas station before heading out), Pi'ilani Highway provides stark and dramatic scenery devoid of a tourist infrastructure found elsewhere on Maui. Take it slow. From Kipahulu it may be 38 miles to Kula, but it will likely take you about two hours to arrive. Fill up on gas and food; it's slim pickin's out here, though at mile marker 35 Kaupo Store hawks a few pricey necessities.

As you wind up toward Upcountry, the road becomes Highway 37 (Kula Highway). Those with time to spare should plan at least a day or two to unravel the wealth of attractions in the region. Whether you stay along the coast in Pa'ia, choose one of Makawao's funky lodging options, or find accommodations higher in the clouds of Kula, you'll appreciate the close proximity to these farms, restaurants, and the volcano.

As the road ascends, you spot the 20,000-acre Ulupalakua Ranch, both a cattle ranch and home to Maui's Winery at Ulupalakua Ranch. I know what you're thinking— wine growing on Maui?!—but the grounds are stunning and the pineapple and passion fruit wine is, er, interesting. Or if you cannot brave Hawaiian Chardonnay, head across the street to Ulupalakua Ranch Store and Grill for elk burgers and cowboy souvenirs.

Five miles north is Keokea, a former Chinese farming community. Today most pass the historic church to hit up the legendary Grandma's Coffee Shop, known for growing organic coffee cherries on the slopes of the volcano. "Grandma" and her ancestors have been roasting beans in this historic clapboard house for ages. Purchase decently strong cuppa joe with a hearty breakfast or a sandwich, both of which are favored by those who wake up before dawn to see the sunrise from Haleakala.

While most travel to Upcountry to experience the farming community of Kula on the way to or from the volcano, the town is experiencing a sort of renaissance. Pop-up restaurants, gourmet farm dinners, and an insurgence of artists make Kula more than a

CAMPING ON THE EDGE OF A VOLCANO

If you'd like to camp out in the cool mountain breeze, Polipoli Spring State Recreation Area offers sites (you need a permit from the state in advance). You need an off-road vehicle to make the trek from Highway 377. Turn onto the windy Waipoli Road and continue for 10 miles to reach the campground. The road is unpaved for the last 4 miles and can be very muddy. There are a handful of hikes for daytrippers, just off Waipoli Road. My favorite is the Boundary Trail, which starts just beyond the end of the paved road, and offers plenty of eucalyptus shade and a glimpse at some native plants along the way.

MAUI COUNTRY FARM TOURS

Piggybacking on the farm-to-table craze permeating the island of Maui, Marilyn Jansen Lopes offers one-day farm tours of Upcountry. She can tailor the tour to your interests, but typical trips include a stop at Ali'i Kula Lavender, Maui's Winery, and Kula Country Farms, with a picnic lunch thrown in for good measure. Marilyn knows the farmers and offers a wealth of information about the area. Plus, she's a mean ukulele player. She'll pick up from Ka'anapali as well if you've already made the trek up to Haleakala and don't want to brave the roads again. Call 808-283-9131. Website www.mauicountry farmtours.com.

name on local menus. To stay up in these hills, 3,000 feet above sea level, means getting to know the unpolished side of Maui, one devoid of surf camps and $40-a-plate dinners. Instead, you'll likely wear your sneakers to traipse through the mud and don a windbreaker after dark, but you'll get a mirror into the soul of the Valley Isle.

Most of Kula's attractions are on (or just off) Kula Highway. It is feasible to pair a minimal exploration of Upcountry and Haleakala in a day, but you won't be able to completely experience either. It's not a bad idea to stay in Kula for a night or two to fully explore the volcano without the schlep from the beach. Affordable and modest, Kula Sandalwoods Cottages is 45 minutes from the summit of the volcano and offers fine views from your lanai. To call the rooms cottages might confuse, as there are no kitchenettes for guests' use. However, the owners operate Kula Sandalwoods Restaurant, which serves breakfast and lunch. Another option is Kula Lodge and Marketplace, which is on the road up to Haleakala and offers chalets decorated with country-style furnishings—think brass beds and floral comforters. Both the chalets and the restaurant (which is not the most inspiring in the food department, but works for a after a long day of hiking) offer postcard-worthy views, especially as the sun sets over West Maui. FYI: If you are

Kula Country Farms sells yummy strawberries.

KUPU MAUI—A POP-UP RESTAURANT

Made popular by urban chefs with little money or space to open a new restaurant, the pop-up restaurant has now come to Maui. Reserve a spot early on the third Saturday of each month to enjoy a coursed gourmet meal at a rotating farm location (sites have included Ocean Vodka and Kula Country Farms), presided over by three Maui locals who like the concept of a movable feast with yummy farm-fresh ingredients. Website www.kupumaui.com.

---

making the trek up the mountain before sunrise, Crater Coffee Cart sets up camp in front of the Kula Marketplace starting at 3 a.m.

Along Highway 37, Kula Botanical Gardens begs to be worshipped. Home to the most *proteas* in Hawai'i, and a few paths that wind past *kukui* trees, streams, bamboo, and *koa*, these gardens promise make visitors appreciate the rich volcanic soil's effect on plant growth. Nearby, pull into Kula Country Farms to purchase some gorgeous produce—their strawberries are out of this world—straight off the farm.

Just up Waipoli Road, O'o Farms is chef James McDonald's (of Pacific'O fame)

Source your own produce at O'o Farms.

source for his produce. Make a reservation in advance for a lunchtime farm tour to explore this organic spectacle of color and cuisine. You'll harvest the veggies yourself, handing them over to the gourmet chef who then crafts a winning meal in the outdoor industrial kitchen. Dine under a trellis in the center of the farm, then amble over to the coffee roaster to enjoy just-roasted beans ground into lattes and paired with exquisite chocolates grown on the farm. At press time, the owners were talking about building accommodations on the farm (can you see me cartwheeling from there?).

If the sweet smell of lavender is a balm for your nerves, don't miss a self-guided walking tour of Ali'i Kula Lavender Farm. High in the Kula hills, with spectacular views of West Maui, these gardens are a lovely place for some medita-

The dormant Haleakala Volcano is a sight to behold.

tion, a lavender scone, and a dash of tea. Bring home unique souvenirs from their cute store.

From Highway 377, turn left on Lower Kimo Road and right on Lower Kula Road. Veer left on Omaopio Road and keep your eyes peeled for Surfing Goat Dairy. You can stop by to tour the grounds, feed the goats, and sample the yummy goat cheese varietals. On select Saturdays, they offer expanded tours where you can milk the goats. Their chèvre was served at President Obama's inauguration—it's that good.

When your belly starts talking, Kula Bistro opened in 2012 and has since been packing the house for three meals daily. The astonishing menu offers fine twists on pastas, while the flaky pastries are divine. For a splash of French gourmet for breakfast and lunch, La Provence delivers savory crepes and insanely good pastries. To get to both of these establishments, you have to pass through the heart of Kula and turn off to Lower Kula Road.

You'll appreciate all this talk of food after a visit to Haleakala National Park. To get here from Kula, follow the signs to Crater Road, known for fogginess that obscures views of the hordes of bikers descending from the volcano, as well as its remarkable vistas of Maui, the Pacific, and the surrounding islands. It is almost redundant to sing about Haleakala's beauty—it's been praised by artists, voyagers, ancients, and mere mortal travelers—yet it is impossible not to marvel in the starkness of the dormant volcano and the palate of colors that remain. A symphony of clouds and sun, rock and weak oxygen add up to literally take your breath away. It's not called "house of the sun" for nothing. Leg-

Silversword plants can only be found on the slopes of Haleakala.

end has it that the demi-god Maui came up here and wrestled the sun (breaking off two of its limbs) to make the days longer for his mother to craft her *tapa* cloth. It is only from your perch atop Haleakala that you truly understand the power of the sun, and the strength attributed to Maui, a god that can break the sun.

If you are like me, getting to the top of Haleakala at sunrise on my vacation (no matter how jet-lagged I am) is not only un-attractive, but also downright impossible. For those of you who do make the trek, I admire you and wish you well. Seeing the sun ascend from beneath the clouds is a life-changing experience. There are a number of ways to experience this. First off, you can wake up a 3 a.m. (one time in your life when you will be thanking your jet lag) and drive the 45 minutes up to Haleakala National Park summit. This way you have time to acclimate to the thin oxygen levels before exploring the volcano.

The staff at the visitors center can assist with hiking maps and plenty of geological and historical facts about the volcano, as well as reminding you to look out for the *nene*, the Hawaiian state bird that roams the parking lot up here.

The second way travelers make it up here to view the sunrise is via a bike tour. Maui Downhill and Haleakala Bike Company offer transport up the mountain, as well as bikes and safety gear for adventurers to pedal 38 miles back down Crater Road (post-sunrise) toward Pa'ia, where the restaurant workers mark time by the arrival of the bikers each day. Book your bike trip online to assure steep discounts. You'll be back in Pa'ia in time for lunch, then an afternoon massage and beach nap.

For the rest of you, know that any time you arrive at Haleakala can be inspiring—I especially like sunset. Whenever you make the trip, dress very warmly (I'm talking win-ter coats). You will be blown away by how cold it is up here. As you ascend Crater Road, there are a number of overlooks, all of which are worth a stop. One of my favorites is the highest point on Maui, Pu'u'ula'ula Overlook, where you can view a silversword gar-den as well as stunning views of the landscape. Teeth-chattering visitors gather in the glass enclosure to keep warm. From here you can view Science City, an array of other-worldly buildings used by NASA and scholars to study space, climate change, and volcanic activity.

Early arrivals and backpackers can hike into the crater on Sliding Sands Trail—a 9-mile adventure that leads to a rustic campsite. Alternatively, those who camp at Hosmer Grove (the only drive-up site in the park), or those interested in a more mellow shaded hike, will like Hosmer Grove Trail, located less than a mile south of the visitors center.

Once you've had your fill of getting wind whipped by the volcano, back on Kula Highway you'll pass through Pukalani, which doesn't offer much for tourists save Pukalani Superette. Here you can gather goods for a picnic (including yummy *bento* boxes), or merely purchase some hydration. Locals are devoted to this historic Upcountry market. People heading up to Haleakala for sunset often grab some snacks here.

Turn right onto Makawao Road, where Upcountry shows off its rolling hills dotted with cattle farms and rainbows. As the road drops you into Makawao, Upcountry begins to stand taller as a hub for farm-fresh cuisine and art galleries. In any other locale, Makawao would be considered a dusty cowboy town. And while you can find many *paniolo* (Hawaiian cowboys) rounding up cattle, you'll also stumble upon innovative artists and foodies who are filling Makawao's aging plantation-style buildings with cherished destinations.

The commercial district stretches along Baldwin Avenue and houses one of Maui's most dense collection of galleries. Specializing in plein air oil paintings of Hawai'i's beaches, produce, and landscapes, New York transplant Jordanne Weinstein has show-

HELICOPTER TOURS

Viewing the islands from the air can be the most memorable part of any Hawaiian vacation. While expensive, these one- to two-hour journeys can provide glimpses of parts of the islands unseen by most. A few too many licensed pilots hawk helicopter tours for my taste, and every year there's another story of a helicopter (or three) in Hawai'i going up in dangerous conditions, only to end in tragedy. The best way to assure a safe trip is to research the company's recent safety record, and book your trip early in your vacation—that way, if the conditions are not ideal for flying, you have time to reschedule.

Warnings aside, if you have cash burning a hole in your pocket, join Blue Hawaiian Helicopters (www.bluehawaiian.com) for a winning ride over Hana and Haleakala. This outfit also offers multi-island trips that pair Maui with Moloka'i or the Big Island. As with most experiences in Hawai'i, you can find significant discounts online.

Makawao's artsy don't seem to take themselves too seriously.

cased her work in her Lanaʻi gallery for many years. Recently, she opened up Jordanne Gallery and Studio in the heart of Makawao. Across the street, Viewpoints Gallery offers the largest collection of art in town—here you are sure to find treasures like paintings of local landscapes or stunning sculptures. Another worthy stop is Hui Noʻeau Gift Shop, where you can see this artists' collective's craft art as well as the historic grounds. If this little town begins to inspire, sign up for a weekend intensive at Hui Noʻeau.

Market Fresh Bistro sources much of its produce and meats from within 100 miles of the spare dining room. But don't let the bland restaurant interiors fool you—the attention has been placed on the cuisine, so gobble up those juicy grass-fed beef burgers, served at a reasonable price. The vibrant Polli's Mexican Restaurant has been treating Makawao residents to hearty margaritas, abundant tostadas, and steamy fajitas for over 30 years. Frankly, while these are both decent options, I recommend continuing on for a few more miles to find one of Maui's most iconic restaurants.

People wanting to really get into the spirit of Upcountry might splurge on the new luxury retreat Lumeria Maui, situ-

A MORNING DELICACY

Across from the library, Komoda Store and Bakery serves legendary crème puffs, doughnuts, and custard-filled long johns. Get here early, because by late afternoon the selection can be disappointing.

AN UNDER-THE-RADAR UPCOUNTRY EXPERIENCE

Repeat visitors, or those staying in Upcountry, will love the crowd-pleasing Piiholo Ranch Zipline: a fun and education way to see nature. Zip over the treetops with a friend at your side and then breeze to your next set of ropes on ATVs. Those traveling with little ones can arrange pony rides at their ranch.

ated on 6 acres between Makawao and Pa'ia. The restored historic buildings offer interiors with a global aesthetic: Japanese poster beds and woven pillows splashed with color. Rooms feature Maui artwork, a rock shower, and an outdoor sitting area. Guests receive complimentary organic breakfast daily as well as yoga and meditation classes. The on-site gardens showcasing rare crystals and Buddha statues, the pool, and Harvest, their farm-to-table restaurant, add charm.

Less of a wallet shocker is Banyan Bed and Breakfast. The plantation house is broken up into a series of smallish rooms with private bathrooms, a shared living space, and simple interiors. The cottages feature kitchenettes and a bit more space. All accommodations offer pool access, complimentary breakfast, and free Wi-Fi. Another Upcountry option is the historic plantation house Hale Ho'okipa. Guests unwind in the organic gardens, sourced to make the generous breakfasts. Charm and Old World style are on the menu in rooms, with plush bedding, wide windows, private bathrooms, cable TV, and free Wi-Fi. A portion of your room fee goes to preservation of the forest. The owners also offer interesting voluntourism opportunities.

Finally, it is not possible to say you've experienced Upcountry without a stop at Bev Gannon's Hali'imaile General Store (if you only have time to dine at one Upcountry restaurant, this should be your choice). The large plantation house features a wraparound porch where you can often see rainbows stretch over the mountains. Inside, the dining room is guarded by a splashy collection of colorful art. The friendly staff cater to families and those here for celebratory meals.

Entrées run the gamut of Thai, Mexican, Italian, and Hawaiian flavors, but the house specialties are crab pizza, ribs, and creative sashimi dishes. Last time I was here, I had a sashimi pizza, which was surprisingly good. To get here from Makawao's Baldwin Avenue, turn left onto Hali'imaile Road and continue for 2 miles. After a nightcap on the porch, take Baldwin Road downhill to Pa'ia.

Hali'imaile General Store's attractive cuisine

IN THE AREA

ACCOMMODATIONS

Banyan Bed and Breakfast, 3265 Baldwin Ave., Makawao. Splurge on a private cottage with a kitchenette on these historic grounds. Call 808-572-9021. Website www.bed-breakfast-maui.com.

Hale Ho'okipa Inn, 32 Pakani Pl., Makawao. Majestic plantation-style home with a delicious breakfast that provides travelers with ways to give back to the community. Call 808-572-6698. Website www.maui-bed-and-breakfast.com.

Hana Kai Maui, 4865 Uakea Rd., Hana. An oceanfront condo complex in Hana with private lanais and free Wi-Fi. Call 808-248-8426. Website www.hanakai maui.com.

Ha'iku Plantation Inn Bed and Breakfast, 555 Ha'iku Rd., Ha'iku. Bargain accommodations in the heart of one of Maui's funkiest towns. Call 808-575-7500. Website www.haikuleana.net.

Huelo Point Lookout Vacation Rentals, 222 Door of Faith, Ha'iku. Ocean-view cottages with outdoor hot tubs surrounded by organic fruit trees. Call 800-871-8645. Website www.maui-vacationrentals.com.

Inn at Mama's, 799 Poho Pl., Pa'ia. Beachfront and garden cottages decked out in retro beach décor. Call 808-579-9764. Website www.mamasfishhouse.com.

Joe's Place, 4870 Uakea Rd., Hana. Modest accommodations with access to shared kitchen and living room, right by Hana Bay and close to town. Call 808-248-7033. Website www.joesrentals.com.

Kula Lodge, 15200 Haleakala Hwy., Kula. Five rustic chalets in near Haleakala, with an on-site restaurant. Call 808-878-1535. Website www.kula lodge.com.

Kula Sandalwoods Cottages, 15427 Haleakala Hwy., Kula. Cozy cottages on the slopes of Haleakala, with an adjacent restaurant. Call 808-878-3523. Website www.kulasandalwoods.com.

Lumeria Maui, 1813 Baldwin Ave., Makawao. Thoughtful Zen resort popular with yogis and contemplative types, with a farm-to-table restaurant, pool, and yoga classes. Call 855-579-8877. Website www.lumeriamaui.com.

Pa'ia Inn, 93 Hana Hwy., Pa'ia. Trendy boutique hotel just steps away from a white sand beach. Call 808-579-6000. Website www.paiainn.com.

Travaasa Hana, 5031 Hana Hwy., Hana. A luxury spa resort with open-air cottages, some with private lanai hot tubs. There are a couple of restaurants, a gallery, live music, and a pool for families. Call 808-248-8211. Website www.travaasa.com/hana.

ATTRACTIONS AND RECREATION

Ali'i Kula Lavender Farm, 1100 Waipoli Rd., Kula. Wander the lavender-infused grounds and sip a lavender tea with million-dollar views. Call 808-878-3004. Website www.aliikulalavender.com.

Alice in Hulaland, 19 Baldwin Ave., Pa'ia. Cute boutique for Hawaiiana, clothing, and home décor. Call 808-579-9922. Website www.aliceinhulaland.com.

Garden of Eden Arboretum, 10600 Hana Hwy., Ha'iku. Pay to hike to a waterfall along the lush Hana Highway. Call 808-572-9899. Website www.maui gardenofeden.com.

Haleakala Bike Company, 810 Ha'iku Rd., #120, Ha'iku. Pedal down the volcano with these master guides. Call 808-575-9575. Website www.bikemaui.com.

Haleakala National Park. Camp, hike, take photos, and marvel at the lunar landscape atop Maui's dormant volcano. Call 808-572-4400. Website www.nps.gov /hale.

Hana Cultural Center and Museum, 4974 Uakea Rd., Hana. Small museum and shop showcasing Hana history. Call 808-248-8622. Website www.hana culturalcenter.org.

Hana Highway Surf, 149 Hana Hwy., Pa'ia. Board rentals, sales, and lessons. Call 808-579-8999. Website www.hana hwysurf.com.

Hasegawa General Store, 5165 Hana Hwy., Hana. Grab groceries, toys, and tools while you are at it. Call 808-248-8231.

Hi Tech Surf Sports, 58 Baldwin Ave., Pa'ia. Surf gear and lessons in Pa'ia. Call 808-579-9297. Website www.surfmaui .com.

Hui No'eau Visual Arts Center, 2841 Baldwin Ave., Makawao. The North Shore's finest cultural enclave offers a gallery and classes. Call 808-572-6560. Website www.huinoeau.com.

Jordanne Gallery and Studio, 3625 Baldwin Ave., Makawao. Plein air paintings pay tribute to the islands. Call 808-563-0088. Website www.jordannefineart .com.

Kaupo General Store, Pi'ilani Hwy. (#31), Kaupo.

Kula Botanical Gardens, 638 Kekaulike Ave., Kula. *Protea* fans look no farther, this is ground zero for marveling at these prehistoric wonders. Call 808-878-1715. Website www.kulabotanical garden.com.

Maui Crafts Guild, 69 Hana Hwy., Pa'ia. Local artists' co-op and gallery. Call 808-579-9697. Website www.maui craftsguild.com.

Maui Downhill Bicycle Tours, 199 Dairy Rd., Kahului. Cycle down Haleakala with helpful guides. Call 808-871-2155. Website www.mauidownhill .com.

Maui Girl, 12 Baldwin Ave., Pa'ia. A fantastic selection of bikinis. Call 808-579-9266. Website www.maui-girl.com.

Maui Hands, 84 Hana Hwy., Pa'ia. Locally made crafts and art. Call 808-579-9245. Website www.mauihands.com.

Ono Organic Farms, 149 Hana Hwy., Hana. Farm tours, tropical fruit, and a touch of that iconic East Maui flavor. Call 808-248-7779. Website www.ono farms.com.

Piiholo Ranch Zipline, 1156 Makawao Ave., Makawao. Zipline trips and pony rides in the Makawao hills. Call 808-572-1717. Website www.piiholozipline.com.

Surfing Goat Dairy, 3651 Omaopio Rd., Kula. Visit a thriving goat cheese farm. Call 808-878-2870. Website www.surfing goatdairy.com.

Viewpoints Gallery, 3620 Baldwin Ave., Makawao. The largest gallery in Makawao features paintings and sculptures. Call 808-572-5979. Website www.viewpointsgallerymaui.com.

DINING

Braddah Hutts BBQ, mile marker 35 on the Hana Hwy., Hana. Food truck serving local-style BBQ plate lunch or fish tacos with pineapple salsa.

Café Attitude. Pass Kipahulu on your way toward Kaupo (if you go by a cow mailbox, you've gone a few driveways too far). Enjoy mostly vegan food and live music. Ask around for days and times—it's that kind of place.

Charley's, 142 Hana Hwy., Pa'ia. Lively restaurant and saloon atmosphere open for breakfast, lunch, and into the wee hours of night. Call 808-579-8085. Website www.charleysmaui.com.

Colleen's at the Cannery, 810 Ha'iku Rd., Ha'iku. Located in an old pineapple cannery, this pizza joint has a devoted following. Breakfasts are also quite good. Call 808-575-9211. Website www.colleensinhaiku.com.

Crater Coffee Cart, 15200 Haleakala Hwy., Kula. Coffee, tea, and locally baked goodies on the way to Haleakala. Call

808-757-1342. Website www.cratercoffee
.com.

Flatbread Company, 89 Hana Hwy.,
Pa'ia. Pizza with gluten-free options and
fresh, organic veggie toppings lure
health-conscious families. Call 808-579-
8989. Website www.flatbreadcompany
.com.

Grandma's Coffee Shop, 9232 Kula
Hwy., Kula. Enjoy coffee from the farm
where it is grown. Breakfasts are a wise
choice as well. Call 808-878-2140. Website www.grandmascoffee.com.

Halfway to Hana Fruit Stand, 13710
Hana Hwy. (just past mile marker 17),
Ke'anae. I have two words for you: banana bread. Website www.halfwayto
hanamaui.com.

Hali'imaile General Store, 900
Hali'imaile Rd., Makawao. Lunch and
dinners feature farm-fresh salads,
sashimi pizza, and tasty steaks sourced
from Upcountry. Reserve a table for dinner. Call 808-572-2666. Website www.bev
gannonrestaurants.com/haliimaile.

Hana Hou Café, 810 Ha'iku Rd., Bldg.
#404, Ha'iku. Spring for the *laulau* or
opakapaka in this Ha'iku fave. Call 808-
575-2661. Website www.hanahoucafe
.com.

Hana Ranch Restaurant, 5031 Hana
Hwy., Hana. Geared toward tourists, this
pricey cowboy-themed eatery offers big
plates of steaks and pastas. Call 808-
270-5280.

Huelo Lookout Fruit Stand, 7600
Hana Hwy., Ha'iku. Get a tropical
smoothie with fresh-squeezed sugarcane juice. Call 808-280-4791 or 800-
471-7435. Website www.huelolookout
.coconutprotectors.com.

Johnny B's Burgers, Shakes, and
Fries, 65 Hana Hwy., Pa'ia. Stop by for a
burger and fries and watch the people of
Pa'ia wander by. Call 808-579-9790.
Website www.johnnybsmaui.com.

Ke'anae Landing Fruit Stands, Hana
Hwy., Ha'iku. Stop off of the Hana High-

way in Ke'anae for fresh-baked banana
bread and produce. Website www.keanae
maui.blogspot.com.

Komoda Store and Bakery, 3674
Baldwin Ave., Makawao. Guava
malasadas and stick doughnuts take you
back to the 1950s. Get here before noon.
Closed Wednesday. Call 808-572-7261.

Kula Bistro, 4566 Lower Kula Rd., Kula.
White chocolate mac nut pancakes for
breakfast, or pork egg rolls at dinner,
reel foodies to Upcountry. Call 808-871-
2960. Website www.kulabistro.com.

Kula Country Farms, 375 Koheo Rd.,
Kula. Gather fresh strawberries, onions,
and corn. Call 808-878-8381. Website
www.kulacountryfarmsmaui.com.

Kula Lodge Restaurant, 15200
Haleakala Hwy., Kula. Open for breakfast, lunch, and dinner (with a wood-
burning pizza oven) daily. A decent
option for exhausted hikers heading
back from Haleakala. Call 808-878-1535.
Website www.kulalodge.com.

Kula Sandalwoods Restaurant, 15427
Haleakala Hwy., Kula. Eggs Benedict
and fluffy macadamia nut pancakes for
breakfast, and pork sandwiches and
onion soup for lunch, please tired hikers. Call 808-878-3523. Website www
.kulasandalwoods.com.

La Provence, 3158 Lower Kula Rd.,
Kula. Crepes and French-inspired
seafood dishes lure romance seekers to
Kula. Call 808-878-1313. Website
www.laprovencekula.com.

Laulima Farms, between mile markers
40 and 41 on the Hana Hwy., Kipahulu.
Fresh salads, smoothies, and coconut
milk lattes.

Mama's Fish House, 799 Poho Pl.,
Pa'ia. Beachfront seafood eatery is
Pa'ia's most upscale eatery. Dinner
reservations are a must! Call 808-579-
8488. Website www.mamasfishhouse
.com.

Mana Foods, 49 Baldwin Ave., Pa'ia.
Grab picnic fixings or goods to stock

your fridge. Call 808-579-8078. Website www.manafoodsmaui.com.

Market Fresh Bistro, 3620 Baldwin Ave., #102A, Makawao. Organic crab-cakes, fried goat cheese, and lamb ragout for brunch, lunch, and dinner. Call 808-572-4877. Website www.market freshbistro.com.

Maui's Winery at Ulupalakua Ranch, Hwy. 37, Kula. Specialty wines made from grape, pineapple, and passion fruit. Call 808-878-6058. Website www.maui wine.com.

Milagros Food Company, 3 Baldwin Ave., Pa'ia. A great happy hour, with chips and salsa to boot, on Pa'ia's busiest corner. Call 808-579-8755. Website www.milagrosfoodcompany.com.

Ono Gelato, 115 Hana Hwy., Pa'ia. Scrumptious gelato in the heart of Pa'ia, ideal for relieving the summer heat. Call 808-579-9201. Website www.onogelato company.com.

O'o Farms, 651 Waipoli Rd., Kula. Farm-to-table tour and luncheon, where guests pick their own produce. Reserve in advance. Call 808-667-4341. Website www.oofarm.com.

Pa'ia Bay Coffee, 43 Hana Hwy., Pa'ia. Good coffee, bagels, and sandwiches, plus free Wi-Fi. Call 808-579-3111. Website www.paiabaycoffee.com.

Pa'ia Fish Market, 100 Baldwin Ave., Pa'ia. Seafood salads and fish burgers reel in locals and tourists. Call 808-579-8030. Website www.paiafishmarket.com.

Polli's Mexican Restaurant, 1202 Makawao Ave., Makawao. What's better than chips and salsa, cold beer and bur-ritos? Call 808-572-7808. Website www.pollismexicanrestaurant.com.

Pukalani Superette, 15 Makawao Ave., Pukalani. *Bento* boxes, snacks, and water populate the shelves of this Upcountry market. Call 808-572-7616. Website www.pukalanisuperette.com.

Thai Food by Pranee, 5050 Uakea Rd., Hana. Local fish, fresh ingredients, friendly service are served up at this Thai food shack.

Ulupalakua Ranch Store and Grill, Hwy. 37, Kula. Beef and elk burgers, hot dogs, turkey and tuna sandwiches, and salads at this take-out joint in Upcoun-try. Call 808-878-2561. Website www .ulupalakuaranch.com/store.

OTHER CONTACT INFORMATION

Maui Visitors Bureau. Website www.gohawaii.com.

New growth on the Big Island

9 The Adventurer's Guide to the Big Island's Southern Belt

FROM KONA TO PUNA

Estimated length: 238 miles

Estimated time: 8 hours, or 5 leisurely days

Getting there: Many US, international, and inter-island carriers have direct flights to Kona International Airport, though there are a handful that stop in Honolulu first. Inter-island connections can be made on Hawaiian Airlines (www.hawaiianairlines .com), Go! (www.iflygo.com), and Island Air (www.islandair.com). It is possible to arrive at Kona Airport and then depart from Hilo International Airport. Most major rental car companies have offices outside the airport, including Thrifty (www.thrifty.com) and Budget (www.budget.com).

Getting around the Big Island is fairly straightforward: The 230-mile Hawai'i Belt Road circles the island's six districts of Kona, Kohala, Waimea, Hilo, Puna, and Ka'u. For this itinerary, you'll be exploring Kona, Puna and Ka'u.

Highlights: Watching lava spew into the Pacific at Hawai'i Volcanoes National Park; snorkeling with tropical fish, dolphins, and manta rays; learning about Kona coffee; viewing Pu'uohonua o Honaunau National Historical Site; and stepping on black, white, and green sand beaches.

The youngest sibling of the Hawaiian archipelago, Hawai'i (or the Big Island) is constantly in flux. While the other islands have their identities cast in lava rock, the Big Island has an erratic spirit that baffles many visitors. As the birthplace of King Kamehameha the Great, this nascent landscape manages to honor its cultural history with more panache than its sister islands. Yet with an active volcano spewing lava into the sea at an unprecedented volume, the land itself seems intent on having the last word—Pele, the goddess of fire, is such a trickster—by burying villages, closing roads, and entertaining the island's brave occupants with the world's most consistent fireworks show. Having to contend with an active volcano, 11 climate zones that range from blazing sun to

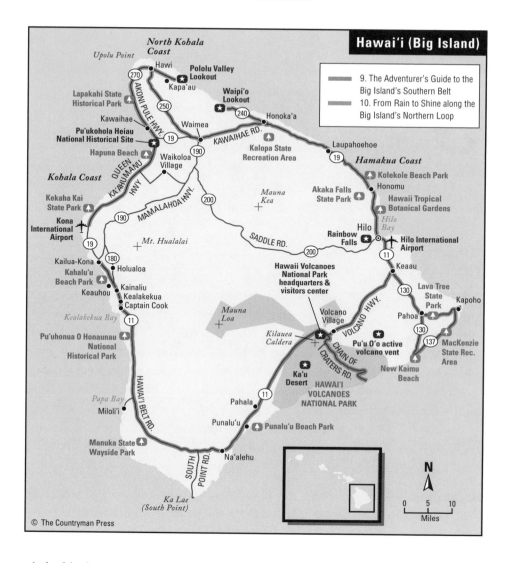

Hawai'i (Big Island)

9. The Adventurer's Guide to the Big Island's Southern Belt

10. From Rain to Shine along the Big Island's Northern Loop

© The Countryman Press

wind-whipping snow (yes, Hawai'i has snow!), and an arid, almost lunar landscape makes Hawai'i's pioneering inhabitants tough as nails, yet friendly as can be.

The intrepid visitors that descend on this otherworldly locale can watch new earth sizzle to life, stand on the southernmost point in the United States, swim with turtles and manta rays, meander along green sand, hike through lava tubes, spend weeks hiking through lush valleys, view some of the state's most sacred sites, or chill out at a resort as your iPhone gets polished. While it is easy to scramble off the beaten path, merely because there is so much to explore, the Big Island caters to all palates.

Begin your journey in the Kona Coast area, which includes Kailua-Kona (Kona), the major commercial district of the Big Island. Kona has been the playland for the affluent since ancient Hawaiian royals sojourned to this former fishing village for dependable sun. This seaside community stretches along Ali'i Drive and is appreciated for its convenience, history, and affordability. Explore the main part of town during a half-day walk. Start at King Kamehameha Beach Hotel's adjacent Ahu'ena Heiau, the former home of King Kamehameha, which at its pinnacle was a startling three times bigger than the remains you see by the Kailua-Kona Pier today. Kona's only slice of sand can be found at Kamakahonu Beach; however, there are better swim areas just south of town.

Drool over Hulihe'e Palace, the former governor's hideaway, and the summer home to King Kalakaua, during a guided tour. Lovingly restored to its former grandeur, the exterior features 1838 coral, *koa*, and lava. Once inside, check out the spear collection, and the attention to detail in the various wooden furnishings throughout the palace. They also offer hula shows on the grounds on the third Sunday of the month at 4 p.m. Across the street, Moku'aikaua Church is the island's eldest tribute to Christianity.

Shoppers will find their fill of island treats like sarongs and dancing hula dashboard trinkets alongside hidden treasures like Hawai'i Titanium Rings for rings crafted from ancient *koa* and palm wood; and Pueo Boutique, which sells locally made clothing for

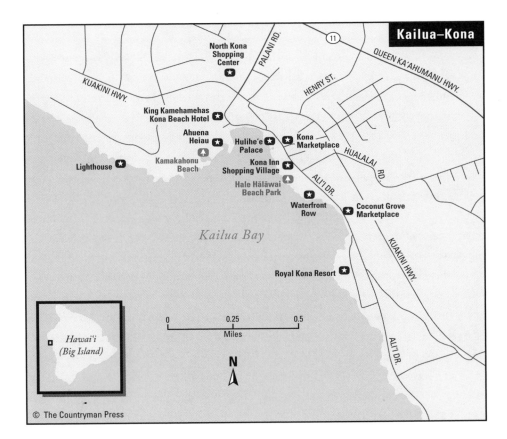

ACTIVITIES AND ADVENTURES IN AND AROUND KONA

When it comes to adventures, the Big Island is ground zero. I have listed additional tour outfitters that depart from Honokohau Harbor and the Keauhou Bay area in those sections. Since there are many experiences worth your time, I recommend selecting one activity per day to fit your needs. In Kona, Jack's Diving Locker is the largest commercial dive center on the island, offering lessons, charters, and trips to just about any underwater adventure you can imagine, including Kaiwi Point and Turtle Pinnacle, and of course those legendary night dive tours to swim with manta rays (more on this later).

Snorkelers can grab gear at Snorkel Bob's, or purchase masks and fins at any ABC Store. On Kamakahonu Beach, Kona Boys Beach Shack rents surfboards and stand-up paddleboards; they also lead trips on outrigger canoes, and offer surf lessons. It's possible to explore the rich underwater world without getting wet on Atlantis Submarines. This trip is ideal for kids over five who aren't afraid of the dark. They take you out and back in about an hour. For those in the market to put on their best linen and take a boozy cruise along the coast, Body Glove Historical Sunset Dinner Cruise offers both two- and three-hour trips.

women and children. It's possible to spend hours in the Coconut Grove Market Place, an oceanfront pageant of places to eat, drink, and spend money; there's a large free parking lot adjacent to the mall. Ali'i Gardens Marketplace houses over 50 vendors hawking crafts, kitschy souvenirs, and coffee. Crossroads Shopping Center is where you'll end up if you need to purchase groceries at Safeway, or see a movie. Another fun place to shop is at Kona Inn Shopping Village: This former hotel features boutiques, galleries, and alfresco dining. On the south side of Kona Town is Kailua Village Artists gallery, showcasing art by Big Island residents.

Eating in Kona is an exercise in diligence. There are so many options, but unfortunately many of them are mediocre. Breakfasts rule at Island Lava Java for *onolicious* pancakes with coconut syrup or eggs Benedict, served on a patio across from the sea while musicians strum guitars. They also serve lunch and dinner, but I usually just come for morning meals. Yogis and spiritual seekers gather at Basik Acai for organic fruit bowls and smoothies punctuated with treats like cacao and spirulina. Big Island Grill is known as *da* spot to grab *loco moco* or Spam and eggs. The pancakes are gigantic, so be prepared to share.

You'll have to do a bit of sleuthing to locate the hole-in-the-wall known affectionately as Da Poke Shack. Lunch features freshly caught *ahi* atop salads or mashed into a variety of *pokes* (like *shoyu* or *dynomite*). Typically, I go for the Shack Special to sample the best they have in stock that day. While I usually avoid places that try to do it all, Lemongrass Bistro manages to craft a mishmash of decent Asian cuisine. I favor their Thai creations like papaya salad, while my husband swears by the oxtail *kimchi* fried rice. The dining room is small, so go early or be prepared to wait a bit.

Jackie Rey's Ohana Grill pleases families in the market for a casual lunch or dinner. Awash in Hawaiian art deco décor, the food is the star, with favorites like *ono* sandwiches, pork egg rolls, and coconut-infused sweet potatoes rocking the house. This breezy outdoor eatery shines during happy hour, when most *pupus* are half price. Make a reservation for dinner, as this is one of Kona's most popular eateries.

Kona's other table in demand is at Huggo's on the Rocks or—as it's called in the morning, when they serve coffee and pastries—Java on the Rock. As you sit over the sea, sipping a piña colada while noshing on Korean tacos or a *kalua* pork sandwich and listening to live music, you've got to wonder if life could get any better. If you'd prefer something more sophisticated for dinner, head upstairs to Huggo's, which is still perched over the crashing waves, but without the casual feet-in-the-sand vibe of its sister restaurant. The chefs prepare the island-fresh catch swimming in a lemongrass *haupia* sauce that still gets me dreamy. Carnivores should opt for the teriyaki steak, their signature plate that has been on the menu since they opened in 1969. Reservations are highly recommended.

It's hard to say, but Kona Brewing Company, lodged in an industrial park on a hill away from the Pacific, might be Kona's most popular restaurant. Locals and tourists line up for growlers, pizza, nachos, and fish tacos. Beer flavors many of the dishes. On your first visit, order the beer sampler to see what these guys do best. Some Saturdays there is live music. While the wait can seem to last for ages, you can start sampling their Longboard lager, so it's not that bad.

Accommodations in Kona run the gamut, and honestly, your best bets are just outside of town. If you'd like to rent a condo, however, you are in luck. There are literally hundreds to choose from. As with the other islands, complexes house independently owned units, which means you need to do your homework. Ask to see photos of units before booking. Some oceanfront complexes to take a look at include Royal Sea Cliff Resort and Hale Kona Kai.

If you'd like to be near the action, but not pay the big bucks for an upscale place to lay your head, check out Kona Tiki Hotel. With 15 simple rooms, a pool, and a fantastic address along the sea, this cash-only hotel lures repeat visitors, especially

Kona Brewing Company is a must on every beer drinker's itinerary.

in winter, when it is nearly impossible to score a room. Splurge for a suite with a kitchenette. The only other hotel in town that I will vouch for is King Kamehameha Kona Beach Hotel, especially if all that matters to you is a beachfront location steps from Kona's restaurants, shops, and attractions. Top it all off with a pool, an activities center, a lu'au, free Wi-Fi, and newly renovated rooms.

As you continue on Ali'i Drive, about 4 miles south of the center of town is White Sands Beach, or Magic Sands Beach. In winter, the tide swallows the sand, making the beach impossible to enjoy. However, when the white sand shows back up, snorkelers, bodyboarders, and sunbathers can't get enough of these strands. About another mile south is one of the Big Island's most popular beaches—Kahalu'u Beach Park. With the sweet St. Peter's Church perched on one end, a collection of ancient historical sites surrounding the bay, and a coral-reef-enclosed sea teeming with tropical fish and sea turtles, this beach caters to all palates. Locals celebrate birthdays here, while visitors go gaga over the abundant sea life and the glorious sunsets. You can easily spend hours at either of these beaches, especially if you've brought along beach toys like snorkels, boogie boards, or surfboards.

By this point you've officially entered the glam Keauhou Resort Area. Unless you are staying here, or heading out on a snorkeling trip from Keauhou Bay, there's not much to add to your itinerary. However, there are a few places to make note of. The gorgeous Outrigger Kanaloa at Kona condos offer spacious units with gourmet kitchens, wide lanais—many of which are perched over the sea—and tastefully decorated interiors. Throw in a pool, Ping-Pong tables, maid service, and a concierge, and you see why these units are highly coveted.

The Keauhou Shopping Center is the community's gathering place and is useful to know about if you are staying nearby for a few days. Besides the farmers' market (see the sidebar), there's a ukulele show on the last Saturday of the month, craft making on Thursday 10–noon, and Friday-evening hula at 6. Shoppers will appreciate the shops like Kona Stories, the best bookstore on the island. There's a cinema here, and plenty of

---

DEEP-SEA FISHING

With a wealth of big fish just 3 miles off the coast, Kona is known for its deep-sea fishing. In August, big-game catchers descend on the coast to participate in one of the world's biggest competitions: the Hawaiian International Billfish Tournament. Just north of Kona, you can hire charters out of Honokohau Harbor to seek out marlin, *mahi mahi*, *ono*, and *ahi*, occasionally weighing over 1,000 pounds. If you'd like to try your hand at snagging a trophy fish, the Charter Desk on the harbor is the main booking area. Bite Me Fish Market also leads fishing trips.

BIG ISLAND'S BEST FARMERS' MARKET

In the Keauhou Shopping Center on Saturday from 8 to noon, it seems the whole island comes out for the farmers' market. Though this is not a sprawling market, each vendor is serious about farming. Score locally grown coffee, fresh-made leis, abundant produce, gifts, and more. There is live music and lots of yummy food.

food. Favorite dining choices include the crepes at Peaberry and Galette and the upscale Hawaiian cuisine at Sam Choy's Kai Lanai, which boasts views of the sea from atop the hill, and glorious *poke*. This center also houses KTA Super Store for groceries.

Cross off a major *to-do* from your bucket list, and arrange a snorkel or dive tour in the waters off Keauhou Bay and Kealakekua Bay. Keauhou Bay is where outfitters take folks on night dives (or snorkel trips) to view the otherworldly manta rays. The waters off Keauhou Bay can often be rough in the evenings, so only go out if you are a strong swimmer. The other adventure cruises departing from this bay are the snorkel and dive trips to Kealakekua Bay, quite possibly Hawai'i's most pristine area to spot sea life. Of the many outfitters who promise both excursions, I've had good experiences with Fair Wind and Sea Paradise. The Kealakekua Bay trips take about 3½–4½ hours and leave in the morning or afternoon (though mornings are better for visibility). The nightly manta ray trips are 1½ hours, and sightings are usually guaranteed. It is wise to know that many get seasick on these tours, as you jump in the water and hold on to a surfboard with lights on it to attract plankton. The manta rays appear like aliens, swimming around your body. This adventure is not for the faint of heart.

The other area specializing in these two adventures is off H 19, 2 miles north of Kona; turn left on Kealakehe Parkway and find Honokohau Harbor. This area is protected by its status as a marine conservation district, making the waters rich with sea life. Outfitters found here include Captain Zodiac (half-day raft trips to snorkel in Kealakekua Bay with dolphins) and Kamanu Charters, which is just one of the gazillion outfitters to lead spooky night dives (and snorkel trips) to view the huge manta rays, but in a less populated area. Adventurers can also arrange kayak trips with Plenty Pupule—they'll tailor trips to fit the skill levels of just about anyone. Surfers can arrange lessons and rent or purchase gear at Ocean Eco Tours on the harbor—ask if they can deliver you to Pine Trees, one of the island's best surf spots, located on Keahole Point, just north of the harbor. In winter, book far in advance for a whale-watching cruise with Captain Dan McSweeney. This researcher pilots his boat out twice daily to view humpback whale

---

DETOUR: KALOKO-HONOKOHAU NATIONAL HISTORIC PARK

Allegedly Kamehameha the Great's final resting spot (his burial grounds have been kept secret), this historic park is one of the island's less-viewed attractions. The ancient Kaloko and 'Aimakapa Fishponds are where native Hawaiians trapped fish for dinner. The visitors center provides trail maps of both the King's Trail and the walking/driving path through the ancient land division that triangles up the lava field. There's a *heiau* and petroglyphs on site. Just beyond 'Aimakapa Fishpond, Honokohau Beach pleases snorkelers who rely on calm seas to spot green sea turtles basking in the sun.

---

breeding grounds. I prefer the morning trips, which are slightly less bumpy. Cruises are three hours long. In summer, Captain Dan usually locates other whale species around the island, but the winter trips are his big seller.

After your journey under the sea, head over to Bite Me Fish Market Bar and Grill on Honokohau Harbor to sample the freshest seafood money can buy. This funky joint caters to the salty sailors at the bar, drinking lager out of their own beer cozies (stored along the bar), talking story about their days at sea. It's fun to watch the fishermen weigh in their catches in the afternoon, and then hand over their fish to the chef to fillet. There's a wall of trophy fish photos and plenty of testosterone provided by the über-cute wait staff. Order the fresh catch, even if other items sound good.

For those wanting to sleep close to Kona, yet up along the breezy Mount Hualalai in Kona's cloud forest, don't miss the charming Honu Kai B&B. Carved wooden poster beds adorned with Hawaiian floral duvets, a hot tub, access to the roof deck, and an abundant breakfast are just some of the ways Wendy and Dave cater to guests. Their attention

Bite Me Fish Market Bar and Grill is a saucy place for a beer.

to detail, from the shared outdoor space to the thoughtful touches like packed lunches with trail mix added in, make this hidden gem one of the island's finest escapes. To get here, take H 19 south from the harbor, and then turn left on Hao Kuni Street.

Continue into Upcountry by taking Highway 180 south to reach the artists' community of Holualoa. This hillside community, rich with galleries and funky shops, slowly exposes herself the longer you stay; budget some time to wander around. In itself, Ipu Hale Gallery is worth the trek up here. Meander through the collection of hand-carved *ipu* (gourds) crafted by local artists, using the traditional

> ## NELHA'S GIFT TO THE WORLD
>
> **B**etween mile markers 94 and 95 on H 19, occupying prime real estate on Keahole Point, you'll find Natural Energy Laboratory of Hawai'i Authority (NELHA). Working to harness clean energy, this lab opens its doors for visitors to experience lectures on solar, wind, and water energy, take abalone farm tours, and visit the Ocean Rider Seahorse Farm. In the surrounding area, their quiet beach has tide pools.

methods of Ni'ihau carvers. Another worthy stop is Kimura Lauhala Shop, packed with woven *lauhala* products like place mats and hats. For those wanting to bring home an authentic ukulele, Holualoa Ukulele Gallery hawks handmade instruments—and if you have a week to spare, you can craft your own in the on-site studio. Studio 7 highlights sculptures and paintings by local artists. Three miles south of the center of town, Donkey Mill Art Center shows off the vision of Upcountry artists.

If you are only passing through for a meal, Holuakoa Café and Gardens occupies a plantation-style house surrounded by gardens. The café offers soups, coffee, and pastries, while the restaurant specializes in slow food served *really* slowly. Locally sourced lunch favorites include a heaping tuna melt and chicken salad sandwich. Dinners feature grass-fed burgers, pastas, or pork trotters. This hidden gem is the most charmed restaurant in Upcountry.

For a stay in the cool uplands of Kona, romance seekers will adore the six-room Holualoa Inn. Bamboo walls, views of the inn's coffee trees and surrounding gardens, local art, and plush bedding are just some of the perks. Additional amenities include rock showers, a shared kitchenette, breakfast, and a pool. This inn is not suitable for small children.

The 22-mile Kona Coffee Belt stretches south from Holualoa and is characterized by verdant rainy hillsides and a low-key vibe that makes you feel as if you're traveling back in time. A string of small towns can satiate your needs for provisions, antiques, or some local flavor. Continue on Mamalahoa Highway, which merges with Highway 11 in Honalo

COFFEE TOURS

There are over 600 coffee farms on this stretch of Upcountry Kona, many of which allow visitors to tour the property. Below are some of my favorites, both for quality and experience. Most tours are less than an hour, so it is easy to pop in on the way to other destinations without taking up a chunk of your day.

Freshly roasted coffee in Kona's coffee country

Mountain Thunder Coffee Plantation, a family business, operates one of the largest organic coffee farms in the state, with free tours on the hour (though with the longer VIP tour you get to roast 5 pounds of beans and take them home as a souvenir). There is a great gift shop focusing on everything from body lotion to mugs for the coffee lover. Tours are informative; you don't get dirty, and strollers and heels are accepted. Plus you get to sample lots of coffee.

Kealakekua's Greenwell Farms offers free tours of their 150-acre coffee plantation—insightful introductions to the craft of urging that caffeine from the cherry to your cup. The farmers have been growing coffee here for four generations.

Other farm tours of note include Hula Daddy, Kona Blue Sky Coffee Tours, and Kona Historical Society's 5½-acre Kona Coffee Living History Farm (a two-hour adventure that explores the rich history of growing and cultivating beans in the area, by taking visitors on a tour of a 1900s coffee plantation).

(the road will be called Highway 11 from now on). You'll pass Daifukuji Soto Mission, a Japanese Buddhist temple, and pull into Teshima Restaurant for classic Japanese eats that have been served up since the 1940s. Even if you aren't hungry, pop in for a nutty green tea and some homey atmosphere.

Five miles south of Kona is the former plantation town of Kainaliu, which is sadly

known for its traffic. Kimura's is a general store like none other that was built in 1927. Another historic building is the 1932-vintage Aloha Theatre, where you can grab a bite to eat at the café, watch indie films, or view community theater in the evenings. If you are hungry, Annie's Island Fresh Burgers serves sweet tropical teas, hearty beef and veggie burgers, and purple sweet potato chips on an outdoor patio.

Continue south on the highway for a mile to Kealakekua, the largest of the Upcountry towns. You can go on a coffee tour (see the sidebar), and if you're interested in a vintage shave ice machine or aloha shirt, Discovery Antiques is the island's most accessible antiques shop. They also have an ice cream bar in the back to help you cool off on a hot day. Another fun antiques shop is Mayme's Attic, literally packed to the roof with trinkets and bric-a-brac from another era.

While it's not the most enchanting of the Big Island's food options, lunches at

Find antique ukuleles in Kealakekua

A vintage shave ice maker for sale at Discovery Antiques

Nasturtium Café are healthy, featuring items like seafood and goat cheese quesadillas or Mexican corn soup. Dinners at Keei Café showcase meaty dishes like the pan-seared rib eye and lamb chops paired with mashed potatoes. The mango cobbler is memorable. The view of the ocean from your perch in the hills isn't bad either. After a day of snorkeling and driving, splurge on a half-hour soak in a hot tub under a thatched roof, and then an hour hot stone massage at Mamalahoa Hot Tubs and Massage—it's the best deal in town. If you'd like to continue the adventure tomorrow, it is possible to return to Kona via the newly constructed bypass road, Haleki'i Street.

As it departs Kealakekua, Highway 11 weaves through lush greenery and approaches Captain Cook, a blink-and-you-miss-it town housing the historic Manago Hotel, built in 1917. The low-key on-site restaurant has been a stopping point for hungry travelers wanting liver and onions or pork chops since its inception. The attached 64-room hotel is similarly modest, with a third of the rooms (in the original building) providing shared baths. Newer rooms have private bathrooms, but these sell out well in advance. Just up the road, between mile markers 108 and 109, on the *makai* side, The Coffee Shack serves breakfast and lunch, as well as Kona coffee, on a spacious lanai overlooking the sea. Don't skip the banana bread. You might want to grab picnic goods or snacks at Choice Mart before continuing with the itinerary.

If you stopped at The Coffee Shack, you have to backtrack a mile or so to take Napoopoo Road west for 4.5 miles to access Kealakekua Bay State Historic Park, one of the most sacred destinations in the entire state. In 1778, after making his rounds to other islands, Captain Cook arrived on the Big Island. It was harvest season, the locals

Pu'uhonua o Honaunau National Historic Park

were generous, and, thinking Cook was the reincarnation of the god Lono, they showered him with women, gifts, canoes, and food. Today you can visit Hikiau Heiau, where Cook was initially welcomed to Hawai'i (it's the lava rock platform by the bathrooms along the bay).

When Cook finally left the island, rough seas battered his ship, forcing him to turn back. The seas on the island had changed as well, and natives weren't as welcoming on the second visit, a mere four months later. In fact, after Cook's longboat was stolen, he went to retrieve it and was massacred by the Hawaiian people. The Captain Cook Monument is a white obelisk by the bay, which is the starting point for a 3-mile trail to the snorkeling beach, Ka'awaloa Cove—though the round-trip hike is quite hot and not recommended if you plan to exert energy in the water, unless of course you are an Ironman or -woman in training. Home to a rich diversity of sea life, including spinner

DETOUR: HO'OKENA BEACH PARK AND MILOLI'I BEACH PARK

To access the gray sand Ho'okena Beach Park, complete with sparkling waters populated with dolphins and whales, between mile markers 101 and 102, follow the sign and head *makai* for 2 miles. The waters are basically calm in summer, making this an ideal spot for snorkeling. It is possible to camp here too, though you may find residents a bit territorial of their slice of heaven.

For another rather isolated beach, take the signed turnoff around mile marker 89 *makai* for 5 windy miles to Miloli'i, a traditional Hawaiian fishing village. Watch native fishermen snag fish to fry at Miloli'i Beach Park.

dolphins, coral reefs, and turtles, Kealeakekua Bay is a snorkeler's dream. There are three ways to access Ka'awaloa Cove: on a boat trip, via kayak, or hiking the Captain Cook Monument Trail. I listed dive and snorkel outfitters that lead trips to this bay earlier in this chapter. As for kayaking, hitch a ride with Kona Boys' tours.

Otherwise, continue south on Pu'uhonua Road to the powerful Pu'uhonua o Honaunau National Historic Park. The 180 acres of beachfront property were once one of the most important destinations to native Hawaiians. In ancient times, if someone had broken a sacred law, called *kapu*, they could be sentenced to death. To mainlanders, the *kapu* system was extreme—someone could be put to death for touching royalty or eating particular foods—but to Hawaiians, this was how they kept order. Luckily the ancients had one get-out-of-jail-free card: If offenders could make it to the place of refuge, the Pu'uhonua, they could absolve themselves and return to society. The newly restored Pacific Islander architecture and statues of this astounding historic site line the sea, and could not be more picturesque. Take a self-guided tour of the thatched-roof *hales*, burial sites, fishponds, ancient games, and the Hale o Keawe *heiau*, a temple constructed in the 1600s. It is possible to snorkel at Two-Step, a clear spot to the north of the park, with nearly perfect visibility. Exploring this park without snorkeling should take between an hour and two hours.

Take Highway 160 east uphill, passing St. Benedict's Painted Church, which was moved from the bay to its perch on the hill; today the walls are painted with biblical scenes that are in need of refreshing. Continue to Highway 11 and if you want a romantic retreat, backtrack north on the highway and travel *mauka* on Tobacco Road for a mile to find Aloha Guest House B&B. The five rooms include poster beds with views of the sea, organic bath products, large lanais, access to the hot tub, and a breakfast to write home about.

As you continue south on Highway 11, you enter the Ka'u District, the South Point area of the island—the largest yet least-populated district, which houses Kilauea Vol-

---

DESCEND INTO ANOTHER WORLD

If you can hold your own in the dark, between mile markers 78 and 79 is Kula Kai Caverns, a 13-mile lava tube. Those wanting a lighter adventure can take a 40-minute guided walking tour. More intense are the half-day excursions. Make a reservation in advance and wear closed-toe shoes.

---

cano. North of mile marker 81 is the shady Manuka State Wayside Park, which showcases native and introduced species throughout the picnic area. There's an easy 2-mile hike—though you'll probably want to hold off on trek for now unless you budgeted a few days to explore this district.

Continuing on the highway, you'll pass Ocean View, 9 miles of houses stretching up a mountain with black lava flow tendrils. Conditions are rough in these parts, which is why this tight-knit community sticks together, not offering much by way of tourist infrastructure. There's a gas station and a couple of mediocre restaurants; unless you are famished, continue on. There is talk of constructing a major resort on a remote beach in the area, but as of press time I have no specifics.

As the road meanders east, you are approaching Ka Le (or South Point), the southernmost point in the USA—from Ocean View it takes about half an hour to get here. Between mile markers 69 and 70, turn right on South Point Road and drive for 12 bumpy miles past a wind farm and a former missile station; at the fork, travel to the right, and then park at the end of the road, which is also the Kalalea Heiau, a sacred site where fishermen made offerings to encourage their luck. Just before the point is Lua 'O Palehomo, a small pond with expansive views. Then head out to the point to experience that remote feeling as the wind whips your face and the ocean pounds below and it feels like anything is possible. This is where Tahitians landed on the islands in a.d. 750, tying their boats to these rocks—you can imagine their strength needed to control their canoes while those waves pounded them against the rocks. A visit here is especially powerful at sunrise or sunset.

To really enhance your exploration of this remote landscape, book a couple nights at Kalaekilohana B&B. Presided over by hosts Kilohana and Kenny, who go out of their way to make sure guests have all their needs met, this B&B occupies a big yellow plantation house. Amenities include locally sourced breakfast featuring specialty items like liliko'i jams and mac nut spreads, plush beds, locally milled wood floors, and marble showers. They even give you credit on your room for every dollar spent in the Ka'u district for up to $50 a day.

Back on Highway 11, you don't know you've arrived in the community of Wai'ohinu until you depart. However, keep your eyes peeled at mile marker 64 for the descendant of Mark Twain's monkeypod tree. The original tree that the author planted in 1866 fell

Punalu'u Beach Park

in the 1950s, but new growth sprang from the roots (how's that for leaving your mark?). Continue for 2 miles on Highway 11 to reach the largest community of the Ka'u District, Na'alehu. Head straight to Punalu'u Bakeshop and Visitors Center and sample some of the island's best *malasadas*—a doughnut injected with crème or jam. They also serve plate lunches, coffees, and other sweets. There are two low-key dining establishments, Hana Hou and Shaka Restaurant, and though both generally leave me wanting, you can get decent sandwiches to fill you up before heading back on the road.

Between mile markers 56 and 57 travel *makai* to Punalu'u Beach Park, a popular black sand beach inhabited by nesting sea turtles (remember that you must stay far away from these turtles; even if you see people getting super close, resist the urge). Unfortunately this beach gets very crowded throughout the day as tour buses dutifully pass through on the way to the volcano. Also a bummer is that swimming is not safe. There are ancient fishponds to the north, accessible by a short trail.

Highway 11 starts to veer north, taking you through the former sugar town of Pahala, and then snakes inland as it enters the domain of Hawai'i Volcanoes National Park. The ride toward the park offers remarkable vistas of black lava fields streaming across barren landscapes. To fully experience the park, I recommend staying for a night (or two) in the nearby town of Volcano, or in Pahoa, about 20 miles away. To reach this village, you'll bypass the park entrance and turn left on Wright Road. As a village, this community seems tapped into a higher power. Living in the shadow of these volcanoes, in a dense fern forest that is often blanketed in vog (volcanic smog), is not for the weak. Artists and renegades have planted roots to offer enchanting B&Bs, galleries, and top-notch eateries with an almost Hobbit-like charm.

DETOUR: GREEN SAND BEACH

On the way to Ka Le, on South Point Road, after 10 miles veer left and park at the grassy field. You'll have to hike for 2.5 miles on a sunny, wind-whipped coastal trail to access Papakolea, Green Sand Beach. Yes, along with volcanoes to blow your minds, the Big Island also has a green sand beach—that is, when the surf doesn't completely eat up the sand. Don't bother swimming. Enjoy the views of the pounding surf and that shiny olivine sand, sediment left from a volcanic eruption. Bring lots of water and go early.

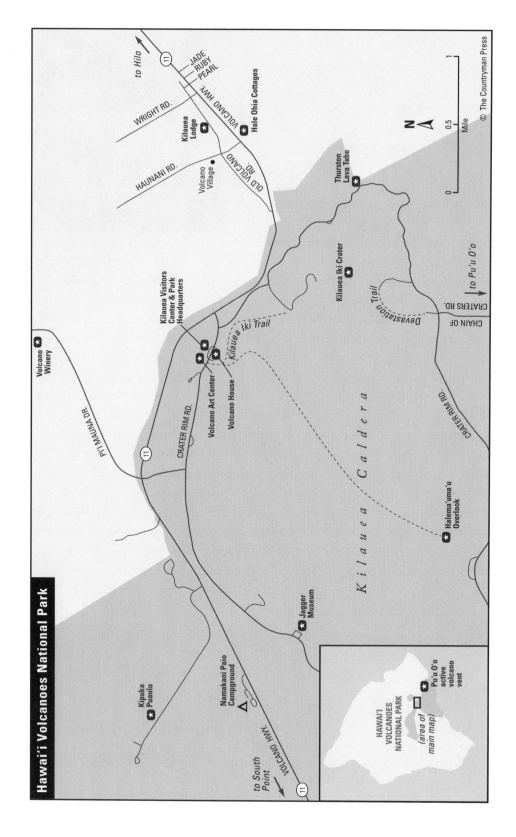

Hawai'i Volcanoes National Park

to Hilo

JADE
RUBY
PEARL

WRIGHT RD.

VOLCANO HWY.

Hale Ohia Cottages

Kilauea
Lodge

HAUNANI RD.

OLD VOLCANO RD.

Volcano Village

Thurston
Lava Tube

Kilauea Visitors
Center & Park
Headquarters

Kilauea Iki Crater

Devastation Trail

Kilauea Iki Trail

Volcano
Winery

Volcano Art Center

Volcano House

CRATER RIM RD.

to Pu'u O'o

CHAIN OF CRATERS RD.

PI'I MAUNA DR.

11

Kilauea Caldera

CRATER RIM RD.

Halema'uma'u
Overlook

Jagger
Museum

Kipuka
Puaulu

Namakani Paio
Campground

VOLCANO HWY.

to South
Point

11

N

0.5   1

0   Mile

© The Countryman Press

HAWAI'I
VOLCANOES
NATIONAL PARK

(area of
main map)

Pu'u O'o
active
volcano
vent

A SUNDAY-MORNING RITUAL

For those lucky enough to be in Volcano Village on a Sunday morning between 7 and 9, Volcano Farmers' Market is the place to be. Held at the Cooper Community Center, this potpourri of organic and biodynamic produce, wacky characters, charming families, delicious food, and artwork is a treat.

Immediately gather the pulse of this community at Volcano Garden Arts, a world heritage site inhabiting a 1908 estate constructed of California redwood trees. The grounds are the brainchild of owner-artist Ira Ono, who wanted a community space for gardeners, writers, and artists to gather. Wander through the gallery to view Ono's whimsical masks, Eastern-inspired sculptures and fountains, and lively paintings. Ono often hosts events and leads nature walks into the upland rain forest. He welcomes guests to rent his one-bedroom guest cottage, decked out in Zen themes, with a private hot tub and a kitchenette. Rounding out his empire, the on-site restaurant Café Ono provides coffee and pastries (after 10 a.m.), as well as salads, soups, and sandwiches for lunch.

There are a handful of restaurants in Volcano, so if you are staying for a night (or two), you will likely sample them all. Thai Thai Restaurant is one of the most popular eateries for miles. Known for fiery curries, plentiful *pad Thai*, and hearty fried rice, you'll have to wait for a table if you show up for dinner, but it is worth the wait. You can find a filling breakfast at Lava Rock Café; breakfast and lunch sandwiches at Café Ohi'a; and groceries at both Volcano Store and Kilauea General Store.

The notable exception for dining feels like it jumped out of a Vermont village. Kilauea Lodge occupies a stately building encircled by grassy lawns with toys and games up for grabs. The interior of the dining room, complete with a blazing fireplace, white tablecloths, and a rock wall evoke that skier's spirit, immediately invites you to order a cocktail, settle in, and enjoy the complimentary bread (food takes a while here). Gamey entrées like venison populate the menu, with vegetarians having limited options—though they will accommodate you as best they can. The restaurant serves three meals and a seriously decadent Sunday brunch. Reservations are recommended, but I have walked in at the last minute and gotten a table. Kilauea Lodge also is a B&B and vacation rental, offering rooms decked out in Hawaiian quilts, poster beds, and local art, along with a full breakfast. The owners rent out four houses as well.

ISLAND VINO?

To say you've tried everything once, sidle into Volcano Winery to sample Pinot Noir grown on the Big Island. Besides the traditional array of styles, they craft honey wine, a guava-grape duo, and a tea-and-honey varietal.

For a serious splurge, however, check into the Volcano Village Lodge, a retreat like none other. The five lodges boast free Wi-Fi, flat-panel TVs, plush bedding, floor-to-ceiling windows, fireplaces, kitchenettes, and full tropical breakfasts delivered to your room. Guests have access to the rain forest hot tub as well.

For a more affordable option, check out Bamboo Orchid Cottage B&B, a sweet little B&B presided over by a friendly host. Rooms seem to have been decorated by a globe-trotting aunt, with Japanese paper fans, silk bedding, or Chinese lamps. Heated beds, fireplaces, continental breakfast, and free Wi-Fi are thoughtful perks. For those wanting more space, their sister property Volcano Tree House offers cottages and suites surrounded by ferns. Kitchenettes, private lanais, and fireplaces, plus the fun raised platforms connecting the units, make it easy to settle in for extended periods.

And then it's time for the show! Hawai'i Volcanoes National Park, which at press time is about 350,000 acres, is like nowhere else on the planet. Since 1983 Kilauea Volcano has been erupting from the Pu'u 'O'o vent (near Pahoa), and while it is challenging to see this particular lava flow unless you have gobs of cash or tons of time, chances are you'll be able to see some version of magnificence to blow your mind. That being said, eruptions are not guaranteed—this is Pele, the goddess of fire, we are talking about, and this lady has her own agenda. When the lava is flowing, people sojourn from all over the world to view it. Start your journey in the visitors center, where a seemingly endless supply of rangers can instruct you on the best ways to plan your time in the park, including ways to see lava flow (if it is happening), information on air quality (vog, a mixture of volcanic sulfur and smog, is quite hazardous to inhale, especially for small

SEE THE FIRE FROM ABOVE

For those with deep pockets and limited time, seeing Hawai'i Volcanoes National Park by helicopter is a once-in-a-lifetime experience. Most tours are about 45 minutes, and many can be chartered to meet your needs. There are a slew of tour outfitters offering trips to view lava, including Paradise Helicopters (www.paradisecopters.com) and Blue Hawaiian Helicopters (www.bluehawaiian.com), which leave from both Hilo and the Kona Coast. Try to sit in the front of the helicopter for the best views. And book your journey well in advance, so if the pilot needs to reschedule, you don't miss your window of opportunity.

lungs, pregnant ladies, and those with respiratory issues), and hiking trails to suit your skill levels. This is also where you can learn about the volcanoes and purchase a sweater in case you've forgotten yours, as it get downright chilly up here after dark.

It's possible to spend days exploring the park, or to experience the highlights in an afternoon—though if you only have a day, you'll want at least three hours to take in the highlights. First-timers start by taking Crater Rim Drive, an 11-mile road that circles the summit's caldera. Next door to the visitors center is Volcano Art Center in the 1877 Volcano House. This gallery showcases some of the Big Island's most interesting artwork, including quilts, prints, and *koa* wood furniture. After a bit of shopping, travel to the Jaggar Museum and become enlightened on the craft of volcanology. The museum offers a sheltered view of Halema'uma'u Crater, home to a lava lake that glows a hellfire red after dark. If conditions are right, motor back here as the sun sets to see the spectacular glowing interior of the crater. During the day, keep your eyes peeled for the endangered *nene* birds that roam the parking lot.

Back on the road, you'll see signs indicating a picnic area; turn into this lot. Kilauea Overlook provides a spectacular view of the 2-mile-wide, 3-mile-long caldera and the crater. Less than a mile farther are the Steam Vents, where groundwater seeps down to the hot volcanic rocks and bubbles to the surface in a steamy show. In the same area, Steaming Bluff is a meadow with vapor rising from cracks along the caldera's edge. Across the street is Sulfur Banks, which is not recommended for pregnant women, small children, and those with respiratory issues. Frankly, I

The lava lake in Halema'uma'u Crater shines brightly after dark.

Dried lava on the Kona Coast

tend to skip this stinky stop, which smells like rotten eggs, but those who think viewing the effects of sulfuric acid turning lava to clay is fascinating should see for themselves.

Park at Kilauea Iki Overlook and take in the former lava lake that, in 1959, had fountains of lava spewing up to 1,900 feet high. The crater is a mile long and 3,000 feet across; the floor is 400 feet below the overlook. You can hike around the rim, or descend into the crater on the 4-mile round-trip Kilauea Iki Trail. If you have limited time, just take the 0.5-mile meander to Thurston Lava Tube (you may also drive there in a jiffy). The Jurassic forest of dripping ferns hugs the lava tube. The sheer size of these roads for lava is humbling.

The Pu'u Pua'i Overlook gives a view of the cinder cone that formed during the 1959 eruption at Kilauea Iki Crater. Winds blew the cinder and ash to form the cinder cone. Half a mile farther is the Devastation Trail, a 30-minute walk through the devastation of the 1959 eruption of Kilauea Iki—though there are other, more interesting trails.

If you still are raring to go and you have two or three more hours of daylight left, continue on Chain of Craters Road to explore the coastal reaches of the park. This road descends 3,700 feet in 20 miles and ends where lava flows crossed the road in 2003. And the road gets shorter all the time. At press time it was about 49 miles to the end (which will likely take you about an hour each way). Expect lovely views of the Pacific and some choice photo ops.

There are a number of trails accessible off the road, so be sure to ask for a map at the visitors center before heading out. The easy 2-mile Pu'u Loa Petroglyph coastal trail at mile marker 16 takes you to view the largest collection of ancient hand-carved drawings in the state. Another striking view is the Holei Sea Arch, before you reach the end of the road, where lava flow disturbed this road's journey to the sea. It's possible to hike to the ocean from here, but it is an eight-hour trip and very arduous. Otherwise, those with sturdy shoes can wander around the lava field and delight in stepping on the newest earth on the planet. Afterward take Chain of Craters Road back to the entrance.

Traveling northeast of Volcano Village, travel for about 15 minutes on Highway 11 to the Puna District, home to the state's most avid granola types and renegades that make San Francisco's counterculture look like Des Moines. You'll pass through Kea'au, stopping to fuel up on caffeine at Hilo Coffee Mill, and then turn right on Highway 130. The soul of Puna is the town of Pahoa, which looks like a dusty western town even though it is home to New Age types and off-the-grid enthusiasts. Strangely, Pahoa is thriving despite being in Pele's fiery sights, growing each day with new arrivals ready to take on the bothersome hassle of the too-close Pu'u 'O'o Vent (which recently closed Puna's beach access road and blanketed nearby villages) for the joys of cheap housing and an anything-goes spirit. Staying for a few days means you might view lava spilling into the sea, scramble through a chilly lava tube, party all night at a ukulele jam, or tune up your core at a yoga retreat; however, the majority of visitors can tour Puna's array of lava-strewn beaches in an afternoon. Since Pahoa isn't cartwheeling for your tourist dollars, turn up the charm and you'll be rewarded with plenty of aloha.

Pahoa's dining scene highlights international cuisine, with Luquin's Mexican Restaurant, Ning's Thai Cuisine, and the Italian flair of Paolo's Bistro satisfying the belly. The most sought-after table is Kaleo's Bar and Grill—a fan favorite for chicken *katsu*, blackened *mahi mahi*, and coconut-crusted *ono* served by cheerful servers who will inspire you to save room for *liliko'i* cheesecake. In the evenings there is some serious bohemian music to boot. For grab-and-go sandwiches and smoothies, plus an array of natural groceries, Island Naturals delivers. On Sunday mornings, there is a sweet Maku'u Craft and Farmers' Market between mile markers 7 and 8 on Highway 130. After dark, check what's happening at the historic Akebono Theater, which often hosts live music performances.

DETOUR: HILINA PALI ROAD

Just off Chain of Craters Road, Hilina Pali is a 9-mile one-lane road; it takes about 45 minutes to reach the end. The beginning section is mostly *ohi'a* trees. At 0.9 mile, you'll see a cliff on your left—that's the Koa'e Fault, made of lava that is about 650 years old. After 3.5 miles you reach Kulanaokuaiki Campground, which offers nice view of Mauna Loa and is a fine (albeit chilly) place to stay the night. Farther along, keep your eye out for *nene* birds as you descend to Hilina Pali Overlook, an expansive coastal and grassland view. There are two trailheads that reach the sea, but these are very rough multiday hikes that you need backpacking gear to attempt. After you've soaked up the views, travel back to Chain of Craters Road.

DETOUR: MAUNA LOA ROAD

While the masses are poking around Crater Rim Drive, exit the park and travel south on Highway 11 then turn up Mauna Loa Road to see the effects of lava scorching a rain forest. This is an 11.5-mile road. At about a mile in you'll see Kipuka Puaulu, known affectionately as Bird Park. Birders can take a 1.5-mile trail through this sanctuary of native species and ancient forest protected by Pele's grace from a major eruption. Continue 3.5 miles, where Mauna Loa Road turns into a white-knuckle one-lane road; go slowly on those blind curves as you ascend the volcano, almost a mile in the sky, and inhale the sweet views of Kilauea and the ocean below. There are trails fit for both Olympians and Sunday hikers up here, so ask at the park's visitors center for trail maps.

If this unruly stretch of the island appeals, Hale Moana B&B offers two suites with kitchenettes and a studio with private bathrooms, free Wi-Fi, and beach gear. The tropical garden immediately calms the senses. Rooms evoke a comfortable feel without being overdone. Imagine thick floral-print bedding, hardwood floors, and gourmet tropical breakfast whipped up by owner, Petra, who is a wealth of knowledge about the area.

Detour south on Highway 130 for an afternoon of exploration. At mile marker 20, Star of the Sea Church, constructed in 1929, features murals lining the walls as well as an interesting bit of information on Father Damien (see chapter 5) and missionary history. And then the highway ends at the lava viewing area. In 1988, lava took over this coastal road; in 1990 it blanketed the village of Kalapana, destroying 100 homes and swallowing Kaimu Beach. The lava has been covering beaches and *heiaus* in its path ever since. There is no guarantee that you can view lava out here, but if Pele is on your side, you may be able to meander out for about a mile and spot the fiery lava oozing into the sea. It's wise to check online or at the Hawai'i Volcanoes National Park Visitors Center in advance.

Highway 130 connects to Highway 137, or Red Road; here and on the right is New Kaimu Beach, which might afford views of lava steam rising from the sea. Out here you'll find a couple of remnants of the former Kalapana village, including lonely houses

DETOUR: LAVA OCEAN ADVENTURES

If Pele is cooperating, a boat trip to view the lava spilling into the sea, creating new land that very second, will be the most memorable facet of your Big Island holiday. Lava Ocean Adventures takes 24 people out on each boat to find the lava. Trips are two hours, and spotting the fiery spew is not guaranteed (you only get $25 refunded if you don't see any). But getting up close with Pele, smelling the sulfur, and feeling the new earth sizzle to life will blow your mind. Tours occur throughout the day and evening. Night tours are especially trippy.

and plate lunch at Kalapana Village Café. In the evening, Uncle Robert's Awa Bar serves kava (a allegedly mind-altering beverage popular in these parts) and live music.

The black sand Kehena Beach Park is at mile marker 19. Though unsafe for swimming, the beach acts as a community gathering place, for both hippies and dolphins. There is plenty of shade, but to access the sand, it is a bit of a scramble—an earthquake in 1979 made the steps drop about 10 feet. Parents and timid beachgoers, be warned: Locals like to bare all here.

Farther north on Highway 137, you'll hopscotch between beaches and lookout areas. Mackenzie State Recreation Area skirts along the lava rocks over the pounding sea. Hikers can traverse the Kings Trail. Picnickers can enjoy a meal under the ironwood trees. Explorers can locate the lava tube and do a bit of poking around. Adventurers can camp here with a permit from the state.

At Pohoiki Road, turn right and park at Isaac Hale Beach Park, or Pohoiki Beach, as it is also called. A choice spot for fishermen, surfers, sailors heading out to view lava, and campers, this sweet yet rocky beach might not be ideal for swimming, but surfers get giddy thinking about these swells. There's an enclosed pool for kiddos, and a hot pond along the trail past the private house. However, I cannot recommend swimming in Puna's famed hot ponds, which are known to house bacterial infections. If you do go in, make sure you have no open cuts and are in stellar health.

A bit farther on Highway 137, Ahalanui Beach Park's thermal pool is a warm-water oasis surrounded by a cement barrier inhabited by tropical fish. Swimming is possible. However, this pool is not flushed out often and germs abound. As with other pools, it is not recommended to swim here if you have open cuts. If you do choose to dive in—this is one of the more popular of the warm ponds—try to visit on a Tuesday or Wednesday, when the pool has had a chance to circulate out some of the weekend warrior cooties. Snorkelers should continue on, turning on Kapoho Kai Drive and then left to find Kapoho tide pools. This is an intricate collection of pools housing octopi, sea turtles, and plenty of colorful sea creatures.

The end of Highway 137 connects with Highway 132 and two other small roads, creating Four Corners around Kapoho. This area was once a rich sugarcane village, but lava flow in 1960 showed the community not to mess with Pele. Take Highway 132 inland for

---

DETOUR: KALANI OCEANSIDE RETREAT

The Big Island's answer to Big Sur's Esalen, Kalani Oceanside Retreat is a 120-acre wonderland for New Age types, hippies, and healers. Even if you don't participate in a retreat here, you can purchase a day pass to enjoy the wealth of yoga and dance classes, workshops, and yummy food. Reserve a massage treatment while you are in the area. They are the Big Island's best.

DETOUR: AN OFF-ROAD ADVENTURE

Those with a four-wheel-drive vehicle can access the amazing snorkeling opportunities at Champagne Pond. To get to this sandy beach, known for its beauty and sea turtle inhabitants, take Highway 137 to Kumukahi Lighthouse, which amazingly still stands, despite begin surrounded by lava. Take a moment to ponder your perch at the easternmost point in the archipelago, and then travel south for 1.5 miles on the bumpy road.

2.5 miles to Lava Tree State Monument. The short trail (just over 0.5 mile) loops through ancient rain forest, past lava molds of trees, an unusual volcanic feat. The highway reconnects with 130, which then allows access to Highway 11 toward Hilo, 7 miles to the north (see chapter 10).

IN THE AREA

ACCOMMODATIONS

Aloha Guest House B&B, 84-4780 Mamalahoa Hwy., Captain Cook. These five guest suites include panoramic views of Kealakekua and Honaunau Bays from the lanai of the guesthouse. Call 808-328-8955. Website www.aloha guesthouse.com.

Bamboo Orchid Cottage B&B, 11-3903 10th St., Volcano. A five-minute drive from the entrance to Volcanoes National Park. Rooms provide luxurious linens atop handmade artisan beds. Call 808-985-9592. Website www.bamboo orchidcottage.com.

Hale Kona Kai, 75-5870 Kahakai Rd., Kailua-Kona. These condos feature oceanfront lanais and fully equipped kitchens with multiple floor plans to choose from. Call 800-421-3696. Website www.halekonakaicondos.com.

Hale Moana B&B, 13-3315 Makamae St., Pahoa. The three rooms available at this B&B have private bathroom and separate entrance, laundry facilities, and a BBQ grill for guest use. Call 808-965-7015. Website www.bnb-aloha.com.

Holualoa Inn, 76-5932 Mamalahoa Hwy., Holualoa. This inn features gar-dens with tropical flowers and an orchard filled with over 5,100 coffee trees. Call 800-392-1812. Website www.holua loainn.com.

Honu Kai B&B, 74-1529 Hao Kuni St., Kailua-Kona. Situated on a lush, 1.3-acre estate, this B&B has a koi pond, garden, Jacuzzi, and expansive lanai. Call 808-329-8676. Website www.honukai.com.

Kalaekilohana B&B, 94-2152 South Point Rd., Na'alehu. Elegant architecture, gourmet breakfasts, and nearby beaches makes this B&B a convenient and comfortable place to stay. Call 808-939-8052. Website www.kau-hawaii.com.

King Kamehameha Kona Beach Hotel, 75-5660 Palani Rd., Kailua-Kona. This centrally located hotel has a pool, tennis courts, a 24-hour fitness center, and a spa that uses locally grown, organic ingredients. Call 888-236-2427. Website www.konabeachhotel.com.

Kona Tiki Hotel, 75-5968 Ali'i Dr., Kailua-Kona. An oceanfront pool and a BBQ area are the main features of this family-friendly hotel. Call 808-329-1425. Website www.konatikihotel.com.

Manago Hotel, 82-6155 Mamalahoa Hwy., Captain Cook. A Japanese garden, a koi pond, and a special room with a *tatami* mat and a futon lure travelers looking for a bargain. Call 808-323-2642. Website www.managohotel.com.

Outrigger Kanaloa at Kona, 78-261 Manukai St., Kailua-Kona. These two- and three-story condos overlook Keauhou Bay amid coconut palms. The property includes tennis courts and swimming pools, as well as the adjoining fairways of Kona Country Club. Call 808-322-9625. Website www.outrigger.com.

Royal Sea Cliff Resort, 75-6040 Ali'i Dr., Kailua-Kona. Studio plus one- and two-bedroom condo rentals are located about a mile from Kona Town. Rooms include full kitchens and washer-dryer units. Call 808-329-8021. Website www.outrigger.com.

Volcano Tree House, 11-3860 11th St., Volcano. This custom-built home features four living units with special touches like exposed-beam ceilings and maple hardwood staircases. Call 808-985-9592. Website www.volcanotree house.com.

Volcano Village Lodge, 9-4183 Rd. E, Volcano. Located only 2 miles from the entrance of Volcanoes National Park, this sumptuous hotel offers private bathrooms, luxury linens, fireplaces in every lodge, garden waterfalls, and a hot tub. Call 808-985-9500. Website www.emmaspencerliving.com.

ATTRACTIONS AND RECREATION

Akebono Theater, 15-2942 Pahoa Village Rd., Pahoa. This live music venue rocks on the weekends with performances by local artists. Call 808-965-9990.

Ali'i Gardens Marketplace, 75-1629 Ali'i Dr., Kailua-Kona. The marketplace features over 50 merchants selling a variety of wares from fresh flowers to *koa* wood products. Daily events include free ukulele and hula-dancing lessons, lei making, and music jam sessions. Call 808-334-1381. Website www.aliigardens marketplace.com.

Aloha Theatre, 79-7384 Mamalahoa Hwy., Kealakekua. A funky, refurbished movie theater with a café where you can buy a pre- or post-movie meal. Call 808-322-3383.

Atlantis Submarines, Kona Pier, Kailua-Kona. Explore Kona in a 48-passenger submarine. You'll see coral reefs and marine inhabitants on your 35-minute journey underwater. Call 808-667-2224. Website www.atlantis adventures.com.

Blue Hawaiian Helicopters, Hilo International Airport, 2450 Kekuanaoa St., Hilo. Enjoy volcano and waterfall views from above on one of the tour packages offered. Call 808-961-5600. Website www.bluehawaiian.com.

Body Glove Historical Sunset Dinner Cruise, 75-5629 Kuakini Hwy., Kailua-Kona. Live entertainment, a buffet dinner, a historical tour, and beautiful views of the Kona Coast at sunset are all rolled into one seafaring experience. Call 800-551-8911. Website www.bodyglovehawaii .com.

Captain Dan McSweeney, Kealakehe Pkwy. and Queen Ka'ahumanu Hwy., Holualoa. Captain Dan McSweeney personally guides all of his tours off the Kona Coast and guarantees you will see a whale. Call 808-322-0028. Website www.ilovewhales.com.

Captain Zodiac, 74-425 Kealakehe Pkwy., Ste. 16, Kailua-Kona. Offers raft, snorkel, dolphin, and whale adventures along the Kona Coast. Call 808-329-3199. Website www.captainzodiac.com.

Charter Desk, Honokohau Marina, Kailua-Kona. Choose the right boat and crew for your trip with this charter company. They offer over 60 boats to choose from. Call 808-326-1800. Website www.charterdesk.com.

Coconut Grove Market Place, 75-5809 Ali'i Dr., Kailua-Kona. A collection of small shops, restaurants, and a farmers' market. Call 808-326-2555.

Crossroads Shopping Center, 75-1000 Henry St., Kailua-Kona. Anchored by Walmart, a Denny's restaurant, and Safeway, this shopping center also includes a mix of specialty shops and restaurants. Call 808-329-4822.

Daifukuji Soto Mission, 79-7241 Mamalahoa Hwy., Kealakekua. Visit this Buddhist temple that offers Zen meditation classes. Call 808-322-3524. Website www.daifukuji.org.

Discovery Antiques, 81-6953 Mamalahoa Hwy., Kealakekua. Look for old trinkets and gadgets as well as vintage kimonos and dresses. Call 808-323-2239.

Donkey Mill Art Center, 78-6670 Mamalahoa Hwy., Kailua-Kona. This art center offers impressive displays as well as workshops in ceramics, drawing, and painting. Call 808-332-3362. Website www.donkeymillartcenter.org.

Fair Wind, 78-7130 Kaleiopapa St., Kailua-Kona. Cruises available include morning and afternoon tours of Kealakekua Bay. Most tours include either a meal or snack, and the *Fair Wind II* boasts a 15-foot waterslide. Call 808-345-0268. Website www.fair-wind.com.

Greenwell Farms, 81-6581 Mamalahoa Hwy., Kealakekua. Tours of the coffee plantation are offered daily and include a walking tour of the coffee fields and free samples. On Thursday, they also offer traditional Portuguese bread-making demonstrations using a wood-fired *forno*. Call 888-592-5662. Website www.greenwellfarms.com.

Hawai'i Titanium Rings, 75-5744 Alii Dr., #190, Kailua-Kona. Shop here for beautiful rings crafted from *koa*, palm wood, and titanium. Call 808-329-8980. Website www.hawaiititaniumrings.com.

Hawai'i Volcanoes National Park, 30 miles southwest on Hwy. 11 from Hilo. Go hiking, biking, or lava-viewing at this national park. Call 808-985-6000. Website www.nps.gov/havo.

Holualoa Ukulele Gallery, 76-5942 Mamalahoa Hwy., Holualoa. This small gallery includes famous brands and vintage ukuleles. You can custom-build your own ukulele at the gallery during a special seven-day workshop. Call 808-324-4100. Website www.konaweb.com /ukegallery.

Hula Daddy, 74-4944 Mamalahoa Hwy., Holualoa. Free coffee tasting, farm tours, and roasting demonstrations are available at this award-winning coffee plantation. Call 808-327-9744. Website www.huladaddy.com.

Hulihe'e Palace, 75-5718 Ali'i Dr., Kailua-Kona. Founded in 1838, this historic site is where the Hawaiian monarchy once resided. Call 808-329-1877. Website www.huliheepalace.net.

Ipu Hale Gallery, 55-3545 Akonipuli Hwy., Hawi. This is your stop for everything gourd related. The gallery features a fascinating collection of hand-carved gourds. Call 808-322-8484. Website www.ipuguy.com.

Jack's Diving Locker, 75-5813 Ali'i Dr., Kailua-Kona. Offers dolphin- and whale-watching tours as well as scuba-diving tours. Try the manta ray night dive, this diving operation's specialty. Call 808-329-7585. Website www.jacks divinglocker.com.

Jaggar Museum, located in Hawai'i Volcanoes National Park, Hwy. 11. This museum features displays on volcanology including working seismographs. Call 808-985-6000. Website www.nps .gov/havo.

Kailua Village Artists, 75-5729 Ali'i Dr., Ste. C-110, Kailua-Kona. Art that uses a variety of different media including glass, wood, and porcelain. Call 808-324-7060. Website www.kailuavillage artists.com.

Kalani Oceanside Retreat, 12-6860 Kapoho Kalapana Rd., Pahoa. Visit

Hawai'i's oldest retreat center for healthy meals, yoga, weaving classes, and massage. Lodging is available for overnight visits. Call 808-965-7828. Website www.kalani.com.

Kaloko-Honokohau National Historic Park, located 3 miles north of the town of Kailua-Kona. Watch for whales, sea turtles, and shorebirds or explore how native Hawaiians once managed to survive in the hot, arid environment. Call 808-326-9057. Website www.nps.gov /kaho.

Kamanu Charters, Kailua-Kona. Featuring a "snorkeling with turtles" option in addition to manta ray snorkeling trips and a cocktail sail. Call 808-329-2021. Website www.kamanu.com.

Kealakekua Bay State Historic Park, located on Lower Government Rd. from Mamalahoa Hwy. in Captain Cook. This park was the site of the first extensive contact between Hawaiians and Westerners when Captain Cook arrived in 1779. Website www.hawaiistateparks.org.

Keauhou Shopping Center, 78-6831 Ali'i Dr., Kailua-Kona. A nice collection of specialty shops and restaurants along with a movie theater. Call 808-322-2603. Website www.keauhouvillageshops.com.

Kimura's, along Hwy. 11, Kainaliu. This old-fashioned general store sells sewing supplies and features a large assortment of Hawaiian fabrics such as brocades and silks. Call 808-322-3771.

Kimura Lauhala Shop, at the top of Hualalai Rd., Holualoa. A fabulous collection of handwoven *lauhala* products including hats, purses, baskets, and slippers. Call 808-324-0053. Website www .holualoahawaii.com/member_sites /kimura.html.

Kona Blue Sky Coffee Tours, 76-973 Hualalai Rd., Holualoa. This 400-acre coffee estate offers complimentary guided walking tours and coffee tastings Mon.–Sat. 9–3:30. Call 877-322-1700. Website www.konablueskycoffee.com.

Kona Boys Beach Shack, 75-5660 Palani Rd., Kailua-Kona. Grab gear for surfing, kayaking, snorkeling, and paddle boarding at this shop. They also offers surf lessons and canoe trips. Call 808-329-2345. Website www.konaboys .com.

Kona Coffee Living History Farm, located on Mamalahoa Hwy. about 14 miles south of Kailua-Kona. Costumed historians tell the story of what life was like on a coffee farm in the 1900s. Visitors can walk through the coffee and macadamia nut orchards, tour the historic farmhouse, and pay a visit to the resident donkey. Call 808-323-2006. Website www.konahistorical.org.

Kona Inn Shopping Village, 75-5744 Ali'i Dr., Kailua-Kona. A family-friendly place on the beach that includes shops, restaurants, and entertainment. Call 808-329-6573.

Kona Stories, in Keauhou Shopping Center, 78-6831 Ali'i Dr., Ste. 142, Kailua-Kona. Stocked with over 10,000 titles, this bookstore carries a wide variety of genres, including books written by local authors. Call 808-324-0350. Website www.konastories.com.

Kulanaokuaiki Campground, located in Hawai'i Volcanoes National Park, Hwy. 11. This camping area is free and available on a first-come, first-served basis. Call 808-756-9625. Website www.hawaiivolcanohouse.com/cabins -campsites.

Kula Kai Caverns, off Hwy. 11, Ocean View. Leading caving expeditions including a twilight tour and a lighted trail tour. Call 808-929-9725. Website www.kulakaicaverns.com.

Kumukahi Lighthouse, past the intersection of Hwys. 132 and 137, Kapoho. This working lighthouse is surrounded by hardened lava.

Lava Ocean Adventures, 14-3782 Pohoiki Rd., Pahoa. This tour company specializes in catamaran tours of lava waterfalls and beaches along the coast. Call 808-966-4200. Website www.lava ocean.com.

Maku'u Craft and Farmers' Market, Kea'au-Pahoa Bypass Rd., Pahoa. Sample lots of delicious, fresh food like green papaya salad while listening to live music. Call 808-896-5537.

Mamalahoa Hot Tubs and Massage, 81-1016 St. Johns Rd., Kealakekua. Enjoy a soak in one of the 6-foot private teak tubs. This spa also offers a couple's massage package. Call 808-323-2288. Website www.mamalahoa-hottubs.com.

Mayme's Attic, 81-6586 Mamalahoa Hwy., Ste. B, Kealakekua. Go hunting for treasures from the 20th century. A 1970s vending machine still sells ice-cold sodas. Call 808-323-3839.

Moku'aikaua Church, 75-5713 Alii Dr., Kailua-Kona. This church was founded in 1836 by Boston missionaries. Call 808-329-0655. Website www.mokuaikaua.org.

Mountain Thunder Coffee Plantation, 73-1944 Hao St., Kailua-Kona. Tasting the award-winning coffee is worth the trip to this organic coffee plantation that offers tours daily. Call 888-414-5662. Website www.mountain thunder.com.

Natural Energy Laboratory of Hawai'i Authority, 73-4460 Queen Ka'ahumanu Hwy., Kailua-Kona. Tours of this sustainability laboratory run Mon.–Thu., 10–11:30 a.m. Call 808-329-8073. Website www.nelha.org.

Ocean Eco Tours, 74-425 Kealakehe Pkwy., Kailua-Kona. Dive, surf, or watch whales. Call 808-324-7873. Website www.oceanecotours.com.

Ocean Rider Seahorse Farm, located in the Natural Energy Lab, 73-4460 Queen Ka'ahumanu Hwy., Kailua-Kona. This organic aqua-farm raises seahorses and other aquatic life. Call 808-329-6840. Website www.seahorse.com.

Paradise Helicopters, 73-341 U'u St., Kailua-Kona. Choose from a variety of tour packages that will provide you with excellent views of the active volcanoes and hundreds of nearby waterfalls. Call 808-969-7392. Website www.paradise copters.com.

Plenty Pupule, 73-4976 Kamanu St., Kailua-Kona. Offers kayak rentals and sailing, snorkeling, and fishing tours. Call 808-880-1400. Website www.plenty pupule.com.

Pueo Boutique, 75-5695 Ali'i Dr., Kailua-Kona. Local brands of clothing for women and children, jewelry, and accessories. Call 808-326-2055. Website www.pueoboutique.com.

Punalu'u Bakeshop and Visitors Center, off Hwy. 11, Na'alehu. Enjoy free samples of Hawaiian sweet bread, and then take home a basket of the goodies for purchase including *malasadas*, coffee cake, macadamia nut shortbread cookies, and Hawaiian-style fruitcake. Call 866-366-3501. Website www.bakeshophawaii.com.

Pu'uhonua o Honaunau National Historic Park. From Kailua-Kona, take Hwy. 11 south for approximately 20 miles. Between mileposts 103 and 104, at the Honaunau Post Office, turn right on Hwy. 160 until you reach the ocean. Explore the ancient royal grounds on a self-guided tour or watch cultural interpreters as they make clothing, weave fishing nets, or carve canoes out of *koa* wood. Call 808-328-2288. Website www.nps.gov/puho.

Sea Paradise, 78-6831 Ali'i Dr., Ste. 144, Kailua-Kona. Join this tour company on a morning or afternoon excursion when there's a good chance you'll see spinner dolphins. The night snorkeling option puts the spotlight on manta rays. Call 808-322-2500. Website www.seaparadise .com.

Snorkel Bob's, 75-5831 Kahakai St., Kailua-Kona. No matter what gear you need for your snorkeling or beach adventure, this place is sure to carry it, from masks and fins to beach towels and T-shirts. Call 808-329-0770. Website www.snorkelbob.com.

Star of the Sea Church, Pahoa Kalapana Rd., Kalapana. The beautiful paintings on this church are colorful and unique.

St. Benedict's Painted Church, 84-5140 Painted Church Rd., Captain Cook. A picturesque church that overlooks the Kealakekua Bay. Call 808-328-2227. Website www.thepaintedchurch.org.

St. Peter's Church, along Ali'i Dr. north of mile marker 5, Kailua-Kona. A quaint clapboard church built in 1889 with beautiful beach views.

Studio 7, 76-5920 Mamalahoa Hwy., Holualoa. This fine-art studio features local paintings and sculptures. Call 808-324-1335.

Volcano Art Center, located in Hawai'i Volcanoes National Park, Hwy. 11. You'll find lots of paintings, sculpture, jewelry, glasswork, and woodwork varying in price from $20 and up. Call 808-967-7565. Website www.volcanoartcenter.org.

Volcano Farmers' Market, 19-4030 Wright Rd., Volcano. Local produce, flowers, crafts, and food abound at this farmers' market. Enjoy fresh-baked bread and pastries and homemade Thai dishes. Call 808-936-9705. Website www.thecoopercenter.org.

Volcano Garden Arts, 19-3834 Old Volcano Rd., Volcano. A world heritage site that includes cultivated gardens, an art studio, greenhouses, and nature trails. Call 808-985-8989. Website www.volcanogardenarts.com.

Volcano Winery, 35 Pii Mauna Dr., Volcano. Tropical fruits like yellow guava are blended with traditional wine grapes for a Hawaiian twist. Call 808-967-7772. Website www.volcanowinery.com.

DINING

Annie's Island Fresh Burgers, 79-7460 Mamalahoa Hwy., Ste. 105, Kealakekua. The burgers here are made with grass-fed beef and topped with local tomatoes and organic lettuce. The house-made purple potato salad and purple sweet potato chips are both a big hit. Call 808-324-6000. Website www.anniesislandfreshburgers.com.

Basik Açai, 75-5831 Kahakai Rd., Kailua-Kona. Known for their delicious bowls of fruit and granola as well as smoothies jam-packed with healthy ingredients like spirulina. Call 808-238-0184. Website www.basikacai.com.

Big Island Grill, 75-5702 Kuakini Hwy., Kailua-Kona. Split one of the huge entrées at this restaurant so you can save room for dessert: The mud pie and sweet potato *haupia* (coconut pudding) cheesecake are both excellent choices. Call 808-326-1153.

Bite Me Fish Market Bar and Grill, 74-125 Kealakehe Pkwy., Ste. 17, Kailua-Kona. Enjoy fresh-caught fish specials daily in a casual environment. Call 808-327-3474. Website www.bitemefishmarket.com.

Café Ohi'a, 19-4005 Haunani Rd., Volcano. If you're craving generously sized sandwiches made on artisan breads (the hearty cranberry macadamia nut is a favorite), then you've come to the right place. Call 808-985-8587.

Café Ono, 19-3834 Old Volcano Rd., Volcano. Stop in for high tea with hearty soups, savory sandwiches, and delicious pastries, or pick up a picnic lunch to go. Call 808-985-8979. Website www.volcanogardenarts.com.

The Coffee Shack, 83-5799 Mamalahoa Hwy., Captain Cook. Decent breakfast and lunch as well as espresso drinks with ocean views. Call 808-328-9555. Website www.coffeeshack.com.

Choice Mart, 82-6066 Mamalahoa Hwy., Captain Cook. Pick up basic groceries as well as fresh fruits and veggies at this grocery store. Call 808-323-3994. Website www.choicemart.net.

Da Poke Shack, 76-6246 Ali'i Dr., Kailua-Kona. As its name suggests, this restaurant is a good bet for *poke*; spicy, sesame, and avocado varieties inspire. Call 808-329-7653.

Holuakoa Café and Gardens, 76-5901 Mamalahoa Hwy., Holualoa. This slow-food establishment serves organic, from-scratch dishes made with locally grown ingredients alongside biodynamic wines. Call 808-322-2233. Website www.holuakoacafe.com.

Huggo's, 75-5828 Kahakai Rd., Kailua-Kona. This oceanfront restaurant serves upscale Hawaiian dishes such as fresh-caught fish and guava-braised baby back ribs. Call 808-329-1493. Website www.huggos.com.

Huggo's on the Rocks, 75-5828 Ka-hakai Rd., Kailua-Kona. Enjoy live music, fish tacos, tropical drinks, and the beautiful view while dining at this lunch and dinner place. Call 808-329-1493. Website www.huggosontherocks.com.

Island Lava Java, 75-5799 Ali'i Dr., Kailua-Kona. Famous for pancakes, pull-apart rolls, and fresh Kona coffee, this place is an excellent start to your day. Call 808-327-2161. Website www.islandlavajava.com.

Island Naturals Market and Deli, 15-1870 Akeakamai Loop, Pahoa. Located just off the main street in Pahoa, this grocery store is a quick stop for natural groceries or sandwiches at the deli. Call 808-965-8322. Website www.island naturals.com.

Jackie Rey's Ohana Grill, 75-5995 Kuakini Hwy., Kailua-Kona. This restau-rant features daily lunch specials like coconut shrimp and stir-fried chicken. For dinner, try the macadamia-nut-crusted *mahi mahi* with a side of purple sweet potatoes. Call 808-327-0209. Web-site www.jackiereys.com.

Java on the Rock, 75-5828 Kahakai Rd., Kailua-Kona. The café-style menu in-cludes pastries, omelets, and granola.

Call 808-322-2411. Website www.javaon therock.com.

Hana Hou Café, 95-1148 Na'alehu Spur Rd., Na'alehu. Stop in for plate lunch specials on the way to the volcano. Call 808-929-9717.

Hilo Coffee Mill, 17-995 Volcano Rd., Mountain View. Coffee samples abound at this café and breakfast place where you can fuel up on pineapple coffee, fresh eggs (straight from the chickens roaming the property), and waffles. Call 808-968-1333. Website www.hilocoffee mill.com.

Kalapana Village Café, 12-5032 Pahoa Kalapana Rd., Pahoa. Try the beer-battered *ono* served with mango vinai-grette, or enjoy a Hawaiian-style burger with fries. Call 808-965-0121.

Kaleo's Bar and Grill, 15-2969 Pahoa Village Rd., Pahoa. Make a stop here for live music and Hawaiian-inspired local favorites such as Pulehu-grilled burgers or coconut-crusted *mahi mahi*. Call 808-965-5600. Website www.kaleoshawaii .com.

Keei Café, 79-7511 Mamalahoa Hwy., Kealakekua. Try the eggplant rolls, which are stuffed with couscous and served with a side of marinara sauce. Call 808-322-9992. Website www.keei cafe.net.

Kilauea General Store, 19-3972 Old Volcano Hwy., Volcano. Stock up on snacks and local items like jam and honey, or take some homemade pastries to go from the bakery. Call 808-967-7555.

Kilauea Lodge, 19-3948 Old Volcano Rd., Volcano. For food with German and Hawaiian flair, this is the place to go. Enjoy the German sausage plate served with potatoes and sauerkraut or the schnitzel made with antelope. Call 808-967-7366. Website www.kilaualodge .com.

Kona Brewing Company, 75-5629 Kuakini Hwy., Kailua-Kona. A favorite for locals and tourists, who wait in an industrial park for ages to sip artisan brews like the Longboard Island Lager and eat heaping plates of nachos and filling pizza. Call 808-334-2739. Website www.konabrewingco.com.

KTA Super Store, 74-5594 Palani Rd., Kailua-Kona. A quick stop for groceries in the Kona Coast Shopping Center. Call 808-329-1677. Website www.ktasuper stores.com.

Lava Rock Café 19-3972 Old Volcano Rd., Volcano. Before exploring Volcanoes National Park, this place is a great stop for French toast with passion fruit syrup. Call 808-967-8526.

Lemongrass Bistro, 75-5742 Kuakini Hwy., Ste. 103, Kailua-Kona. This Asian restaurant combines Japanese, Chinese, Thai, Korean, and Vietnamese cuisine at reasonable prices. Call 808-331-2708. Website www.lemongrass-bistro.webs .com.

Luquin's Mexican Restaurant, 15-2942 Pahoa Village Rd., Pahoa. From tacos to flan, you'll find all your favorites at this Mexican joint. Call 808-865-9990. Website www.luquinsmexicanrestaurant hawaii.com.

Nasturtium Café, 79-7491 Mamalahoa Hwy., Ste. B, Kealakekua. The food on this menu is healthy and organic, featuring desserts made with spelt flour and lots of fresh produce. Call 808-322-5083. Website www.nasturtium-natural-cafe .weebly.com.

Ning's Thai Cuisine, 15-2955 Pahoa Rd., Pahoa. Try the pineapple curry or the green papaya salad. Call 808-965-7611.

Paolo's Bistro, 1529-51 Pahoa Village Rd., Pahoa. The black ink squid pasta with *ahi* is a local favorite. Save room for tiramisu! Call 808-965-7033.

Peaberry and Galette, 78-6831 Ali'i Dr., Kailua-Kona. This French-style *crêperie* serves both sweet and savory crepes in addition to specialty espresso drinks and other French favorites such as quiche Lorraine and Niçoise salad. Call 808-322-6020. Website www.pea berryandgalette.com.

Sam Choy's Kai Lanai, 78-6831 Ali'i Dr., Ste. 1000, Kailua-Kona. People come here for the fresh *poke* and breathtaking sunset views. Call 808-333-3434. Website www.samchoy.com.

Shaka Restaurant, mile marker 64, Hwy. 11, Na'alehu. A Hawaiian bar with a flair for *ono* fish-and-chips and cold beers served in frosty mugs. Call 808-929-7404.

Teshima Restaurant, 79-7251 Mamalahoa Hwy., Kealakekua. Try the sashimi, tempura, or *miso* soup at this traditional Japanese restaurant. Call 808-322-9140.

Thai Thai Restaurant, 19-4084 Volcano Rd., Volcano. The *pad Thai* and curry dishes are favorites at this Asian restaurant located just outside Volcano National Park. Call 808-967-7969. Website www.lavalodge.com.

Uncle Robert's Awa Bar, end of Hwy. 137, south end of Kalapana-Kapoho Rd., Kaimu. Feast on fresh pizza, pulled pork, and green papaya salad while browsing the flea market goods and enjoying live music.

Volcano Store, 19-4005 Haunani Rd., Volcano. Make a quick stop for groceries and beer at this local grocery store. Call 808-967-7210.

OTHER CONTACT INFORMATION

Big Island Chamber of Commerce, 117 Keawe St., Ste. 205, Hilo. Call 808-935-7178. Website www.hicc.biz.

Big Island Visitors Bureau, 250 Keawe St., Hilo. Call 800-648-2441. Website www.gohawaii.com.

A sunset on the Kohala Coast

10 From Rain to Shine Along the Big Island's Northern Loop

HILO TO THE KOHALA COAST

Estimated length: 130 miles

Estimated time: 5 hours, or 6 leisurely days

Getting there: Many US, international, and inter-island carriers have direct flights to Hilo International Airport, though many also stop in Honolulu first. Inter-island connections can be made on Go! (www.iflygo.com), Mokulele (www.mokulele.com), Hawaiian Airlines (www.hawaiianairlines.com), and Island Air (www.islandair.com). It is possible to arrive at Hilo Airport and then depart from Kona International Airport. Most major rental car companies have offices outside Hilo Airport, including Dollar (www.dollar.com), Hertz (www.hertz.com), and Budget (www.budget.com).

The 230-mile Hawaii Belt Road circles the island's six districts of Kona, Kohala, Waimea, Hilo, Puna, and Ka'u. For this itinerary, you'll be exploring Hilo, Waimea, and Kohala, though it is helpful to know that as you reach the northern section of the itinerary, the road switches names a few times—I've noted this in the itinerary.

Highlights: Spotting rainbows; picnicking in Hilo's Lili'uokalani Park; snorkeling with Technicolor tropical fish on the Kohala Coast's white sand beaches; gazing into some of the planet's most picturesque valleys; dining in Waimea; shopping for art in Hawi; watching 'Akaka Falls plummet into a fern-hugged pool.

Hilo, and by association the rugged Hamakua Coast, sits in the shadows of the Big Island's major attractions. One of the rainiest cities in the United States, with no sandy beach to speak of and relatively meager food offerings for a college town, Hilo doesn't immediately lure tropical vacationers. Yet those who settle into the slow pace will find plenty to enjoy in the walkable downtown and the abundance of nature within a short drive.

In the 1900s, Hilo was rich port town, drawing on an ethnic stir-fry of immigrants to shuttle the sugarcane between fields and buyers. People built lovely houses along the

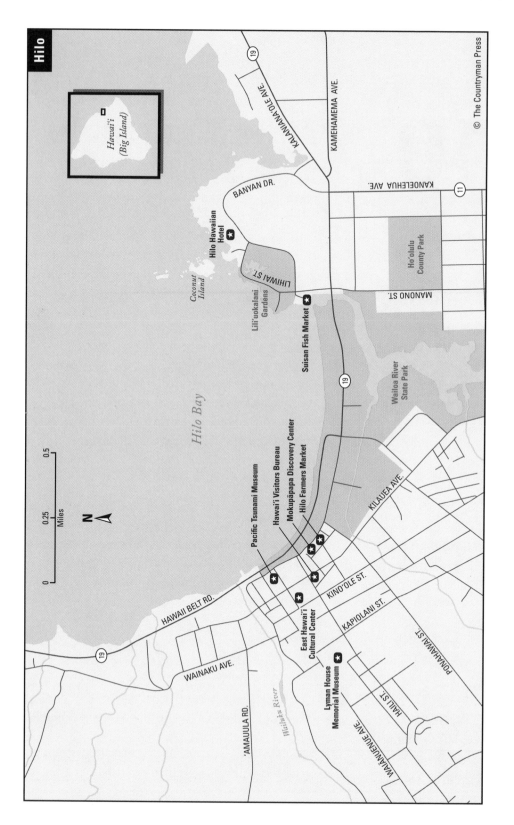

Hilo

Hawai'i
(Big Island)

BANYAN DR.

Coconut
Island

Lili'uokalani
Gardens

Hilo Hawaiian
Hotel

LIHIWAI ST.

Suisan Fish Market

Hilo Bay

Miles

0   0.25   0.5

N

Pacific Tsunami Museum

Hawai'i Visitors Bureau

Mokupāpapa Discovery Center

Hilo Farmers Market

19

Wailoa River
State Park

Ho'olulu
County Park

KANOELEHUA AVE.

11

MANONO ST.

KAMEHAMEMA AVE.

KALAKANA'OLE AVE.

19

HAWAII BELT RD.

WAINAKU AVE.

'AMAUULA RD.

Wailuku River

East Hawai'i
Cultural Center

Lyman House
Memorial Museum

KINO'OLE ST.

KAPIOLANI ST.

KĪLAUEA AVE.

PONAHAWAI ST.

HAILI ST.

WAIANUENUE AVE.

© The Countryman Press

coast, within walking distance to the tin-roof downtown. And then Hilo was devastated by not one, but two tsunamis in 1946 and 1960, and the good luck dried up. Today, besides housing the University of Hawai'i–Hilo, this region still hosts one of the island's most diverse populations, as well as a thriving agricultural scene.

Start in downtown, where you can park your car and explore the historic buildings filled with the museums and shops. On Kamehameha Street, the Pacific Tsunami Museum is a terrifying and educational glimpse into the power of the surrounding ocean that has swallowed up parts of this island so many times, it's a wonder people still inhabit the coastline. The researchers and staff are an amazing wealth of knowledge.

Another experience for the upping your Big Island trivia IQ is the Lyman Museum and Mission House, a habitat for natural and social history artifacts. Learn about various types of lava, ancient Hawaiian rituals, sports and laws, and then pop into the adjacent 1839 Mission House to gain information about missionary history. All in all this should take about 45 minutes, unless you tack on the half-hour guided tour of the Mission House.

For a kick, head over to the Hilo Public Library, where outside you'll find the Naha and Pinao stones. Legend has it that King Kamehameha I moved the gargantuan Naha stone when he was 14 (without the help of tools). Ancients believed whoever could move the stone could unify the Hawaiian Islands. Imagine if we made our leaders perform such a feat!

Shoppers can spend an hour wandering through the galleries around Hilo's downtown. Sig Zane Designs is an institution in Hilo—these wildly colored (and expensive) fabrics will be among your favorite souvenirs. Browsing the stacks at Basically Books is one of my favorite rainy-day activities. The owners stock this bookstore with toys as well as a fantastic collection of titles. Peruse the antique aloha shirts and Hawaiiana at Alan's Art and Collectibles. The caliber of art in Dreams of Paradise gallery is astounding. Grab some edible souvenirs of *mochi* at Two Ladies Kitchen, or crack seed (a salty-sweet concoction) at Kawate Seed Shop. A bit out of town (and a good choice when you want to escape the rain), Prince Kuhio Mall is Hilo's largest shopping center; there's a cinema if the weather's got you down.

Breakfast in downtown is a crapshoot. I've experienced yummy morning meals—and then other times, I've wandered around for an hour because nothing was open. The best place to score a hearty breakfast is a bit too far to walk to from the center of Hilo, so hop in the car and head to Ken's House of Pancakes. This 24-hour diner has been slinging *ono grindz* since 1971. Whether you favor mac nut pancakes or chili *loco moco*, you won't leave hungry. Nearby in the Wailoa River State Recreation Area, Café 100 promises huge and inexpensive varieties of *loco moco*, pancakes, and eggs with Portuguese sausage. After you eat, wander around the river area to see the bronze Kamehameha statue, or enter the state-run Wailoa Center, showcasing locally made paintings and sculptures.

Coffee drinks, breakfast sandwiches, and smoothies at Surf Break Café makes a reasonable choice. This small gallery and café caters to students and offers a sweet community vibe. Another funky café, Bayfront Coffee Kava and Tea, is a Hilo experience where the tripped-out staff offer free samples of the mind-altering kava beverage in coconut bowls.

For lunch, if the sun is out, piece together a picnic from Abundant Life Natural Foods (those wanting less expensive groceries can grab supplies at KTA Super Store), gathering fresh *ahi poke* at Suisan Fish Market and *liliko'i* cupcakes at Short N Sweet. Take your bounty to Lili'uokalani Park to sit under a banyan tree (the trees along Banyan Drive are marked with the name of the famous person who planted them). The Japanese gardens, quiet ponds, and green-hugged paths make this area the most peaceful place in town. You can cross the bridge and access Mokuola (Coconut Island) to jump into the sea. Locals like to fish and stand-sup paddle from this popular location, rain or shine. If you want to try the island's newest favorite sport, grab a board at Sun and Sea Hawai'i before driving this way.

If rain has foiled your picnic plans, you can still enjoy a decent lunch at Café Pesto. This is downtown's best restaurant (and it is also open for dinner). Whether you prefer thin-crust gourmet pizzas, bowls of pasta filled with veggies, or heaping salads packed with goodies, this airy eatery delivers consistently good food. They have another outpost up in Kawaihae, which is just as good.

Cacao for sale at Hilo's Abundant Life Natural Foods

Hidden in the old Waiakea Villas overlooking Waiakea Pond, Miyo's is a local favorite for a rustic Zen dining experience sourced almost entirely from the nearby waters. While the food can be hit or miss, don't bypass the *genmacha*, the sesame chicken, or the fresh catch of the day. Some might find this restaurant more expensive and hyped than it deserves. Reservations are a must at dinner.

For quick eats, Ocean Sushi Deli serves super-fresh sashimi and sushi rolls injected with fruit or mac nuts. For piping-hot bowls of house-made noodles, Nori's

---

HILO FARMERS' MARKET

On Wednesday and Saturday from 6 a.m. to 4 p.m., the Hilo Farmers' Market features over 200 stalls hawking produce and crafts under a dreary overhang on Mamo Street and Kamehameha Avenue. This is not the hotbed for organics grown locally; for that you'll want to travel up to Kino'ole Farmers' Market on Saturday morning, or Pahoa's lively affair (see chapter 9). However, this is a fun place to see Hilo's aunties in action as they wheel and deal over apple bananas and papayas.

Saimin and Snacks delivers dependably rich soups at the right price. Fans of Thai food should pop over to Sombat's for sweet *pad Thai* and a perfectly pitched green curry.

Hop in the car and head over to 'Imiloa Astronomy Center of Hawai'i to view one of the state's most informative museums. The world's largest telescope sits atop Mauna Kea, and this is the place to learn about what otherworldly knowledge we are gaining from that massive view into space. The museum educates on ancients' abilities to navigate by using the stars as well. The planetarium show and the 3-D theater are also worth some time.

Afterward take Waianuenue Avenue inland for 1.5 miles to Rainbow Falls. Easy to access, this 80-foot waterfall can be seen from the parking lot, so expect heaps of others there as well. If you continue driving uphill for another 2 miles, you reach another lovely vista point, offering views of Pe'epe'e Falls and boiling pots, a waterfall plummeting into bubbling sulfur pools.

Pass back through Hilo as the humidity kicks it up a notch and grab some yummy shave ice at Wilson's by the Bay, or Itsu's Fishing Supplies. Or, if you prefer ice cream, take Kalaniana'ole Avenue south to Hilo Homemade Ice Cream, where tropical delights bring out the kid in just about every grown-up who visits.

In late afternoon, it seems everyone heads to the sea. Along Kalaniana'ole Avenue, you'll find a variety of ways to access the sea, depending on your abilities. Most people will find satisfaction at Onekahakaha Beach Park, a family-friendly grassy beach area with a shallow rock and sand-bottomed enclosed pool. There are tide pools on the northern edge, packed with sea cucumbers and sea stars. More experienced swimmers and snorkelers should head to the next beach, James Keahola Beach Park, which is 4 miles from downtown. Locals like to catch winter swells in the rough western side of the sea. At the end of the road, Richardson Ocean Park is a black sand beach popular with surfers and summertime snorkelers (sea turtles often hang about the rocks).

When it comes time for dinner, hidden in a strip mall outside downtown (take Highway 11 west for 3 miles to Makaala Street) is Hilo Bay Café. Ignore the strange location;

PANA'EWA RAINFOREST ZOO AND GARDENS

Hilo's free Pana'ewa Rainforest Zoo and Gardens is a small affair. That being said, this 12-acre oasis houses enough wildlife to please *keikis*—especially the lemurs, peacocks, and Bengal tiger. Garden fans will appreciate the tropical flora and fauna doted over by an array of loving hands.

this is Hilo's best dining establishment. Focus is on sustainability, while the ambience is as urban as can be with fancy cocktails and experienced staff. Favorites include a mushroom potpie, truffled mac and cheese, and the salmon sandwich. They also serve lunch. After dinner, check to see what's happening at the 1925 neoclassical Palace Theater, downtown's event destination for art house films and live music.

Hilo houses a slew of places to stay. And while many make Hilo their base for exploring Hawai'i Volcanoes National Park (see chapter 9), the 45-minute drive each way usually annoys this exhausted hiker. Instead I recommend using Hilo as a place to stop for a night or two to explore Hilo (and use Volcano Village as a base for Kilauea instead) before moving on to sunnier pastures.

Hilo Hawaiian Hotel is perched on the bay along Banyan Drive. With a small pool, modest rooms, an on-site restaurant, and lanais, this hotel is a great choice for those wanting to be surrounded by nature *and* be close to downtown. Affordable and popular with repeat visitors, Dolphin Bay Hotel offers fresh flowers in rooms, lanais, kitchenettes, and a tropical fruit breakfast. You can book a one- or two-bedroom apartment for a longer stay. Upscale and classy, the Orchid Tree B&B looks like it jumped off the pages of *Sunset Magazine*. With hardwood floors, Hawaiian quilts atop poster beds, a pool, and an abundant house-made breakfast, this B&B is a favorite with discerning guests want-

Onekahakaha Beach

ing to stay near Hilo, but not be based in the heart of town.

In the morning, travel north on Highway 19, passing the surfer-inhabited waters of Honoli'i Beach Park to explore the Hamakua Coast, arguably the Big Island's most pristine environment. While it is possible to explore this stretch of coastline while staying in Hilo or at one of the sweet B&Bs off the highway, you can also drive the ribbons of roads along the coast in a day to arrive in the North Kohala Coast for some sun, sea, and serious *grindz*

Hilo Bay Café's scrumptious eats

by dinnertime. Between mile marker 7 and 8, veer right onto the Old Mamalahoa Highway for the gorgeous Pepe'ekeo Scenic Road. This 4-mile drive gives a glimpse at what makes Maui's Hana Highway so spectacular, but with far less of a time commitment. Traverse one-lane bridges, drive through lush rain forest, and view waterfalls streaming down the mountain as your car hugs the Pacific Ocean.

At the beginning of this scenic road is Hawaii Tropical Botanical Gardens. The nature preserve features over 2,000 tropical plants along an hour-long trail hugged by banana trees and banyans, ending in Onomea Bay. Once you reach this small beach, keep your eyes peeled for Hawaiian monk seals, and remember, if you see them, you must stay back at least 50 feet.

Back on the main highway, between mile markers 13 and 14, turn left on Highway 220 and drive for 4 miles to reach 'Akaka Falls State Park. A 0.5-mile loop descends into the rain forest past the smaller Kahuna Falls and deposits you directly in front of the 426-foot 'Akaka Falls. It is well worth the trek, even if it's pouring—this just adds to the ambience.

Once you depart the park, travel back downhill to the community of Honomu's Main

HILO CELEBRATIONS AND EVENTS

Across the state, celebrations flair up for Lei Day (May 1) and King Kamehameha Day (June 11)—and Hilo is no exception. The grandmother of all Hawai'i festivals is April's Merrie Monarch Festival, a tribute to the best hula dancers and musicians around the world. Each Easter since 1964, this wild party and competition has brought thousands to Hilo's shores, packing hotels and restaurants with participants and their families. Purchase your tickets well in advance; the event sells out every year.

Hilo Hawaiian Hotel

Street. **Mr. Ed's Bakery** is housed in the 1910 Ishigo Bakery building. Whether you purchase their tropical jams and jellies pumped into pastries, the Kona coffee butter, or the fluffy Hawaiian bread, it's well worth stopping for a post-hike treat.

'Akaka Falls State Park

Traveling north on Highway 19, pass **Kolekole Beach Park**, another surf break at mile marker 15; at mile marker 16, travel *mauka* to follow the signs to **World Botanical Gardens**, a fun green space and activity hub for families. There's a giant maze for kids, a zipline adventure where you soar over the treetops, a Segway tour through the gardens, and an orchid-lined hiking trail, leading to a lovely waterfall. While this garden is a bit pricey, there is much to appreciate, especially if you have oodles of time on your hands.

At mile marker 25, you approach the former sugarcane community of **Laupahoehoe**. In 1946, a tsunami washed out a schoolhouse (sadly, with the *keikis* inside), forcing the town to move uphill. Today you can learn the history of this region's short-lived affair with sugarcane, trains, and industry at the **Laupahoehoe Train Museum**. Take a quick detour on the 1.5-mile scenic road to **Laupahoehoe Beach**

DETOUR: SADDLE ROAD AND MAUNA KEA

The spiritual and geographic center of the Big Island, Mauna Kea reaches a staggering 13,796 feet into the sky. (Serious scientists, of course, like to remind us that we actually measure mountains like this from below the ocean floor. By that calculation, this is the world's tallest mountain—take that, Everest!) This desolate mountain houses endemic plants, the world's largest collection of super-powered telescopes at the Mauna Kea Science Reserve, and the alluring alpine Lake Waiau.

In Hilo, gas up and bring plenty of water, food, sunblock, and warm clothes, as the average temperature at the visitors center (a mere 9,000 feet in the air) is 30 degrees Fahrenheit. You'll want to make sure that you did not go diving within 24 hours; and those of you who want to drive to the summit need a four-wheel-drive vehicle.

Take Saddle Road for 32 miles (this will take about an hour) to the Mauna Kea Access Road. Continue for 6 miles to the Onizuka Visitors Information Center. Stop here to learn about this dormant volcano and the area's hiking trails (though if you are hiking, remember that the air up here is thin and altitude sickness is very common). You can also experience the evening stargazing program—one of the best things to do on the island, especially since it is clear up here almost year-round. Besides a nightly view of the celestial world, there are star parties, meteor extravaganzas, and even music on select nights.

To continue up to the summit for the last 8 miles (most of which is unpaved and requires four-wheel drive), you can join a caravan tour from the visitors center, or brave this road yourself. Without stops, it takes about half an hour to reach the summit. Know that the air is particularly thin up here, and altitude sickness is almost a requirement for visitors. Hiking can be challenging for even the most fit individuals. Pregnant women, young people under the age of 16, and those with respiratory difficulties are not allowed. Hawaii Forest & Trail offers decent summit tours.

At mile marker 6, turn off for Keanakako'i, an ancient quarry and the trailhead to Lake Waiau, about an hour's hike each way. Or just continue on to the summit area. At the peak, enter the W. M. Keck Observatory visitors gallery for a warmer view of this moonscape world. In January and February, you may notice people skiing on the snow that briefly appears. It's more a novelty than anything else; there are no true slopes or services. After you descend the mountain, it is possible to take Saddle Road to the Kona side of the island. (The trip takes about an hour once you reach Saddle Road).

Park to view the massive banyan tree perched over the sea (this is where the schoolhouse once stood). If you are hungry and not signed up for the Hawaiian Vanilla Company's luncheon (see below), Back to the 50s Highway Fountain Diner serves traditional greasy fare while 1950s tunes serenade you up along the highway.

Otherwise continue on Highway 19 north and turn left on Haula Road. Turn left on Old Main Road, right on Pohakea Road, and then right on Paauilo Mauka Road to find Hawaiian Vanilla Company. You need to reserve in advance for their educational luncheon, which infuses everything from tea to chicken to ice cream with their vanilla, explaining how to grow, extract, and cook with this sweet pod. Their gift shop is sweet (literally), and as long as it is not too soggy, the tours are worth experiencing.

Back on Highway 19 north, those not heading out to Waipi'o Valley might want to budget the cool forest of eucalyptus and *ohi'a* trees at Kalopa State Recreation Area into the itinerary. Turn *mauka* on Kalopa Drive and continue for 3 miles. There are picnic areas and camping cabins available as well as mellow forest trails and more advanced 4-mile hikes. Again, those with limited time will want to skip this option.

In these lush hills, feed a fantasy of becoming a farmer on the Big Island and stay at Keolamauloa Farm. The private two-bedroom red farmhouse includes a full kitchen, plenty of produce and eggs, laundry, free Wi-Fi, and charming interiors. Rates are reasonable, making this a good choice for hikers and those wanting to escape the traditional tourist areas of the island.

Just off Highway 19, follow the signs to Honoka'a, a surprisingly sophisticated small town perched over the sea. Once a thriving sugarcane community, this village now houses organic farms, decent restaurants, and cute antiques shops. This is also the gateway to the Waipi'o Valley. Breeze through Honoka'a's cute collection of shops, including Symbiosis, where secondhand kid's clothing and toys, hang about organic women's shirts and leggings. Taro Patch Gifts is ground zero for local art and kitschy gifts. Fans of chocolate don't miss a stop into Hamakua Fudge Shop. Honoka'a Trading Company is a cluttered antique shop ideal for stumbling upon local treasures. If you continue on the road as it approaches Waipi'o Valley in Kukuihaele, Waipi'o Valley Artworks sells exquisitely carved *koa* wood bowls and paintings.

Eaters will find a surprisingly large collection of restaurants strung along Mamane Street. Simply Natural is your best bet for healthy lunches, smoothies and hearty pre-

GUIDED HIKING TOURS

Interested in exploring the Big Island's most enchanting outdoor destinations, but prefer going with a trustworthy local? Hawaiian Walkways offers educational guided hiking tours of the Kona Cloud Forest Sanctuary (a 70-acre haven of greenery in the hills above Kona), waterfalls, Waipi'o Valley, Mauna Kea, and Kilauea Volcano. They can tailor a trip to your needs and abilities. Another outfit worth checking into is Hawaii Forest and Trail for their exemplary Mauna Kea stargazing experience as well as treks into Hakalau Forest National Wildlife Refuge.

FARM TOURS

With everything from tomato farms to tea plantations, coffee farms to honey ranches, the Hamakua Coast agriculturists are taking advantage of fertile soil and relatively cheap abundant land. Sign up for a farm tour vie Earth Bound Tours to visit Volcano Island Honey Company, Hawaiian Vanilla Company, Mauna Kea Tea, Long Ears Coffee, or Original Hawaiian Chocolate Factory. Tours vary by styles and lengths and must be booked in advance.

---

hike breakfasts. Café il Mondo is the go-to spot for pizzas and ravioli. BYOB. Up on Highway 19 is the wildly popular Tex Drive In, famous for *malasadas*, though they also serve gut-sticking plate lunches crafted in a open-kitchen above the sea.

If you'd like to stay in or around Honoka'a, you are in luck. Some of the island's most unique and lovely properties skirt Highway 19. My favorite is Waianuhea B&B, an upscale artsy affair offering five rooms surrounded by greenery. Rooms feature bright color schemes, thick duvets, luxurious bathrooms, a full breakfast, and dinner upon request. Guests gather by the rock fireplace in the evenings to enjoy wine and talk story about their treks into Waipi'o Valley.

For a bit less cash, Waipi'o Wayside B&B provides family friendly accommodations, just north of town in a 1932 historic plantation home. The hosts offer full organic breakfasts, a guest refrigerator, and funky rooms honoring Chinese, Hawaiian and lunar themes. About seven miles out of town in the small community of Kukuihaele, Waipi'o Rim B&B offers spectacular views of the Waipi'o Valley and plenty of privacy. Enjoy your own second floor unit with a lanai, free Wi-Fi, a flat-panel TV, and hardwood floors. Breakfast is delivered to your door in the morning and the hosts provide heaps of aloha spirit.

Highway 19 then veers inland, traveling west (in these parts it's more commonly referred to as Mamalahoa Highway). Continue for about 15 miles to the farming community of Waimea (or Kamuela as it is also called). Waimea is experiencing a foodie renaissance like no other destination on the island. Characterized by emerald rolling hills dotted with cattle, small farm-to-table restaurants, and a cool climate ideal for farming, Waimea is worlds away from both the hot Kona Coast and the rainy Hilo area.

As you enter town from the east, to your right in Church Row, housing the 1857 *koa*-wood-constructed Imiola Congressional Church, as well as the Ke Ola Mau Loa Church, a Buddhist temple, a Mormon temple, and a handful of other places of worship. Just up the road is the W. M. Keck Observatory Office; if you didn't make it up to Mauna Kea's summit, pop in to view the video feed from the summit's cameras, without the cold, the shortness of breath, or the itinerary-filling drive.

DETOUR: WAIPI'O VALLEY

From Honoka'a, take Highway 240 until it ends at the Waipi'o Valley, one of the Big Island's most stunning vistas, known in ancient times as Valley of the Kings. As with most of this coastline, this was once a thriving agricultural community as well as the choice home for ancients. However, the 1946 tsunami forced most to relocate uphill. Today a host of renegades still call the valley home, growing *pakalolo* and living off the grid in makeshift homes. Locals won't necessarily be greeting you with leis, or even smiles. This fiercely insular region prides itself on its remoteness. Respect this as you trek downhill.

Most will stop at the overlook to snap photos of this 6-mile deep verdant valley rich with waterfalls and taro fields that seems to spill into the Pacific. Able-bodied hikers can walk the 45-minute trail (if you have a four-wheel-drive vehicle you can drive it in 15 minutes) down into the valley to Waipi'o Beach, a wild surf beach known for housing sharks and serious swells. On the way into the valley, you'll spot Hi'ilawe Falls, the tallest in the state. There are loads of backcountry hikes for the determined, as well as guided hikes around the valley (see the sidebar). Ask around Honoka'a for information should you desire this type of adventure.

The center of town is a patchwork of restaurants and shops, strip malls and green spaces. On the left, just before the road intersects with Kawaihae Road, Parker Ranch Center is a large strip mall housing the best burger joint in the state—Village Burger. Indulge in grass-fed burgers sourced from local cattle ranchers, thin-cut fries, and yummy milk shakes in this funky new spot that has quickly become the pride of the community. Afterward, you can book a two-hour horseback-riding trip with Parker Ranch Horseback Riding Tours at the desk in the mall's food court. Tours offer the chance to

Waimea's bucolic hills

explore the massive ranch operated by the largest beef producer in Hawai'i.

Back in the car, turn right onto Kawai-hae Road; on the right side in Waimea Park you'll find Isaacs Art Center, a renovated schoolhouse morphed into a thriving art gallery. There are local creations, including some impressive *koa* wood sculptures, as well as some international pieces that will make art buyers giddy. Across the street in Waimea Square is my favorite shop on

Bone and bead necklaces for sale at Waimea's Gallery of Great Things

the island, Gallery of Great Things. The name could not be more accurate as you explore the well-curated collection of a Hawaiian and Asian art, jewelry, and photography. Parker Center also houses Waimea Coffee Co., this area's best crafter of lattes, drip coffees, and sweet pastries.

When it comes to breakfast, no one on the island does it like Hawaiian Style Café. Wait in line with the faithful for huge plates of *loco moco*, griddle fare, or lunch sandwiches. For lunch (or dinner, if you cannot get a table at Merriman's), Pau serves quinoa salads, fish sandwiches, or seasonal pizzas. If you prefer organic BBQ, *kiawe*-smoked meats, or seafood snagged that morning, the Fish and the Hog Market Café offers upscale comfort food, and also holds court as Waimea's brewpub of choice.

Dinners are ruled by Peter Merriman's namesake Merriman's Restaurant, a haven for fresh seafood, prime cuts of meat, and a gorgeous selection of vegetables laid out in colorful salads. The cocktail menu is as inspirational as the food. Make sure to save room for dessert. Merriman's coconut crème brûlée is legendary. Reservations are required—the masses head up here from the coast for dinner.

Despite the cheesy name, Aaah the Views B&B pleases those wanting to stay in Waimea for a few days. With cozy floral bedding, cable TVs with DVDs, and plenty of space, country style emanates from each well-thought-out guest quarter. A couple of the rooms share a bath, making these quarters more affordable than those with private washrooms. If you prefer to have your own cottage, Tina's Country Cottage is a sweet two-bedroom affair with expansive grounds and a fully equipped kitchen.

It is possible to travel from Waimea west to the Kohala Coast's resorts to then make the coastal resort area your base for exploration of the following area. However, those wanting to getting off the beaten path should instead take Highway 250 north toward Hawi, weaving among rolling hills as you approach the least-explored part of the island, the North Kohala Coast: the Big Island's hidden oasis of art, organic living, hiking, and history. This is the birthplace of King Kamehameha I. And while the region was once a thriving sugar town, today you'll stumble upon a healthy mix of native Hawaiians, off-the-grid hippies, artists, and musicians. The drive through the mountains offers fantastic views of the volcano peaks, rolling hills, the sea, and the neighboring islands in the distance.

As the road approaches Hawi, there are a handful of working cattle ranches offering that *paniolo* experience. Kahua Ranch offers horseback riding and ATV adventures as well as an evening BBQ, complete with a campfire and live music. If you really like playing cowboy, inquire about staying the night in their two-bedroom country cottage. Another choice way to gallop along the rolling hills is with Paniolo Riding Adventures. This outfit is known for their array of horseback rides through the working cattle ranch (the three-hour ride and picnic is the way to go).

When the highway approaches Hawi, it turns into Hawi Road and meets up with Highway 270, a lip of road along the sea punctuated by cliffs backing beaches. Park the car along the highway to explore the two blocks of Hawi, which is packed with galleries and shops inhabiting plantation-era homes awash in color. My favorites include the Gallery at Bamboo, for local music and crafts; Living Arts Gallery, a fantastic art co-op showcasing paintings, sculptures, and photography; As Hawi Turns, which shows off vintage wares, ukuleles, and artwork; and Elements Jewelry and Crafts for designer accessories and wall hangings.

Hawi has a surprisingly decent selection of restaurants for such a small town. Those passing through will appreciate the Kohala Coffee Mill, a community gathering space and art gallery with a nice outdoor patio for coffee, sandwiches, and ice cream throughout the day. In the evenings, the back section of the café turns into a kava bar. If you want to grab picnic fare or a cold beer, Lighthouse Deli is the spot for thick pastrami or turkey sandwiches. Zest Kitchen offers farm-to-table café cuisine that highlights everything from Asian fusion to Latin cuisine. I've had some killer homemade ice cream here as well. It is a casual affair for Cuban sandwiches and goat cheese dips for lunch. Dinners kick it up a notch with blue crab ravioli. BYOB.

People come from around the island to party it up at Sushi Rock, a Japanese restaurant that specializes in sushi packed with local treats like papaya or mac nuts. I like the fresh-caught *mahi mahi* smothered in *umami*-inducing sauces. Other favorites are the baked mac nut chèvre and the purple potato cheesecake. Reservations are highly recommended for dinner. Lunches are a bit less in demand.

The main event in town is Bamboo Restaurant, a large café and gallery, with live music from local legends like John Keawe and his family in the evenings. Start with the *liliko'i* martini, and then engross yourself in the *kalua* pork BBQ burger or coconut *mahi mahi*. Desserts are on the small side, making it easy to share a Belgian chocolate mousse tart after a large meal.

RACE THROUGH THE KOHALA DITCH SYSTEM

Kohala Ditch Adventures is not for the faint of heart, though adventurers in the market for a heart-racing adventure can take a 2½-hour kayak trip through the backwater plantation ditches of the Hawi area. Pass through rain forests, flumes, and 10 tunnels as you race toward the end of the line. Tours leave every 1½ hours, until 1:30 p.m. This is a wild adventure, not to be missed.

Continuing east on Highway 270, you arrive in another former sugarcane town, Kapa'au. As you pass through town, notice the Kohala Artists Cooperative Project and Kenji's House Museum, where you can view local art and undersea treasures found by the late diver Kenji Yokoyama. As you continue east for a couple of blocks, pass the Kamehameha the Great statue in front of the Kohala Civic Center. This is the original version of the one that stands in Honolulu. This statue sank on its way from Italy; another was crafted from the mold. Once divers found this one, they brought it to the region of the great leader's birth, where it stands today. On King Kamehameha Day, there's a fantastic parade and plenty of leis draped over this statue.

Two miles east of Kapa'au, on the *mauka* side of the road, is Kamehameha Rock, a large boulder that Kamehameha the Great supposedly carried uphill to show his strength. Continue on until the road ends at Pololu Valley Lookout, a gorgeous emerald valley that gapes toward the raging sea. It is possible to hike the steep mile-long Pololu Valley Trail to a black sand beach backed by lush greenery, though don't bother trying to brave these rough seas.

Travel west on Highway 270, backtracking through Kapa'au and Hawi to find one of the most elegant yet understated places stay on the island, Puakea Ranch. This country estate avoids being pretentious with six bungalows and a five-bedroom B&B house providing upscale amenities like copper bathtubs, poster beds with luxurious linens, a lava rock pool, and free Wi-Fi in a community-centered atmosphere—think summer camp, without the counselors or panty raids. B&B guests receive a complimentary breakfast, as well as access to the pool, horses, and gardens. The ranch also features a couple of Upcountry bungalows for those wanting to stay closer to Waimea.

History buffs, detour off Highway 270 west and travel *makai* on Old Coast Guard Road between mile markers 18 and 19 for a mile, then park on the side of the road by the cattle gate. Walk through the gate and hike for a bit to find the oldest *heiau* in the state, Mo'okini Luakini Heiau. Legend has it that Menehune constructed this temple in just under 24 hours for the most royal *ali'i*. As is the case with most of Hawai'i's most sacred places, human sacrifices were performed here, making this both a contemplative and a

Pololu Valley Lookout

slightly spooky destination. Back on Old Coast Guard Road, about a quarter of a mile south of the *heiau* is King Kamehameha's birthplace.

As you continue on, another historic site can be found south of mile marker 14 at Lapakahi State Historical Park. This former fishing village is spread across 260 acres, showcasing the remains of houses, shrines, and ancient games. Portions of the park are considered sacred, so please treat the crystal blue waters and the ruins with the utmost respect. There is no shade here, so bring plenty of water.

Twelve miles from Hawi on Highway 270, you come across the port town of Kawaihae. King Kamehameha I used the harbor as a setting-off point to conquer the other Hawaiian Islands. The harbor is where many whale-watching, snorkeling, and diving trips depart from. The local Kohala Divers leads dive trips in these waters rich with dolphins, turtles, and sharks. Ocean Sports takes snorkelers and whale-watchers out on their dependable and educational tours (and they also have a couple of shops in the Waikoloa area).

In town there is an outpost of Hilo's popular Café Pesto. There are a handful of take-out joints and food trucks scattered throughout town, most of them fine for a quick bite. The most interesting of the lot is Blue Dragon, a renovated restaurant, music venue, and bar that makes almost anyone who steps inside a fan. The blue walls, killer cocktails, and lively music scene make this a must on your itinerary. Make a reservation in the evening to enjoy organic salads, blackened fish tacos, and tequila shrimp. While it is possible to stay in the area, I'm not swooning over any of the options around here.

About a mile south of Kawaihae, on the *makai* side between mile markers 2 and 3, is Pu'ukohola Heiau National Historic Site. When King Kamehameha I was in the process of "unifying" the archipelago, he was struggling with the pesky islands of the Big Island, Kaua'i, Ni'ihau, and O'ahu. Ancients had made the prediction that the man who constructed a coastal *heiau* would gain power over all of Hawai'i. Up went the *heiau* dedicated to the god of war. To celebrate the new temple, Kamehameha invited his foe (who was also his cousin) to a "party"; he then killed his rival and became the leader of the island. Today there is not much to see save some lava rocks along the sea, but this is a very sacred destination for locals, so please be respectful.

At mile marker 2, Spencer Beach Park might be an unsightly beach, but it's popular with local families wanting a safe place for kids to swim and bring a picnic to take a break from the raging heat. Alternatively, take a 10-minute walk south to find the lovely Mau'umae Beach, a popular snorkel area, with white sand and a shady spot to beat the pounding sun. When I snorkeled here, I saw reef sharks, turtles, and a wealth of tropical fish. Sometimes snorkel boats anchor here in the morning. You can also access this beach from Mauna Kea Resort to the south.

As you continue, Highway 270 turns back into Highway 19 south. You've entered the South Kohala Coast, a barren landscape more akin to the moon than a tropical isle. Rivers of black lava stream down the mountain, spilling toward the sea. Locals graffiti the lava with stark white coral messages. The coastal reaches are strewn with some of the state's most gorgeous white sand beaches dotted with upscale resorts that consistently win international awards as the best of just about everything. Food and services are expensive, but if you want that tropical vacation experience, there is no better region on the island to have it. I recommend ending your Hawai'i adventure with a couple of nights of chilling by the beach, sipping *mai tais* and toasting yourself for being such a brave and respectful adventurer.

The first resort area that you reach is Mauna Kea, which houses Mauna Kea Beach Hotel and Hapuna Beach Prince Hotel—both haute golf destinations, with their own world-class greens, fronting the jaw-dropping beaches of their namesakes. All amenities are interchangeable with these sister resorts, including shuttle service between the two. Mauna Kea is the more upscale, newly renovated and

Snorkelers love the rich Big Island waters.

founded by Laurance S. Rockefeller, with 258 rooms featuring Hawaiian wood and luxurious bathrooms, international art, a lu'au, koi ponds, shopping areas, four restaurants, a clambake, an outpost of the Mandara Spa, and cultural activities like lei making. Even if you are not staying here, pop in for a glass of bubbly and a *kurobuta* pork porterhouse bathing in mango brown butter at Manta and Pavilion Wine Bar, and then head over to Mauna Kea Beach to watch the sunset.

South of mile marker 69, travel *makai* on Hapuna Beach Road to find one of the island's most picturesque beaches, Hapuna Beach State Recreation Area. The 0.5-mile-long white sand strand is a choice spot for plenty of sun, tide pools, and summer snorkeling. Winter brings decent swells for bodyboarders. There are a handful of rustic cabins along the beach, though you need a permit from the state. You can camp here, or grab a pricey room in the adjacent Hapuna Beach Prince Hotel. I like to settle into the hotel's Reef Lounge for *pupus* and sunset cocktails.

The huge coastline seems endless as you travel south on Highway 19. Between mile markers 70 and 71, Puako is no more than a stretch of houses along the coast, save the hidden tide pools. Travel *makai* on Puako Beach Drive and take one of the six paths marked BEACH ACCESS to find the Puako Tide Pools, lava rock bowls sheltering generous glimpses into sea life. You'll see coral, sea stars, tropical fish, and more.

Farther south, it is hard not to be smitten with the Mauna Lani Resort Area. Not only are the resorts, cuisine, and beaches glorious, living up to that holiday ideal that many dream about, but there is also something accessible, almost honest about the experience. Sure, you'll pay an arm and a leg to stay at Mauna Lani Bay Hotel and Bungalows or Fairmont Orchid, but this is vacation! Take Mauna Lani Drive *makai* and veer right before Fairmont Orchid to find Holoholokai Beach Park. Besides black sand, decent summer snorkeling, and a great picnicking area, this beach park also houses the Puako Petroglyph Preserve, the island's largest collection of preserved petroglyphs. The trail should take about half an hour; wear sturdy shoes and plenty of sunscreen.

The stark South Kohala Coast's lava fields

Next door, the Fairmont Orchid is a 32-acre beachfront resort that is an essay in luxury. Rooms are subdued, decked out in earth tones, with wide lanais, free Wi-Fi, and flat-panel TVs. With five restaurants and bars, a children's program, a sweet snorkeling beach, tennis courts, golf, a lu'au, and the award-winning Spa Without Walls (which showcases treatments using the local bounty), you'll be hard pressed not to relax while in this sophisticated oasis. The on-site Brown's Beach House Restaurant serves sustainable seafood and meat highlighted with Japanese flavors in a lovely oceanfront location that will make you want to take out a second mortgage just to stay a bit longer.

A lazy sea turtle resting on the Big Island shores

Off Mauna Lani Drive, splurge for a few nights at Mauna Lani Bay Hotel and Bungalows, one of the island's most luxurious properties, which is at once grandly sophisticated and laid back. Whether you opt for a traditional room with ocean views, a lanai, Wi-Fi, and flat screen TVs, or the indulgent condo rooms, complete with fully equipped kitchens, you can enjoy the hotel's green pedigree (it is almost entirely solar powered), the cultural activities, the lively pools, and the three beaches (non-guests can also experience the hotel's bays, which are ideal for snorkeling and stand-up paddle boarding). The hotel is an exercise in culture, with a slew of activities like lei making and fish feeding, as well as a winding river of tropical fish and turtles. Throw in the only non-plantation outpost of Mountain Thunder Coffee Company, the astoundingly good oceanfront Canoe House Restaurant (presided over by chef Allen Hess of Allen's Table, known for his *furikake*-crusted *ono*, goat tacos, and a gorgeous collection of desserts that still make this gal swoon) as well as a handful of lounges perfect for watching the sunset with your sweetheart. The hotel also shelters the world-class Mauna Lani Spa (where you should spring for the *lomilomi* hula treatment), two golf courses, morning snorkeling or whale-watching cruises, and access to the Kalahuipa'a Historic Trail, which skirts the sea, passing historic ruins, lava tubes, and ancient fishponds. Told you it was astounding!

Just across the road is the Shops at Mauna Lani. Those in the market for resort wear, ukuleles, or art can spend an hour or two breezing the shops. There's a Snorkel Bob's to rent gear, a Foodland Farms market, a coffee shop, and a juice bar. Eaters populate this outdoor marketplace for upscale noodles and sushi at Monstera (reservations recommended), steaks and seafood at Ruth's Chris, or chicken tacos at Just Tacos. This marketplace is geared toward those staying at the resorts, and frankly you don't need to spend too much time here; instead, head a bit south to the Waikoloa region, where shopping is a bit more varied.

Around mile marker 76 is Waikoloa Resort Area, the largest collection of resorts, condos, and hotels on this coastline. While it may seem a bit too bustling for those wanting to escape the masses, you can find a few choice accommodations, some exciting cuisine, and one of this area's best beaches. Waikoloa Village is on the *mauka* side of the highway, and honestly doesn't offer much by way of tourist services or dining.

As you first enter the area, to the right are the King's Shops and to the left is the Queen's Marketplace shopping area, though these names are no indication of the offerings. The King's Shops features live music on Tuesday and Friday evenings, a farmers' market on Wednesday morning, and guided tours of the nearby petroglyph trail at Waikoloa Petroglyph Preserve (though if you go on your own, it takes about 20 minutes of beating sun for you to get the gist of these 16th-century carvings). You'll find the usual array of stores offering everything from sandals to Hawaiian art. Serious shoppers appreciate Louis Vuitton, Tiffany, and the local Honoloa Surf Co. Diners flock here to for the casual eats at Merriman's Market Café, where *mahi mahi* tacos, truffle fries, and Hamakua mushroom pizzas steal the show. Superstar chef Roy Yamaguchi has an outpost of his empire called Roy's Waikoloa Bar and Grill that offers his sensational butterfish or *mahi mahi*, as well as a yummy pineapple upside-down cake. New on the scene is Three Fat Pigs, a gastropub from Food Network star Ippy Aiona. Small plates like oyster shooters with *yuzu* lemon sauce and Hamakua mushroom salads populate the innovative menu.

Across the road is Queen's Marketplace, which also features hula and music on Wednesday through Friday evenings. There are a handful of shops like Reyn's for aloha shirts; look for upscale resort-wear and designer blue jeans at Persimmon. Another worthy stop is at Hawaiian Quilt Collection for those emblematic floral quilts adorning many locals' beds. There's a food court where you can score Food Network chef Ippy Aiona's Ippy's Hawaiian BBQ, as well as a the wildly popular Sansei Seafood, Steak and Sushi Bar for Japanese favorites like teriyaki as well as decent sushi and sake—though his crab ramen steals my heart every time (reservations are required for dinner). You can pick up essentials to stock your kitchens at Island Gourmet Market. Ocean Sports has an office here to arrange snorkel tours and whale-watching cruises—they also have a small shack on A Bay (see below) where they rent gear and lead glass-bottomed boat tours.

Follow the tour buses to 'Anaeho'omalu Beach Park, otherwise known as A Bay. This glassy bay is one of the island's best spots for snorkeling, swimming (watch out for flying boogie boards and tour boats coming and going), and SUPping. The beach is backed by Waikoloa Beach Marriott (which has a decent Sunday brunch overlooking the bay) and a couple of ancient fishponds, though my favorite part of the bay is to the south, where sea turtles come to shore and the crowds thin out.

If you'd to stay in the area awhile, you'd prefer a condo, and you're okay with not being on the beach, Aston Waikoloa Colony Villas are spectacular. Lofty ceilings, a full kitchen, and access to the adjacent golf greens please families.

On the north edge of the resort area is Hilton Waikoloa Village Resort, a massive tribute to Hawai'i, with a man-made lagoon populated with sea turtles and tropical fish that begs you to kayak or snorkel in their midst. Rooms offer plenty of comforts, from flat-screen TVs to luxe linens. But the draw is the activities: You can swim with (or train) dolphins at Dolphin Quest; play on the waterslide; SUP on the lagoon; ride the monorail; get a massage at the spa; delight in the lu'au; enjoy nine restaurants; or play on the beach. Even if you don't want to stay in this resort, if you have kids, you may want to spring for a day at the pools, or just come view the dolphins jumping around.

For a unique place to stay, grab one of the four beach chic cottages at Lava Lava Beach Club, literally on the sand on the southern edge of A Bay. Romance seekers love the outdoor rock showers, the private lanais, the complimentary cocktails and *pupus* delivered to your door in the evenings, the individual coffeemakers, and the kitchenettes. Not to be missed is the adjacent sand-in-your-toes alfresco Lava Lava Beach Club Restaurant, featuring fruity cocktails, great beers, and a host of sustainable dishes like pork nachos and burgers. This is the perfect place to watch the sunset as you listen to live music on your last night in Hawai'i.

Before your flight, travel south to Kekaha Kai State Park to have one last go at the island's untouched splendor. These white sand beaches will inspire you to take one last jaunt into the impossibly blue waters before heading back home. This beach is definitely screensaver material.

Lava Lava Beach Club offers a chilled-out place to spend an afternoon—or a week.

IN THE AREA

ACCOMMODATIONS

Aaah the Views B&B, 66-1773 Alaneo St., Waimea. Centrally located in Waimea, between Hilo and Kona, this B&B can accommodate singles, couples, and families. Call 808-885-3455. Website www.aaahtheviews.com.

Aston Waikoloa Colony Villas, 69-555 Waikoloa Beach Dr., Waikoloa. One-, two-, and three-room villas are available at this luxurious condo resort. Each villa has a fully equipped kitchen, central air, and a washer-dryer unit. Call 877-997-6667. Website www.astonhotels.com.

Dolphin Bay Hotel, 333 Iliahi St., Hilo. This laid-back hotel offers affordable rooms and a sweet and simple breakfast of coffee, fresh papaya, bananas, and pastries from a local bakery each morning. Call 808-935-1466. Website www.dolphinbayhotel.com.

Fairmont Orchid, 1 N. Kaniku Dr., Kohala Coast. With six restaurants, golf, tennis, swimming, and a year-round children's program, there's something for each member of the family at this 32-acre luxury resort. Call 808-885-2000. Website www.fairmont.com/orchid-hawaii.

Hapuna Beach Prince Hotel, 62-100 Kauna'Oa Dr., Kamuela. This hotel is situated on 32 acres of oceanfront property on Hapuna Beach. Of the 350 guest rooms, scoop up one of the 36 that face the ocean. Call 888-977-4623. Website www.princeresortshawaii.com.

Hilo Hawaiian Hotel, 71 Banyan Dr., Hilo. With a freshwater pool, nine-hole golf course, and garden, this hotel offers plenty of opportunities to relax and enjoy the area. Call 808-935-9361. Website www.castleresorts.com.

Hilton Waikoloa Village Resort, 69-425 Waikoloa Beach Dr., Waikoloa. Along with the usual hotel amenities, this resort offers canal boat rides, hula demonstrations, dolphin swimming, and lei-making classes. Call 855-256-0287. Website www.hiltonwaikoloavillage.com.

Keolamauloa Farm, 43-1962 Paauilo Mauka Rd., Hamakua Coast. Each suite includes a private entrance, fully equipped kitchen, living room, and two bedrooms. Amenities include Wi-Fi access, a foosball table, and the relaxing surroundings of a working farm. Call 808-776-1294. Website www.keolamauloa.com.

Lava Lava Beach Club, 69-1081 Ku'ualii Place, Waikoloa. Beach-chic cottages on the sand at historic A Bay, with outdoor rain shower, private lanai, kitchenette, and a fun on-site restaurant make this new destination a fantastic choice for romance. Call 808-769-5282. Website www.lavalavabeachclub.com.

Mauna Kea Beach Hotel, 62-100 Mauna Kea Beach Dr., Kamuela. Play a round of golf on the world-class golf course, or enjoy the swimming pool and tennis courts at this beachfront restaurant. Its 258 luxury guestrooms feature nightly turndown service, private lanais, and luxurious bath amenities. Call 808-882-7222. Website www.princeresorts hawaii.com/mauna-kea-beach-hotel.

Mauna Lani Bay Hotel and Bungalows, 68-1400 Mauna Lani Dr., Kohala Coast. With a tropical Asian aesthetic, the mountain-, garden-, and ocean-view rooms and bungalows provide access to the pool, a gorgeous beach, a world-class restaurant, and free activities like hula dance classes. Call 808-885-6622. Website www.maunalani.com.

Orchid Tree B&B, 6 Makakai Place, Hilo. Conveniently located minutes from downtown Hilo, this B&B still offers beautiful views and privacy in a 600-square-foot suite with access to a large, covered lanai, swimming pool, and Jacuzzi. Call 808-961-9678. Website www.orchidtree.net.

Puakea Ranch, 56-2864 Akoni Pule, Kohala Coast. These beautifully restored ranch houses and bungalows offer private swimming pools and round-the-clock concierge service. You can even pick your own fresh fruit from the orchards on the grounds. Call 808-315-0805. Website www.puakearanch.com.

Tina's Country Cottage, 65-1396D Kawaihae Rd., Waimea. This two-bedroom cottage has a fully equipped kitchen, dining room, and two bathrooms; it's within walking distance of the shops and restaurants in Waimea. Call 702-525-0289.

Waianuhea B&B, 45-3503 Kahana Rd., Honoka'a. This relaxing B&B features a full gourmet breakfast, wine, and *pupus* served daily. A Jacuzzi that looks out over the ocean and a massage room complete the peaceful experience. Call 808-775-1118. Website www.waianuhea.com.

Waikoloa Beach Marriott, 69-275 Waikoloa Beach Dr., Waikoloa. Fronting the Anaeho'omalu Bay beach and several ancient fishponds, this 15-acre resort has a spa, fitness center, and pool. The hotel also offers Hawaiian cultural activities such as ukulele lessons and lei-making classes. Call 888-236-2427. Website www.marriott.com.

Waipi'o Rim B&B, 48-5561 Honoka'a-Waipi'o Rd., Honoka'a. The single studio available includes a private covered deck, an ocean view from the shower, and beautiful hardwood floors. Call 808-775-1727. Website www.waipiorim.com.

Waipi'o Wayside B&B, 46-4226 Honoka'a-Waipi'o Rd., Honoka'a. Each of the five rooms available at this B&B includes organic bath products, luxurious bathrobes, and a homemade organic breakfast. Call 800-833-8849. Website www.waipiowayside.com.

ATTRACTIONS AND RECREATION

'Akaka Falls State Park, end of 'Akaka Falls Rd., 3.6 miles southwest of Honomu. Enjoy a self-guided walking tour through lush tropical greenery to scenic vistas that offer views of Kahuna and 'Akaka Falls. Website www.hawaiistateparks.org.

Alan's Art and Collectibles, 202 Kamehameha Ave., Hilo. Search for antique lamps, jewelry, and furniture at this waterfront store. Call 808-969-1554.

As Hawi Turns, Akoni Pule Hwy., Hawi. *Whimsical, unique*, and *delightful* are just a few of the words that describe the mix of treasures you can find at this funky store. Look for straw hats, kitschy jewelry, and vintage items. Call 808-889-5023.

Basically Books, 160 Kamehameha Ave., Hilo. Stop in this bookstore for Hawaiian literature, a large collection of local music, and detailed maps of the islands. Call 808-961-0144. Website www.basicallybooks.com.

Dreams of Paradise Gallery, 308 Kamehameha Ave., Ste. 106, Hilo. Many well-known Hawaiian artists sell their creations here. Call 808-935-5670. Website www.dreamsofparadisegallery.com.

Dolphin Quest, 425 Waikoloa Beach Dr., at Hilton Waikoloa Village, Waikoloa. A fun, interactive dolphin experience for the entire family that includes a learning center lagoon and a swim-with-the-dolphins adventure. The Hilton Waikoloa Village runs this program. Call 808-886-1234. Website www.hiltonwaikoloavillage.com.

Earth Bound Tours. Featuring a variety of themed tours from culinary to agricultural and horticultural experiences. Take a cooking class, tour a working coffee plantation, or visit the botanical gardens. Call 808-864-0556. Website www.earthboundtours.com.

Elements Jewelry and Crafts, 55-3413 Akoni Pule Hwy., Hawi. Look for colorful, high-quality jewelry, pottery, lava glass, and paintings. Call 866-719-1289. Website www.elementsjewelryandcrafts.com.

Gallery of Great Things, 65-1279 Kawaihae Rd., Kamuela. Chock-full of artsy Hawaiian, Polynesian, and Asian treasures. Call 808-885-7706. Website www.galleryofgreatthingshawaii.com.

Hakalau Forest National Wildlife Refuge, 60 Nowelo St., Hilo. A prime place for bird-watching, this wildlife refuge is home to many native birds such as honeycreepers, flycatchers, and Hawaiian hawks. Call 808-443-2300. Website www.fws.gov/hakalauforest /index.html.

Hawaiian Walkways, 45-3674 Mamane St., Honoka'a. Offers walking tours of Kilauea Volcano, Kona Cloud Forest, and Saddle Road as well as a trek in which a helicopter takes you to the starting point of your hike. Call 808-775-0372. Website www.hawaiianwalkways.com.

Hawaiian Quilt Collection, 201 Waikoloa Beach Dr., Waikoloa. Quilted bags to wall hangings. Call 808-886-0494. Website www.hawaiian-quilts.com.

Hawai'i Forest & Trail, 74-5035 Queen Ka'ahumanu Hwy., Ste. B, Kailua-Kona. This tour operation offers volcano tours, bird-watching tours, and adventures to Mauna Kea's summit. Call 808-331-8505. Website www.hawaii-forest.com.

Hawai'i Tropical Botanical Gardens, 27-717 Old Mamalahoa Hwy., Papaikou. There are two major hiking trails at this nature preserve and sanctuary, each featuring a wide variety of tropical flowers, trees, and plants such as jackfruit trees and Alexandra palms. Call 808-964-5233. Website www.htbg.com.

Hilo Farmers' Market, on Mamo St. and Kamehameha Ave., Hilo. Over 200 local farmers and artisans sell produce, crafts, and gift items at this outdoor market. Call 808-933-1000. Website www.hilofarmersmarket.com.

Hilo Public Library, 300 Waianuenue Ave., Hilo. Outside this building you'll find the Naha and Panao stones. Call

808-933-8888. Website www.hilopublic library.org.

Honoka'a Trading Company, on Mamane St., Honoka'a. This secondhand store features finds like vintage business signs and aloha shirts. Call 808-775-0808.

'Imiloa Astronomy Center of Hawai'i, 600 'Imiloa Place, Hilo. This museum compares and contrasts the creation views of native Hawaiians and modern astronomers. Call 808-969-9700. Website www.imiloahawaii.org.

Imiola Congregational Church, 65-1084 Mamalahoa Hwy., Waimea. Stop in to view the dark *koa* wood interior of this church, first built in 1832. Call 808-885-4987.

Isaacs Art Center, 65-1268 Kawaihae Rd., Kamuela. This gallery includes a large inventory of artwork from paintings to ceramics, furniture, and Hawaiian quilts. Call 808-885-5884. Website www.isaacsartcenter.hpa.edu.

Kahua Ranch, Kohala Mountain Rd., Waimea. Explore the working ranch's grounds and ocean vistas by ATV or horseback, or go on the guided historic walking tour. Call 808-882-4646. Website www.kahuaranch.com.

Kekaha Kai State Park, on Queen Hwy. 19, 2.6 miles north of Keahole Airport. Hike to the summit of a 342-foot-high cinder cone that offers an excellent view of the coastline, or enjoy a picnic on the beach at this beachfront park. Website www.hawaiistateparks.org.

Ke Ola Mau Loa Church, Church Rd., Kamuela. The vibrant green exterior of this church is quite striking. Call 808-885-7505.

King's Shops, 250 Waikoloa Beach Dr., #B10, Waikoloa. This shopping center includes name-brand stores as well as local shops and restaurants. Call 808-886-8811. Website www.kingsshops.com.

Kino'ole Farmers' Market, 1990 Kino'ole St., Hilo. Local farmers grow all of the produce at this market. Products include vegetables, herbs, fruit, and baked goods. Call 808-938-4545.

Kohala Artists Cooperative Project and Kenji's House Museum, Akoni Pule Hwy., Kapa'au. Downstairs is an informal museum; upstairs is the cooperative where exhibits from local artists are on display. Call 808-884-5556. Website www.kenjishouse.com.

Kohala Ditch Adventures, Akoni Pule Hwy., Halaula. This tour operation runs kayak tours along a privately owned trail that has been maintained to preserve the natural Hawaiian flora and fauna. Call 808-889-6000. Website www.kohala ditchadventures.com.

Kohala Divers, located 1 mile from the intersection of Hwys. 19 and 270 in the Kawaihae Shopping Center. This dive operation will take you on a trip to see hidden lava tubes and interesting sea creatures. Call 808-882-7774. Website www.kohaladivers.com.

Lapakahi State Historical Park, on Akoni Pule Hwy., 12.4 miles north of Kawaihae. Take a self-guided tour of this partially restored ancient Hawaiian settlement to learn about the traditional Hawaiian lifestyle. Website www.hawaii stateparks.org.

Laupahoehoe Train Museum, 36-2377 Mamalahoa Hwy., Laupahoehoe. This small, community-based museum displays photographs, railroad artifacts, and memorabilia highlighting the history of railroads on the island of Hawai'i. Call 808-962-6300. Website www.thetrain museum.com.

Living Arts Gallery, 55-3435 Akoni Pule Hwy., Hawi. Artist co-op gallery features watercolors, Chinese brushwork, jewelry, and paintings. Website www.livingartsgallery.net.

Long Ears Coffee, P.O. Box 915, Honoka'a. Nestled in the foothills of Mauna Kea Mountain, this 8-acre coffee plantation offers tours that teach visitors about the entire coffee process, from planting the trees to husking and roasting the beans. Call 808-775-0385. Website www.longearscoffee.com.

Lyman Museum and Mission House, 276 Haili St., Hilo. Showcases exhibits such as traditional Hawaiian feather artwork and special events about Hawai'i's people and historical traditions. Call 808-935-5021. Website www.lyman museum.org.

Mandara Spa, 62-100 Mauna Kea Beach Blvd., Kohala Coast. Signature services at this spa include hot stone therapy, seaweed massages, and an enzyme facial. Call 808-882-5630. Website www.mandaraspa.com.

Mauna Kea Tea, 46-3870 Old Mamalahoa Hwy., Honoka'a. Organic green and oolong teas are the specialty at this tea plantation. Farm tours are available and include a walking tour of the plantation and tea samples in the tasting room. Call 808-775-1171. Website www.maunakea tea.com.

Mauna Lani Spa, 68-1400 Mauna Lani Dr., Kamuela. Try a traditional Hawaiian *lomilomi* massage or a warming and cooling body wrap using cooling *pa'akai* (Hawaiian salts) and a warming *pikake* essential oil. Call 808-881-7922. Website www.maunalani.com.

Ocean Sports, 69-275 Waikoloa Beach Dr., Waikoloa. This sailing operation will take you to see whales and dolphins. They also offer canoeing options, snorkel cruises, and scuba diving. Call 808-886-6666. Website www.hawaiiocean sports.com.

Onizuka Visitors Information Center, 177 Maka'ala St., Hilo. Open daily 9 a.m.–10 p.m., this center features informational videos about Mauna Kea, high-powered telescopes that allow visitors to view constellations, and a gift shop. Call 808-961-2180. Website www.ifa.hawaii .edu/info/vis.

Original Hawaiian Chocolate Factory, 78-6772 Makenawai St., Kailua-Kona. Tours of the farm are offered every Wednesday and Friday at 9 a.m. and include a one-hour walking tour of the orchard and factory as well as a sampling of the chocolate. This farm also grows coffee and macadamia nuts. Call 808-332-2626. Website www.ohcf.us.

Pacific Tsunami Museum, 130 Kamehameha Ave., Hilo. Check out the museum's exhibits that interpret the history of tsunamis in places such as Hawai'i, Japan, and Alaska. Call 808-935-0926. Website www.tsunami.org.

Palace Theater, 38 Haili St., Hilo. This historic theater offers unique films and live music. Call 808-934-7010. Website www.hilopalace.com.

Pana'ewa Rainforest Zoo and Gardens, 800 Stainback Hwy., Hilo. This zoo houses a Bengal tiger, birds, and primates. There is a petting zoo 1:30–2:30 p.m. Call 808-959-9233. Website www.hilozoo.com.

Paniolo Riding Adventures, mile 13.2, Kohala Mountain Rd., North Kohala. Go horseback riding on this 11,000-acre working cattle ranch for views of Mauna Kea, Mauna Loa, and the volcanoes. Themed rides include a three-hour picnic ride, a sunset ride, and a less rigorous option for beginners. Call 808-889-5354. Website www.panioloadventures.com.

Parker Ranch Center, 67-1185 Mamalahoa Hwy., Waimea. Shop for food at the grocery store, visit several specialty clothing boutiques, or enjoy a meal at one the restaurants or cafés in this shopping center. Call 808-885-7178. Website www.parkerranchcenterads.com.

Parker Ranch, 67-1304 Mamalahoa Hwy., Waimea. This historic homestead founded in 1879 is the largest ranch in Hawai'i. Walking and horseback tours are available Mon.–Sat. 10–4. Call 808-885-7311. Website www.parkerranch.com.

Prince Kuhio Mall, 111 E. Puainako St., Hilo. Anchored by Macy's and Sears, this mall has several mainstream shops and restaurants. Call 808-959-3555. Website www.princekuhioplaza.com.

Puako Petroglyph Preserve, Holoholokai Beach Park, Mauna Lani Resort, Kohala Coast. Enjoy a 30-minute hike to large slabs of lava rock covered in ancient petroglyphs.

Queen's Marketplace, 201 Waikoloa Beach Dr., Waikoloa. This is the largest shopping center on the Kohala Coast. It includes several clothing and apparel shops, two jewelry stores, a food court, and a few gift shops. Call 808-886-8822. Website www.queensmarketplace.net.

Shops at Mauna Lani, 68-1330 Mauna Lani Dr., Kohala Coast. The open-air walkways at this mall lead to fashionable name-brand stores as well as chic local boutiques. Call 808-885-9501. Website www.shopsatmaunalani.com.

Sig Zane Designs, 122 Kamehameha Ave., Hilo. The designs at this clothing store make use of indigenous designs to create unique and vibrant apparel for men and women. Call 808-935-7077. Website www.sigzane.com.

Spa Without Walls, 1 N. Kaniku Dr., Kamuela. This spa features private outdoor huts where you can enjoy the scents and sounds of the ocean and gardens while you're being pampered. Call 808-885-2000. Website www.fairmont.com.

Sun and Sea Hawai'i, 224 Kamehameha Ave., #102, Hilo. This dive shop and rental operation has something for every sport, whether it's snorkeling, diving, or paddle boarding. Call 808-934-0902.

Symbiosis, 45-3587 Mamane St., Honoka'a. A cute secondhand children's clothing store that also sells women's apparel and toys. Call 808-775-0333.

Taro Patch Gifts, 45-3599 Mamane St., Unit D, Honoka'a. A large collection of

Hawaiiana including prints, books, ceramics, soaps, and apparel. Call 808-775-7228. Website www.taropatchgifts.com.

Volcano Island Honey Company, 46-4013 Puaono Rd., Honoka'a. The organic raw white honey here is a favorite. Tours of the farm and hives are available and include an educational movie, a live beehive demonstration, and free samples of fresh honey. Call 808-775-1000. Website www.volcanoislandhoney.com.

Waikoloa Petroglyph Preserve, South Kohala Coast, Waikoloa. Many of the petroglyphs etched here date back to the 16th century. The King's Shops offer a daily one-hour tour of the petroglyphs at 10:30 a.m.

Wailoa Center, in Wailoa State Park, 200 Piopio St., Hilo. An art and culture gallery that regularly rotates exhibits on everything from art to dolls and quilts. Call 808-933-0416. Website www.hawaiimuseums .org/mc/ishawaii_wailoacenter.htm.

Waipi'o Valley Artworks, 48-5416 Kukuihale Rd., Kukuihale. A wide variety of artwork including *koa* wood furniture, ceramics, porcelain dishes, and pine bowls. Call 800-492-4746. Website www.waipiovalleyartworks.com.

W. M. Keck Observatory Visitors Gallery, 65-1120 Mamalahoa Hwy., Kamuela. Comprising two 10-meter telescopes, this visitors center also provides information on equipment and movies about Mauna Kea. Call 808-881-3827. Website www.keckobservatory.org.

World Botanical Gardens, Hwy. 19 at mile marker 16, 15 miles north of Hilo, Hakalau. World Botanical Gardens offers zipline and off-road adventures as well as tours through gardens filled with orchids, tropical fruit trees, and other exotic plants. Call 808-963-5427. Website www.worldbotanicalgardens.com.

DINING

Abundant Life Natural Foods, 292 Kamehameha Ave., Hilo. This natural grocery store offers a wide variety of natural groceries. Call 808-935-7411. Website www.abundantlifenaturalfoods .com.

Back to the 50s Highway Fountain Diner, 35-2704 Mamalahoa Hwy., Laupahoehoe. Serving up traditional diner fare, this 1950s-style diner includes affordable plates heaped with pancakes, French toast, or burgers and fries. Call 808-962-0808.

Bamboo Restaurant, 5-3415 Akoni Pule Hwy., Hawi. This restaurant serves fresh island-style cuisine such as coconut prawns and seafood risotto, but also doubles as a gallery that features *koa* wood furniture and jewelry. Call 808-889-1441. Website www.bamboo restaurant.info.

Bayfront Coffee Kava and Tea, 116 Kamehameha Ave., Hilo. Enjoy a cup of kava, coffee, or tea at this café that also serves up moist kava brownies. Call 808-935-1155. Website www.bayfrontkava .com.

Blue Dragon, 61-3616 Kawaihae Rd., Kawaihae. Enjoy fresh fish, lamb dishes, and pastas at this restaurant that also serves as a live music venue. Call 808-882-7771. Website www.bluedragon restaurant.com.

Brown's Beach House Restaurant, 1 N. Kaniku Dr., Kamuela. For a taste of fine dining on the Kohala Coast, this beachfront restaurant serves grilled chipotle pork chops, filet mignon, and a seafood trio. Call 808-885-2000. Website www.fairmont.com.

Café 100, 969 Kilauea Ave., Hilo. The expansive menu at this diner features tons of cheap breakfasts, daily plate lunch specials, and an entire section dedicated to varieties of *loco moco*. Call 808-935-8683. Website www.cafe100.com.

Café il Mondo, 45-3626 Mamane St., Ste. A, Honoka'a. An Italian pizzeria and coffee bar that serves yummy stone-baked pizzas. Call 808-775-7711. Website www.cafeilmondo.com.

Café Pesto (two locations) 61-3665 Hwy. 270, Kawaihae; t 308 Kamehameha Ave., #101, Hilo. Start your meal with a passion fruit iced tea and Asian-style shrimp nachos, move on to a heaping plate of seafood risotto, and then finish the meal with a warm coconut tart. (Kawaihae) 808-882-1071; (Hilo) 808-969-6640. Website www.cafepesto.com.

Canoe House Restaurant, 68-1400 Mauna Lani Dr., Kohala Coast. The restaurant's ocean views pale only in comparison with chef Allen Hess's fanciful dishes, like coastal salad and the furikake-crusted ono. Reservations recommended. Call 808-885-6622. Website www.maunalani.com.

Fish and the Hog Market Café, 64-957 Mamalahoa Hwy., Waimea. This is an excellent stop for salads, sandwiches, classic BBQ, and fresh-caught fish. They use organic produce and fresh ingredients. Call 808-885-6268. Website www.thefishandthehog.com.

Hawaiian Style Café, 65-1290 Kawaihae Rd., Kamuela. Best known for their loco moco, gigantic banana mac nut pancakes, and haupia pudding. At press time there was talk of another location opening in Hilo. Call 808-885-4295.

Hawaiian Vanilla Company, 43-2007 Paauilo Mauka Rd., Pa'auilo. If it's made with vanilla, you can be sure it's on the menu (and maybe in some surprising ways, too, like vanilla bacon or vanilla fried rice). Call 808-776-1771. Website www.hawaiianvanilla.com.

Hilo Bay Café, 315 Maka'ala St., Ste. 109, Hilo. This trendy restaurant serves organic meals like vegetarian sweet potato flax burgers and mushroom potpie. For dessert, try the molten chocolate lava cake served with a side of Kona coffee ice cream. Reservations recommended. Call 808-935-4939. Website www.hilobaycafe.com.

Hilo Homemade Ice Cream, 1477 Kalanianaole Ave., Hilo. The ice cream menu includes flavors like salted caramel macadamia nut and mocha almond fudge. Call 808-959-5959. Website www.hilohomemade.com.

Hamakua Fudge Shop, 45-3611 Mamane St., Ste. 105, Honoka'a. Over 25 flavors of fudge such as chocolate orange mango and chocolate caramel macadamia nut. Call 808-775-1430. Website www.hamakuafudge.com.

Island Gourmet Market, 69-201 Waikoloa Beach Dr., Waikoloa. Gourmet food items from Hawai'i and around the world like dragon fruit and lychee. The deli serves a made-to-order sandwiches or pizza. Call 808-886-3577. Website www.islandgourmethawaii.com.

Ippy's Hawaiian BBQ, 69-201 Waikoloa Beach Dr., Waikoloa. A great pulled pork sandwich or a refreshing coconut lime smoothie. Call 808-886-8600.

Itsu's Fishing Supplies, 810 Pi'ilani St., Hilo. This small café serves shave ice, burgers, and fried chicken. Call 808-935-8082.

Kawate Seed Shop, 1990 Kinoole St., Hilo. This little shop serves hot dogs, hamburgers, shave ice, and crack seed (a snack made of dehydrated and preserved fruit). Call 808-959-8313.

Ken's House of Pancakes, 1730 Kamehameha Ave., Hilo. Top your pancakes with the signature guava, passion fruit, and coconut syrups at this breakfast spot. Call 808-935-8711. Website www.kenshouseofpancakes.com.

Kohala Coffee Mill, 55-3412 Akoni Puli Hwy., Hawi. A coffee shop and ice cream parlor that serves yummy mac nut ice cream, Kona coffee, and fresh bagels. Call 808-889-5577.

KTA Super Store, 50 E. Puainako St., Hilo. A quick stop for groceries or bento boxes. Call 808-959-9111. Website www.ktasuperstores.com.

Just Tacos, 68 1330 Mauna Lani Dr., Ste. 108, Kohala Coast. Casual Mexican fare, such as house-made margaritas and fish tacos, is served at this cantina. Call 808-885-8484. Website www.justtacos.com.

Lighthouse Deli, 55-3419 Akoni Pule Hwy., Hawi. This delicatessen supports local farmers, so expect lots of fresh local produce when you try one of their salads or sandwiches. Call 808-889-5757. Website www.lighthousedeli.square space.com.

Manta and Pavilion Wine Bar, 62-100 Mauna Kea Beach Dr., Kamuela. An exhibition kitchen showcases the chefs as they prepare dishes like grilled lamb chops, *ahi* tuna, and fresh seafood *cioppino*. Call 808-882-5810. Website www.princeresortshawaii.com.

Merriman's Market Café, 250 Waikoloa Beach Dr., Ste. J 106, Waikoloa. This Mediterranean-style restaurant serves hummus, Greek-style fish tacos with an avocado *tzatziki* sauce, and a vegetarian antipasto platter made with handcrafted cheeses and olives. Call 808-886-1700. Website www.merrimans hawaii.com.

Merriman's Restaurant, 65-1227 Opelo Rd., Kamuela. Make a stop at this restaurant for seasonal fresh fish like the local pink snapper served in an apricot sauce. Reserve a table in advance. Call 808-885-6822. Website www.merrimanshawaii.com.

Miyo's, 681 Manono St., Hilo. This Japanese restaurant serves a wide variety of sushi and curries. Open Mon.–Sat. 11–2 and 5:30–8:30. Make a reservation for dinner. Call 808-935-2273.

Mr. Ed's Bakery, 2816 72 Government Main Rd., Honomu. Homemade jams, jellies, and chutneys are for sale alongside fluffy pastries and buttery shortbread. Call 808-963-5000. Website www.mredsbakery.com.

Monstera, 68-1330 Mauna Lani Dr., Ste. 111, Kohala Coast. A hip, casual sushi and noodle house open for dinner starting at 5:30 daily. Reserve a table in advance. Call 808-887-2711. Website www.monsterasushi.com.

Mountain Thunder Coffee Co., 68-1400 Mauna Lani Dr., Kohala Coast. Open daily 6–4, this outpost serves coffee on the lanai of the Mauna Lani Bay Hotel. Call 808-885-6622. Website www.maunalani.com.

Nori's Saimin and Snacks, 688 Kinoole St., Ste. 124, Hilo. Roasted pork *loco moco* and *saimin* are the specialties, as is the chocolate *mochi* cake. Call 808-935-9133.

Ocean Sushi Deli, 239 Keawe St., Hilo. Affordable sushi and deep-fried *mochi* ice cream are the big draws at this Japanese-style restaurant.

Pau, 65-1227 Opelo Rd., Waimea. Fresh seasonal fast-food options include salads, sandwiches, and pizza. Call 808-885-6325. Website www.paupizza.com.

Reef Lounge, 62-100 Kauna'Oa Dr., Kamuela. Sip your tropical drink in open-air seating with a spectacular view of the ocean while listening to the sounds of live guitar. Call 888-877-4623. Website www.princeresortshawaii.com.

Roy's Waikoloa Bar and Grill, 250 Waikoloa Beach Dr., Waikoloa. A Hawaiian restaurant that melds European-style sauces with Asian spices. Try the mussels and clam hot pot or the duck confit dim sum. Call 808-886-4321. Website www.roysrestaurant.com.

Ruth's Chris, 68-1330 Mauna Lani Dr., Kohala Coast. Start off with some barbecued shrimp, and then move on to one of the signature steaks or fresh lobster. Call 808-887-0800. Website www.ruths chris.com.

Sansei Seafood, Steak and Sushi Bar, 201 Waikoloa Beach Dr., Waikoloa. The *panko*-crusted *ahi* rolls and the mango crab salad rolls lure repeat visitors. Make a reservation. Call 808-886-6286. Website www.sanseihawaii.com.

Simply Natural, 45-3625 Mamane St., Honoka'a. This healthy restaurant serves up taro burgers and taro pancakes. The breakfast burritos are also popular. Call 808-775-0119.

Short N Sweet, 374 Kinoole St., Hilo. This scrumptious bakery offers delicious pineapple bread pudding, artisan breads, bagels, and croissants. Call 808-935-4446. Website www.shortnsweet.biz.

Sombat's, 88 Kanoelehua Ave., Hilo. The owner of this restaurant grows her own herbs and uses locally sourced veggies in her tasty Thai dishes. Call 808-969-9336. Website www.sombats.com.

Suisan Fish Market, 93 Lihiwai St., Hilo. The *ahi poke* at this fish market is no joke. Call 808-935-9349. Website www.suisan.com.

Surf Break Café, 13 Haili St., Hilo. Stop in for breakfast or lunch at this local café. They serve huge breakfast burritos and lunch wraps as well as blended coffee drinks. Call 808-934-8844.

Sushi Rock, 55-3435 Akoni Pule Hwy., Hawi. The organic, locally grown wasabi at this Japanese restaurant is a nice complement to handmade sushi creations like the purple passion roll made with *ahi poke*, purple sweet potato, and apples. Call 808-889-5900. Website www.sushirockrestaurant.net.

Tex Drive In, 45-690 Pakalana St., Honoka'a. Look no further for *malasadas*. Call 808-775-0598. Website www.texdriveinhawaii.com.

Three Fat Pigs, 69-250 Waikoloa Beach Dr., Waikoloa. A gastropub dedicated to serving juicy pork belly sandwiches, baby back ribs, and a large selection of beer. Call 808-339-7145.

Two Ladies Kitchen, 274 Kilauea Ave., Hilo. This is the stop if you're craving *mochi*, a Japanese cake made of glutinous rice; the flavors include strawberry, passion fruit, and peanut butter. Call 808-961-4766.

Village Burger, 67-1185 Mamalahoa Hwy., Kamuela. The burgers here are made with antibiotic- and hormone-free pasture-raised beef. For a non-beef variety, try the *ahi* burger. There are also two vegetarian burger variations. Call 808-885-7319. Website www.village burgerwaimea.com.

Waimea Coffee Co., 65-1279 Kawaihae Rd., Unit 112, Kamuela. Enjoy an espresso and fresh-baked goodies at this café at Parker Center. Their "Obama Blend" coffee, which is a mix of Hawaiian, Kenyan, and Sumatran beans, is a big hit. Call 808-885-8915. Website www.waimeacoffeecompany.com.

Wilson's by the Bay, 224 Kamehameha Ave., Hilo. *Lychee*, vanilla, and pineapple shave ice help beat the heat. Call 808-969-9191.

Zest Kitchen, 55-3435 Akoni Pule Hwy., Hawi. Try a glass of house-made lemonade alongside the eclectic menu that includes blue crab ravioli, *kalua* pig, and lasagna. Call 808-889-1188.

OTHER CONTACT INFORMATION

Big Island Chamber of Commerce, 117 Keawe St., Ste. 205, Hilo. Call 808-935-7178. Website www.hicc.biz.

Big Island Visitors Bureau, 250 Keawe St., Hilo. Call 800-648-2441. Website www.gohawaii.com.

INDEX

3295301197402 1